CABLE COMMUNICATION

CABLE COMMUNICATION

Thomas F. Baldwin
Michigan State University

D. Stevens McVoy
Coaxial Communications

Prentice-Hall, Inc., Englewood Cliffs, N.J. 07632

Library of Congress Cataloging in Publication Data

BALDWIN, THOMAS F.
  Cable communication.

  Includes bibliographical references and index.
  1. Cable television. I. McVoy, D. Stevens.
II. Title.
HE8700.7.C6B34   384.55'56   82-7584
ISBN 0-13-110171-4   AACR2

Editorial/production supervision and
  interior design by Richard C. Laveglia
Cover design by Diane Saxe
Manufacturing buyer: Ed O'Dougherty

Printed in the United States of America

10 9 8 7 6 5 4 3

ISBN 0-13-110171-4

Prentice-Hall International, Inc., *London*
Prentice-Hall of Australia Pty. Limited, *Sydney*
Prentice-Hall Canada Inc., *Toronto*
Prentice-Hall of India Private Limited, *New Delhi*
Prentice-Hall of Japan, Inc., *Tokyo*
Prentice-Hall of Southeast Asia Pte. Ltd., *Singapore*
Whitehall Books Limited, *Wellington, New Zealand*

To Jan Baldwin and Sue McVoy

Contents

Chapter 3   Distribution Plant / 26

Chapter 4   Home Drop / 48

Chapter 5   Two-Way Technology / 56

Part II   SERVICES / 81

Chapter 6   Over-the-Air, Access, Community, and Automated Channels / 83

Chapter 7   Satellite-Delivered Programming and Cable Radio / 111

Chapter *11*   Franchising / 188

Part **IV**   ORGANIZATION AND OPERATIONS / 237

Chapter *12*   Ownership / 239

Chapter *13*   Audiences and Programming / 253

Chapter *14*   Marketing and Advertising / 267

Preface

This book is written for all those who have a need or a desire to learn about the cable communications industry—college students studying communication and communication systems; professionals in cable and the other communication industries seeking a single source of information about all the aspects of cable; citizens and government officials active in franchising, supervision of franchises, and refranchising; investors looking for an overview of this industry that will need substantial new capital in the next few years; producers of programs for cable; and finally, the general reader with an interest in communication. To the general reader, we suggest that cable is a fascinating industry with a potentially significant role to play in human communication. Widespread knowledge of this communication system, still in its formative stages, is probably necessary to the fulfillment of its promise.

A great many people made substantial contributions to this book. Georgella Muirhead, former public information officer for the City of East Lansing, supplied information about the operation of government channels. Randy VanDalsen, national coordinator of local origination programming for United Cable, made suggestions and provided material used in the public access and community channels sections. Mindy Snyder, access coordinator for United Cable in East Lansing, advised us on access rules and supplied the sample used in Appendix B.

Barry Litman, associate professor in the Department of Telecommunication, Michigan State University, read the pay cable chapter, making a number of suggestions. The model of the effects of repeat showing on viewer utility is his. Jane Moyer, regional coordinator for the South Central Region, HBO, had answers for a number of questions. Genie

Zerbinos, now teaching at Marquette University, thoroughly researched videotext and made those findings available to us. James Cragan, former Rockford, Illinois, fire chief, James Wright, then with Rockford Cablevision and Martin Block, John Eulenberg, Bradley Greenberg, and Tom Muth were all involved in the Michigan State University, Rockford, Two-Way Cable Project that provided technical and applications knowledge reported in Chapters 5 and 9. Geoffrey Gates, director, Software Technology, Cox Cable Communications read Chapters 5 and 9 making numerous useful suggestions.

At the National Science Foundation, Charles Brownstein, program manager, supported work reported in Chapters 5, 9, and 16. Stuart Feldstein, a cable specialist in the Washington law firm of Fleishman and Walsh and former chief counsel to the National Cable Television Association, answered a number of questions on communications law.

Alec Fritsch, formerly with the Michigan Senate Special Committee on Cable Television and Governmental Activity/Information Telecasting; Susan McAdams of the national League of Cities; Lonnie Moffett of the Cable Television Information Center; Donald Whitson and Eugene Yee of the San Diego County Cable Television Review Commission; and Ted Baldwin, news media representative of Bethlehem Steel, all supplied materials used in the franchising chapter.

Robert Yadon, instructor in the Department of Telecommunication at Michigan State, read several sections on business organization and made suggestions that were incorporated. Dean Krugman of the Michigan State University, Department of Advertising, contributed to the section on audience. Edward Niner, director of marketing, QUBE; Leo Brennan, general manager, and Charles Boyle, director of marketing and programming, Coaxial Communications of Columbus, Ohio; Mike Harrigan, regional marketing manager, Mid States Region, ATC; Dean Gilbert, sales manager, Eastern Michigan Regional Offices of Continental Cablevision; and Rudy Tober, marketing manager, Continental Lansing, all made contributions to the marketing chapter. Doug Miller and Dave Hanson, former Michigan State students now with HBO, also helped with the marketing chapter.

Gil Hernandez, Brian McNamara of Coaxial Communications, contributed parts of the chapter on business organization and helpful information on other sections. John Quarrier, Union Commerce Bank of Cleveland, supplied information on cable finance. Genelle Armstrong, director of Customer Service, and Harry Cushing, director of Field Operations, Coaxial Communications, provided the basic information for the section on customer service. Harry Cushing also reviewed the chapter on distribution plant design and construction. Doug Grace, chief engineer for Coaxial Communications, reviewed the chapter on headends. Cindy Thompson, Coaxial Communications programming, reviewed Chapter Seven.

John Abel, chairman of the Department of Telecommunication and co-principal investigator of the Media Environment Study, with Rick Ducey and Janet Bridges, graduate students in the Mass Media Ph.D. Program at Michigan State, were collaborators on the research from which much of Chapter 16 was drawn. Rick Ducey read and commented on several other chapters. Students in a class at Michigan State taught by Thomas Muth and Walter Mathews read drafts of several chapters and made helpful comments.

Several people were most helpful in searching out photographs and illustrations: Jessica Baron, Warner Amex, Cincinnati; Sally Cahur, HBO; Linda Holland, Tocom; Shirley Leslie, FCC; John Feight, Scientific Atlanta; Leo Murray, Warner Amex; Harry Cushing, Coaxial Communications; David Anderson, Cox; John Reinhart, United Cable.

Stephanie DeSmith and Lynn Hendricks made excellent contributions in proofreading galleys.

John Duhring recognized the need for this book and was responsible for its publication by Prentice-Hall.

Keeping us organized and typing the manuscript were Ann Alchin in East Lansing and Sharon Caldwell and Toni Brooks in Columbus. Our families were interested in the project and were patient.

To all these people, we are very grateful.

PART I

TECHNOLOGY

1

Introduction

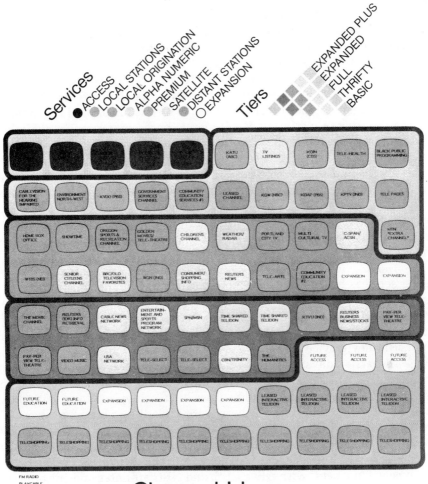

Channel Lineup

Channel lineup, Rogers Cablesystems, Portland, Oregon.

CABLE PROMISE

Cable television has exploded suddenly into a communication system of significance, viewed by cities as a major public service medium, by businesses as growth investment in an otherwise dull economy, and by media and common carrier competitors as a major threat. All this happened over a few short months because of the discovery of what economists suggested many years ago was a consumer underinvestment in television. According to Noll, Peck, and McGowan, "The available evidence from both STV [subscription TV] and cable experience suggests the existence of a considerable unfulfilled demand for television programming, both of the conventional type and a few categories not well represented in the present program logs."[1] This point was not proven until the late 1970s, when satellite-delivered movies induced substantial numbers of consumer households to spend $15 to $30 per month and more on multiple tiers of service. The industry itself was shocked by the revelations of the high subscriber counts and the willingness of many households to buy as many channels of pay service as were offered. And this newly discovered appetite for television, which is far beyond the dreams of the industry of just a few years ago, is based on presently available entertainment services that are only a fraction of the future entertainment and service potentials seen by industry visionaries.

By the mid-1970s, most cable industry people were saying that cable could not make it in the bigger cities where plenty of television stations were already available over the air. Indeed, at that time cable companies were not seeking major-city franchises. Now there are several bidders for each big-city franchise and blue-chip corporations are buying cable companies.

Bidding for franchises is so fierce that cable companies are promising services beyond tested technical capability at the time of application—services such as home security systems and automatic utility meter reading and videotext. Capitalizing on the frenetic bidding for franchises, cities are quite creative in their demands and expectations, pushing cable into still new service areas.

In earlier days, demand for cable services was stable and quite predictable. In a community with no clear channels available off air, 95 percent of the households would subscribe to cable; in a town with only one TV station, 80 percent; if there were already two stations, about 60 percent; and a town with all three network affiliates represented by nearby broadcast stations would still sign up 40 percent of the homes by bringing in some independent stations from the nearest larger cities. In television "markets" with ABC, CBS, and NBC affiliates and one or more independent local stations, not enough subscribers could be found to justify the investment in cable lines unless there were reception problems due to terrain or ghosting from large buildings. The recent success of satellite pay movie channels and, to a lesser degree, superstations and specialty networks (sports, religious, childrens', cultural, ethnic, etc.) has proven that subscriptions could be sold even in a television-rich environment such as metropolitan New York.

Now the expectation is that the whole nation, save a few sparsely populated areas, will be wired by cable in a few years. The newer systems will have upwards of 30 entertainment channels, plus home security, electronic text, two-way polling, games, instruction, government services, and more.

Early on cable captured the imagination of scholars of communication, critics of television, communication policymakers, and others who saw more promise for television than the products of limited-channel commercial television. We review the alleged defects of the broadcast system and suggest the promise of cable in relation to each.

Diversity

Technical factors require separation of broadcast television channel assignments. Adjacent channels (e.g., channels 7 and 8) cannot be assigned to the same place.[2] They would interfere with each other. Two stations on the *same* channel must be separated by 150 miles or more, so that their signals don't overlap in the middle and make a muddle of the signals for people there. It would have been possible for the FCC to have created a system of high-powered regional stations so that every household would have six or more stations available, but this would have sacrificed local service, which was a crucial goal of the FCC in creating the assignment table. As the table was worked out, most places in the United States had three or fewer stations. This effectively limited the number of networks to three.

In programming television networks, it made better economic sense for each of the networks to aim for the mass audience with similar tastes, that is, to seek the "lowest-common-denominator" programs that would attract a one-third share of the majority.[3] Following this strategy, the networks, and also individual stations programming their own option time, imitated each other's successes, and all television stations were pretty much alike. People who didn't conform to the interests of the mass audience were left out entirely. Critics and intellectuals railed at this development, but the economic incentives of the commercial television system, under a table of assignments that limited channels, all favored the system as it existed.

Cable offered an answer—*unlimited* channels: 12, 30, 54, 108. With this abundance, new networks could arise, and since the commercial broadcast networks served the mass audience well, the new networks would have to be more specialized. With signals beamed from communication satellites to cable system earth stations, this hope for diversity has actually been realized, and plans have been laid for still greater variety. Even the commercial broadcast networks are now developing alternate services for cable.

New Opportunities

Another complaint against the broadcast television system arising from the limited-broadcast-channel assignments was the monopoly of communication power it gave to a few corporations. The three commercial broadcast networks controlled prime time and much of the rest of the day. This presented a tight market to creative talent. Very few could break in. There was no room to experiment with new ideas. Some felt that, in news and public affairs, television was dominated by a few men in New York and Washington, and in entertainment by men in New York and Hollywood.

Cable could loosen the hold of the networks and their affiliates and open television to new talent and fresh ideas. Certainly cable has provided new options in prime time as the satellite cable networks have emerged. As cable reaches a higher proportion of U.S. homes (some say 30 percent, others 50 percent), much more new entertainment material will be produced originally for cable, thereby increasing the market for talent. Now there is a Cable News Network (CNN) with headquarters not in New York but in Atlanta, Georgia.

More News

Many have said there is no depth to broadcast news. Television is only a headline service. Commercial television stations have expanded news time to what they believe to be the tolerable limits, economically. Only for transcendental news events can entertainment programming be sacrificed to news broadcasts.

Cable can devote whole channels to news. A cable system may have CNN's 24-hour news and two or three full-time text news channels. Cable can present *raw* (unedited) news—gavel-to-gavel coverage of the U.S. House of Representatives, city council meetings, school boards, trials, special events, and so on.

Many neighborhoods and communities within metropolitan areas are too small for attention by the big media—newspapers, television, and radio—that must cover the entire metro market. Cable can offer local newscasts, either full audiovisual programs or alphanumeric text.

Access

Critics of broadcast television have lamented the fact that not everyone can own a station. There is no access to the airwaves comparable to the freedom to print a newspaper or a handbill. Efforts to impose some elements of free expression on broadcast television have produced the FCC's Fairness Doctrine and other federal rules that encroach on the freedom of the broadcaster. None is an entirely satisfactory solution.

Cable can provide a community soapbox, giving over one or more channels to the public. Although no longer required of cable systems by the FCC, many cable franchises require a public access channel. Cable systems find the concept and the programming attractive to some subscribers, and none would bid a new urban system without promising it.

Less Commercial Intrusion

Some people are offended by television commercials, although Americans are generally tolerant. The critics say that commercials interrupt program flow, influence television content, are tasteless, and invade viewer privacy.

The cable subscriber can experience commercial-free television on channels other than PBS. Some channels have no commercials. Other channels use commercials to subsidize programming, much like magazines use advertising to supplement subscriptions, by discreetly inserting commercials between programs.

Education and Government

Educators and public service providers note that in most countries TV first serves public communication and education needs and then commercial interests, if at all. In the United States it is the other way around. Commercial broadcasting dominated the system and took the best channels first. Education was second, and government public service channels operated in only a handful of cities.

Cable has room for government, education, and library channels. Some cities and cable systems are proud of the innovative uses and accomplishments of these channels.

Interactive Television

Finally, almost everybody is somewhat uneasy about hours of passive television viewing. It doesn't seem healthy for kids, and adults feel guilty too.

Interactive two-way cable can offer a modicum of involvement to the television user. Through polling, viewers can have some sense of the rest of the audience. Viewers may even control the content of the television by choosing particular options for themselves or participating with others in voting for particular outcomes. Television can be used as a reference service where the user may order text and graphic information to serve a variety of individual needs.

HISTORY

The origins of cable are humble. There was no vision of the services and impacts just outlined. When broadcast television became a reality for many areas of the country in 1948, people shielded from the signals by mountains, or slightly out of range, felt a sense of deprivation. Appliance stores and radio repair shops in these areas were denied the booming new business in television. The most imaginative of the appliance dealers and repairpersons in these areas began to look for a way into the market. Several of them laid claim to the original community antenna television (CATV) system.

One is Robert J. Tarlton of Lansford, Pennsylvania, a radio sales and service person. Lansford was only 65 miles from Philadelphia, close enough to receive weak television signals, but cut off by the Allegheny Mountains. A few venturesome people bought television sets. The reception was terrible. Tarlton went to the top of the mountain in 1949 and tried to set up individual antennas for the set owners. It worked, but it would have resulted in a mountain-top forest of antennas and rivers of cable coming down the hill with tributaries all over town. Tarlton thought of a better way. He found some friends to invest with him in a company called Panther Valley Television. They built a master antenna at the mountain summit, amplified the weak signals from Philadelphia, and distributed them house-to-house by coaxial cable hung on poles. Panther Valley charged an initial installation fee of $125, and $3 per month. The system brought in the three Philadelphia television stations clearly, and Tarlton began selling television sets.[4]

At the same time, in Astoria, Oregon, Ed Parsons at KAST radio was experimenting with antennas to get television from Seattle for his wife. He ran the wire from his home to a hotel lobby across the street and to a nearby music store. Even earlier, in 1948, John Walson, a power and light maintenance employee and appliance dealer in Mahanoy City, Pennsylvania, claimed to provide a master antenna-cable system. However all his records were wiped out in a fire.

From 1949, the number of cable systems grew slowly but steadily. By 1961 there were 700 community antenna TV systems. Growth accelerated at this point so that in 1971 there were 2,750 systems serving nearly six million homes.[5] During this period, cable was first providing television to homes that were entirely out of rooftop antenna range of any television stations. Later, cable came to be a business of filling out the complement of television services in communities that had less than the three commercial networks. Through much of this period cable was viewed as ancillary to the broadcast service, simply a community antenna. There was no intent to bring in anything except the nearest television stations, although some CATV systems reached out a fair distance to get those stations with the help of microwave relay stations.

In the 1970s, the concept of originating programs at a cable system was established. The programs were fed directly into the cable. This meant that cable systems became more than an extension of broadcasting stations. They became a programming *source*. The cable systems being built in the 1970s were 30 or 35 channels, up from the 5- or 12-channel systems of the early years. To go beyond the 12 channels that could be tuned on the VHF dial of the set required a converter, a device for selecting channels on the cable from across a frequency spectrum from 54 to 300 megahertz.

The cable systems of the 1970s were capable of *two-way* communication. This meant that their amplifiers were constructed to accommodate signals *from* the receiving household as well as *to* the household if the demand ever arose for such a service. For the most part, however, two-way cable was still experimental. Now cable construction is 400 megahertz, meaning a single cable capacity of 54 channels. Two-way service including home security, information retrieval, and interactive instruction will be required of most systems built in the 1980s.

In 1985 cable will be serving more than 40 million homes; 47 percent of the television households in the United States. Of these subscribing households, 25,000,000 will be pay cable subscribers.[6] In only a few years there has been a radical shift in cable communication from 12-channel systems averaging about 2,000 subscribers to 100-channel, bidirectional systems with 100,000 or more subscribing households. There is a dramatic difference between community antenna television and the 100-channel broadband communications systems of today.

Significant maturation for cable is expected through the 1980s. Existing systems will be adding services and customers. Franchises are being granted in the big cities with the major portion of the nation's population. By the end of the decade, cable will probably serve a majority of the U.S. households and have developed its own character as a communication medium.

This book is in five parts. Part I is the technology of cable, tracing a cable system from the control center, or headend, through the distribution plant to the home. A separate chapter presents the special technology of two-way cable.

Part II describes cable services, present and future, including over-the-air television and radio; automated channels; public, government, and education access channels; community channels; satellite-delivered programming, with a chapter on pay television; and two-way services.

Part III is public policy—the Congress, FCC, copyright law, state regulation, local franchising, and privacy.

Part IV is the business of cable. It includes ownership patterns, finance, accounting, audiences and programming, marketing, advertising, customer relations, maintenance, engineering, and personnel. Part IV also contains a section on professional resources.

Part V, a single long chapter, discusses other new communication technologies as they relate to each other and to the general media environment in different community types. We conclude with a discussion of the potential social impact of cable.

NOTES

[1]Roger G. Noll, Merton J. Peck, and John J. McGowan, *Economic Aspects of Television Regulation* (Washington, D.C.: The Brookings Institution, 1973), p. 32.

[2]This is true except for channels 6 and 7, which have the entire FM band separating them.

[3]For a discussion of the economics of programming, see Bruce M. Owen, Jack H. Beebe, and Willard G. Manning, Jr., *Television Economics* (Lexington, Mass.: Lexington Books, 1974), chap. 3.

[4]Ralph Lee Smith, *The Wired Nation* (New York: Harper Colophon Books, 1972), p. 3.

[5]Sloan Commission on Cable Communication, *On the Cable* (New York: McGraw-Hill, 1971), p. 31.

[6]"Cable Stats," *Cablevision*, April 26, 1982, p.248.

2

Headend

Base of antenna tower and satellite receive stations at the headend, Warner Amex Cable Company, Cincinnati, Ohio.

OVERVIEW

A cable television system is in essence a method of distributing television, radio, and data signals from a central originating location to residences and businesses by way of coaxial cable. It consists of three main elements. First is the *headend,* which is the point at which all the program sources are received, assembled, and processed for transmission by the distribution network. Second is the *distribution network,* consisting of coaxial cable leaving the headend on power or telephone company poles or, in some cases, buried underground, and going down each street within the community served. Third is the *subscriber drop,* which consists of the coaxial cable going from the street into the individual subscriber's home or business, and the related equipment required to connect the cable to the subscriber's television receiver and other devices.

The operation of a cable television system can be compared with the operation of a municipal water system as shown in Figure 2-1. In a water system, the supply of water comes from either a well field or a reservoir. In cable television, the headend is the source for the signals to be transmitted to the subscribers.

Water mains leave the well field to carry the water into individual areas of the community to be served. In the cable system, the trunk cable serves a similar function for transmission of the television signals.

Along the way, friction in the water pipes slows down the flow of water, and pumping stations are required to bring the water flow up to the required rate. In a cable television system, electronic signals diminish as they travel through the cable, and amplifiers are required periodically to boost the signal back up to an acceptable level.

Within individual neighborhoods, a water system branches out, with smaller-diameter pipes along each street. Similarly, in a cable system, smaller-diameter cables are used to transport TV signals down individual streets. Each water system customer is connected to the pipe at the street by a junction box located near the street, typically next to the sidewalk. A portion of the water is tapped out of the pipe and is sent into the customer's home. In a cable television system, a *tap* serves a similar function, with electronic signals tapped from the distribution cable and fed over a small-diameter cable into the subscriber's home for connection to television and radio receivers.

THE CABLE TELEVISION HEADEND

As mentioned, the headend is the originating point for all the services carried on a cable television system. Over the years, it has grown in complexity from perhaps ten pieces of electronic equipment in a small

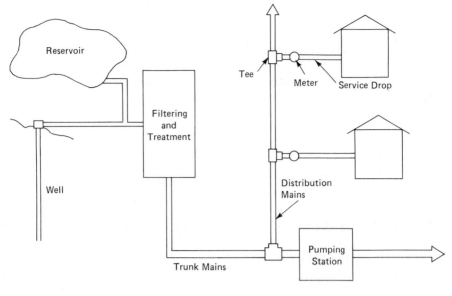

Water System

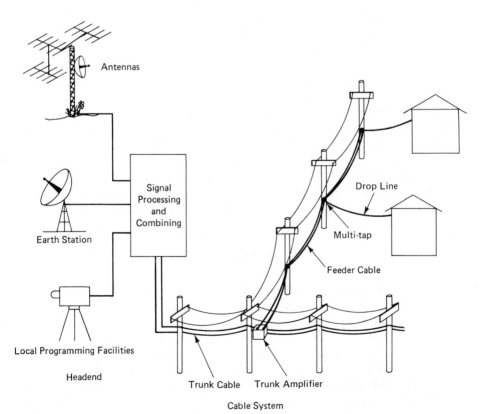

Cable System

Figure 2-1. Cable system compared to a water system.

utility building to a multimillion dollar control center consisting of thousands of pieces of equipment, including satellite-receiving equipment, towers, antennas, computers, TV production studios, and radio and television receivers.

OVER-THE-AIR CHANNELS

Early cable television systems served only one purpose: to pick up distant television channels that could not be received by residents of a community, and to deliver those channels to subscribers. Typically, a cable television headend would be located on the top of a mountain near the community. In many cases, a very tall tower (300 to 1,000 feet) was built and antennas were installed to bring in stations from distant cities. A small building was constructed at the bottom of the tower to contain *signal processors* (devices that "clean up" the pictures from the desired television channel). Since these channels came from some distance away, they would often vary greatly in signal strength. One of the signal processor's purposes is to level out the strength of these signals so that they are more uniform. Another is to eliminate interference from adjacent channels. After each of the signals has been processed, all are joined together in a combining network and fed into the cable distribution plant.

Later, cable television operators began originating some of their own services, most commonly a time and weather channel. At the headend, a television camera was mounted on a motorized platform that would rotate back and forth televising a thermometer, a barometer, a windspeed indicator, and a clock. To put this television picture on the cable system, a *modulator* is required. A modulator is a miniature television transmitter that generates a signal on a television channel. The output of this modulator is combined with the other channels in the headend combiner for transmission over the cable distribution plant. (Figure 2-2.)

MICROWAVE

Another source of signals for the cable television headend is *microwave* transmission. Sometimes, when a cable operator wishes to provide its subscribers with a distant television station, it is impossible to receive that station with an antenna located on a tower. In this case, the cable television operator has two options. First, if there is an existing *common carrier* microwave network in the area, the operator might contract with that common carrier for delivery of the channels desired to the headend. Common carriers are licensed by the FCC to deliver television channels to a number of cable television systems on a *tariff* (fee schedule)

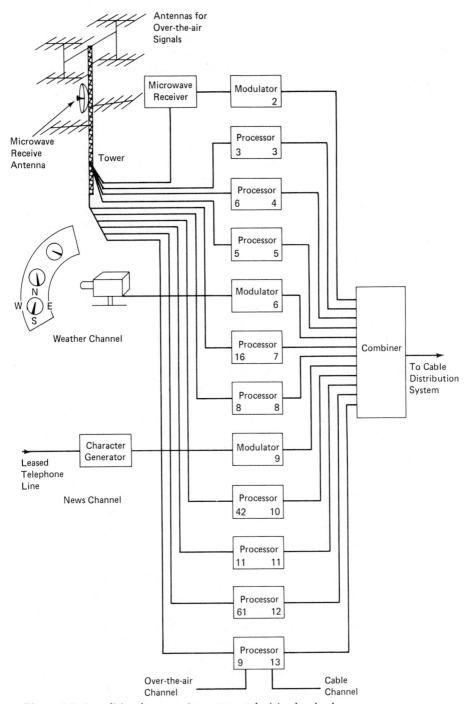

Figure 2-2. A traditional community antenna television headend.

established by the company and approved by the FCC. In this case, the common carrier company would provide a microwave-receiving antenna on the cable company's tower, and the necessary receiving equipment in the headend. The cable operator would provide only the modulator to put the desired channels on the cable system.

The alternative is for the cable TV company to build its own CARS (community antenna relay service) microwave system. The cable operator purchases or leases land close enough to the desired television station to receive a good picture, and installs a small building and tower and the necessary microwave-transmitting equipment to relay the signal to the headend. In some cases intermediate relay points are required.

A microwave signal can travel approximately 25 miles before it must be retransmitted. Microwave is also being used for interconnection of cable systems for exchange of programming, and many regional microwave networks are emerging.

SATELLITE EARTH STATIONS

During the mid-1960s, the technology became available for distribution of telephone, data, and video signals via communications satellite. These satellites are located in a *geosynchronous orbit* 22,300 miles above the earth. At this altitude, they make one revolution per day around the earth so that they appear to be standing still in relationship to the ground below.

Communications satellites are broadcast relay stations. They pick up signals that are beamed from *uplink* stations on the ground and retransmit them back down toward the earth to a *receiving station,* often called an *earth station,* a TVRO (TV receive only) or simply a "dish."

Communications satellites use *transponders* to receive the signals from the ground and relay them back to the earth stations. Although there are many types of communications satellites, the ones used for cable purposes are capable of transmitting either 12 or 24 TV channels, together with a number of *subcarrier* audio and data channels within each TV channel.

Because of the great distances from earth and the state of the art in satellite design, the signals that arrive at an earth station are extremely weak. For this reason, large-diameter receiving antennas are required, together with sophisticated preamplifiers and receivers. When communications satellites were first used for cable service, cable operators were required to install antennas that were 10 meters in diameter. These earth stations cost in excess of $100,000. Later, the FCC authorized the use of 5-meter earth stations, which, with a few exceptions, are the standard in use today in the cable industry.

In some areas of the country, and particularly in Hawaii and Alaska, the signal from the satellites is weaker than in other areas, and larger-diameter antennas are required. For instance, in Alaska a 10-meter earth station is almost always necessary. In the southern portion of Florida, a 7-meter antenna is usually required.

Before an earth station is installed, an engineering study must be performed to determine that the antenna size is sufficient to produce a good quality picture and that nearby microwave transmitters will not interfere with the reception of the satellite signals. This work, called a *frequency coordination study,* is performed using a computerized listing of all the existing microwave transmission facilities in the United States. A cable operator usually relies on a consulting service to provide this study.

There is no advantage in putting in an earth station larger than the one necessary for good quality reception. If a 7-meter station is called for by the engineering study, installation of a 10-meter station will not provide better picture quality; however, installation of a 5-meter station will most likely produce inferior results.

Two major types of earth stations are in use today. The first and most common is the *parabolic reflector.* This type of antenna looks like a giant dish and is mounted on a concrete slab and aimed toward a point above the equator where the satellite is located. (See photograph on the chapter title page.) Satellites are located at different positions above the equator approximately 4 degrees apart and transmit on the same frequencies. By aiming an earth station at one satellite, and aligning it carefully, transmission from other satellites will not interfere with the desired signal.

The second type of earth station is called a *conical horn* and looks like an immense horn of plenty. The conical horn is substantially more expensive than the parabolic reflector, but it is often necessary in areas with interference from nearby terrestrial microwave sources.

Each earth satellite is capable of transmitting several channels, and a single earth station is capable of receiving all of them. A receiver and modulator are necessary for each channel received from the satellite.

Cable systems started using satellite earth stations in the mid-1970s when Home Box Office leased a transponder on the RCA satellite. Shortly after that, Ted Turner's channel 17, the independent TV station from Atlanta, was put on the satellite.

At first, only a few channels of satellite programming were offered, and there was no problem getting them all on a single satellite—the RCA Satcom 1. (See picture at the opening of Chapter 7.) However, as new services became available, the RCA satellite filled up, and program suppliers were forced to go to additional satellites. Until mid-1981, each satellite required a separate earth station. At present, most cable systems have only one earth station. A growing number are installing two or even three earth stations to take advantage of all the programming that is available. Now it is possible to receive several satellites on a single *multiple-beam satellite antenna.*

Even with all the services mentioned, a headend building with no more than 200 square feet is required, and the headend can be operated unattended. Most cable system headends now in operation in the United States are similar to those just described.

AUTOMATED CHANNELS

With the advent of cable systems in major markets, however, the complexity of cable headends has increased dramatically. In addition to all the signal sources noted, cable systems have started originating a large number of TV channels. Most of them are *automated services;* that is, they are alphanumeric channels, such as news, weather, sports, channel listings, stock market quotations, and community bulletin boards. A device called a *character generator* is required to provide these channels. A character generator is nothing but a special-purpose computer that accepts input from a keyboard, or telephone line, and formats the information in a pleasing way to be displayed on a television screen. Initially, character generators were used by cable systems to provide national and international news services from the existing news wire services, such as The Associated Press or Reuters. The cable operator leases a telephone line from the nearest Reuters or AP center and connects it to a character generator. The telephone line transmits digital information to the character generator at the cable headend, where it is formatted and displayed on a TV channel.

As more channels of alphanumeric information were required, cable operators began installing complex *multichannel character generators.* These systems have the capability of programming on 10 or more different television channels and can store thousands of pages of information. A typical multichannel character generator system has some channels programmed by a keyboard (the program schedule, community bulletin board, etc.), some channels programmed by a leased telephone line (AP, Reuters news), and some channels programmed by automatic sensors (weather).

Another form of automated program origination that is similar to the character generator channels is the *frame store* channel. In new cable systems, particularly in major markets, these channels are becoming more common. The two most popular uses of the frame store technique are slow-scan news and weather radar. Frame store technology involves the transmission of a television picture at slow speed over a telephone line or satellite channel to a frame store device at the cable system headend for display on a television channel. In the case of the slow-scan news services, still pictures are transmitted over a *subcarrier* (an unused segment of a satellite channel that does not interfere with its main television program). It takes about ten seconds for a full black and white picture to be transmitted in this method. The subscriber sees a succession of still pictures appearing on the television screen and hears an accompanying audio description.

Weather radar operates in a similar fashion. The National Weather Service provides the capability for connecting a slow-scan formatting device to its radar system nearest to the cable system's headend. The information from this radar picture is transmitted in digital form over a telephone line to the slow-scan storage device at the cable system headend, where it is reformatted to produce a video display of the weather radar scan.

HEADEND AUTOMATION

As cable systems have become more sophisticated, headends have changed from unmanned sheds located on the outskirts of town to large operation centers manned 24 hours a day. (See Figure 2-3.) Originally, each cable channel carried only one program source, such as an off-the-air television channel or the time and weather display. With the enactment of FCC rules on program exclusivity and blackouts (discussed in other chapters), cable systems were required to start switching program sources. For instance, if a distant independent television channel was the normal program source on a cable channel, the cable operator would be required to black out the program. Rather than leaving that channel blank, many cable operators would opt to insert a program from another television station in its place. To do this, switching equipment would be required. In the early days of cable, the switching was often done manually or with crude rotating drums. As the drum rotated, switches would be activated to enable or disable different program sources. Later, computerized systems were introduced which could be programmed several days in advance to provide the switching function.

Newer cable systems have extensive switching requirements with dozens of program sources being switched. However, because of the complexity of the switching operation, and because of last-minute changes in program schedules, automation is not, in itself, sufficient. Many major market cable systems today provide around-the-clock monitoring of program quality and switching to assure that subscribers are receiving the programs and quality that they expect.

Usually this monitoring is done by video operators who constantly check high quality television monitors. The operators look sequentially at each of the signals carried on the cable system to make certain that

Figure 2-3. Interior of the Qube Cable headend, Cincinnati, Ohio. Racks contain modulators for each channel.

the picture quality is good. The operators also check to make certain that the proper program is being carried on the proper channel at all times. Often cable systems have alternative sources for programming. For instance, if a network program is being carried on the system and the picture quality is poor from one station, the video operator may switch to a second broadcast station signal. Also, the operator will have spare satellite receiving equipment to be used in case of a failure of one of the satellite-delivered channels.

FM RADIO SERVICES

Cable systems carry audio services, utilizing the FM radio spectrum of 88 to 108mHz (megahertz, millions of cycles per second). In the headend, radio signals are processed similarly to video signals. For over-the-air FM stations, signal processors convert stations to a different frequency and stabilize the signal levels. For locally generated radio signals, such as cable radio, a modulator is used to put the audio signal on an FM radio frequency.

Audio programming is also carried on satellites and microwave paths using subcarriers. To put these signals on a cable system, *subcarrier receivers* extract the audio from the video channels. Modulators are then used to produce the FM radio frequency.

Up to 40 audio channels can be carried on a cable system in the FM band. However, many engineers are concerned about the effects of carrying a large number of FM stations, especially in 50-channel systems. They fear that degradation of video services could occur. In addition, it is difficult to provide undegraded FM audio service, since the signals are distorted as they pass through amplifiers in the distribution plant, a liability that will become more critical as FM receivers and home stereo equipment improve. However, as cable amplifiers improve in quality, it is likely that the problems cited will be solved.

LOCAL ORIGINATION FACILITIES

Most modern cable television systems offer locally produced programming on at least one television channel. Up until as recently as two years ago, a typical cable system might install a small studio and control center consisting of two or three low cost cameras and perhaps a *portapak* (portable videotape-camera combination). Such a studio might cost $75,000 to $100,000 and might be staffed with two full-time and three or four part-time employees. Maintenance is usually handled by the chief engineer of the cable system or perhaps a part-time video engineer.

With the explosion of the franchise competition in 1979 and 1980, cable operators began promising more elaborate local origination facilities. It is not unusual in present proposals to see capital investments of $1–2 million for local origination equipment. In most cases more than one origination studio is promised, equipped with broadcast quality cameras and videotape machines. Expensive mobile production vans are also promised, with a substantial number of portapaks. Portable microwave equipment is included to allow the production of live programming from anywhere within the community. Major city franchise applicants often promise 50 or more employees for local program production, with operating budgets of several million dollars per year.

A sample of the proposed facilities for a major city franchise is included as Appendix A.

HUB INTERCONNECTION

Cable television systems are limited in size to a radius of about 5 miles from a headend location. A detailed explanation of these limitations is provided in Chapter 3. To service large metropolitan areas, a single headend is not sufficient. However, it is desirable to centralize the chan-

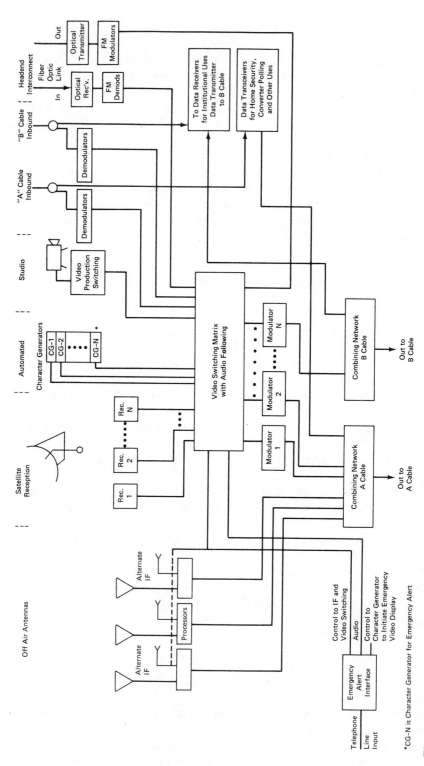

Figure 2-4. Diagram of the headend in a major city cable system.

*CG-N is Character Generator for Emergency Alert

22

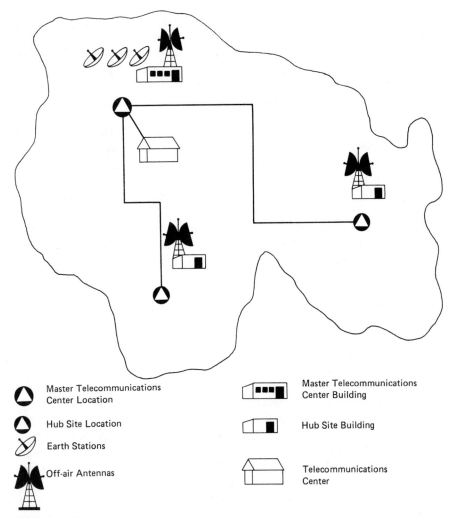

Master Telecommunications
Center Location

Hub Site Location

Earth Stations

Off-air Antennas

Master Telecommunications
Center Building

Hub Site Building

Telecommunications
Center

Figure 2-5. Hub system.

nel origination, processing, switching, and monitoring at one location. To serve large metropolitan areas, a *hub* system is typically used. (See Figure 2-5.) The area around the main headend is served by trunk lines leaving the headend. Other areas of the community are served by remote hubs, each of which serves an area with a radius of about 5 miles around the hub. To deliver the television programming from the main headend to each of the hubs, two techniques are employed.

The first is microwave. A complex microwave transmitter is installed at the main headend feeding a multitude of antennas, one directed at each of the remote hubs. At each hub, a relatively inexpensive microwave-receiving system is installed, which converts these microwave channels to regular television channels for carriage on the cable system within that hub. This system is highly reliable and provides excellent picture quality.

Because new systems are promising large numbers of channels (50 to 100), conventional microwave techniques cannot be used. The amount of microwave spectrum space required is prohibitive. Instead, a system called AML (amplitude modulated link) is used. AML systems have proven reliable and capable of delivering good quality television signals in many locations. However, they have two major drawbacks. The first, a failure of the transmitter system at the main headend, will cause loss of service to all the hubs and therefore all subscribers in the cable system. Redundant equipment is extremely expensive. Second, and more important, AML systems are not reliable in areas with frequent and severe thunderstorms. Rain attenuates the microwave signals very dramatically, and during heavy periods of rainfall, AML microwave signals deteriorate. AML hub interconnection, therefore, is not a wise solution in many locations.

A second interconnection method is the use of a *supertrunk*. A large-diameter cable interconnects the main headend with each of the hubs. This cable is equipped with high quality cable amplifiers. In some cases, FM transmission of television signals is utilized over the supertrunk, reducing the signal degradation. Another approach is to use *feed-forward* amplifiers, which are expensive, but have substantially less distortion than conventional cable amplifiers.

Supertrunk interconnection of hubs also has two disadvantages. First, signal degradation may be greater over a supertrunk interconnection than over AML microwave in certain cases. Careful design techniques, however, can keep this degradation to an insignificant level. Second, a supertrunk line is susceptible to outages caused by failure of amplifiers or by physical damage to the cable plant. For instance, an automobile accident that involves knocking down a utility pole could put a supertrunk out of operation for hours.

Reliability in modern cable television systems is of extreme importance, especially when home security services are offered. Interconnection of the main headend with hubs, therefore, must be designed so as to provide almost flawless reliability. Redundant paths from the main headend to the hub provide one solution. For instance, interconnection might be done using both AML and supertrunk, or two supertrunks utilizing different physical routes might be employed. Either of these approaches is costly, but given the complexity and reliability requirements of modern cable systems, redundancy is becoming an essential element.

As cable systems become more involved in two-way communication, headends become even more sophisticated. Large, complex, minicomputer systems are being installed for home security services, videotext, and other interactive cable television services. Chapter 5, on two-way cable systems, discusses these headend systems.

HRC AND IRC HEADENDS

Many new cable systems are designed using HRC (harmonically-related carrier) or IRC (interval-related carrier) type headends. In Chapter 3, signal degradation due to distortion in cable equipment is described. These distortions can cause poor picture quality. Their severity increases as the number of channels carried on the system is increased. HRC and IRC headends provide one way of minimizing the problem.

HRC and IRC headends tie the television channels to a common frequency reference, which causes the distortions that are created in amplifiers to cancel each other out or to occur at places where they are less visible to cable subscribers. HRC and IRC techniques will allow a cable operator to increase the system size without adding more headends or hubs, or to increase the performance of a cable system of a given size.

There is much debate now in the cable industry over the use of these types of headends. Although improvements can be made in picture quality using them, the distortions are still present, only hidden, and in fact, some system designs utilizing these headends do not meet FCC technical standards. Future services, such as videotext, may cause these distortions to become visible again. Also, certain other problems such as signal ingress (see Chapter 5) are made more severe using these headends.

For these reasons a prudent cable operator will use HRC and IRC headends as a method of enhancing system performance rather than extending system size or reducing the number of hubs.

3

Distribution Plant

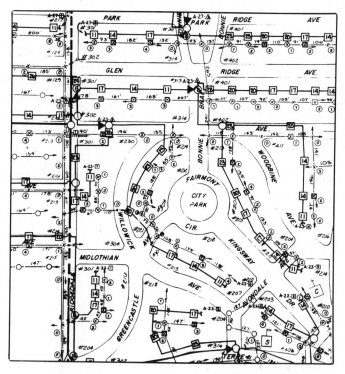

Section of a system design map, Temple Terrace, Florida.

THE NATURE AND FUNCTION OF THE
DISTRIBUTION PLANT

In contrast to the cable headend, the complexity of cable television distribution systems has changed very little from the early days of cable. However, many improvements in reliability, performance, and channel capacity have been made.

The Cable Spectrum

To understand cable television systems, a knowledge of the television spectrum is required. (See Figure 3-1.) Each television channel occupies 6mHz of space in the electromagnetic spectrum. Over-the-air TV broadcasts take place in three regions of the electromagnetic spectrum: channels 2 through 6 are broadcast at 54 to 88mHz, and channels 7 through 13 are at 174 to 216mHz. The third band, the UHF channels 14 through 83, are in the range of 470 to 890mHz.

The very earliest cable distribution systems consisted of coaxial cable about a half an inch in diameter. The cable had a copper center conductor (which carries the TV signals), surrounded by a plastic insulator with a braided copper shield (which prevents cable signals from leaking *out of* or over-the-air signals from leaking *into* the cable) surrounding the insulator. A plastic jacket was placed around the cable for protection from moisture and physical damage. The amplifiers, which maintain signal strength throughout the system, were located in utility boxes on poles. A single amplifier was required for each channel carried on the cable system, and for this reason, three to five channels were all that could be carried.

These amplifiers used electron tubes, which have a limited life and which deteriorate in performance with age. Maintenance of this type of cable television system was extremely costly and difficult.

In the next version of cable TV systems, single-channel amplifiers were replaced with *broadband* amplifiers. These amplifiers were capable of carrying 54 to 108mHz (5 channels), and later 54 to 108 and 174 to 216mHz (12 channels) simultaneously. At first, these amplifiers also used tubes and had the same maintenance and reliability problems.

Later, in the mid-1960s, transistorized amplifiers began to appear. Although promising greater reliability than electron tube amplifiers, they were less reliable for the first several years after their introduction. Transistors are much more susceptible to damage by lightning and surges of electrical current than are electron tubes.

During the early 1960s, the braided copper cable was replaced by a solid sheathed aluminum cable with a copper, or copper-covered alu-

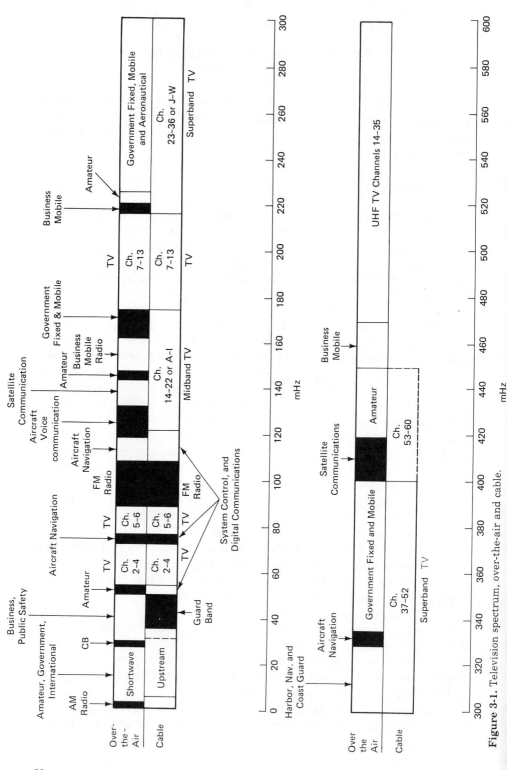

Figure 3-1. Television spectrum, over-the-air and cable.

28

minum, center conductor, which with minor variation, is the type of cable in use today. (See Figure 3-2.)

In the early 1970s, the first *hybrid* cable amplifiers were developed. An outgrowth of *integrated circuit* development, a hybrid is a packaged device that contains integrated circuits and individual electronic components. An integrated circuit is a silicon chip, the surface of which is processed ("printed") to create transistors and other devices that are connected to make an electronic circuit.[1] The hybrid amplifiers, using integrated circuits, offer much higher reliability and performance than do the older transistor amplifiers.

About the same time, cable system amplifiers became capable of carrying 20 TV channels with reasonable performance. To increase a cable system's capacity from 12 to 20 channels, the space in between channel 6 and channel 7 (121 to 174mHz) is utilized. These frequencies are used by over-the-air broadcasters for other purposes such as aircraft communication, police and fire, amateur radio, and military communications. However, since the cable system distributes signals only within a wire and not over the air, it can share these same frequencies without interference.

A normal television receiver cannot tune these *midband* channels (commonly labeled channels A–I or 14–22 in cable systems). To receive them, a converter is required. (Converters are described in Chapter 4.)

Going from 12 to 20 channels was not as simple as providing amplifiers that covered the frequency range of 54 to 216mHz. This is because amplifiers are not perfect and introduce distortion to television pictures. All cable TV systems, no matter how well designed, contain these distortions, but in a well-designed and well-maintained system, these distortions are small enough that they are not visible to cable TV subscribers. As the number of channels is increased on a cable system, the severity of the distortion increases substantially. So going from 12 to 20 channels requires amplifiers with a great deal higher performance to produce good quality television pictures. In the late 1960s and early 1970s, this distortion problem was the main limitation on the number of channels that

Figure 3-2. Coaxial cable.

could be carried on a cable system, and in fact, today, it is a major problem with the 50-channel systems that are being constructed.

In the early 1970s, channel capacity was increased to around 30 channels, and by the mid-1970s, 35 channels could be carried with excellent performance. To go from 20 channels to 35 channels required amplifiers to cover the frequency range of 54 to 300mHz, with the extra channels being carried above channel 13 in the *superband* (216–300mHz). These channels are commonly labeled channels 23–36 or channels J–W. The most recent cable TV systems carry 54 to 60 channels. This is accomplished by increasing the amplifier's frequency spectrum up to 400–450mHz.

There is much confusion about the actual channel capacity of these systems. Systems that carry from 54 to 400mHz are variously described by different equipment manufacturers and cable operators as being 50-, 52-, or 54-channel systems. The actual channel capacity depends on FCC regulations concerning use of frequencies in the aeronautical, navigational, and communications spectrum. Many cable systems are prohibited from using channel A in the midband, and some cannot use other channels in the midband or superband.

Manufacturers are presently making 450-mHz amplifiers, which add another six channels to the capacity of systems using this equipment, for a total of 60 channels.

The Trunk

A cable TV distribution plant consists of two major elements: the first is the trunk system; the second is the feeder network. The trunk system (shown in Figure 3-3) consists of a large-diameter cable (three-quarters to one inch in diameter) leaving the headend or hub and going through a community, splitting at various points, and finally terminating at the extreme of the service area. The trunk's only purpose is to deliver television signals to individual neighborhoods of the community. No subscribers are served directly from the trunk; instead, *bridger* amplifiers are located periodically along the trunk at intervals of approximately 0.35–0.50 miles to take signals from the trunk and feed them to the feeder network. Typically, there is about one mile of trunk cable for every three to four miles of feeder cable in a cable system.

Trunk Amplifiers

Signal strength diminishes as the signals pass through coaxial cable. This loss is referred to as *attenuation*. Amplifiers are located so as to counteract attenuation whenever the signal level is reduced to the point where it would result in *visible noise* in the television picture. Noise

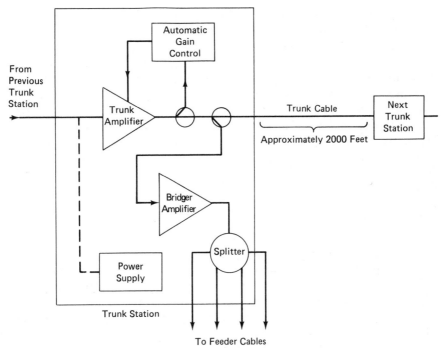

Figure 3-3. Trunk system.

appears to the cable subscriber as a snowy picture. Before the television signal is attenuated to the point where noise is visible, an amplifier is installed, which boosts (adds *gain* to) the signal by an amount equal to the attenuation of the previous section of cable. Therefore, the amount of signal coming out of each amplifier will be equal throughout the entire cable system. In cable television, the *decibel* (or *dB*) is used as the measure of attenuation and gain. Typically, a trunk cable will have an attenuation of approximately 20 dB between amplifiers.

The industry standard of approximately 20 dB of amplifier gain was derived from the distortion characteristics of amplifying equipment. If a cable amplifier were perfect, that is, created no distortion, then one large amplifier with a gain of, say, 500 dB could be placed at the cable headend, which would produce a signal strong enough to compensate for the loss of all the cable in the entire cable system. No amplifiers would be required in the cable plant. However, amplifiers produce increased distortion as their gain is increased. This distortion, actually a combination of different types of distortion (intermodulation, second order, triple beat, etc.), appears in subscribers' pictures as wavy lines or faintly visible pictures from other TV channels in the background. Amplifiers must be operated well below the point at which this distortion becomes visible in subscribers' pictures. The gain of 20 dB, the industry standard, allows a typical cable amplifier to be operated so that the subscriber will have degradation neither from noise nor from distortion.

It should also be mentioned that both noise and distortion increase each time a television signal is passed through an amplifier. Each time the number of amplifiers connected together, called *cascading,* is doubled, the amount of distortion and noise approximately doubles. For this reason, the length, or cascade of trunk lines, is limited to approximately 32 amplifiers in a modern cable system. With about three amplifiers per mile, the maximum trunk length is limited to about ten miles. In practice, however, both shorter and longer trunk lines are found. A well-designed 35-channel system will have trunks of no more than about five miles in length.

Automatic Gain Control

The attenuation of coaxial cable does not remain constant at all times. As temperature changes so does attenuation. As it gets colder, attenuation decreases; as it gets hotter, attenuation increases. This effect is significant and can easily cause a ten percent change from the normal attenuation of the cable, or about plus or minus 2 dB between each pair of trunk amplifiers. Although this effect is insignificant through a single trunk span, it is additive, and at the end of 20 trunk amplifiers, the signal level will change up or down by 40 dB over the temperature range normally experienced. During the summer months, the increased attenuation decreases the signal level entering each amplifier. Since the amount of noise that an amplifier adds is constant, this reduction in signal level reduces the ratio of signal-to-noise, causing the noise to be more visible. By the time the signal reaches the end of the cascade, signals are 40 dB weaker than normal, and the noise and signal are approximately equal, resulting in a totally unviewable picture.

In the winter, attenuation decreases, causing signal levels entering amplifiers to be higher. Since amplifier distortion increases as output signal level is increased, distortion becomes severe at only a few amplifiers down the cascade.

To cope with this problem, a technique called *automatic gain control,* or AGC, is employed. In a typical cable system, AGC modules are provided at every second trunk amplifier. These modules measure the strength of the television signals leaving the amplifier and compare them with a reference standard (the signal level that the amplifier is specified to put out). The amplifier's gain is then adjusted automatically to keep its output signal level at a constant point. In this way, fluctuations in temperature do not affect the signal quality at the end of the trunk line in any appreciable way. It should be noted that as channel capacity is increased on cable systems, the performance of all elements of the cable systems becomes more critical. For this reason, many state-of-the-art systems use AGC modules at every trunk amplifier location. The trunk station is pictured in Figure 3-4.

The Bridger Amplifier

As mentioned, the purpose of the trunk is to carry signals with a minimum of degradation to each neighborhood in a community. To feed the signal into the neighborhood, a *bridger amplifier* is used. The bridger amplifier is usually located in the same *housing,* or enclosure, as the trunk amplifier. A small portion of the signal is taken off the trunk and is fed into the bridger amplifier, which amplifies the signal to a level substantially higher than the level carried on the trunk line. It is then split into up to four *ports* that are used to supply feeder cables leaving the bridger. Bridger amplifiers usually have no AGC, but they are generally of the same quality as trunk amplifiers.

Passive Devices

At various points in the trunk system, the trunk must be split to serve different sections of the system. A device called a *splitter* or *directional coupler* is used. A splitter divides the signal equally into two, three,

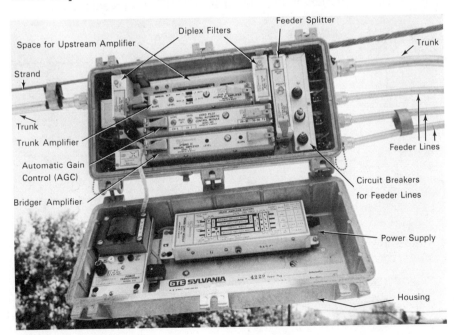

Figure 3-4. Trunk station.

or four different *legs*. A coupler, on the other hand, removes a portion of the signal from the main trunk and feeds it to a single output leg. Splitters and couplers are often referred to as *passive* devices since they have no electronic amplifying or control circuitry. Amplifiers may be referred to as *active* devices.

Connectors

Anytime the coaxial cable enters an amplifier, splitter, or coupler, a *connector* must be used. Connectors are made of aluminum. A small copper tube within the connector makes contact with the copper center conductor of the cable. The outer aluminum shield of the cable slips inside a larger tube in the connector, and a nut is tightened on the connector to squeeze a small metal ring around the aluminum outer conductor to make good contact. Connectors also contain rubber seals to keep moisture from entering the cable.

The Feeder Network

The *feeder system,* sometimes called the *distribution system,* is the network that parallels each street within a neighborhood to which subscribers connect. It is illustrated in Figure 3-5. Feeder cable is typically half an inch in diameter. Because of its smaller size, feeder cable has a

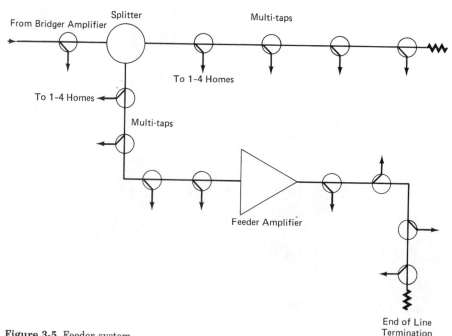

Figure 3-5. Feeder system.

higher attenuation than does trunk cable, but it is substantially lower in cost.

Unlike the trunk system, the feeder system rarely has more than two amplifiers in cascade. As a result, amplifiers can have a higher signal output than trunk amplifiers and still provide acceptable distortion levels. And again, because only two are in cascade, AGC is rarely provided.[2]

The *feeder amplifier*—also called *line extender amplifier* and *distribution amplifier*—is much less complex than a *trunk station,* is substantially smaller physically than a trunk amplifier, and costs only a fraction of what the trunk amplifier costs. Feeder amplifiers usually have 30 to 35 dB of gain. (The word "station" is used to describe the enclosure containing the trunk amplifier, the AGC device, the bridger amplifier, and other modules.)

Multitaps

After the signal leaves the port on the output of the bridger amplifier, it passes through a series of *multitaps* (diagrammed in Figure 3-6). A multitap is a device that takes a small portion of the signal off the feeder cable and feeds it to subscribers. Multitaps are available to service two, four, and eight subscribers from a single location. In an *aerial* cable system (one built on utility poles), a multitap is located in the feeder

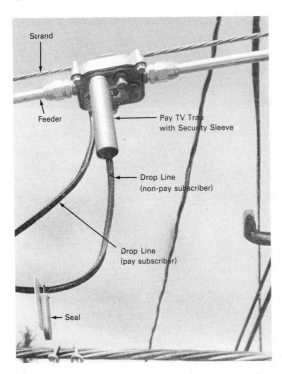

Figure 3-6. Multitap.

cable about every second utility pole, with the capability of connecting four homes. The cable plant is usually designed to follow the existing utilities, that is, telephone and electric service. Generally, if a home receives electric and telephone service from a particular pole, the cable multitap will be located there. In an *underground* system, multitaps and amplifiers are installed in *pedestals,* small containers usually located on the rear property line near the telephone company pedestals. (See the following section on construction for more details.)

It is important that a multitap *tap off* from the feeder system only the amount of signal necessary to provide good quality pictures. To accomplish this, multitaps are made in different *tap off values;* that is, different amounts of signal are removed from the feeder line. When a multitap is located immediately following a bridger or feeder amplifier, signal levels within the feeder cable will be high, and only a small amount of signal needs to be taken off the feeder line to provide the subscriber with adequate signal. Farther down the feeder cable, less signal will remain in the cable, and a greater percentage will have to be tapped off to serve subscribers. Finally, there will not be enough signal left in the feeder line to service a subscriber, and a feeder amplifier must be installed or the line must end.

Dual Cable

An increasing number of new franchises granted have been to companies proposing *dual cable* systems. Dual cable is not a new concept. It orginated in the early 1970s, as a means of increasing channel capacity. Duplicate 12-channel cable systems were built serving exactly the same area, each with its own cable, amplifiers, and subscriber connections. Twelve channels were carried on each cable system, and a switch was installed in the cable subscriber's home allowing access to a total of 24 channels. As franchise competition increased in 1979 and 1980, cable companies, in their attempt to provide higher numbers of channels, proposed the same type of arrangement. Today however, 35 or even 54 channels are carried on each cable. Dual cable systems do not differ significantly from single cable systems. In some cases a common housing is used for amplifying equipment for both cables, and the powering equipment is common to both.

Dual cable systems, although offering double channel capacity, cost only about 50 percent more than comparable single cable systems.

Institutional Network

Most of the new cable systems being built today, whether single or dual cable, include an additional cable referred to as an *institutional cable* or *institutional network.* This cable is typically another trunk cable paralleling the route of the trunk network. Its purpose is to provide interconnection of governmental and commercial institutions. (The proposed uses of the institutional networks are described in Chapter 6.) In addition, the institutional network's signals can be routed to the cable subscriber network, allowing programming to be originated at an institution and viewed by all cable subscribers.

Institutional cables differ from conventional trunk cables in that they are designed to carry an approximately equal number of channels in each direction. A 400-mHz institutional cable might carry 20 channels in one direction and 30 channels in the other direction.

Since institutional networks are basically trunks, they involve no feeder systems and sometimes no bridger amplifiers. Signals are fed into and tapped off the trunk as the trunk passes institutions that are connected to the network.

Amplifier Redundancy

Even using a hub system design, a trunk line in a cable system serves thousands of subscribers. The failure of a trunk amplifier near a hub or headend can result in loss of service to thousands and sometimes even tens of thousands of subscribers.

When cable was providing only entertainment services, such a failure was not critical. With the offering of home security services, however, a large-scale failure could result in loss of property or life.

Cable operators are beginning to experiment with techniques of providing *redundancy* for critical amplifier locations. One method utilizes trunk stations with dual amplifiers and automatic circuitry for switching from one to the other should the main amplifier fail. Very few of this type of amplifier have been installed by the cable industry, and no data are yet available on the effectiveness of this approach.

A second approach utilizes a bypass switch. If an amplifier fails, a bypass jumper is automatically connected between its input and output. The signals passing through the amplifier will not be amplified, and the signal levels will be about 20 dB lower than normal. Television pictures that subscribers receive will be substantially degraded, but home security systems, which require lower signal levels, will still operate properly. This approach, as with the redundant amplifier approach, is new and is in operation in only a few systems.

It is likely that as cable systems carry increasingly important services, new methods of redundancy will be developed.

Powering

The amplifiers used in cable systems require electric power for operation. In the early days of cable, each amplifier was connected individually to the power line. Later, methods were developed for multiplexing electric power with cable signals on the coaxial cable. Power supply units are now located at convenient points in the cable system. Each feeds power over the coaxial cable along with the TV signals to nearby amplifiers. Approximately one power supply is required for every one to three miles of trunk and feeder plant served.

A major source of outage in cable systems is the failure of electric power. If the first trunk amplifier leaving a headend is without electric power, subscribers all down the line will be without cable service. For this reason, cable operators have begun to install battery standby power supplies, and most new systems being built in large cities today utilize such power supplies. A bank of batteries will take over to power the cable system for four or more hours if the electric power service is interrupted.

System Rebuild

As cable technology changes and the demand for cable services increases, older systems face the problem of upgrading their facilities. Almost all the original 5-channel cable systems have rebuilt to 12-channel capacity, and very few systems still exist that utilize the braided type of coaxial cable. Most coaxial cable of the solid sheath aluminum variety can carry signals up to 300mHz and in many cases to 400mHz.

Upgrading or rebuilding of cable systems can take several forms. In the simplest, a cable system carrying 12 channels can add one or more midband channels simply by adding the required headend equipment and putting the channels on the system. (For the subscriber to see these channels, a converter, which will be described in the next chapter, must be used.) Most 12-channel cable systems can be expanded by at least one channel to add a pay TV channel without removing any channels from its basic service.

To add the full nine channels to the midband in older systems often requires the replacement of amplifiers and, in some cases, relocating the amplifiers. Some cable operators faced with this problem have taken the approach of installing an HRC headend as discussed in Chapter 2. This is a headend in which the cable television channels are put on special frequencies so as to make the distortions created by cable plant amplifiers less visible to subscribers. The effect is that several midband channels can be added without replacing amplifier equipment. HRC headends are relatively expensive, but when compared with the expense of replacing amplifiers in a large cable system, the approach is generally less costly.

To go beyond midband channels requires installation of new amplifiers and, in many cases, new multitaps. Such a rebuild can convert a 12-channel system into a 30- or 35-channel system at a relatively low cost ($2,000 to $3,000 per mile of cable plant).

Finally, some cable systems must be totally rebuilt to increase channel capacity. In this case, a new duplicate cable system is built, and subscribers are switched over to the new system. The old system is removed and sold to a salvage company. The cost of this kind of a rebuild often equals or exceeds that of building a new cable system.

Frequently, other elements of the cable system, such as powering equipment or subscriber drops, must also be replaced to increase channel capacity.

Cable manufacturers have now introduced 54-channel equipment covering the frequency spectrum from 54 to 400mHz, and it is likely that the frequency limit will be pushed even higher. Soon, 80-channel equipment will probably be offered. In anticipation of increased channel capacity, many new cable systems today are being built with system designs to allow for upgrading to a higher channel capacity by replacing only amplifiers. For instance, many of the present 300-mHz systems are designed for eventual 400mHz operation, and all cable and multitaps are specified to operate up to 400mHz. At some future date, 300-mHz amplifier modules can be removed and replaced with 400-mHz modules, thus increasing the channel capacity from 35 to 54 channels.

The next generation of cable systems may be built with 400-mHz amplifiers but designed to accommodate 500-mHz amplifiers when they are available, permitting further expansion in channel capacity.

FCC Regulations

For many years now, the FCC has regulated the technical performance of cable television systems through a series of technical standards. These standards are found in subpart K, Sections 76.601–76.617 of the 1972 rules.[3] All cable television systems operating in the United States must meet or exceed these specifications. Because the specifications were written to cover all types of systems, including those built ten or more years ago, the standards are minimal. Most of the new franchises being granted have specified technical standards that are substantially stricter than those of the FCC. This is in the nature of a "freely made contract" to exceed the FCC's standards.

The FCC's standards require that certain minimum and maximum signal levels be delivered to subscribers' television sets, that the signal-to-noise ratio and various types of distortions do not exceed certain limits, and that sufficient isolation at the multitap, or in the splitter for a multiple set installation, is provided so that there is no interference between neighboring subscribers or receivers.

The regulations also strictly limit the operation of cable systems in the frequency bands of 108–136 and 225–400mHz, namely, those used by aircraft communication and navigation signals. Cable operators are required to *offset,* or move, signals carried on the cable away from frequencies used at nearby airports.

In addition, the technical standards define how various measurements are made and require the cable operator to conduct periodic performance tests to assure that all FCC technical standards are being met or exceeded.

DISTRIBUTION PLANT CONSTRUCTION

Cable television systems are constructed on telephone and power company poles (aerial construction) or are buried in the ground (underground construction). In this section the procedures involved in each type of construction are explained.

Aerial Plant

Most utility poles are owned either by the local power company or by the telephone company. Both have contractual arrangements that allow attachments of other types of lines to their poles. For a cable system to install its lines on a power company pole, a contract is signed with the power company giving the right to attach to that pole. An annual rental fee is charged averaging $4.00 to $8.00 per year. In recent years, telephone companies have been eliminating installation of new poles wherever possible. As a result, most poles now in use are owned by the electric companies.

For uniformity and safety, there are established *spaces* for attachment by each occupant of a pole and consequent *clearances* to be built and maintained by all users. These clearances usually conform to National Electric Code standards, but they can be modified by local or regional practices. Telephone lines are at the bottom of the poles, and cable lines are located above the telephone lines. Telephone lines must be located a certain minimum distance above the ground, and there must be a minimum clearance between the telephone line, cable line, and power lines. In many cases, poles were installed without cable systems in mind, and telephone lines were located too close to the power lines to allow installation of cable lines without relocation of the phone lines. The process of making space on the pole for installation of cable lines is called *make-ready*. Make-ready, which is performed by the owner of the pole, can be time consuming and expensive. It is a major cause of delay in construction of cable systems.

The process of installing an aerial cable plant is long and complex, involving many steps. The following is a basic outline of the process.

First, a *base grid map* system is set up. Many times this grid may be duplicated from a city or utility grid in existence. A utility may be most anxious for the cable company to duplicate its grid to simplify pole permit procedures. Then *strand mapping* is done. The entire area to be served by cable is mapped by a cable employee or contractor. Again, existing utility company maps are often used as a reference. In the strand mapping process, the location of all utility poles, the number of residences served from each pole, and the distances between poles are noted. Also, notations are often made as to what make-ready might be required on each pole.

The strand mapping information is placed on the *base maps* that will serve as the map on which the cable system design is placed.

The next step is the design of the cable system. Using the specifications for cable attenuation, amplifier gain, amplifier cascade limitations, and multitap losses, the designer lays out a cable route which will efficiently serve all subscribers within the franchise area. (A portion of a system design appears at the opening of this chapter.) Often the design process is aided by the use of the computer, since the calculations are long and arduous.

The specifications for equipment performance, cable attenuations, amplifier gains, and multitap losses come from the manufacturers of the various equipment, but many cable operators will add their own safety factors to the manufacturer's specifications.

Proper cable TV system design is crucial. Many earlier cable systems were built without proper attention to the various tolerances and limitations of cable and equipment. Not only do today's requirements have to be considered, but the future must be considered as well. Some of the factors that must be taken into account in designing a cable system include the following:

1. *Operating temperature.* The system must be designed to meet all technical standards over the entire range of temperatures that are expected.
2. *Equipment tolerances.* Often equipment specifications are given for an average amplifier or piece of cable as well as *worst case* specifications for the equipment. A prudent cable designer will use the worst case figure rather than the average figure in design calculations.
3. *Increased attenuation as a result of additional splices.* A prudent designer will include a factor in the design to compensate for additional splices over time. As splices are added to the cable, losses between amplifiers will increase.
4. *New homes in existing neighborhoods.* A cable design should include provisions for residential lots on which homes have not yet been built. A multitap should be installed for all locations, even the vacant lots.
5. *Subscriber drop length and number of TV sets.* A designer should include an estimate of the length of the subscriber's drop and number of TV sets to be served in the design calculations. For instance, in wealthy neighborhoods with homes on large lots it can be expected that each house will have several TV sets and that a long drop line will be required to reach the house. Adequate signal strength must be present at the multitap to serve these houses.
6. *System expansion.* As communities grow, cable operators must extend

their trunk lines to cover the new areas. The cable designer should take the projected growth into account when designing the trunk system, since cable system degradation increases as the amplification cascade is increased.

7. *Human and test equipment error.* A margin of error should be built into the system design to allow for inaccuracies in test equipment and errors made by technicians in balancing and operating the system.

The difference in cost between a system designed with the factors just cited taken into account, and one designed to meet the technical specifications as cheaply as possible, can be substantial. In the long run, however, it is sensible for the cable operator to design the system with adequate margins. In analyzing proposals for new franchises, a great deal of care should be paid by the franchising authority to the standards used by the cable company for system design. Systems not designed with adequate safeguards, though capable of providing good quality pictures initially, may not provide high quality service as the franchise area grows and subscribers are added.

Once the system design is completed and put on the base maps, the cable company applies to the utility companies for permission to attach to poles that are needed. Each utility company has a different process for this application, but generally they require *proof of authority* (a franchise) to operate a cable system, *proof of liability insurance* and, in many cases, posting of a *bond.*

Next, a joint pole inspection, commonly referred to as a *walkout* is scheduled. A representative of the cable company and of all the utilities renting or owning space on the pole go to each pole on which cable facilities are to be attached. Poles found to not have sufficient space for addition of cable lines are measured to determine what changes are necessary. Often, the pole already violates the *clearance* requirements, and the utility company must make changes at its own expense. Otherwise, the utility company prepares an engineering estimate of the cost of performing the make-ready required, and submits this estimate to the cable company. If there are no problems, the cable company then authorizes the utility company to proceed.

All make-ready costs that relate to the installation of cable TV lines are paid by the cable company. In some cases, the cable company may elect to change its system design and avoid a particularly costly make-ready location. For instance, if the utility pole is too short to allow rearrangement of the telephone company lines to make room for the cable lines, the whole pole must be replaced, and the make-ready cost could be in excess of $1,000. In this case, the cable company might choose to redesign its system and avoid using that pole. It should be remembered that all costs are estimated and that the cable company can be entitled to a refund or may have to pay more when all make-ready work is completed. The utility company will then proceed with the rearrangement of the facility on the poles. This process sometimes takes weeks and even months, and as the pace of the cable TV construction accelerates, the delays are increasing.

Once the make-ready is completed, the installation of *strand* can begin. Strand is a galvanized steel supporting cable approximately one-quarter inch in diameter that is strung from pole to pole. At specified intervals, this strand must be grounded and *bonded* (connected) to other utility strands for lightning and safety protection. *Guy wires* must be installed to relieve stress on the utility poles. Proper tensioning of the strand and proper grounding are important factors in the life and reliability of the system.

When the strand installation is complete, the cable can be installed. A device called a *lasher* is used to connect or *lash* the cable to the strand. The lasher wraps a very small stainless steel wire around both the strand and cable to hold the cable in place. At this stage of construction, great care must be exercised by the construction personnel. Coaxial cable is susceptible to kinks and dents that will degrade the performance of the cable system.

If the cable system is a dual cable system or if there is an institutional network, all the cables are lashed to a common strand. All trunk cables or multiple cable runs should be *double lashed* for extended life. This requires a second wrap from the lasher, but the process is relatively easy as most lashers are equipped for two spools of lashing wire.

After the cable has been installed, *splicing* can begin. Splicing involves installation of the electronic components and the splitters and multitaps that will tie the cable system together. Splicing is, perhaps, the most critical of all cable construction steps, since an improperly installed connector can result in serious degradation of performance and moisture leaking into the cable, which can cause permanent damage. Cable companies that use contractors for installation of strand and cable often use their own employees to perform the splicing, since it is felt to be so critical. Special *bending tools* are used to form *expansion loops* in the cable at all connections. These loops allow for expansion and contraction of the metal cable components.

In certain climates, near the seacoast or areas of high industrial pollution, for instance, special precautions are taken to protect the cable from corrosion. In these locations, coaxial cable with a polyethylene jacket is used in place of one with a bare aluminum jacket. Special sealing materials are used around all connections to make certain that they are completely watertight. Cable splicers may use a test device such as a continuity checker to verify each connection as it is spliced, thus speeding up activation time.

Underground Plant

Underground cable systems are constructed either on publicly owned *easements* (the right to use these easements is granted in the franchise) or on private easements granted by individual property owners. In new subdivisions, easements are often granted to the cable companies by the developers of the subdivisions. In existing subdivisions, however, cable companies are sometimes required to obtain individual easements from property owners before installing cable.

As in the case of aerial construction, underground cable systems generally follow the same route as the power and telephone companies. The cable is usually buried in the same area, and cable *pedestals* are located near the telephone company and electric company pedestals. A pedestal is a junction box where cable television equipment is located.

Next, the cable route and system design are established. Most states and many counties have requirements for permits before underground cable can be installed. From the system design, the cable company can determine which streets it needs permission to use and which private easements it must obtain.

Getting easements from individual homeowners where dedicated cable easements do not exist is a difficult and costly process. First, subdivision plat maps must be obtained and the ownership of lots determined. Then, a door-to-door team visits each homeowner to get the easement document signed. Often the document must be notarized and filed with the local government, and a nominal fee of $1.00 paid to the homeowner.

Because of the complexity and cost of this approach, many cable companies take short cuts in the easement process. For instance, a cable operator may be willing to take the risk of not having an easement agreement notarized and filed with the county court house. In this case, the easement may not be binding on the next property owner, should the property be sold. However, the practical risk of a future homeowner's demanding removal of cable facilities is small, and when compared with the savings in the easement procurement process, the risk may be justified. When using this simplified procedure, easements may be obtained by mail.

In many cases easements are not required. For instance if a cable is to be located in the front yard, county or city right-of-way may be used for cable installation. In this situation, the cable operator is under no requirement to even notify the homeowner or resident of the intention of installing cable. A prudent cable operator will, however, mail a letter or deliver a door hanger to each home well before construction is to begin, to inform them of the company's construction plans.

As in the case of aerial construction, the underground construction process begins by mapping the area to be served. Utility company maps sometimes serve as a starting point, or, in many cases, subdivision plat maps are used. In this mapping process, the location of property lines, existing utilities, easement lines, and obstructions that might make underground construction difficult (e.g., a fence or garden) are noted.

As cable companies attempt to get permits and easements, problems may be encountered. Often homeowners may refuse to sign the cable easement, or the location of existing underground utilities may make the original cable route impossible. Underground cable systems are frequently redesigned several times before final installation, as the cable company attempts to balance the availability of easements and the problems with existing utilities against the most economical system design.

Once the design has been completed and all necessary easements and permits have been obtained, a public relations process begins. No matter how careful cable companies are in underground construction, some disruption will occur. Residents are very sensitive about digging on or near their property, and great care must be taken by the cable company to inform residents of exactly what to expect. Although cable installations are usually quite neat, often residents will have an exaggerated idea of the damage that will occur from experience with the more complex construction of gas, water, or sewer lines. Cable companies sometimes use slide presentations or photographs to show residents how little disruption will occur.

Just prior to the beginning of construction, the utility companies must be notified so that they may *spot* their facilities. The power, water, gas, and telephone companies mark the route of their cables by using stakes or spray paint so that cable installation crews can avoid them.

The cable installation can take several forms, depending upon the terrain, soil conditions, local regulations, and the policies of the cable company. The most common technique in use today is the direct burial method, utilizing a vibratory plow or small trencher. The vibratory plow causes substantially less disruption of the ground than does a trencher, but its use is restricted to areas where soil conditions are amenable.

The coaxial cable used for underground construction has an outer jacket of polyethylene. In between this jacket and the aluminum coaxial cable is a *flooding compound,* a tarlike substance that will spread and seal any puncture that may occur in the outer jacket. Cable is usually buried at a depth of 12 to 36 inches.

Caution is necessary in laying and burying the cable. Aluminum, if left in contact with the soil, will corrode in a matter of weeks, so great care must be taken to install the cable in such a way as to avoid puncturing the plastic jacket. Rocks can cause kinks or dents in the cable, which will affect the cable system's performance.

Some cable companies use *armored* cable for underground construction. Armored cable has stainless steel bands wrapped around the outer jacket, with another jacket on top. Armored cable is an effective way of providing protection from damage, but the extra cost is significant.

In some cases, cable is installed in plastic or metal pipe called *conduit.* In this case, a trencher digs a hole in which the conduit is laid. Later, cable is pulled through the conduit. The conduit method provides some additional protection against cable damage, but it is substantially more expensive than the direct burial method. Another advantage of a conduit system is the relative ease with which faulty cable can be replaced.

In high density downtown areas, utilities are often in duct systems located underneath the streets and owned by the power company or phone company. Cable companies, in this case, lease space in the ducts. A similar arrangement is used for crossing rivers where conduit may have been attached to a bridge or buried under water.

The next step is the installation of pedestals and the splicing. Pedestals are located above the ground, sticking up a foot or two. Sometimes, however, *vaults,* which are installed flush with the ground surface, are used. Care must be taken when installing these pedestals so that they are not subject to physical damage and do not allow water to enter the cable or its components. In underground systems, waterproofing is essential, and special sealing materials are used to protect all connectors from leakage.

After the installation of the cable and pedestals comes the most sensitive part of the installation process, the restoration of the ground. The ground must be compacted and seeded where grass may have been destroyed. Shrubs and trees that may have been damaged must be replaced. Success of the cable system's marketing effort will depend on the care taken in the restoration. Many cable systems that did a poor job in the final stage of underground construction many years ago are still living with low penetration in those areas because of the ill will created.

In some circumstances, the procedure for installation of underground cable will be slightly different from that just outlined. In new subdivisions, for instance, *joint trench* arrangements are often used. In this case, a single trench is dug by one of the utilities, and telephone, electric, and cable lines are placed in the same trench. All three companies share the expense equally.

Plant Costs

Costs for 400mHz single cable plant are about $10,000 (in 1982 dollars) per mile for aerial construction including labor, materials, design and make-ready. The second cable for a dual system adds $5,000 per mile. The cost for underground cable in a residential neighborhood averages about $15,000. Underground cable in urban areas may be $50,000 per mile or more. These figures do not include the drop which is about $30 for aerial. Dual cable and underground construction add about $10 each.

Balancing and Proof of Performance

At this point, the cable system construction is completed. Electronic technicians then follow to perform the *balancing* and *proof of performance.* Balancing is the adjustment of each of the cable television amplifiers to its specified operating level and testing to make certain that the losses between amplifiers are exactly as anticipated in the system design. As in the case of splicing, balancing is often done by cable television employees rather than by contractors. Proof of performance testing involves the use of sophisticated test equipment on a completed cable system to make certain that the system operates as designed. Tests are usually made for signal-level uniformity, various types of distortion, signal-to-noise ratio, *hum modulation,* and *signal ingress.* Hum modulation is distortion of the TV signals by the electrical current necessary to operate the amplifier and appears in TV pictures as dark or light horizontal bars moving through the picture. Signal ingress, which will be discussed more thoroughly in Chapter 5, is the leakage of over-the-air broadcast signals into the cable.

If the cable system is a *turnkey* installation, in which a contractor supplies a complete operating cable plant to the cable company, the proof of performance test serves as a quality check before final acceptance by the cable operator. Whether the cable system was built by a contractor, a combination of contractors and cable company employees, or entirely by cable company employees, the proof of performance serves as a final check before connection of subscribers.

The cable system is now ready for installation of subscribers. Many cable companies prefer to wait a period of time before connecting subscribers. Electronic components have their highest rate of failure during the first few hours of use, and allowing a cable system to "cook" for a few days before connecting subscribers reduces the possibility of a new subscriber being annoyed by a failure in the first days of service.

NOTES

[1]Roger S. Walker, *Understanding Computer Science* (Dallas, Tex.: Texas Instruments, 1981), p. G-3.

[2]Some feeder amplifiers utilize *thermal compensation,* a simplified system of AGC to adjust gain under different temperature conditions.

[3]*Cable Television Report and Order,* 36 FCC 2d 143 (1972), Sections 76.601–76.617.

4

Home Drop

User with a handheld keypad/converter accessing videotext information. Photograph courtesy of Cox Cable Communications, Inc.

THE SUBSCRIBER DROP

This chapter deals with the connection of the subscriber to the cable distribution plant. The connection to the plant is made through a *drop line,* which is a small-diameter (about one-quarter of an inch) coaxial cable leading from the multitap in the cable plant to the subscriber's television receiver.

The drop line is similar to the coaxial cable used in the distribution plant except that its outer sheath is generally braided copper or aluminum (sometimes with an aluminum foil wrapping) covered by a plastic jacket. These sheath materials are used instead of solid aluminum because the drop wire must be flexible.

Generally, if the cable system plant is aerial, the drop will be aerial; if the cable system plant is underground, the drop will be underground. The drop enters the house at some convenient location and is routed to the subscriber's TV receiver. A *matching transformer* is used to connect the coaxial cable to the antenna terminals on back of the TV set. The purpose of this matching transformer is to mate the coaxial cable, which carries all the signal in its center conductor, with the two antenna terminals on the TV set, each of which must be provided with a portion of the signal.

If more than one TV set is to be connected, a *splitter* is used to route the signal to two or more TV receivers. If the cable operator offers FM radio service, TV/FM splitters are installed to route FM frequencies (88–108-mHz) to the FM receiver and TV frequencies (54–88 and 121-mHz and above) to the TV sets.

CONVERTERS

As noted in the discussion of cable distribution plants, a cable system carrying more than 12 channels carries the additional channels in areas of the electromagnetic spectrum between channel 6 and channel 7 (midband) or above channel 13 (superband). Most TV receivers will not tune these frequencies, although recently some TV sets have been built with the capability to receive midband and superband channels.

For many years, cable companies have been urging TV set manufacturers to make sets that would be *cable ready,* that is, could be connected to a cable system without a converter, thus eliminating an expensive investment by the cable operator. Until recently, manufacturers were moving in that direction.

In recent years, however, with the emergence of scrambling techniques for pay TV, the cable-ready trend has stalled. When standardization exists for descramblers, if ever, TV set manufacturers may begin to incorporate converters and descramblers into TV sets.

TV sets will tune to the UHF spectrum (channels 14 through 83), the channels in the frequency range of 470 to 890mHz. Because cable TV systems at present only carry up to 400mHz, it is not possible to use the UHF tuners in TV sets to tune cable frequencies. Therefore, to tune the mid- and superband channels carried on cable systems, a converter is required. The purpose of a converter is to convert the special cable channels to VHF television channels that can be tuned on a TV receiver.

There are two basic types of converters: block converters and tunable converters. *Block converters* are used mainly in small cable systems that carry a few midband or superband channels. Block converters have a two-position switch. In the *normal* position, the subscriber tunes 12 TV channels on the VHF selector. In the *midband* position, seven different channels appear on channels 7 through 13 of the selector. Block converters are simple and very inexpensive and offer the small cable system a low cost way of increasing channel capacity. Another type of block converter shifts the midband or superband channels to the UHF band.

With the *tunable converter,* the subscriber's television receiver is tuned to an unused VHF channel (typically channel 2, 3, or 4). All channel tuning is done using the converter. The converter has a knob, slide switch, series of push buttons, or a keyboard that selects the desired channel. Many of these converters allow the subscriber to turn the TV receiver on and off using the converter.

Tunable converters come in three varieties: set-top, wireless-remote, and wired-remote. The *set-top version* is self-contained for location on top of the subscriber's television receiver. The *wired-remote converter* consists of a unit located behind the subscriber's television receiver connected by a thin wire to a hand held control unit. The *wireless converter* is similar to the wired-remote, but uses infrared light or ultrasonic sound for communication from the hand held control unit instead of a wire.

Recently, with the introduction of inexpensive microprocessors, cable converters have become more sophisticated and complex. Some now offer the ability to control the volume or the capability of restricting channels by requiring a special authorization code to be entered before the channel can be viewed. With this feature, the subscriber is given a four digit number at the time of installation. When one of the restricted channels is tuned, for instance a channel with "R"-rated programming, the subscriber must enter the four-digit code following the channel entry or the screen will remain blank.

Some of the new converters also permit preprogramming of up to ten of the subscriber's favorite channels in a memory and recalling them with the push of a button.

New types of converters include other features, such as built-in clocks and the ability to program in advance the channels that the subscriber wishes to view. The converter automatically tunes to those channels at the appropriate time. In addition, some of the new converters include videotext capability and are used as entry keyboards for interactive services. (See Chapter 6.)

Addressable Converters

Many of the new converters are *addressable.* As subscribers are offered a multitude of channels on a tier basis, it becomes desirable for the cable operator to be able to control which services a subscriber receives without making a service call to the home. Addressable converters provide the solution. If a subscriber wishes to receive Home Box Office, for instance, the cable company is called and the subscriber's converter is "addressed" with instructions to allow the Home Box Office channel into the home.

Addressable converters are new and have been installed in only a few systems. Questions remain as to their reliability and whether their added cost is justified. In addition, addressable converters, though providing more protection than standard converters, are subject to piracy of unauthorized signals, a problem that presently plagues the cable industry and will continue to do so for some time.

Addressable Taps

The forerunner of the addressable converter was the *addressable tap.* Multitaps were built with electronic circuitry in them to allow the cable operator to turn on or off a subscriber's drop from the headend. In addition one, and in some cases two channels of pay TV could be controlled. Addressable taps were installed in some systems on a test basis but never found wide acceptance. A major limitation of addressable tap technology is that control of more than two individual channels is difficult. Cable operators need more flexibility in controlling tiers of programs, a problem which addressable converters solve.

TRAPS

When pay television was introduced, cable operators were faced with the problem of how to deliver it only to those subscribers who paid for the service. Some early pay systems used an inexpensive converter and carried the pay TV channel in the midband. But many subscribers soon learned how to receive the pay television channel without paying for it. TV repairpersons would retune the subscriber's television set to receive these channels, or converters designed for other purposes were used to tune in the pay television channel.

Today, two methods are generally used to provide security for premium TV service. One of these is the *trap*. A trap is a device that is located between the output of the multitap and the subscriber's drop. Traps block the transmission of a particular TV channel to a subscriber's drop line. If a subscriber does not desire a premium television service, a trap for that channel is placed in the line, making it impossible to receive the channel.

Traps have two major advantages. First, they are very inexpensive ($5.00 to $10.00 each). If the penetration of a particular premium service is high, traps can be a very low cost method of providing security (traps are put on all nonpremium subscribers' drops, so as the number of premium subscribers increases, the number of traps required decreases). If the penetration on the premium channel is low, traps are relatively expensive. Second, traps are extremely secure. To steal a premium service, the subscriber must climb a utility pole, remove the trap, and reconnect the drop line. Most cable operators use *security sleeves* and connectors that require special tools to remove. It is very difficult, therefore, for a subscriber to steal service in a system using traps.

However, traps have disadvantages too. For one thing, they are difficult to administer. A special record must be kept of the location of the installation, and when a subscriber disconnects from a premium service, a trap must be installed in the line. Another disadvantage to traps is that, with few exceptions, a trap is required for each channel to be blocked. When only one pay TV service was typical, traps provided an ideal solution. However, with multiple tiers of pay TV being offered, traps became cumbersome and expensive. In practice, no more than two, or perhaps three, channels may be secured using traps.

DESCRAMBLERS

The second method of providing security for premium services is *scrambling*. The television signal is scrambled at the headend in such a way to make it difficult or impossible for a subscriber TV set to get a good picture. In some systems, the sound is also scrambled. In the subscriber's home, a *descrambler* is provided to those customers paying for a premium service. Often the descrambler is incorporated inside the converter. Descramblers are more expensive than traps. Included as a part of the converter, the additional cost of the descrambler is around $20.

Descramblers have the advantage of being able to descramble many TV channels with little if any additional cost above the cost of descrambling one channel. When combined with a programmable or addressable converter, they can be used to descramble an almost infinite variety of channel combinations for different subscribers purchasing different program packages.

Many different techniques are used for scrambling TV pictures, with little compatability among techniques used by different manufacturers. Most methods alter the synchronizing signals that make TV pictures hold still on the TV screen. The descrambler then adds the synchronizing signals back in their proper location.

Descrambling systems fall into two major categories. The first is the *out-of-band* technique. In this method (the earliest used for descrambling), a separate *pilot signal* is transmitted on the cable system to the descrambler to facilitate reconstruction of the TV picture. Although the out-of-band system is inexpensive, only two or three TV channels can be scrambled. The second method is the *in-band* system in which the information for reconstructing the TV picture is carried within each television channel. Descramblers for this type of system are more expensive; however, an unlimited number of channels can be scrambled.

If the penetration of a particular premium service is low (below 30 percent of basic cable subscribers), descramblers can actually be cheaper than traps. However, descramblers have a serious liability. As more premium services are added to cable systems, the incentive for theft of service will increase. In new major market systems, the total monthly charge for all services combined may reach $50 to $60. A market will be created for bootleg equipment to receive these signals.

Descramblers must be relatively inexpensive for the cable operator to afford them. Yet they must be complex enough to make it difficult for a subscriber to defeat. As the incentive for stealing pay services increases, more subscribers will be tempted to purchase bootleg descramblers (which can be designed and built by an average TV repairperson). In fact, designs for descramblers have already appeared in *Popular Electronics* and *Radio Electronics,* two major electronic hobbyist magazines. Furthermore, it has not been clearly established that the sale of bootleg descramblers is illegal. It may be difficult or impossible for the cable operator to keep descramblers off the market.

It should be noted that addressable converter-descramblers do nothing to solve this problem. A standard converter combined with a bootleg descrambler will allow viewing of all the channels carried on the cable system.

Converter Costs

A 36-channel set-top converter without a descrambler cost the cable system about $45 in 1982. A 120-channel wireless-addressable converter was about $180. Converters with lesser options fall in between.

FUTURE SECURITY SYSTEMS

The technology of cable security is in its infancy. New methods are being developed to solve the security problems. Already three systems have been developed that are steps in that direction. The first is being used by broadcast subscription (STV) pay television operators.

The television picture is scrambled in a random fashion when transmitted. The code to unlock the scrambling is transmitted separately over the telephone line only to those subscribers who have paid for the service. Since the descrambling code is transmitted by phone line or along with the television signal, and there are millions of possible code combinations for descrambling the picture, it is virtually impossible for a bootleg descrambler to work. This system in its present configuration is quite expensive, but large-scale integrated circuit development may bring the price down in the future.

A second approach involves placing the converter outside the subscriber's home on the utility pole or in the pedestal. The subscriber would be sent only one channel at a time down the drop to the TV receiver. If the subscriber is not authorized to receive a particular channel, it will not be sent down the drop. This system has several serious limitations. First, each converter unit would take a substantial amount of space, and the converters to serve four homes would not fit in standard pedestals for underground construction. Second, the cost per home for this equipment is exceptionally high. And third, a converter and drop line would be required for each TV set served by the cable system, meaning that second and third TV sets within homes would each require a converter unit and drop line. Two manufacturers have announced tests of outdoor-type converters.

A third design that attempts to solve many of the problems noted, and also provides many of the two-way services, has been proposed by one of the authors of this book and is presently in the patent-pending stage. This converter design splits the converter into two units, with half located outside the subscriber's home and half within. The unit located outside is in communication with the headend utilizing a small microprocessor. When a subscriber wishes to view a channel, the channel number is entered on a small keyboard at the TV set. The request travels up the drop line to the outside unit where the channel selection is done. The channel request is relayed to the headend where the subscriber's authorization to receive this channel is checked. If the subscriber is authorized, the converter allows the subscriber to view that channel. Since all requests for channel viewing are transmitted to the headend, it is easy to keep track of which channel a subscriber is viewing for pay-per-view pay television and audience rating purposes. More than one subscriber's TV set may be connected to a single drop line utilizing frequency division techniques.

Other devices may also communicate with the outside unit. For instance, home security terminals or information retrieval keyboards located within the home may communicate over the drop to the outside unit. The information requests or data can then be relayed by the outside unit to the headend. Such a system is being field tested. In this design, many of the two-way services described in Chapter 5 may be provided.

Clearly, the cable industry is faced with problems of theft of service. The incentives, however, for solving the problem and avoiding the loss are significant, and it is likely that a solution will be found in the next few years.

With the advent of two-way services, the subscriber drop is changing and is becoming substantially more complex. In Chapter 5, two-way services and the related subscriber equipment are described in detail.

5

Two-Way Technology

Computer (left) which controls videotape and character generator and records "upstream" communication in an experimental two-way cable system, Rockford Cablevision, Rockford, Illinois.

TWO-WAY

Cable systems are capable of transmission of audio, video, and data signals not only from the headend to subscribers but also from subscribers back to the headend. This is possible using a technique called *frequency division multiplexing.* Cable systems use frequencies above 50mHz for transmission of video, audio, and data information into subscribers' homes (referred to as *downstream* transmission). The coaxial cable itself can carry frequencies below 50mHz as well by installing amplifiers that have bidirectional capability (described later in this chapter). Signals in the frequency range of 5 to 35mHz can be transmitted from points in the distribution network back to the cable headend (referred to as *upstream* transmission).

Two-way capability in cable systems has been in use for many years. In the late 1960s, two-way communication was used by some cable systems to transmit local origination programming from a downtown office or studio to a headend located outside of town. Some cable systems use portions of their trunk to send video signals from remote locations such as schools or auditoriums back to the cable headend, where they are then processed and retransmitted in the downstream direction on a cable television channel to subscribers. In these applications, only a portion of the cable system, usually the trunk, is equipped for two-way transmission.

In the early 1970s, cable operators began experimenting with two-way distribution plants where the entire system was equipped with bidirectional amplifiers. Three companies produced small quantities of interactive cable terminals that were tested in several cities, including El Segundo, California; Overland Park, Kansas; and Orlando, Florida. All these terminals were of the *transponder* type. A digital address command was transmitted down the cable from the headend to the home terminal. The home terminal, in turn, recognized its proper address and responded with a digital message upstream to the headend.

These systems were plagued with problems, the most serious of which was *signal ingress*—the leaking of over-the-air radio signals into the cable, which caused interference with the upstream cable communications.

In addition to the technical problems with these terminals, the cable industry expanded too rapidly in the early 1970s and overestimated the speed with which two-way services would develop. As a result, none of these experiments ever proceeded beyond a small-scale test.

In the mid-1970s, two other two-way technologies emerged. One, pioneered by Tocom, involves a transponder system similar to the earlier experimental systems. Tocom installed its first system in The Woodlands, Texas, a planned residential community of upper-income homes. Because the cable system of The Woodlands was quite small, problems with signal ingress were controllable and the system has functioned reliably. Over the years, Tocom has installed several of these systems in planned communities like The Woodlands and is now a major supplier of two-way terminal equipment to the cable industry.

The second technology that emerged is the Coaxial Scientific Corporation *area division multiplexing* technique. In this system, which will be described in more detail later, the home terminal is not a transponder, but only a transmitter, sending out its message from the home continually. Code-operated switches (COSs) within the cable plant route these signals back to the headend. The Coaxial Scientific system was first installed in Columbus, Ohio in 1974 as part of a pay-per-view television system. At its peak, the system had over 6,000 home terminal units in operation. The Coaxial Scientific system solved the ingress problems associated with the transponder technology and also allowed the home terminal's cost to be reduced to less than half that for the transponder-type home terminal. The Coaxial Scientific system is now in use for home security and interactive TV in several U.S. and Canadian cities.

In the late 1970s, Warner Communications introduced its Qube system also, coincidentally, in Columbus, Ohio. The Qube system uses transponder-type home terminals, coupled with a code-operated switch (or bridger switch), an element borrowed from the Coaxial Scientific system. Qube's two-way terminals have proven to be reliable, but quite expensive. Qube systems are being installed in most of Warner Amex's systems now under construction.

During 1980 and 1981, several new transponder-type technologies emerged from suppliers. All these systems utilize a transponder-type technology in one form or another, and all are similar in price.

The Two-Way Distribution System

Two-way cable distribution systems are identical to the description in Chapter 3 with two exceptions. First, the amplifiers must operate in two directions. This is accomplished by utilizing two separate amplifier modules, one of which covers the frequency range of 50mHz and up and the other of which covers the frequency range of 5 to 35mHz (called channels T7–T11). At the input and output of each of these amplifiers are diplexing filters (Figure 3-4, p. 33). *Diplexing filters* split cable signals into two frequency bands, routing frequencies above 50mHz to the downstream amplifier and those below 35mHz to the upstream amplifier.

For a variety of reasons, diplexing filters cannot be designed that allow the use of all the spectrum. A *guard band* must be provided, and frequencies above 35mHz in the upstream direction or below 50mHz in the downstream direction cannot be used.

The coaxial cable itself is insensitive to which direction frequencies are transmitted, so it is possible to transmit frequencies above 50mHz downstream and below 35mHz upstream over the same cable. The frequencies between 50 and 54mHz are used for control and data transmission, but not for video.

All these modules are installed within the same housing and use a common power supply. Most two-way cable systems incorporate some form of automatic gain control in the upstream direction. In some cases, AGC circuitry similar to that described in Chapter 3 is used. In other cases, thermal compensation systems, which regulate an amplifier's gain in accordance with the outside air temperature, are used.

The Code-Operated or Bridger Switch

As mentioned earlier, signal intrusion is a major problem with upstream communications. This is because the frequency spectrum occupied by upstream transmission is used over the air by many high power transmitting sources, such as international shortwave broadcasts, amateur radio operators, business and military communications. Signals can leak into the cable because of a break in the aluminum sheath or because a connector that has become corroded or loose. (There is also a condition called *signal egress,* in which cable signals leak from the cable into the air. The FCC has put strict limitations on cable's use of frequencies used for aircraft navigation and communication because of possible interference due to leakage from cable systems.)

The code-operated switch, designed to solve the ingress problem, is located at each bridger amplifier and allows the downstream signals to pass unimpeded from the trunk into the feeder system and from there to subscribers' homes (Figure 5-1). Upsteam signals from each feeder area, however, are routed through an electronic switch. A computer at the cable system headend can turn on or off each code-operated switch in the system.

In operation, the computer turns on one code-operated switch at a time, allowing only signals from one bridger area to enter the trunk and travel up the trunk to the headend. If signal ingress occurs within a feeder area, only signals from within that feeder area will be affected, since the ingress will be switched off when the code-operated switch is disabled.

The code-operated switch is used in a different way by Cox Cable. Normally, all switches are turned on and data is gathered from all home terminals in the system. If a fault occurs, such as signal ingress, the switch serving the area in which the fault is located is turned off. In this method, the code-operated switch serves as a diagnostic tool, and to limit the effects of ingress and faults to one area of the system.

At this time, there is some disagreement in the cable industry as to whether code-operated switches are necessary. Some engineers claim

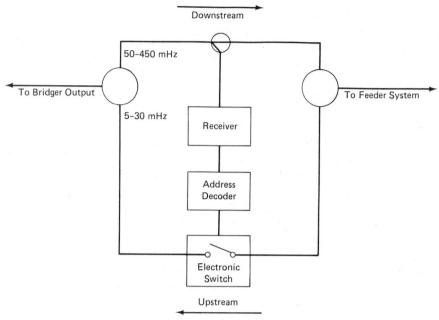

Figure 5-1. Code-operated switch.

that modern construction practices and good maintenance procedures can eliminate the problems of signal ingress. However, it should be noted that three cable operators with long term two-way cable experience (Warner Communications, Coaxial Communications, and Rogers Cablesystems) all incorporate code-operated switches in their system designs.

The Two-Way Headend

Additional equipment is required at the headend for two-way services (Figure 5-2). Although certain elements are standard to any two-way system, equipment needs are dictated by the two-way services to be provided.

The heart of a two-way cable headend is a minicomputer or microcomputer system. This computer polls code-operated switches and home terminals to retrieve the desired data. It then formats the data and presents it to the cable operator in usable form.

These computer systems can be relatively simple and inexpensive, if only a few subscribers are involved and if the two-way service offering is limited, or the system can be quite complex and expensive. For instance, a two-way system offering only home security service to a few hundred subscribers might have only a small microcomputer and floppy disk drives, a $10,000 to $15,000 investment.

If other services are offered, more sophisticated computer installations are necessary. The Rogers Cablesystems, Syracuse, New York system offers home security, opinion polling, channel monitoring, and system status monitoring using dual DEC PDP-11/34 computers, together with four disk drives and related equipment (over $100,000 in cost). The system automatically switches from the main computer to a backup in case of failure, thus assuring uninterrupted home security service.

Newer cable systems use even more sophisticated computers, with four or more minicomputers, costing over $500,000. It should be noted that much of the equipment and software being proposed for new systems is experimental and that the final hardware and software configurations have not evolved.

To connect the computer system to the cable system, data modulators and demodulators (or receivers) are required. A data modulator takes the digital output from the computer system and places it on an unused section of the downstream cable spectrum (typically between 108 and 121mHz). The data demodulator takes the upstream signals from the cable system and converts them to digital signals for processing by the computer.

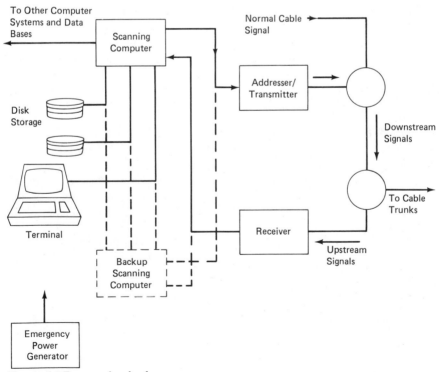

Figure 5-2. Two-way headend.

Two-Way Design and Construction

Although a two-way cable plant is similar to a one-way system, special care must be taken in the design process. In the past, many cable operators have designed their systems for downstream performance only, believing that upstream signals could be successfully added later.

Experience has shown, however, that calculations must be made for both upstream and downstream signals. Those cable operators with two-way experience have developed design criteria based on their operating experience, assuring that the two-way plants they build will work properly. Some cable operators may have difficulties in operating reliable two-way distribution plants, although Cox has been successful in converting its relatively old San Diego system to two-way by tightening up the plant. There was no redesign.

During construction, care must be taken to assure the integrity of all connections, since upstream frequencies are more susceptible to ingress than downstream. Connectors must be chosen to assure good upstream performance. Waterproofing is very important.

Because of the special problems of upstream cable, and because of the importance of reliability in new services, especially home security, many operators are installing automatic system status monitoring devices in the cable plant.

Status Monitoring

Status monitoring involves the installation of transponder units in various places in the cable distribution system. A computer at the headend interrogates these units, instructing them to send data on signal levels and picture quality back over the upstream path to the headend. The computer tabulates the information and presents it to the maintenance personnel. In this way the cable operator knows the condition of the system at all times and can respond immediately to outages. In addition, minor problems which may not yet be visible to subscribers can be detected and cured.

Status monitoring has been available since the late 1960s but has not yet become widespread. Most status monitoring equipment is expensive ($150 to $300 per location) and will monitor only the trunk lines. Since cable operators constantly monitor the condition of their trunks using field tests by technicians, status monitoring offered little benefit. Today, however, concerns with reliability have forced cable operators to include status monitoring in new systems. Several types of equipment are available.

Many amplifier manufacturers offer status monitoring modules for their trunk stations, costing about $150. These modules provide reliable information about trunk performance, but they tell nothing about feeder performance. Also, only two channels out of the total of 35 to 50 are monitored. In most cases, this provides reliable indication of system performance, but occasionally problems occur that will not be detected by this type of monitor.

Some manufacturers offer status monitoring devices that are in separate housings, allowing installation at any point, trunk or feeder, in the plant. These units are costly, however, and feeder monitoring is rarely provided.

Since feeder lines make up 70 to 80 percent of the mileage in a cable plant, feeder monitoring is desirable. One low cost status monitoring system now available was developed as an outgrowth of the Coaxial Scientific Corporation's two-way system in Columbus, Ohio. This method utilizes status monitors costing $20 to $30 each which monitor all channels in a system. The entire cable plant, trunk and feeder, can be monitored for about $150 per mile in extra capital cost. A strong signal is sent repeatedly into the system at two frequencies between television channels. The signal may be ten times the strength of normal signals. Detectors located remotely in the system read the signal and send it back. If it is greater or less than the strength of the original, the system is not performing properly. The high level signal is not visible because it is transmitted at frequencies between television channels and is only momentarily on the system, but if trouble is indicated, the entire spectrum is swept manually to read each channel. The bursts of signal appear momentarily as a black line on a home television receiver. This type of status monitoring, developed jointly by Coaxial Scientific and Rogers Cablesystems, is in use in several U.S. and Canadian cities.

The Two-Way Subscriber Drop

Two-way subscriber drops do not differ significantly from one-way drops. Again, special care must be taken to assure that connectors are tight and waterproof, and drop cable must be chosen to have good shielding characteristics to prevent ingress.

Some cable operators install *high-pass* matching transformers or filters in the drops of subscribers not taking a two-way service. These devices pass the downstream signals to TV sets but block upstream frequencies. In some cases, TV sets can actually act as antennas to pick up over-the-air signals and send them up the drop into the cable system. High-pass filters and matching transformers eliminate this problem. Newer systems, in which all subscribers have converters, do not require such filters.

The Two-Way Home Terminal

The two-way home terminal is a device that sends data from a subscriber's home to the cable headend. Data can be from many sources, including fire and smoke detectors, intrusion detectors, utility meters, or keyboards. Terminals are often included as part of the converter, although such designs have liabilites if home security or other monitoring services are provided (all the wiring from the detectors for these services must be routed to the back of the TV set).

There are two basic types of terminals. The transponder and the transmitter type.

The Transponder-Type Terminal

A transponder terminal (Figure 5-3) consists of a digital receiver, which is "talked to" by the computer at the headend; a transmitter, which "talks to" the computer; and a microprocessor, which controls all the functions of the terminal.

The headend computer sends a digital message to all terminals simultaneously. Part of this message is an *address,* a digital code that is different for each terminal. When a terminal recognizes its address, it responds by turning on its transmitter, which sends back upstream a digital message containing its address plus data from the various devices that are monitored by the terminal. For instance, one "bit" of the message sent might indicate the presence or absence of a fire alarm; another group of bits might contain the channel numbers to which the subscriber's converter is tuned.

After the message is sent, the transmitter is turned off, and the terminal waits for the next transmission of its address.

The microprocessor in the terminal performs the address recognition, transmitter control, and data transmission functions.

Transponder terminals are the most common form of two-way terminals in use today, being manufactured in one form or another by many suppliers. They have the advantage of allowing communication *into* the home for such services as power load management as well as *out* of the home. Their disadvantages are cost ($200 to $400) and the fact that they all share a common upstream channel, making them susceptible to signal intrusion and even intentional jamming. The use of code-operated switches (described earlier) in conjunction with transponder terminals solves this problem.

Oak Industries has designed a terminal for Cox which is a modification of the transponder method. It is called a *contention* terminal. When a subscriber enters data, the terminal listens to the downstream command channel to find out if the system is in use. If the system is free,

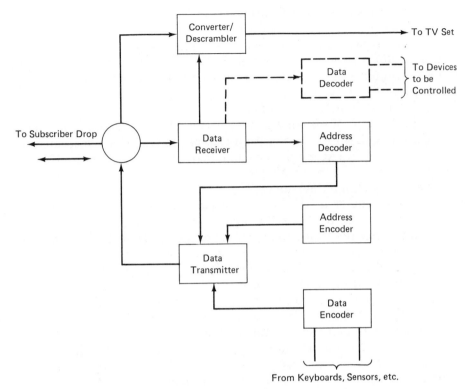

Figure 5-3. Transponder-type terminal.

the data is transmitted by the home terminal. At the headend the data from the home terminal is sent back over the command channel. The home terminal listens to its own message to make certain that it was received in an ungarbled fashion by the headend. If not, the terminal repeats its message.

The advantage of the contention-type terminal is that data is almost instantaneously transmitted from the terminal to the headend. Another advantage is that only new data is transmitted from the terminal so that a great deal more data can be transmitted on a given upstream signal bandwidth. This may be important in the future when new services are added.

The main drawback of the contention system is that failure of a terminal may not be recognized for many hours since the terminal is not continuously polled to determine its status. In a contention system, a "global" poll of all terminals to determine their status is done periodically. In this mode, each terminal is requested to respond to assure that its operation is normal. Global polling, however, takes place only periodically and in between global polls a terminal can fail.

The Transmitter-Type Terminal

The second two-way home terminal type is the Coaxial Scientific/Rogers Cablesystems area division multiplex transmitter-type home terminal (Figure 5-4). This device consists of only a transmitter and a few digital *chips* (integrated circuits). A code-operated switch is required at each bridger amplifier.

In this type of system, the home terminal sends its digital message continuously. Each terminal within a feeder section has a separate upstream frequency. At the bridger amplifier, where upstream feeder signals are routed into the trunk, the code-operated switch controls the flow of these signals into the trunk.

The computer at the headend instructs one code-operated switch (COS) to turn on. It allows the signals from all homes in that feeder section to enter the trunk and to travel to the headend. At the headend, the computer receives and stores the data from all these homes simultaneously. Then, the COS is turned off. The next COS is turned on and so forth until all the plant has been scanned.

Transmitter-type terminals are in use in several cities and have been adopted by Rogers Cablesystems, presently the largest cable operator in the world, for use in all its systems.

This system has two major advantages. First, and most important, is cost. With its limited capability and fewer components, a complete home security terminal costs under $50, compared with $200 for a comparable transponder-type. Second, the system is less vulnerable to signal ingress and intentional jamming than the transponder-type.

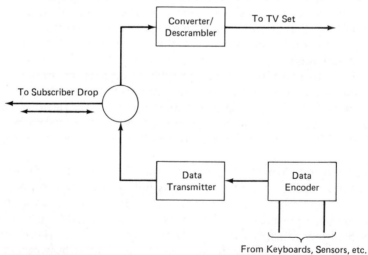

Figure 5-4. Transmitter-type terminal.

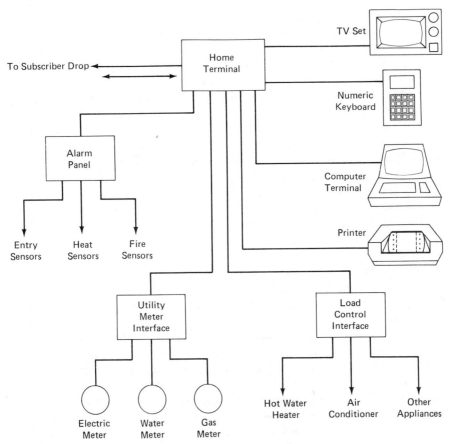

Figure 5-5. Connection of data sources to a home terminal.

The system's disadvantages are that it occupies slightly more spectrum space in the upstream direction (4 to 10mHz compared with 2 to 6mHz for transponders), and that commands cannot be sent into the home, making services such as utility load management impossible. However, a receiver module can be added to the terminal to allow such services. This add-on could be provided only for those subscribers requiring the service.

Connection of Alarms, Keyboards, etc.

A two-way terminal can be connected to any number of data *sources*. For home security, an alarm *panel* is installed that is an interface between the intrusion detectors (door switches, motion detectors, etc.) and the home terminal. This panel also has the necessary subscriber controls to enable and test the alarm system. (Figure 5-5.)

To connect a home terminal to utility meters, a special meter must be installed, which electrically encodes the meter dials. A connection is made to an interface circuit, which is located inside the home terminal.

For monitoring television viewing, a connection is made to the channel selector circuitry inside the converter. Often, the keyboard used as part of the converter to select channels is also used as a subscriber response keyboard. With this approach, opinion polling, interactive TV programming, or home shopping is possible.

The most sophisticated source for connection to a home terminal is the full alphanumeric keyboard. With this configuration, the terminal becomes a computer terminal, with full data retrieval capability. Home computers, such as the Apple and Radio Shack, can be connected to home terminals to provide this capability. (See the videotext section following for more on information retrieval.)

The State of the Art

It should be remembered that two-way services are new and basically experimental. Manufacturers are rushing to introduce equipment to the marketplace, often without adequate testing or design. Cable operators are uncertain as to what capabilities they want and what services will emerge. Problems with standardization of equipment will occur, and today's front-runners in equipment sales may be gone tomorrow.

New developments are occurring daily, and the final design for two-way home terminals is some time away. In the meantime, claims and promises for two-way services and equipment should be carefully evaluated.

Videotext Services

Videotext information retrieval systems are becoming standard in franchise applications. Videotext technology has been around in experimental form for several years, mainly in Europe.

Videotext service uses telephone lines, over-the-air TV, or cable to distribute information to subscribers' TV screens. It can be one-way or two-way, although to the subscriber there is little difference in operation. The information transmitted in digital form is stored in a decoder at the subscriber's home and is displayed as text or simple graphics on the subscriber's TV set.

One-Way Cable Videotext

Over-the-air videotext systems (teletext) in which text information is transmitted on a broadcast TV channel utilize a system in which digital information is sandwiched within TV pictures in an area called the *ver-*

tical blanking interval. The subscriber is provided with a *decoder,* which extracts this information, stores it, and formats it as a still TV picture.

Information for 200 to 300 *pages* of display is transmitted sequentially, with the transmission of each whole cycle of 200 to 300 pages taking 5 to 10 seconds. The videotext terminal has a selector switch or keyboard that instructs the terminal to "grab" the desired page as it is transmitted. The subscriber has to wait only a few seconds for the desired page.

When one-way videotext service is offered over a cable system, many channels can be used in this manner, so several thousand pages of information can be accessed by the subscriber.

A variation of this approach uses an entire TV channel to transmit several thousand pages. A few manufacturers have introduced terminals for one-way cable videotext ranging in price from $200 to $300 including a 54-channel converter.

Two-Way Videotext

In the two-way system, a large computer at the headend stores hundreds of thousands of pages of information. Often, the computer is interconnected with other *data bases,* giving it access to millions of pages of data.

The home decoder has the ability to recognize a unique address and can store a page and format it on a TV screen. The decoder is connected to a two-way interactive terminal.

The subscriber enters the desired page number on the two-way keyboard, and the two-way computer at the headend receives the request and sends it on to the videotext computer. The videotext computer then sends out the subscriber's digital address, followed by the desired page. The videotext decoder recognizes its address and "grabs" the page, which it then formats and displays.

Page capacity is limited only by the size of the headend computer system, and access time is independent of the number of pages desired. As opposed to a one-way videotext terminal, terminals for these types of services are more expensive, ranging from $300 to $400 with the two-way circuitry and a converter.

Time-Shared Videotext

Rogers Cablesystems recently introduced a system that may solve the major problem with videotext—high terminal cost and uncertain subscriber revenue—that has prevented cable operators from making the necessary investment.

The company began to test the service in 1982 in Portland, Oregon and the suburbs of Minneapolis. It is a two-way videotext system, but instead of installing a decoder in each home, decoders are located in the cable plant, shared by many homes. The decoder is similar to the device used in the two-way cabletext system except that it is put in a housing which can withstand weather extremes.

One drawback of this system is that all homes served by a decoder can tune in the information from that decoder. Confidential information, such as electronic banking, cannot be provided.

By combining this time-share method with addressable converters, the communication could be made private, since only the subscriber currently using the videotext channel would have its converter addressed. All other subscribers who tuned into that channel would find it blank.

Another disadvantage of this system is the possibility of subscribers finding all videotext channels in use, the equivalent of a busy signal on the telephone network. Careful planning by the cable operator could keep the waiting time to a minimum, since the number of decoders could be increased in proportion to the usage of the system. In addition, subscribers who desired individual decoders, which would allow immediate and private access to the service, could be provided with decoders if they were willing to pay.

The great advantage of this approach is that videotext service can be provided with a very low investment per home. As videotext services are developed and become economically viable, more private decoders can be installed.

Home Computers

Another method of providing videotext service involves the use of home computers. Several dial-up telephone networks exist that allow home computers to access large data bases (e.g. The Source, Compu-Serve Dow Jones). With these services, home computer owners dial a local telephone number and are connected to a large computer system. Users are billed on a per-minute basis with charges ranging from $4.00 per hour during nonprime time to $50.00 or more per hour during prime time. Several experiments in the cable industry involve simply replacing the telephone line as the communications path between the home computer and the data bases. On a very small scale, this is easy to do in a cable system. A dedicated narrow bandwidth channel is provided for each user in both the upstream and downstream direction. As the number of users increases, however, the amount of spectrum space consumed increases to an unacceptable amount.

If cable systems are to serve as a mechanism for tying together home computers, a more efficient method of communication will have to be developed. Furthermore, it will have to be compatible with other information retrieval (videotext) services offered by the cable company, since for the next several years only a small percentage of cable subscribers will have home computer systems.

System Standards

The cable operator has another problem with offering videotext services—the problem of standards. At the present time, many different methods for providing text information exist. The systems, all of which were developed overseas with government assistance, vary greatly in capability and complexity.

The simplest system and the oldest is the British Prestel System—a system developed by the British Post Office and presently in use over the British telephone network and British over-the-air television. The decoders for this system are relatively simple and inexpensive, but the display is limited to simple alphanumeric characters and crude graphic symbols. The most sophisticated of the systems is the Canadian Telidon system, which allows tremendous flexibility in the visual effects that can be created, but the decoding equipment is also complex and expensive.

Recently, AT&T announced the results of its study of the various systems and introduced a new standard of its own which could become compatible with both the Telidon and the French Antiope systems, but not with the Prestel system. As was the case with color television, stereo radio, and videocassette systems, it will likely be many years before complete standardization exists.

Cable operators who wish to offer videotext service are caught in the middle. On the one hand, the franchising battles are providing incentive for offering videotext services immediately. On the other hand, standardization does not exist; decoders are expensive (and experimental), and services are unproven. Cox Cable is to date the only cable operator that has attempted to establish its own standard for videotext with its Indax system. The system is best for text. Its fairly low resolution for graphics leads to "blocky" figures, but this may be a practical tradeoff for the low cost terminal.

Security

Many types of information retrieval do not require a high level of privacy. For instance, requests for information from a video newspaper, weather information, stock market reports, and the like could all be provided with little or no security. Services that involve financial transactions, however, are a different story. If home banking or home shopping is ever to be offered using videotext systems, privacy will become a major concern. The cable system is poorly suited for privacy since it is, in essence, a giant party line. Tapping into the system and listening to electronic conversations between the headend and the home is simple. If security is to be provided for financial transactions, some type of complex and effective data encryption will have to be installed in each home decoder. The cost may be prohibitive.

FUTURE TECHNOLOGY

This section outlines emerging technologies that may shape the future of cable television. As mentioned in Chapter 3 on distribution systems, there has been a trend over the years toward increased bandwidth on cable systems to increase channel capacity.

Higher Bandwidth Systems

At present, amplifier technology limits cable to approximately 60 TV channels. The upper frequency limit of cable amplifiers is 450mHz. But some passive equipment suppliers are offering multitaps and splitters that operate up to 500mHz. In addition, cable is presently available which has good specifications up to and above 500mHz.

There is little difficulty in increasing the frequency coverage of amplifiers to 500mHz and above. In Europe, many cable systems cover the entire UHF spectrum (up to about 800mHz). The limiting factor to upward expansion of channel capacity in cable systems is the distortion characteristics of amplifiers. Present 400-mHz equipment is inferior to 300-mHz equipment, requiring system designs with shorter trunk cascades and lower operating levels. In the very near future, manufacturers will be producing 400-mHz amplifiers with performance that equals or exceeds today's 300-mHz equipment, and it is only a matter of time before 500-mHz amplifier equipment will be available. It should be noted that increasing cable system bandwidth is a very economical way of adding additional channels. Going from 300 to 400mHz, for instance, increases the cost of the cable system by only about 10 percent, whereas channel capacity increases from 35 to 54 channels, an increase of almost 60 percent. An increase from 400 to 500mHz would add 17 more channels at a nominal increase in system cost.

There is no theoretical limit to the number of channels in future cable systems, and it is likely that over the next decade, systems will be built with 100 or more channels carried on a single cable. Of course converter technology has to keep pace.

Bandwidth Compression

As mentioned earlier, a standard television channel occupies 6mHz of spectrum space. It is possible, using advanced digital techniques, to compress a television picture into a smaller amount of spectrum space. This is done by eliminating *redundancy* in the television picture. Rather than transmitting 30 complete individual television pictures per second, as the present TV system does, each picture is compared with the previous picture and only the differences are transmitted. The difference between any two pictures, or *frames*, will be transmitted except when there is a scene change, in which case an entire new picture must be transmitted. The total amount of information transmitted however, is less, and as a result, the bandwidth required for transmission is reduced a great deal.

Although bandwidth compression techniques have been in existence for some time, the decoding equipment is still extremely expensive. In the next ten years, however, integrated circuits will likely be developed that will bring the cost of the decoder down to a reasonable figure. Jones Intercable, a small MSO (multiple system operator), has announced development of such a bandwidth compression technique and will market decoders.

If a television picture could be compressed to 2mHz instead of the present 6mHz, a cable system could carry substantially more channels than at present. For instance, a 400-mHz system could carry 150 channels.

A second advantage of bandwidth compression is that it is in itself a form of scrambling, since a normal TV receiver would not get a picture on a cable system using bandwidth compression.

Fiber Optic System

Over the last ten years, a whole new communication transmission medium has emerged. Rather than transmitting electrical impulses through a wire as the telephone and cable networks do, optical fiber systems utilize a thin strand of flexible glass. A light source such as a small laser, at the transmitting end, and a photodiode at the receiving end allow the transmission of impulses of light through fiber optic cable.

Fiber optic systems have many advantages over coaxial cable. First, very great bandwidths are possible—several times that of coaxial cable. Second, ingress and egress problems are nonexistent. Third, illegally tapping a fiber optic cable is much more difficult than is tapping into a coaxial cable or telephone wire. And finally, some time in the future, fiber optic systems are likely to be cheaper than coaxial cable systems. Fibers are made of glass, a relatively inexpensive material, whereas coaxial cable is made of aluminum and copper, both of which have been increasing in cost over the years. Fiber is also light weight and smaller.

Most fiber optic development in the past has been in the telephone industry. The telephone company presently utilizes copper wire or coaxial cable to tie together switching centers within cities. In the major cities, these cables are in ducts located beneath the streets. As ducts fill up, and new ducts must be installed, tremendous capital investment is necessary. Since a single optical fiber can carry as many telephone conversations as a massive cable with several thousand individual wires, telephone companies have seen the advantages of replacing present wire circuits with fibers to increase the communication capacity in existing ducts.

At the present time, fiber optic systems for telephone companies have passed the experimental stage and are entering the operational stage. Although fiber optic systems are still more expensive than comparable wire systems, the cost of fiber systems is coming down as the cost of wire systems is increasing. By 1985, it is very likely that it will be economically feasible for telephone companies to use fiber optics for interconnection of most switching centers.

The advantages of fiber optics for individual telephone circuits into residences and businesses are not as great. It will be some time before optical fibers are installed in place of wires for individual telephone circuits. This is because of the cost of the equipment to be located in the subscriber's home. In addition, phone lines typically have a useful life of 30 to 40 years. Even if optical fibers become economically feasible for individual lines by 1990, it would be another 20 years before a majority of lines are optical fiber. In certain specialized applications, such as high-speed digital communications, optical fibers may be in use relatively soon because of their high information carrying capacity. If new services are introduced by the phone company, such as picturephone or even some form of entertainment TV service, the incentive to add fibers would increase, since wire circuits cannot handle such services.

There has been some use of optical fibers in cable systems. All have been "supertrunk" situations where two headends are to be tied together or headends are to be interconnected with hubs. At the present time, the cost of these systems is far greater than is the cost of a comparable coaxial cable system, and this channel capacity is substantially below that of coaxial cable systems.

Over the next few years, however, it is likely that optical fiber development in the telephone industry will bring the cost of fiber systems for supertrunk applications down below coaxial cable systems.

Fiber systems for trunk and feeder use are far less developed. The telephone network is called a *star network* (Figure 5-6). In a star network, individual lines run from a central point (the switching center) to each home. Every subscriber has a private line (except for party lines, where several homes share one line). Party lines have become much less common over the years.

A cable system is a *tree network*, with common signals all leaving a central point (the headend) on a single trunk. The signals are branched out into individual feeders and then to homes. In essence, all subscribers share one large party line.

Star networks are not new to cable TV. For many years Redifusion, the largest British cable operator, has run star-type cable systems in Hong Kong and England. These networks use small switching centers

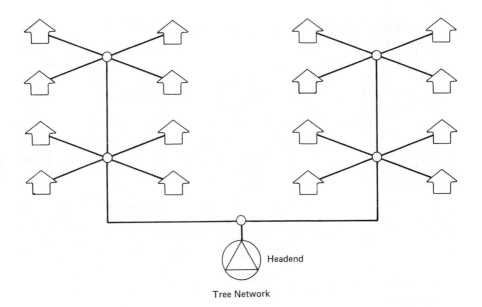

Tree Network

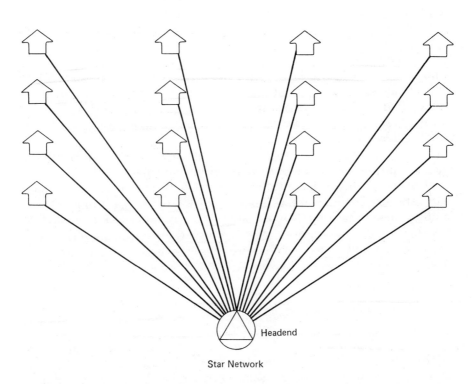

Star Network

Figure 5-6. Tree and star networks.

serving a few hundred subscribers each, with individual drop lines from the centers to homes.

In the early 1970s, a Redifusion system was installed in Hyannis, Massachusetts. Another star system, called "Discade," was tried in a suburb of San Francisco. Although both systems worked well technically, the cost per subscriber was unacceptable.

Fiber optic systems development has concentrated on technology for the star network, and little has been done to develop equipment for tree networks. When optical systems are manufactured in large quantities, only star hardware components will be available at reasonable costs. Therefore, if fiber is used for new cable-type services or in rebuilding or replacing coaxial cable systems, it is probable that it will be used in a star network system design, not the traditional cable tree network. However, large-scale fiber systems will probably not be in use for cable-type services until the mid-1990s. Video frequency-large capacity switching equipment remains to be developed. Substantial capital will be necessary and the capital investment already made in cable is also a deterrent.

With a star network, channel capacity is unlimited. Rather than sending all channels down a single cable and allowing each subscriber to choose one, as is done in a tree network, the star network sends only one channel at a time as requested by the subscriber, down each individual line.

A star network need only have a two- or three-channel capacity (one for each TV set in the house) on each line. Channel offerings can be as great as is desired, limited only by the amount of headend equipment rather than by subscriber equipment. Also, star network designs solve security and privacy problems, since only authorized channels are sent down a subscriber's line.

In the future, cable systems and phone networks will be almost indistinguishable in capability. Both will be star networks utilizing optical fibers. Both will have sufficient bandwidth to handle video, audio, and data services, and both will be switched allowing point-to-point communications. In fact, by the year 2000, either network could handle both telephone and cable services. Whether both these networks will survive side by side and which services will be offered on what network are questions to be answered by regulatory and economic conditions in the future.

High Definition Television

The present U.S. TV system was developed in the 1930s and 1940s. In the 1950s, the system was adapted for color. In other parts of the world other systems were developed, some of which are far superior to that in the United States.

The U.S. system, called the NTSC (National Television System Committee), has several disadvantages. First, the *resolution,* or sharpness, of the TV image is limited. With small-screen TV sets, the fuzziness is not noticeable; on large-screen sets, however, and especially on projection-type sets, pictures are truly inadequate.

Second, the color technique used by the NTSC system is not very stable. It is difficult to maintain natural looking color with the system. In addition, *color resolution* is even poorer than black and white, resulting in smeared areas of color, especially in lettering and small detail.

Finally, the system does not presently allow stereo sound or, in the future, three-dimensional TV pictures.

Over the years, many improvements have been made to transmitting and receiving equipment. However, the limits of improvement with the present system are close to being reached now.

Changing TV standards create two main problems. First, the new standard would probably not be compatible with the NTSC system. For many years, as TV sets of the present style were phased out, programming would have to be transmitted on two different channels, one for each standard. Both Britain and France did this in the early 1950s when they switched to newer, higher resolution systems.

Second, the new standard will almost certainly require more bandwidth than the NTSC system. There is already a scarcity of spectrum space at TV broadcast frequencies, so it is not likely that this new system will be broadcast over the air as is true for present programming. The two best candidates for transmission of high definition TV (HDTV) are DBS (direct broadcast satellite, discussed in Chapter 16), and cable.

Before a new standard can be established, years of study will take place, followed by intense competition between rival technologies, until a standard is finally decided. In this process, many questions have to be answered. For instance, what features are desirable? Should videotext be part of this standard? How about three-dimensional TV? How sharp a picture is desirable? Should digital transmission be used?

It is also likely that an attempt will be made to make the new standard international. Because of the complexity of the decision and the economic implications, it is unlikely that a new standard will emerge before 1990.

Several organizations including the Society of Motion Picture and Television Engineers (SMPTE) and the International Radio Consultative Committee (CCIR) have been studying high definition television. Field tests have been conducted in Japan, and in the United States. CBS has proposed to use high definition standards for their direct broadcast satellite service.

The overall goal of the SMPTE, for example, is to provide a television picture which is equal in quality to 35 millimeter film. To do this, they have concluded that the new standard should:

1. consist of a TV picture with about 1,100 lines compared to the present 525 lines,
2. have an aspect ratio (the ratio of horizontal to vertical screen dimensions) of 5:3 or 2:1 as opposed to the present 4:3 ratio, thus making the screen dimensions resemble the movie screen,
3. improve the method of transmitting the color information to provide greater color sharpness and detail,
4. increase the sharpness of detail by increasing the bandwidth utilized for video information.

These changes will require a bandwidth of 30mHz per channel as compared to the present 6mHz channel width. Bandwidth compression techniques (described earlier) would reduce the spectrum required, but it is unlikely that a high definition TV picture could be compressed to fit in the present TV channel.

Integrated Terminal Equipment, TV Components

Today, a typical cable home contains one or more TV sets, a converter, and a telephone. As two-way and information retrieval services develop, more hardware will be added, such as data terminals, videotext decoders, keyboards, and home computers.

Many of these devices could be consolidated into one unit. For instance, a TV set could incorporate a converter at a minimal extra cost. The same is true of some forms of videotext decoders. Typically, a significant proportion of the cost of a device is in the power supplies and cabinets, so that any design that consolidates two or more devices that share these costs will be cheaper than the combined cost of the separate devices.

The problem with integration of hardware lies in the way in which services develop. Each service must be tested, implemented, and proven, one at a time. Only after a service is well established, and standardization accomplished, can its hardware be consolidated into another device. For this reason, TV components (as in stereo components) will be more common. The consumer can build up the components to the desired TV system from among the separate components such as monitors, converters or tuners (pick one), videotext decoders, and stereo sound systems.

It is possible that more than one communication center will evolve for the home. The telephone of the 1990s will most likely contain a computer terminal and video display. A "Home Information Center," consisting of a telephone, microcomputer, display screen, and modems (modulator-demodulators) for connection to both cable and telephone networks, may evolve which will serve the information retrieval, storage, and display functions within the home. All the services forecasted for cable (and the telephone network) will be handled by the center.

One manufacturer, Zenith, has already introduced a TV set that will tune all 54 cable channels and also contains a telephone. Many manufacturers are looking at similar possibilities, including the incorporation of videotext decoders.

PART II

SERVICES

6

Over-the-Air, Access, Community, and Automated Channels

Public access studio and control room, United Cable, East Lansing, Michigan.

OVERVIEW

A great assortment of programs and services is now available from cable systems and more are planned. These include local and distant television stations; automated news, weather, and shopping channels; local and distant radio stations; government, education, public, and specialty access channels; community channels for news, performing arts, religious, ethnic, children's, and sports programs; special pay channels of movies, sports events, and specials; and two-way services for instruction, information retrieval, pay–per-program entertainment, home security systems, automated meter reading, polling, and games. These cable services are described in this and the following three chapters. Only the most recently built systems offer all these services. For all systems, the problem is to package the available programs to maximize subscriber satisfaction and revenue.

12-Channel Systems

The earliest of the cable systems were 5- or 12-channels and are referred to today as *classic systems*. The cable channels were selected by using the VHF detent tuner built into the receiver. These systems offer all the network-affiliated television stations, add one or more independent, nonnetwork-affiliated stations, and then fill out the 12 channels with automated news and weather. There may also be a channel of locally originated community programming. The monthly charge averages about $8.00. One of the channels might be an optional pay movie channel available for an additional fee of about $8.00.

12-Channel System with Optional Channels

Many of the original 12-channel systems can offer 18 to 23 additional channels by installing a converter. The cable company need only provide the converter to those subscribers who want the extra channels. These channels are the satellite-delivered networks described in Chapter 7, most of which are advertiser supported. The additional package might be about $4.00 per month. In this multilevel system, the original 12 channels are often *basic* cable and the next level *expanded basic*. Since these channels depend on satellite reception, such a system would almost always have at least one optional satellite-delivered pay movie channel at around $8.00.

30- to 35-Channel Systems

Cable systems that are originally built and marketed as 30- to 35-channel systems, where a converter is installed in every home, may have a *universal* service, which includes cable company originated channels and access channels programmed by community institutions and private individuals. This is provided without any monthly service charge after the installation fee has been paid. To offer this service in the application for a franchise may be impressive, but cable companies expect few people to accept this option and few do. Those who do may be eventually converted to other options. How to package the remaining channels is now a debate within the industry. One option is to put every available program service, except the pay channels, into a single package that would be priced at $10 or more. The other is to break the channels into a basic service and an optional expanded basic package.

54- to 108-Channel Systems

Program packaging strategies for the single or dual 400 plus-mHz systems have not been tested. Many are divided into *tiers* with each new tier of service including the previous one. Another approach, now quite common, is to offer several separate packages of services (e.g., basic and several different pay channels) and allow the subscriber to choose any combination. The basic service may be offered at a very low price, perhaps $2.00, or at no charge at all. Still another is to create a new kind of basic by combining two-way interactive services, home security and a pay channel with the usual basic services at a relatively high price (e.g. $19.50).

Somewhat strangely from a marketing standpoint, tentative internal industry labels for service such as "basic," "pay cable," and "extended basic" and "tier" have been introduced to the public. Some confusion has resulted. Professional marketing people would prefer trade names that are clearly identified with a package of services.

Programming and pricing strategies are discussed more fully in later chapters. This chapter deals with over-the-air television, access, community and automated channels. Chapter 7 outlines the satellite-delivered, nonpay, program services, Chapter 8 deals with pay TV, and Chapter 9 discusses two-way service.

A sample of a tiered system appears in Chapter 1.

OVER-THE-AIR TELEVISION

The foundation of the cable television service in most communities is still the delivery of off-air television signals. This is not true, of course, in the bigger cities that have an abundance of clear television station signals available to any television receiver with rabbit ears. But, in towns that have strong signals from *fewer* than the three networks and one independent station, a principal appeal of cable is the supply of the missing broadcast television stations. As a matter of fact, commercial network television, with its news, sports, and popular entertainment series and specials, is the most valued television service, even in cable households with 30 or more channels including commercial-free pay cable movies. Surveys of cable audiences with a full range of cable services available consistently find the predominance of viewing time to the commercial broadcast networks.[1] Adding an independent station to network service provides a schedule of off-network syndicated programs especially popular with children, more movies, and sports. Cable homes with more independent stations available spend four times as much time viewing independent stations as do noncable homes.[2]

These off-air signals are the entire service for the old 5-channel and some 12-channel cable systems. For a very small system, under 500 subs, it may not be practical to build an earth station to receive additional signals by satellite or to build a studio for local production.

FCC Signal Carriage Rules

For systems built since 1972, the FCC mandates carriage by cable companies of local broadcast television signals. These are referred to as the *must-carry* rules. In addition to the nearby local stations, cable systems must also carry *significantly viewed* stations. These are stations, wherever located, that have a good following in the cable area. More details are in note 3 pages 108-109.[3] Furthermore, the local network affiliate is protected from a cable system duplicating its network programming by simultaneously carrying the same network programs from a more distant station. This *nonduplication* (or network exclusivity) rule allows the cable system to carry only the most local station in these circumstances. The cable system may put the local station programming on the distant channel to avoid a "blacked out" channel. Cable systems serving 1,000 or more subscribers may not carry home team, at-home sports events carried by distant stations if the same sports events are not broadcast by local stations. For example, if the Detroit Tigers baseball team were playing the Chicago White Sox in Detroit and Chicago station WGN were carrying the game, but none of the Detroit television stations were carrying the game, a cable system within 35 miles of Detroit could not carry it even if WGN were a part of its regular cable service.

The rules protect local broadcast stations from the economic impact of a loss of the cable households that would force advertising rates down. Furthermore, the rules make sure that cable subscribers have access to whatever local television information is available.

The must-carry rules are being contested by Turner Broadcasting System, Inc., owner of WTBS, the superstation, and CNN, the Cable News Network. Turner would like to see cable systems, particularly the older 12-channel systems, have the option of dropping "must-carry" stations to accommodate one or both of his services. He bases the argument on the First Amendment (free speech) rights of cable operators.[4]

AUTOMATED SERVICES

To fill excess channel capacity, cable systems have always offered certain automatically functioning, *alphanumeric* (letter and number text) channels that provide marginal, but valuable services. In newer systems with 35 channels and up, automated services make up a significant proportion of the total number of channels. This is partly because not enough video programming is available. Listed now are some of the common automated services.

Weather. The earliest form of automated channel positioned a rotating camera in front of a barometer, thermometer, and wind velocity gauge connected to instruments on top of the building. In most systems this crude arrangement has given way to character generated weather (temperature, forecast, wind velocity) and time. Upper and lower portions of the weather screen may also be used for other information such as the program guide, news, shopping guides, and advertising.

Program guides. Multichannel cable systems provide so many program options that a separate channel to index all the others is useful. Each pay channel and some of the other cable networks produce their own program guides. The average family no doubt loses track of one or more of these guides before the month is up. Comprehensive printed program guides are not available for all cable systems, and even when they are, they may not be entirely reliable. The complication of cable program listing is illustrated by a cable *network preempt* channel, where the cable system substitutes another network affiliate that is carrying a preempted program. As a result, desired network programs may not appear on the usual, or nearest, channel. The program guide channel can be kept up to date with these schedule changes.

On a daily routine, some cable employee must punch in the schedule for the day, hour by hour, channel by channel. Once programmed into the character generator, the schedule repeats automatically, every few minutes.

News channels. The Associated Press, Dow Jones, Reuters, United Press International, Consumer News, and others offer news services to cable systems. The AP, Reuters, and Consumer News are alphanumeric text services; North American Slow-Scan provides a voice delivery over *slow-scan* still pictures that wipe across the screen. The news services come to the cable headends by telephone wire, automatically operating a character generator that feeds the intended channel. Reuters has a new teletext news service delivered via satellite. The cable system does not need to buy a character generator, but simply leases a decoder for about $50 per month, in addition to the monthly charge for the news service that is the same however delivered.

The news character generators can be programmed to reveal the text at the average readers pace, or a "page" at a time, filling the screen all at once and holding for the reader to finish.

Stock ticker. Dow Jones supplies running stock prices (delayed 15 minutes) and other business news to cable systems by telephone line in the same manner as AP and Reuters general news. Only a small percentage of the cable subscribers actually use this service, but presumably it is very important to those who do and may indeed be worth the monthly cable service charge in itself.

Local news. A number of cable systems and newspapers have collaborated to supply local news by character generator. The *Coos Bay Reporter,* a *weekly* newspaper in Oregon, produces a *daily* cable version of the paper.

Shopping channels. Consumer shopping channels present comparison marketbaskets. The cable company, or a syndicated service, shops commonly purchased items at major local supermarkets each week and lists the prices, usually ranked from lowest to highest. The service may also provide a total price for the category adjusted to a quantity suitable for a family of a particular number (e.g., total meat items, total sundries, total produce) and the total adjusted price over all categories.[5] See Figure 6-1.

Classified advertisements. The future of classified advertising by cable is in two-way cable, where desired categories of ads can be called up by an individual household (see Chapter 9). Nevertheless, cable can serve for general interest classifieds such as "garage sales" and the kinds of items on "Tradeo" programs on radio. Help wanted, used cars, and real estate may also work on cable. Still pictures can be used with the text. Teleprompter's Worcester, Massachusetts system and the *Worcester Telegram and Gazette* offer classifieds on cable or in print. The classified customer can take either or both. The cable classifieds run six times per day in 15-minute segments.

Bulletin board. Community bulletin boards are included in many systems. It may be a message wheel rotating in front of a fixed, black and white camera, or a character generator. The announcements may appear on a single channel or several different channels sponsored by the government, educational institutions, libraries and other agencies.

ACCESS CHANNELS

In its 1972 rules, the FCC required larger cable systems to make available separate channels free, for education, government, and the public. Further, the cable systems were to have additional channels avail-

CONSUMER SHOPPING GUIDE			CONSUMER SHOPPING GUIDE	
SIRLOIN STEAK	PER LB		TOTAL MEAT COST	
SAFEWAY	2.29		SAFEWAY	65.49
A & P	2.39		KROGER	68.51
KROGER	2.69		A & P	68.72
ALPHA BETA	2.79		ALPHA BETA	69.63
INDEPENDENT	2.98		INDEPENDENT	75.42

ITEM FRAME   *TOTAL FRAME*

Figure 6-1. Sample shopping guides.

able for lease on a common carrier basis, permitting access to these channels to anyone, without discrimination, who could pay. These channels, known collectively as the *access* channels, were supplied in return for the privilege of using off-air broadcasting signals. The requirement was imposed in response to frustrations with the broadcast system which did not accommodate much local government and education programming and could not offer adequate citizen access. The monopoly effect of cable franchises was supposed to be mitigated by leased access which permitted other users of the cable system.

In a case known as *Midwest Video II,* the federal courts struck down the FCC access rules.[6] But the concept had already been established. Many cable franchise agreements and city ordinances required education, government, and public access channels separately or in some combination. Now, bidders in the cable franchising contests are all offering access channels, often substantially in excess of the original FCC requirements.

Educational Access

Educational access channels are used mainly for *external communication*—community relations, the essential communication between public school systems and citizens and taxpayers. School millage issues, school programs, and other general interest information may be on the channel. This could include school board meetings, live and/or taped for replay, and school board informational programs and community debate on issues (e.g., redrawing of school boundaries). More narrowly, the channel may serve the homes of students with instrumental information such as school menus and the calendars of events. Meetings of parents' associations are sometimes conducted by cable. With interactive cable, the meeting chairperson could poll members to determine opinions on issues and take votes on officers and motions.

Further use of the education channel(s) may be in continuing education for adults. This is often a responsibility of the secondary schools and almost always a responsibility of community colleges. Where the nature of the course is not principally social (a chance to get out of the house and meet new people), and the instruction can be adapted to television, cable may be used to lessen the travel burden of students and limit the physical plant needs of the educational institution. In a large community with huge continuing education enrollments, a single cable channel does not go very far. If continuing education by cable were successful, however, schools and colleges might lease channels beyond the number specified in the franchise.

A special category of use for educational channels is in the training of the homebound and the handicapped. Several experiments have established that people can learn well and respond favorably to one-way and interactive instruction to the home via cable.[7]

Television production may be a course or extracurricular activity in the schools. A good argument can be made for bringing elementary and secondary school students into the modern communication age by giving them experience with the full range of communication techniques, including television. The education access channel is an outlet for the television production student as well as for students of the performing arts. A wider audience through television and the excitement of being on television gives their work additional meaning.

Education access channels may be used for school sports. Although cable systems sometimes do school sports on other channels, educational institutions may elect to put school sports on their own channels, promoting the use of the channel and perhaps covering television costs by inviting *underwriting* by local businesses.

For a bulletin board announcement of the school calendars, menus, board agenda, and so on, it is only necessary for the school system to have a character generator (or television camera and rotating message wheel). In a few minutes, a staff member can type in the messages each day. For use of cable as a distribution system for audiovisual materials, the schools must have a videocassette or videodisc playback machine for materials prepared for television and a film chain for instructional films and slides. Someone must set up for each use, although it is possible to automate the play of the videocassettes and videodiscs.

Original television production requires studio space and studio and control room equipment. Portable equipment is necessary for remote work. Operation of this equipment requires at least one professional. Students could be trained to serve as crew, and schools that offer television production as a curricular or extracurricular activity quickly develop a cadre of conscientious and competent video "freaks." It becomes an engrossing experience for a number of students and can lead to careers in communication.

In planning for use of cable, some educators neglect to budget for maintenance and equipment replacement. A conservative sum (perhaps one percent per month of the original purchase price) should be set aside for maintenance and replacement or the system will soon be useless.

It is most convenient if the school system feeds the cable system from its own location. This can be accomplished by use of a special cable between the school system studio or audiovisual center and the cable headend. In most newer cable systems, the link between the schools and the cable system is the institutional network, described in Chapter 3 and discussed later in this chapter. For each channel in use, the educational institutions must provide a modulator. Cable systems may want to maintain the modulators themselves so that the signal quality meets their standards. Almost all cable franchises specify a free cable drop for each school building in the cable service area. If the schools wish to connect more than one room, the schools' maintenance staff can do the wiring to cable system specifications or the cable company will do it at its own expense. Newer franchises may require cable company wiring of whole school buildings.

In a small community, administration of the education channel(s) is not difficult. The channel is turned over to the public school system which generally serves an area at least as broad as the cable franchise. If there is a private school in the community, its needs are accommodated through the public schools. In larger communities, several school districts, community colleges, and universities may all desire a channel. Depending on the cable system design, and the franchise, there may be one channel each for the community college, the universities, and the public school districts. Each public school district might be served by a different hub of the cable system.

Government Access

Government access channels can serve purposes quite similar to those of the educational channels—communication between government and taxpayers, interconnection of geographically separated units (e.g., fire stations, police precincts, district courts), and training programs.

Many government channels are used as bulletin boards—with such mundane but essential information as trash pickup schedules for holiday weeks, tax notices, city council agendas, street closings, city job listings, and recreational facilities (e.g., status of the ice rinks).

These bulletins are produced on character generators from information generally already at hand in various printed reports and from information supplied especially for cable by the city departments. The character generator should have enough capacity (e.g., 16 pages) so that on heavy information days, old but current items do not have to be bumped to accommodate new items. Sixteen pages allow room for attractive and functional spacing of items and is sufficient, because the time of a complete cycle of information cannot be too great or users will have a long wait for the particular piece of information desired. Incidentally, some cable bulletins contain one index page to inform users of the contents at any time. By reviewing the index page, the user can determine if there are items of interest or if a particular item sought is available.

Usually the bulletin is updated daily by a clerical person designated to collect the materials, but it can be updated more often if desired. The cable bulletin is extremely useful in government public information programs, especially for cities and suburbs swallowed up in metropolitan areas where there is no other local media source for detailed information.

The automated bulletin is available 24 hours per day on most cable government channels except when preempted by other information programming in the audiovisual format. A study of government channels in seven communities indicated that about three hours per day is *not* automated programming.[8] These programs are principally live and taped replays of city council and other government meetings, a valuable part of the government cable service. In East Lansing, Michigan, for example, the average viewership for each council meeting is 4.9 percent of subscribing households (about 250).[9] The capacity of the council meeting chamber is only 100.

Other informational programs are created especially for cable on topics of interest. These include explanations of new ordinances, budget presentations, employment opportunities, in-service training of government personnel, regular phone-in programs for access to elective and city department personnel, public safety programs (e.g., fire and crime prevention), and annual reports of various government units.

The nonautomated programs are usually scheduled at an established time so that the community can come to expect these programs. They are repeated often and promoted heavily through all media, to maximize the audience. Since the city council meetings are viewed most heavily, the public information officer in East Lansing, Michigan creates brief spot announcements promoting other programs for running before, after, and during breaks in council meetings.

It takes many *years* to establish a government channel. Both the government and the citizens must learn to use the channel. Through time, the city, with the help of experience and user feedback, makes better use of the channel. Very gradually cable subscribers become aware of the service, discovering the channel accidentally while sampling cable offerings or hearing about it by word of mouth and publicity. A council meeting dealing with a controversial issue for a particular neighborhood, or the need to know the schedule of leaf pickup in the fall may be the first exposure to the channel. Eventually (after about five years), most people in the community are aware of the channel and make good use of it on an irregular basis.

It is possible for the government channel to become a platform for the promotion of individuals and points of view. The City of East Lansing has established a policy that the channel not be used for advocacy:

> Programming shall be information rather than advocative. This does not preclude the cablecasting of public hearings, city council meetings, and other governmental meetings where advocacy may take place.[10]

In East Lansing, the city council members appear on the government channel only as a group, not individually. If a city council member wants to advocate a particular point of view, the public access channel is used.

The government channel is especially effective for the training of city employees. Firefighter training is a good example. Firefighters train continuously to stay familiar with infrequently used equipment and information and to learn new equipment and techniques. A substantial proportion of this training is cognitive (legal, technical, factual) rather than manipulative. The training is done through company officers (of uneven instructional capability and motivation), self-study (requiring strong self-discipline), and the local fire training academy (requiring removal from operational service). Cable, usually providing a free drop to each fire station, can be used to train firefighters in their stationhouses where they are free to respond to an emergency in their districts. The instruction may be live, with telephone contact with the instructor, or via videocassettes, which can be used conveniently for each shift of firefighters and as often as necessary for new recruits and refresher training.

Cable was very effective for firefighter training in Rockford, Illinois via one-way television and in the interactive mode.[11] Cable television is used regularly for firefighter training in Miami-Dade County, Florida; Lansing, Michigan; Jackson County, Michigan; Spokane and Tacoma, Washington; and other cities. Increasingly, ready-made materials are becoming available in the television format through commercial training materials producers and exchange programs among television users.

Using the government access channel for training has some disadvantages since the channel is also available to the general public. For example, certain elements of an emergency medical training program might be upsetting to some adults and children. If available, institutional network channels, which are received only by the institutions on the network, are better for training and other internal communication.

The cable system may have an emergency notification system. If so, the city government public information office usually takes the responsibility for the organization, and the public safety director or police chief for its implementation. This service provides a one-line crawl message and/or an audio message on every single channel in case of an emergency (flood, hurricane, and tornado warning, gas leak, etc.). A visual message can be prepared on the same character generator that is used for the automated bulletin. An audio message can be taken over the phone from the emergency dispatch office and may be somewhat more convenient for public safety personnel. A Cox "Cablealarm" service offers subscribers an option of having their sets come on antomatically in time of emergency, in ever-increasing volume, as a continuous alert.

The full use of the government channel is costly. An original outlay for equipment is necessary. The city channel requires full- or part-time people to coordinate use of the channel and produce program materials. Albany, New York employs a full-time television coordinator and video production aide; East Lansing, Michigan, a full-time television coordinator and the public information officer who devotes about one-fourth of her time to cable information activities; Madison, Wisconsin, a full-time program coordinator, a full-time assistant program coordinator, and a full-time administrative clerk-technician; New York, a full-time executive producer and a full-time executive director; Spokane, Washington, one full-time media technician and a full-time clerk typist; Tacoma, Washington, a full-time program manager, a full-time production coordinator, and a full-tme technician; and Tulsa, Oklahoma, a general manager, a producer-director, a clerical person, and an engineer—all full time—and a half-time artist. Most of these organizations also report use of volunteer personnel and college interns.[12]

Operational budgets for the government channels include personnel, maintenance, and production costs. For the sample communities reporting, annual figures (1980) are Albany, $63,500; East Lansing, $18,000 (not including public information office contributions); Spokane, $25,000; Tacoma, $100,000; Tulsa, $130,000.[13] These budgeted funds may come from franchise fees.

Public Access

The public access channel is one of the most interesting developments in cable television. In modern times the concept of free expression, in the mode of Tom Paine, is impractical. The audience is too vast, printing is too expensive, and broadcast channels are scarce. Perhaps somewhat romantically, public access channels on cable were conceived as an opportunity to provide free expression to any individual. In the abundance of cable channels, one or more set aside for this purpose, on a trial basis, seemed to have merit. Most of the access channels (public, educational, and government) went unused, and the FCC eventually reduced its access requirement to a single channel for all three purposes not long before a federal district court eliminated the requirement altogether. But in a few places, the public access channel took hold to become a vital and diversified communication channel for the community. For reference, some of the communities where public access has been successful are New York; East Lansing, Michigan; Madison, Wisconsin; Bloomington, Indiana; Kettering (Miami Valley), Ohio; Marin County, California; Hayward, California; Austin, Texas; Rome, Georgia; Columbus, Indiana; San Diego, California; Dubuque, Iowa; and Sun Prairie, Wisconsin. Now, as noted, almost every franchise bid includes a public access channel.

It is appropriate here to elaborate the public access concept. The public access channel, under the American notion of freedom of speech, is available to any resident of the community on a first come, first served basis, to communicate whatever is desired. To many people some of the content may be thought to be totally without merit, indeed even harmful. Nonetheless, in the concept of public access, this is irrelevant. No one is to judge another's message. Minority ideas and tastes and eccentric communication have as much status in public access television as do communications from the mainstream of society. In fact, the public access channel may be one of the few places in which novel ideas may be introduced to the marketplace of ideas.

To maintain a public access channel, where no one imposes a judgment on the merit of another's communication, requires great tolerance on the part of the cable company, citizens, and the franchising authority. Some of the community will find some of the programming offensive, trivial, and worthless. Some will consider it a squandering of cable spectrum. However, under the principles of free speech and democracy, it is important for the community to have an available outlet for expression. Furthermore, the public access channel has instrumental value to individuals and groups. It is an inexpensive and effective means of communication available to the entire community. In various places it has been used by politicians of all stripes, the Boy Scouts, the Visiting Nurses Association, the entire spectrum of religious groups, amateur entertainers, public affairs commentators, PTAs, minority groups, handicappers, 4-H Clubs, arts groups, artists, social services, economists, professors, fire chiefs, the Beanblossom Bluegrass Festival, the owners of a boa constrictor snake and Nikki the cougar, and people taking baths, to name only a few.

Here are some examples. In Bloomington, Indiana, "every other Thursday, after school, Channel Three is invaded by children who come to make television. They arrive in twos and threes, some to run camera, some to direct, some to do interviews and skits . . .". The program they produce, "Kids Alive," features conversations with local sports figures, educators and artists, parodies of commercials, and critical reviews of books, movies, and restaurants. Children's library people schedule workshops, arrange field trips, conduct planning sessions, and help the children through the productions. Otherwise, the kids do it all.[14]

Out-of-school, out-of-work teenagers in St. Johnsbury, Vermont have produced shows on teen unemployment, vandalism, alienation, education, parenting, religion, the draft, stock car racing, and nuclear energy—a substantive education, one presumes, along with the practice in communication skills and the opportunity for meaningful activity.[15] In the same town, the Gray Panthers are also active in public access television. There is a lively interaction through telephone lines.[16]

PACE (Public Access Cable Television by and for Elders) of San Diego presents this report:

> As of December 1, 1979, PACE has produced over forty one-half hour programs. It has trained 200 seniors in basic studio production. Broadcast quality public service announcements have been made for nonprofit agencies. Forty demonstration projects have been given. A recent PACE research project indicated that 10,000 seniors have watched PACE on public access. Program topics include oral history, consumer information, legal services, adjustments to aging, arts, sports, advocacy and health.[17]
>
> Consumers Power Company and Dow Chemical Corporation, both in Michigan, use public access cable for communication to employees.

Portable Channel in Rochester, New York has produced documentaries titled: "Free to Be," on an alternative elementary school; "New Kid in Town," a fictional treatment of youth peer pressure and prejudice; and "Women/Ministers," a program featuring an "irregularly" ordained Episcopalian priest. Many of the productions are played on a program called "Window" in rough edited form to get audience feedback.

The purpose of Portable Channel may serve to describe all public access efforts: "to make television more creative, diverse, human and personal, and to continue the successful integration of art, media and community."[18]

In speaking to the cable industry at the 1980 National Cable Television Association Meeting, FCC Chairman Charles Ferris said,

> Your industry's experience with local access channels has shown that there are in many communities local video producers willing to provide exciting and innovative program ideas, and that there is local interest in cable programs on community issues and events . . . while you look to the sky for new programming ideas [a reference to satellite networks]. I hope you are not ignoring them in your own backyard.[19]

In large communities, it is now relatively certain that the public access channel will be active and filled with original and taped material produced locally or elsewhere. More and more people are capable of producing television programs. Periodic workshops increase the numbers with that competency. In large cities, there is a sufficient range of ideas and communication needs and limited means for communication available at low cost. In smaller towns the need may be less because of alternative communication opportunities and limited cable system and community resources. For the smaller towns, public access periods on a more generally used community channel might be more appropriate than a full channel. In this case the concept of entirely open access on a first come, first served basis can be maintained during the public access periods.

The law in most states does not adequately support the fullest implementation of the public access concept. *Both* the access channel user and the cable system are likely to be held responsible for libel and obscenity. This puts the cable system at risk for all the content on the public access channel. Therefore, some cable systems reserve the right to review public access programming in advance, ruling out live programs. If live programs are permitted, the cable company may make stringent rules and require outlines of proposed content.

Ideally, to preserve the freedom of the public access user, cable franchises, supported by state law, would hold the user *solely* responsible for the content on the public access channel and exonerate the cable company from any action resulting from public access channel. This would eliminate the need for any monitoring of the users.

Obscenity is a cable company and community problem. Occasionally, the public access channel will present content that some people in the community are likely to judge as obscene or at least in bad taste. This creates a major public relations problem for both the cable company and the city that provides the franchise. There is no immediate solution.

It is difficult to convince offended citizens that the First Amendment applies even to material they may consider obscene. Many Americans do not subscribe, in practice, to the principles of free speech.[20] The city and the cable company are put in the position of explaining complex constitutional law and may appear to be defending the offending content. Although this is no consolation to cable executives and city officials who must deal with the problem in the present, over time the existence of public access channels may develop a more mature understanding of free expression that will generally strengthen the American character and help to resolve the problem.

The FCC does *not* apply its Fairness Doctrine and rules on equal opportunity for political candidates, lotteries, obscenity, and sponsorship identification to access programming.[21] These rules *do* apply to local origination programming, where the cable operator has editorial control (as discussed in the next section on community channels).

Administration of a public access channel may be accomplished in a number of ways: through the cable company, the city, or a nonprofit corporation. There are advantages and disadvantages to each. If the cable company manages the channel, it can be held responsible for its effective use under the franchise agreement. The *cable company* always has technicians available for maintenance. On the other hand, since there is some cost in public access, even if subsidized by franchise fees, there are disincentives for a profit-maximizing cable company in making public access channels widely used. The *city government* may be able to manage the public access channel, efficiently sharing government channel personnel. Certain equipment might also be shared. An independent, *nonprofit corporation* is insulated from the politics of city government and has different incentives from the private, profit-making company. There are strengths and weaknesses in any of these administrative schemes, but from the variety of experience with all of them, it is clear that any plan can be made to work. Some communities have agonized over the decisions on administrative structure for years without getting public access started.

Two elements are crucial in public access: a coordinating person or staff and a budget. The coordinator may be an employee of the city or the cable company. The principal functions are to *promote* and *facilitate* use of the channel. The first task is to get people to use the channel. After a few years, as people become aware of the channel and facilities through the promotion and public relations work of the coordinator, the job becomes more administrative and instructional. The coordinator teaches people to use the tools, and programs the channel so that it is of maximum value to users and audiences.

Budget is necessary to pay the coordinator and staff, if any, and to keep equipment functioning. It is also necessary to have funds for videotape and graphic materials. The best source of budget is a portion of the franchise fee. This should be a fixed, dedicated fund so that the channel staff and users do not have to curry favor with the city council members to keep their programs alive, violating the basic principle of public access and free expression. If the cable company itself assumes the burden of funding public access under the franchise agreement or ordinance, it must set aside adequate funds. In this case, the franchising authority should require an accounting of the efforts and funds expended for public access.

It is necessary that certain rules of procedure be established to assure an orderly function of the public access channel and also to prevent any individual or group from monopolizing production facilities and channel time. These procedures must not be overly complex and thereby forbidding. Further, there should be no clause that permits disguised censorship. For example, a rule could state that materials presented for play on the public access channel must meet certain technical standards. Ostensibly, this rule would maintain a basic level of quality on the public access channel, but could also be used as a device for rejecting materials not suitable to someone on grounds of *content.*

A sample set of rules that has evolved over several years of application and amendment is included as Appendix B. These rules could be adapted to the public access channel in most communities.

Ordinarily, public access channels do not charge for initial production facilities and channel time. Some charges may be made for studio and equipment use beyond a maximum free time. Since most public access channel users are people of modest means or members of nonprofit groups who cannot afford to buy time or space for their messages in other media, free or low cost access is important to the purpose of the channel.

Equipping a public access channel is a problem. Durability is highly desirable since some users may be inexperienced. Maintenance is not only costly but puts the equipment out of service. Simplicity is also important so that public access does not become a private domain of the technical elite. Increasing the complexity of equipment selection is the constant change in the state of the art. Fortunately, there is now midline equipment, even in color, that suits most production needs and holds up well under public access channel use. For cities and companies without experience in the use of public access channel equipment, it is wise to seek advice of *public access channel personnel* in other communities. Because public access production is unique, the advice of people knowledgeable in other areas of television production is less valuable. The information provided by manufacturers and suppliers is valuable, of course, but self-serving.

Equipment should probably be purchased for public access channels in installments, starting with basic equipment and adding to it as the demand evolves, since it is difficult to anticipate the kinds of production that might develop for a particular public access channel. Availability of maintenance service and parts is important, particularly where the city or cable company does not have service personnel assigned to public access channel responsibilities.

An inevitable function of the public access channel is training. Even an established public access channel will have a continual flow of new users needing basic training in television production. Most cable public access channels have a routine training sequence as part of the checkout procedure for first-time portable equipment users. Workshops are presented periodically for prospective users of the studio equipment and those who want to refine skills. Two publications by United Cable Television Corporation are useful handbooks for the development and operation of public access channels.[22]

Multiaccess

A trend in 100-channel systems, to fill channels, has been to assign separate access channels to every conceivable purpose. For example, the Storer application for Dallas-Fort Worth included 24 channels identified as access channels: action clearinghouse/job bank, library, educational (6), government, interfaith, public, older citizen, black, Hispanic, health, women's, youth, fine arts, commerce, environmental, regional, public affairs, and college (2).

It is relatively easy to propose access channels because programming is not the responsibility of the cable operator. Facilities and production money are another matter. In the Dallas-Fort Worth case, five studios, four mobile units, and $500,000 per year in programming-production money were pledged.

Some of these access channels shared time with other programming. For example, the youth access channel also had Penny Arcade and Calliope; the black access channel, Black Perspectives and the Black Entertainment Network. The advantage of clearly identified, vertically programmed access channels is the continuous availability of that special interest. The older citizen channel always has programming targeted to older citizens, whereas a single access channel would be serving up a *potpourri* of programs. The latter is difficult to promote. Viewers with specific interests must know when programs addressed to those interests are scheduled.

But, can 24 channels be used effectively? The supply of programming and the cadre of producers needed is immense even for a place the size of Dallas-Fort Worth. Just the administrative costs in producing and scheduling programs for 24 channels would be overwhelming. With all the special interest access channels, is their anything left for a general public access channel?

Some public access coordinators advocate a *single,* horizontally programmed public access channel to represent a composite of the community. Public access may help various subcultures within the community to maintain their distinguishing characteristics, yet at the same time expose others in the community to different people and different interests.

Despite these questions, the experiment with multiaccess channels will be informative. Perhaps the programming resources will be found. Perhaps there is program material for 576 daily hours of channel time available (24 channels). As long as there is little other competition for channels in the 100-plus systems, the effort may be worth making. If the capacity is there, program experiments and new ideas may be tried.

Leased Access

Cable companies lease channels, sometimes for nominal fees, as might be done to add channels for educational institutions and as a business. Examples of the latter are data channels. The cable industry and independent communication companies are also now talking about cable providing the within-city, "local loops" to intercity communication carriers. As noted earlier, the FCC once required leased access channels. The object was to mitigate the effect of the cable monopoly. Others could use the system; no person or business would be foreclosed from communicating via cable as is the case in common carriers such as telephone and telegraph. Under this system, outsiders could actually compete with the cable company (e.g., home security systems, pay TV channels, videotext services).

The cable industry does not want to be considered a common carrier. It would like to have control over its channels and lease only at its own discretion.

Many cable companies have not decided how to handle alarm and other services. Will they lease channels to the alarm security industry or enter that business in competition with the alarm industry?

INSTITUTIONAL NETWORKS

In Chapter 3 we described a second cable trunk line following the distribution trunk through the main arteries of the community. It is referred to as the institutional network, or sometimes the "B cable" or "B trunk." This trunk passes all the major institutions of the city or may reach them with short extensions. Because some of the channels go in one direction from the headend (downstream) and the rest in the opposite direction (upstream), the institutional network can be used for two-way communication or teleconferencing. The institutional network, which serves only institutions on the trunk, may also be switched to the main distribution trunk and feeder system to reach all the subscribers to the system—the subscriber network. Thus, the institutional network is a means of feeding the entire cable system, remotely, from any location on the network. Since most of the institutions are served by their own channels on the subscriber network (e.g., government, education access), the communication system is complete.

Part of the institutional network may be assigned to data and audio transmissions. Therefore, the institutional network is capable of a variety of communication modes: two-way television, two-way audio, two-way data; one-way television with return audio or data; one-way audio with return data; one-way television; one-way audio; one-way data.

To use the institutional network, each location must have a source (data terminal, microphone, television camera), a modulator to introduce the signal to the cable, a return active cable drop, and a receiver (FM radio, television receiver, CRT, or printer). Most institutions are already equipped to use the institutional network, with the exception of the modulator which costs about $1,500 and may be portable to serve more than one location.

The following are some examples of uses for the institutional network. The "institutions" may be private (businesses) or public.

One-Way Distribution of Information to Institutions

With several channels available, schools and government agencies may find the institutional network a convenient, low cost means of distribution of live presentations or audiovisual material for in-service training.

Most institutions have a continuing need for in-service training—for example, teachers, firefighters, police officers, social workers, and medical personnel. These people usually work at locations scattered throughout the city. It is costly and inconvenient to have them travel to central training or meeting facilities for all types of training. The institutional network is useful and effective for some of this training.[23]

The network is also useful for instructional materials distribution for schools. Distribution via cable permits greater use of the materials because the time for physical delivery and pickup is eliminated. The instructional materials center maintains better control of the materials if they are handled only by staff people in a central location. Most audiovisual materials can be adapted to cable distribution—slides, films, and, of course, videotape or cassettes. (Certain of these materials may require a larger screen than the conventional television receiver; therefore, institutional cable network distribution may not entirely supplant vehicle or mail distribution of films or slides.)

The institutional network may also be useful for announcements and briefings. This means of communication may be more effective than memos and newsletters and more efficient than passing information down an organizational hierarchy from one individual to another.

One-Way Distribution of Information to Households

The institutional network may be a convenient link to the government and education access channels that reach all subscribing households in the cable system. It avoids physically delivering the tapes or other materials to the cable headend and permits live cablecasts from the institutional locations (e.g., city council and school board meetings).

As noted earlier, this means of communication may be useful for announcements (e.g., winter highway conditions, school closings, meeting agendas, available capacities in public recreational facilities). It can be used for instruction of school children and adults, home security, and fire safety information. Community cultural events produced by schools, colleges, and community performing arts groups may also be televised through the facilities of the institutional network.

Two-Way Instruction to Institutions and Households

The two-way instructional systems discussed in Chapter 9 may make use of the bidirectional institutional and subscriber networks.

Teleconferencing

Television teleconferencing is achieved by use of the institutional network to interconnect the conferencing parties. Each location must have at least minimal television studio equipment and a modulator. The most advanced systems are automated on multiple channels. Where a large number of conferees and more than one camera exist at each location, the dominant voice automatically switches to the camera that covers the microphone picking up that voice. It is also possible to conduct teleconferences with a chairperson or an associate determining which location will be active at any time and switching manually to that location.

The cable system in Reading, Pennsylvania has had an operational teleconferencing system for use, principally by the elderly, as an information resource, a means of exchanging views, and for entertainment. The project was initiated by the New York University Alternate Media Center under funding by the National Science Foundation.[24]

The teleconferencing need not be confined to a single cable system if two or more systems are interconnected by terrestrial or satellite links.

Data Communication

The cable system may supply the data communications link between institutions at no cost. If the franchise is written to include this capability at no cost to the participating institutions, substantial sums could be saved by changing this function over to cable.

Administration

At the present level of use for institutional networks, very little coordination is necessary. There are more than enough channels for the users. As the institutional networks are "discovered" by eligible institutions, the channels could become filled. Before this point is reached, the franchising authority may need to make upstream and downstream channel assignments and establish a procedure for sharing time on channels among occasional users.

COMMUNITY CHANNELS

Signals that begin at the cable system headend, and are not automated, are generally referred to as *local origination*. This distinguishes such signals from off-air and satellite-delivered signals. Access channels are also local origination, but often the term is used to refer more specifically to channels filled by the cable operator rather than access users. To avoid confusion, we will refer to operator-controlled, locally produced programming as *community channels.*

Community channels are programmed by the cable system or under the auspices of the cable company and where the company *has editorial control* as opposed to the access channels which are programmed independently by educational institutions, government, or the public on a first-come, first-served basis and the cable company *has no editorial control.* Since cable company may involve any number of voluntary groups in community channel production, the difference between community channels and public access may not be apparent. In large cities, cable systems may have several community channels or programs "narrowcast" to different neighborhoods and a great variety of special interests.

Under the old FCC rules that orginally established access channels, they were to be noncommercial. No such constraints were placed on the other local origination channels. Community channels are likely to contain advertising, and there is a major movement in the cable industry to increase advertising revenues by selling commercia time in locally originated fare. It is probable that packaged advertising plans will develop so that local advertisers will have an opportunity to participate in all the channels available for commercial spots. It is also probable that local programs will be provided for very specialized interests; for example, a program for philatelists, where the local stamp dealer sponsors and perhaps even produces the program. Three types of programming constitute the bread and butter of community channels: local sports, news, and government-political.

In earlier days of cable origination, *sports events* such as regional high school tournaments were the principal programs on community channels. There were certain audiences, local sponsors to cover the cost, and usually volunteers to handle the production. Now many cable systems cover high school, youth and adult leagues, community college, and college sports. Dynamic Cablevision of Hialeah, Florida covers high school football games, cablecast simultaneously on multiple channels, in two languages—English and Spanish. In 1980 the games were sold out to Burger King in *both languages.*

News is an important product for community channels. As discussed in the introductory chapter, many communities served by cable are engulfed by metropolitan media. Only the most heinous crimes and unusual human-interest stories from the community would ever come up on broadcast stations and in the daily newspapers.

For example, metropolitan Pittsburgh encompasses 698 local governments. The City of Pittsburgh, itself, has only one-fifth of the population of the Pittsburgh television market. But, on average, Pittsburgh television stations give Pittsburgh a 40 percent share of the news coverage of the market. The other 697 localities with four-fifths of the population divide up the rest of the time, so that it is a rare month that most are even mentioned.[25]

Cable, in text or video forms, can serve the information needs of these communities. Co-anchor of the "Totalvision Community News" and "The Northwest Spotlight," of Lone Star Video Cable Television, Patty Tobias, says "Network and local television stations feature state and national news and we feel that our job is to serve the particular needs of Northwest Houston."[26] "The Northwest Spotlight" covers only a small corner of greater Houston, lost in the reporting of the big media. This is a critical potential value of cable television. It can provide an *identity* for a neighborhood or area within a community that has been swallowed up by the metropolitan media that must necessarily appeal to a much broader audience.

The owner of an AM-FM combination radio station and cable system in Naples, Florida produces a half-hour evening cable newscast five nights a week using a writing and production staff pooled for the three media. An April 1980 Nielsen survey showed a 23 percent share of the audience among subscribers, beaten at that time period only by an NBC affiliate in Fort Myers, Florida. The program first runs at 6 P.M. and is repeated with updates, if necessary, at 8, 9, 10 and 11 p.m.[27]

With six reporters and three electronic newsgathering (ENG) crews and a stringer, Guam Cable TV provides the only television news to 70 percent of the homes on that Pacific Island—a one-hour newscast at 6 P.M. and a half-hour update at 10 P.M.[28]

Colony Communications produces a half-hour newscast in the Portuguese language in cooperation with a Portuguese-language newspaper for New Bedford and Falls River, Massachusetts. The news comes from the newspaper, a single ENG crew and a video news service of the Portuguese government with news and sports highlights from Portugal. Many of the 50,000 Portuguese-speaking people in the two towns are recent emigrants from Portugal. Director of community programming, Joseph Langhan, says that news is "one of the most valuable services you can offer. . . . I don't think any cable system can be embedded in the community until it does some news."[29]

Cable systems do not usually have the journalistic resources for news programming, and it has not been established how such programming would be paid for other than through advertising revenues and system subsidy. News consumers are not accustomed to paying directly for television news, and advertisers are only beginning to consider cable. The news-gathering resources of local weekly and daily newspapers, and radio stations have been applied to cable, however. The *Florida Times-Union* and *Jacksonville Journal* provide a channel of text news via cable, supplemented by occasional taped and live video programs. The *Phoenix Gazette* and *Arizona Republic* have leased three channels on the Camelback Cable System.

Cable, with its potential for experimentation in format and style need not be like broadcast television news. Colony Communications Woburn, Massachusetts cable system put together a 60-minute documentary on what was called New England's largest uncontrolled hazardous waste dump by the Environmental Protection Agency. It was followed by more than two hours of panel discussion with environmental experts, community leaders, and state and federal representatives who were glad to have an opportunity to speak in detail on the subject. The *Woburn Daily Times* reporter participated with the cable system community programming director in the panel and co-authored the documentary. The cable system made use of the well-established contacts of the newspaper, and the paper was able to promote its staff by the participation. Over several weeks, more than 40 hours of coverage was given to the issue.[30]

A third area of community channel programming is *government-political*. This includes cablecasts featuring local, state, and federal government officials; public interest representatives; and candidates for political office. Many of these are weekly or monthly programs on tape prepared by legislators in state or congressional facilities, and professionally produced information programs by government agencies. Before elections, cable systems invite candidates for office to make campaign presentations individually or arrange panels or debates among candidates for the same office. As a general rule, cable can provide much more time to the discussion of issues than can the broadcast media, and can cover minor candidates.

A survey released in 1980 by the National Cable Television Association received responses from 1,167 cable systems, representing about 30 percent of all systems. These systems served 49 percent of the total number of cable subscribers at that time. Of those responding systems, 819 (70 percent) offered local programming to nearly 7 million homes. Two hundred and eighteen carried sporting events, 79 produced their own newscasts (with 59 doing so on a daily or weekly basis), 200 produced public affairs programming, and 232 produced government-political programs.[31]

Just as narrowcast news can provide an identity to neighborhoods within a metropolitan area, narrowcast programs can provide an identity to special interests *across* the community. In the first case, the programming is cablecast narrowly to a unique geographic area. In the second, the interests of a few people in a much wider geographic area (the whole cable system) are aggregated to make programming feasible. The special programming may be oriented to political, ethnic, career, hobby, academic, religious, or arts interests.

Community Channel Rules

In programming community channels, unlike the access channels, the cable company must follow the same rules that the FCC and the U.S. Criminal Code prescribe for broadcasting by candidates for public office, handling of controversial issues of public importance (Fairness Doctrine), lotteries, wagering, obscenity, fraud, and sponsorship identification. The full statement of these rules is in Appendix C.

Briefly, the rules on political candidates require that, if the cable system permits any legally qualified candidate for any public office to use the community channels, then all other candidates for the same office must be afforded equal opportunities. This rule excludes newscasts, news interviews, news documentaries, and on-the-spot coverage of news. Under the Fairness Doctrine the cable system is obligated to afford reasonable opportunity for discussion of conflicting views on issues of public importance.[32]

According to the U.S. Criminal Code, whoever utters obscene, indecent, or profane language is subject to fine and imprisonment.[33]

Schemes using information transmitted by wire to defraud are also prohibited by the U.S. Criminal Code.[34]

Cablecasts of advertisements or information concerning lotteries, gift enterprises, or similar schemes offering prizes, dependent in whole or in part upon chance, are prohibited.[35] Advertisements, lists of prizes, and other information concerning a lottery conducted by a state are exempted from this prohibition.[36] Using wire communication for wagering or betting, except where legal under state law, is prohibited in the U.S. Code.[37]

For any cablecast for which money, service, or other consideration is received, at the time of cablecast, an announcement must be made that the matter is sponsored, either in whole or part, and by whom.[38] This rule applies to paid political cablecasts and, if the political cablecast is more than five minutes long, the announcement must be made at the beginning and at the end of the cablecast.

NOTES

[1]"Nielsen Gets First Good Grip on Viewing Levels," *Broadcasting,* August 4, 1980, p. 27.

[2]"Cable Viewing Facts, Beyond the Ratings," *Arbitron,* May 1979, p. 5.

[3]The must-carry requirement varies by community type. For cable systems *wholly outside any television market* (more than 35 miles from any commercial television station) the rules state that the system must carry:

(1) Television stations within whose Grade B contours the cable system, in any part, is located. The Grade B contour is a radius of about 70 miles. It is the effective broadcast range of the station.

(2) Television translator stations, with 100 watts or more power, licensed to the community of the cable system.

(3) Noncommercial educational stations within 35 air miles of any part of the cable system.

(4) Commercial stations that are significantly viewed in the cable system community.

For cable systems located in the *smaller markets* (markets outside the top 100 largest markets as designated by the FCC) the rules state that the cable system must carry:

(1) Television broadcast stations within 35 air miles of any part of the cable system.

(2) Noncommercial educational television stations within whose Grade B contour the cable system lies, in any part.

(3) Commercial television stations licensed to other smaller markets if the cable community is located within the Grade B contour of those stations. (Example: If a small market station is not designated as being in the market in which the cable system is located, but still puts at least a Grade B signal over any part of the cable community, it must be carried.)

(4) Television stations licensed to other communities which are considered part of the smaller television market. These are the "hyphenated markets," such as Burlington, VT - Plattsburgh, NY, where stations may be located in each of the communities.

(5) Television translator stations with 100 or more watts power that are licensed to the cable community.

(6) Significantly viewed commercial television stations.

For cable systems in the *largest 100 television markets* (according to an FCC listing) the must-carry rules are the same as for smaller markets with the exception of number 3 which does not apply.

The FCC definition of "significantly viewed": "Viewed in other than cable households as follows: (1) For a full or partial network station—a share of viewing hours at least 3 percent (total week hours), and a net weekly circulation of at least 25 percent; and (2) for an independent station—a share of viewing hours of at least 2 percent (total week hours), and a net weekly circulation of at least 5 percent." To establish "significantly viewed" stations, the FCC used a May 1972 American Research Bureau report. (The significantly viewed stations are printed in rules or may be obtained from the Cable Bureau of the FCC.) The object of these rules is to "assure that 'local' stations are carried on cable television systems and are not denied access to the audience they are licensed to serve" *Cable Television Report and Order,* 36 FCC 2d 143, 24 RR 2d 1501 (1972).

⁴In the matter of "Petition for Rulemaking to Delete the Cable Must-Carry Rules," FCC, RM 3786, October 14, 1980.

⁵"Consumer Shopping Guide," Vector Enterprises, Inc., Santa Monica, California.

⁶*FCC* v. *Midwest Video Corp.,* 440 U.S. 689 (1979).

⁷Erling S. Jorgensen, Thomas F. Baldwin, Stephen L. Yelon, and John B. Eulenberg, "Final Report, Project 'CACTUS'—Computers and Cable Television in a University Setting," Michigan State University, East Lansing, September 15, 1976; Peg Kay, "Social Services and Cable TV," NSF/RA-760161 (Washington, D.C.: G.P.O., 1976).

⁸Scott M. Spaine, "A Sample of Government Access Facilities in the United States," City of Arlington, Virginia, June 24, 1980.

⁹"Cable Television Public Channel Viewership Survey," City of East Lansing, Michigan, 1979.

¹⁰"Programming Policy for Channel 22," City of East Lansing, Michigan, East Lansing Cable Commission, January 18, 1978.

¹¹Thomas F. Baldwin, Bradley S. Greenberg, Martin P. Block, John B. Eulenberg, and Thomas A. Muth, "Michigan State University-Rockford Two-Way Cable Project: System Design, Application Experiments and Public Policy Issues," Volume II. Final Report, NSF Grant No. APR 75-14286, Michigan State University, East Lansing, June 1978.

¹²Spaine, "A Sample of Government Access Facilities in the United States."

¹³Ibid.

¹⁴Don R. Smith and Rebecca McKelvey, "Bloomington's Popular 'Kids Alive': A New Kind of Children's Television," *Community Television Review,* January 1980, p. 6.

¹⁵Lise Steinzor, "Vermont Community Television Project Teaches Life Skills to 'Delinquents'; Brings Issues to Community," *Community Television Review,* January 1981, pp. 12–13.

¹⁶Tom Borrup, "Overcoming Passive Program Format Is Emphasis of Vermont Group," *Community Television Review,* January 1980, pp. 10–11.

¹⁷Rita M. Wolin, "Community Video Center's Popular PACE Project," *Community Television Review,* May 1980, pp. 4–5.

¹⁸Ann Stonehocker, "Portable Channel: A Community and Documentary Video Center," *NFLCP Newsletter,* Winter 1978, pp. 8–9.

¹⁹Charles Ferris, address to the National Cable Television Association Convention, Dallas, Texas, May 1980.

²⁰John Immerwahr, Jean Johnson, and John Doble, "The Speaker and the Listener: A Public Perspective on Freedom of Expression," The Public Agenda Foundation, New York, New York 1980.

²¹In the matter of "Amendment of Part 76 of the Commission's Rules and Regulations Concerning the Cable Television Channel Capacity and Access Channel Requirements of Section 76.251," Docket No. 20508, November 4, 1980.

²²Randy Van Dalsen, "Access Center Handbook," United Cable Television Corporation (4700 South Syracuse Parkway, Denver, Colorado 80237), 1981. "Cablecasting & Public Access in the Eighties," United Cable Television Corporation, 1981.

[23]Peter Clarke, "Telecommunication in the Workplace," Department of Communication, University of Michigan, Ann Arbor, September 1979; Baldwin et. al., "Michigan State University-Rockford Two-Way Cable Project."

[24]Mitchell Moss, ed. *Two-Way Cable Television: An Evaluation of Community Uses in Reading, Pennsylvania*, April 1978.

[25]William C. Adams, "Local Television News Coverage and the Central City," *Journal of Broadcasting*, Spring 1980, pp. 253–265.

[26]"Northwest Harris County Viewers Served by Lone Star Video Cable Programming," *TVC*, February 1, 1980, p. 36.

[27]"Cable TV: Going After Small Markets," *Broadcasting*, December 1, 1980, pp. 78–84.

[28]Ibid.

[29]Ibid., p. 82.

[30]"Cable Owner Pushes Documentaries," *Broadcasting*, November 24, 1980, p. 66; "Colony Hazardous Dump Site Documentary Wins Rave Reviews from Civic Officials." *TVC*, October 1, 1980, p. 40.

[31]"NCTA Report on Local Cable Programming," *Broadcasting*, September 1, 1980, p. 42.

[32]47 U.S.C.A. 315 (1964).

[33]18 U.S.C.A. 1464.

[34]18 U.S.C.A. 1343.

[35]18 U.S.C.A. 1304.

[36]18 U.S.C.A. 1307.

[37]18 U.S.C.A. 1084.

[38]*Cable Television Report and Order*, 36 FCC 2d 143, 24 RR 2d 1501 (1972).

7

Satellite-Delivered Programming and Cable Radio

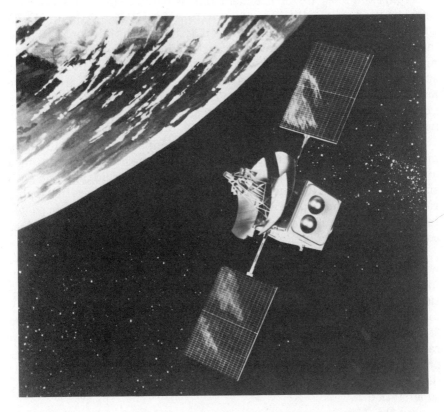

Communications satellite in orbit (drawing), RCA Satcom I. Photograph courtesy of RCA.

Satellite delivery of programming to cable systems has opened up the opportunity for cable television and radio *networks*. At the beginning of 1982, there were three domestic satellites ("domsats") serving cable (satcom IIIR, RCA American; Comstar D-2, AT&T/GTE; Westar III, Western Union) with about 35 channels available (some as backups). Ten more satellites are projected for launch by the end of 1984.[1] At least 12 satellite programming categories, not necessarily exclusive, may now be identified: superstations, news and public affairs, cultural, religious, ethnic, children's, sports, general, regional, educational, radio, and pay. These are discussed in the order outlined with examples of each. Although subscriber counts and number of cable systems in satellite networks change rapidly, May-June 1982 figures are provided to indicate the scope and relative breadth of service for each.[2]

SUPERSTATIONS

Superstations are independent television stations that have been retransmitted via satellite. In service in 1981 were WTBS, Atlanta; WGN, Chicago; and WOR, New York. They may be carried full-time or added late at night after other stations have gone off the air. Cable systems may carry the superstation's entire schedule or pick and choose. The stations are programmed 24 hours daily. While these stations are licensed broadcasters with responsibilities to the city of license, they may be programmed and may sell national spot advertising on the basis of the national cable audience.

Ted Turner's WTBS, Atlanta, is the original superstation. It promotes 40 movies a week and syndicated and sports programming aimed at the cable audience. Most cable systems value the service and find good subscriber response. It is interesting to note that cable viewers in Albany, New York spend more time watching Atlanta-based WTBS than do people in the Atlanta audience for the station.[3] (May 1982 system/subscriber count: 4,144/21,190,000.)

WGN, Chicago, provides a service quite similar to that of WTBS, with Chicago professional sports and somewhat more emphasis on original programming. WGN is retransmitted by an independent organization, without the cooperation of the station, which may fear for its ability to negotiate for syndicated programs in competition with other Chicago stations or to be excluded entirely from the bidding. There have been cases in which syndicators have refused to sell to superstations that carry programs into the syndicators' other potential markets.[4] (April 1982 system/subscriber count: 2,719/8,405,198.) Such a station is called a *passive* superstation.

WOR, New York, has similar services with heavy coverage of New

York area professional sports. (April 1982 system/subscribers count: 1,-327/4,911,148.) WOR is also a passive superstation, being retransmitted without its cooperation. All three superstations charge cable systems a few cents per subscriber per month.

An unlimited number of superstations could develop. However, there *is* a limit on the value of *time differentiation* (availability of the same programs at different times) for off-network syndicated shows and a limit on the number of movies and sports events available. Superstations will have to have *product differentiation*, now being approached by emphasizing and increasing program origination. Superstations may develop a strong regional appeal based on the professional sports carried. The superstations are in direct competition with other satellite network services that may carry similar services without the local obligation imposed by the broadcast license.

NEWS AND PUBLIC AFFAIRS

In 1980, Ted Turner made a dramatic new entry into the cable programming pool—with CNN, the Cable News Network. The television news channel offers news, features, sports, and weather around the clock. The network has the capability of presenting live news events as they are occurring, while the three broadcast television networks wait for an apocalyptic event to interrupt other programming. The $3 million a month news operation was considered a colossal gamble at the outset. Would enough cable systems sign up at 20 cents per month a subscriber; 15 cents if also a WTBS system? Would cable viewers use the news service? Would advertisers support it? Could the company handle the logistics of such a massive news operation? Could the network hold on at substantial financial losses until the bigger markets got cable? Now, the answers to most of these questions appear to be affirmative.

Cable operators who added CNN have received favorable feedback from subscribers but only sparse audience data are available. Early studies in San Diego and Cumberland, Maryland show 52 and 74 percent awareness of CNN, respectively, among cable subscribers.[5] A national study of audiences indicates CNN is doing well in the early evening (4:30–6:30 P.M.) with a 5.6 percent share of the audience and during Saturday morning, as an alternative to cartoons, with a 6.3 percent share.[6]

National advertiser support for the network has been strong. Advertisers have been anxious to get in on the ground floor to test the cable medium, seeking the presumed *upscale* (high-income) CNN audiences and wanting to reach people hard to get in other television formats. Bristol-Myers made a ten-year, $25 million commitment. Others have been Procter & Gamble, GTE Sylvania, GE Credit, *Life* magazine, Buick, Atlantic Richfield, Duracell, and General Foods.[7] Two minutes of every CNN cablecast hour are available for local advertising sales.

Group W Satellite Communications in association with the ABC television network intends to compete with CNN by offering two Satellite News Channels. CNN responded with the initiation of CNN-2, a 24-hour television headline news service. (CNN May 1982 system/subscriber count: 2,255/13,040,000. CNN-2 subscriber count 140/1,200,000.)

Another unique cable news service is C-SPAN, Cable-Satellite Public Affairs Network. It is the service that carries the U.S. House of Representatives, live, using video provided by the House staff. At rare times of high-interest legislative action, this service is valuable to cable audiences available during the hours that the House is in session. It is also a useful tool for government political science courses in secondary schools and colleges. C-SPAN has added to the House coverage, National Press Club speeches, panel talk shows (some of which permit call-in questions), and other programming. One C-SPAN special program was "three hours in the life of the *Washington Star*," before that life expired, where the cameras went into the editorial meetings, eavesdropped on editorial cartoonist Pat Oliphant as he worked and interviewed editors and reporters.[8]

While the cable industry is not yet sure of its value in attracting subscribers, it is certain of C-SPAN's utility in obtaining franchises. C-SPAN is also good national politics. Cable operators and the national associations feel that cable's image in Washington will be enhanced by carriage of C-SPAN. Both these things are well worth the charge per month per subscriber. C-SPAN, like CNN, is proposed in almost all applications for new cable franchises.

Some operators theorize that C-SPAN and CNN, particularly CNN, will help to reach the "upscale," better educated people who may otherwise shun cable. (C-SPAN April 1982 system/subscriber count: 1,-000/11,000,000.)

CULTURAL NETWORKS

For critics of television who lament the limited attention to culture and the performing arts, the rush to launch cultural networks for cable is welcomed. Several major cultural networks are already available or are in planning.

These networks base their hopes on an assumed, unmet demand for programming appealing to a higher level of taste than that served by commercial television and an unstated assumption that others can serve that demand better than PBS and the local public broadcasters. The ABC cable network (ARTS), one of the entrants in this arena, conducted a $1 million survey that concluded that about 90 million viewers would have at least "mild interest" in cultural fare.⁹ Most of the new cultural offerings will be presented with a showbiz approach and an attempt to personalize the artists. ABC's Herbert Granath says the hosts for programs "will be David Hartmans and Alan Aldas. They will definitely not be Alistair Cookes."¹⁰ The progamming mix will not be all opera, ballet, Shakespeare, and symphony orchestras. Plans include jazz, night club performances, folk festivals, and upscale life-style features.

Bravo, the first cable performing arts network, began service in December 1980. It opened with its regular 60-minute newscast that featured opera baritone Sherrill Milnes and a dance class conducted by Jacques d'Amboise of the New York City Ballet, for ghetto youths, and then premiered the two-hour, eightieth birthday tribute to Aaron Copland. Bravo is a pay service at first peculiarly coupled with an adult movie service called Escapade. Bravo had two days a week, Escapade five. Later the services were split into separate packages.

ABC (ARTS) and CBS Cable offer advertiser-supported services at an extremely high cost-per-thousand viewers figure—about $40. CBS is also considering forms of pay TV. Ads would be placed between performances or at intermissions. ABC has teamed up with Warner Amex to have immediate access to a large subscriber base. ABC started with three hours of programming nightly, piggybacked on Nickelodeon; CBS has 12 hours daily. CBS includes programs on science, anthropology, psychology, and investments. (ARTS December 1981 system/subscriber count: 1,350/-6,200,000. CBS Cable, April 1982, 350/4,000,000.)

Another service delivered by cable is RCTV, operated by New York's Rockefeller Center in partnership with RCA (NBC). Called The Entertainment Channel (TEC), it transmits BBC programming, children's programming, feature films, theater, and performing artists. It is a pay service that might be supplemented with advertising revenues from institutional advertisers in informational blocks of about five minutes. RCTV has a ten-year contract for exclusive rights to all the BBC's programming.

A coalition of local arts, education, and humanities groups has formed the Cultural Cable Channel of New Orleans to secure a lease on the cable franchise to be granted in New Orleans. Five hours of programming per day would be devoted to the cultural image of New Orleans.¹¹

These developments have posed problems for public broadcasting. Not only has public broadcasting lost first rights to the BBC, which formerly provided some of its most popular programming, but the new networks will be directly competitive in areas that were once the exclusive province of public television. Before any of the cultural networks were launched, the Carnegie Corporation proposed that public broadcasting operate a pay cable service called PACE (Performing Arts, Culture and Entertainment). Months later CPB and PBS were still contemplating the prospect of the Public Subscriber Network, while faster-moving organizations were going into service. Public broadcasting may find much of its function taken over by cable with its new, specialized, satellite networks in cultural, educational, ethnic, and children's programming. On the other hand, cable offers to public television much of what it has needed all along—more channels to serve its special purposes and narrow audiences. Services proposed by public broadcasting would have to be considered seriously for any franchise proposals, although this advantage may be lost through public broadcasting delays.

In the meantime, some individual public broadcasting stations are independently pursuing cable opportunities. WGBH, Boston, one of the major suppliers to PBS, has formed NovaCom, a company to distribute programs to cable. At first they will come from its own library of programs including the science program "Nova," "Evening at Pops" with Arthur Fiedler, and the "French Chef" with Julia Child.[12] WHA of Madison, Wisconsin will feed the local cable channel with overflow programming from PBS (about 30 percent) that for one reason or another does not get on the air.[13]

According to *Newsweek* magazine, diversity of choice in specialized cable has so far "been limited to fans of sports, news, and popular movies." Now cable is reaching out to a new audience: "in the democracy of the new TV marketplace, even elitists will get equal time."[14]

RELIGION

Almost as soon as satellites became available for cable system interconnection, religious networks emerged. They are free to cable systems, sustained by viewer contributions, and, in one case, advertising. A very interested group of viewers uses the services, as cable operators discover if they attempt to drop one of the channels. These channels were added to cable systems as they became available and before other programming options in basic and pay were anticipated. Some operators now have second thoughts about the channels. Many carry more than one or all of the channels, but worry about redundancy. There is a community concern that the religious cable networks are draining funds from local churches. Religious network operators deny this, arguing that the networks stimulate interest in religion and result in more money to both places.[15]

A second concern is the narrow, evangelical fundamentalism that characterizes present channels. Although the religious networks actively seek programming representing all faiths, mainline religions have hesitated to participate because of a reluctance to be associated with the evangelical programming and their own greater interest in community-based religion. Therefore, the cable company carrying one or more of the channels is presenting a somewhat unbalanced perspective on religion.

Gill Cable of San Jose, California dropped a religious network (CBN) in favor of its own religious channel representing area churches. The hope is to represent a wide range of religious faiths through live discussion programs and sermons. The channel will solicit funds for expenses with the money staying in the area.[16]

A final issue for cable is the political activism of many of the cablecasts. Some of the religious programs are slanted decidedly to the political right, giving cable systems carrying the networks another dimension to the balance problem.

Whatever the difficulties, cable is a useful medium for religion, reaching people with many more opportunities for worship, teaching, and discussion of theological issues than broadcasting, which limits religion to undesirable fringe times or brief "thoughts for the day."

Biggest of the satellite-delivered religious networks is CBN—the Christian Broadcasting Network. It is experimenting with advertiser support nationally and makes local availabilities.[17] CBN intends to make a somewhat broader appeal by including sports and family entertainment. Others are People That Love (PTL) and Trinity Broadcasting Network.

These networks have polished production and some nontraditional religious broadcasting formats such as talk shows. According to Scott Hessek, satellite manager for CBN,

> We want to let people know that what we will produce is not going to be mamby-pamby, dry, quiet or dull religious programming. What we will produce is good material—serials, drama, magazine-type formats, children's shows, even game shows. We will go whole-hog and pull out all the stops in production.[18]
>
> (CBN April 1982 system/subscriber count, 2,860/16,200,000; PTL, 600/5,200,000; Trinity, 170/1,587,000; National Jewish Television, 90/1,896,-`800.)

ETHNIC

Minority audiences, aggregated over hundreds of cable systems, may be served by cable-satellite networks. BET (Black Entertainment Television) offers a full daily schedule of programming on its own transponder. Advertiser supported (Anheuser-Busch is the charter advertiser), BET programs black college football and basketball, black-oriented feature films, specials, talk and gospel shows. (April 1982 system/subscriber count: 845/9,100,000.)

The National Spanish Television Network, or Spanish International Network (SIN), operated by a broadcast television group of five stations, is available to cable systems outside the broadcast areas on a paid basis—10 cents per month *to* the cable system for every Hispanic subscriber. (The trade ads say "SIN Pays.") The network, supported by advertising, provides Spanish-language movies, sports, comedies, "novellas," and news. (May 1982 system/subscriber count: 488/24,652,500 estimated Spanish-speaking cable and broadcasting households.)

GalaVision is a pay television network, with no advertising, also operated by SIN. The network offers mainly Spanish-language movies, "novellas," some sports, and variety. Cable systems pay GalaVision a portion of the rate charged to subscribers or a minimum fee, whichever is higher. (April 1982 system/subscriber count: 134/100,000.)

CHILDREN

Children also have cable-satellite networks. One, Nickelodeon, is a 14-hour daily service distributed by Warner Amex to its own systems and others. It carries no advertising. Nickelodeon costs the cable operator 10 cents per month per subscriber. The programming is *age specific;* that is, it is prepared and targeted to particular age groups. ("You can't think of children as one group from 2 to 15 years of age like most of the broadcasters do," says Peggy Charen, president of Action for Children's Television.)[19] A sampling: "Pinwheel," for ages two to five, is educational entertainment using puppets and character actors; "Kids Writes", for ages 6–12, offers stories, jokes and poems submitted by kids; "What Will They Think of Next," for ages ten through teens, is programmed with science-related animation and on-location films (how to preserve rare books by freezing them to destroy insects); "Livewire," for ages 12 through 17, is a talk show for teens with celebrity interviews, consumer information, career planning, and so on.[20] (April 1982 system/subscriber count: 1,725/7,700,000.)

Calliope, on the USA network, runs children's films one hour daily.

SPORTS

ESPN (Entertainment and Sports Network) is a 24-hour, advertiser-supported sports network running live and taped replays of popular sports and other sports previously unknown to television (polo, rugby, table tennis, handball, karate, etc.). ESPN has contracted to cover many of the NCAA's minor sports. Heavy on sports news, the network covers some news live such as the NFL player draft. ESPN may broaden the American knowledge of sports, extend the *range* of television sports, and provide an around-the-clock opportunity for the eclectic sports fan.

ESPN pays cable systems a small per-subscriber fee for carrying the network. Other popular networks such as CNN and USA insist, against some cable system pressure, that a small subscription fee paid by the system will be necessary for quality programming. (April 1982 ESPN system/subscriber count: 3,685/15,848,692.)

GENERAL

Some of the cable networks transmit a *potpourri* of sports and entertainment features, something like a superstation without the broadcast license. Although launched fairly early, they are still experimenting with format and searching for programming to attract audiences.

USA Network originated as an outlet for Madison Square Garden Sports and expanded it to include BET, Calliope, and the "English Channel," featuring non-BBC British productions from companies such as Granada and original programs such as health and preventive medicine. (April 1982 system /subscriber count: 1,800/11,000,000.) It is now partially owned by Time, Inc. and represented to affiliates by HBO.

Another network ignores sports and concentrates on entertainment and information. SPN (Satellite Program Network) contains celebrity interviews and other talk, women's news (with still pictures), classic movies sometimes packaged by category such as Saturday night's "Cowboy Flicks," and "Telefrance-USA," which is French entertainment and news in English or French with English subtitles. (April 1982 system/subscriber count: 460/4,591,505.)

These two networks are advertiser supported and permit local ad inserts by the affiliates as does ESPN.

REGIONAL

Many of the satellite-cable networks might be considered regional, although most do not advertise it. The superstations each concentrate on the hometown sports teams and may be strongest in those regions; the Hispanic networks are strongest in the Southwest and Florida.

One network, PRISM®, is avowedly regional. It combines pay movies, specials and exclusive Philadelphia sports delivering the package by microwave to cable systems within a 100-mile radius of Philadelphia. This is a unique combination. It can be expected that each other major region will have its own sports coverage—through superstations or PRISM-like regional linkages.

EDUCATIONAL

Some networks are dedicated to education, information, and public service. The Appalachian Community Service Network consists of public affairs programming, educational material, teleconferencing, and community service. It charges independent cable operators one cent per month for each subscriber and multiple system operators half a cent, but for courses cable operators get $3.00 per student enrolled. (April 1982 system/subscriber count: 217/1,431,271.)

Modern Satellite Network is an advertiser-supported educational and informational programming service during daytime hours. No charge is made to cable systems. (May 1982 system/subscriber count: 541/4,-338,664.)

OTHER NETWORKS AND PROGRAMS

A profusion of other networks or programs is now available or proposed. These include Music Television (MTV) with 24-hour audiovisual taped performances of popular musical groups in concert (April 1982 system/subscriber count: 600/4,000,000); a 24-hour weather channel; classic films; financial news; signed programming for the deaf, a "cable college"; how-to; health programming; a woman's network; cartoons; harness racing with a "Call-a-Bet" plan for telephone wagering; the Nashville Network with Grand Ole Opry; black-oriented music; the Cinemerica Satellite Network to meet the needs of the over-50 age group; a network called "Window" to showcase independent producers; and a number of "video publishing" services drawing on the resources of several major magazine groups (examples: Charter: *Ladies Home Journal, Redbook;* Hearst: *House Beautiful, Sports Afield, Harper's Bazaar*).

Advertising agencies, now interested in the cable opportunity, are beginning to become program suppliers. This harks back to the early days of radio and television broadcasting when the agencies owned and produced the shows for the sponsors they represented. Benton & Bowles, a major ad agency, has created a wholly owned subsidiary to produce for cable. Other agencies will follow.

The cable networks with a single type of programming, such as ESPN, CNN, and the religious networks, are said to be *vertically programmed* as opposed to the *horizontally programmed* USA network which has something for every interest.

Some of the networks described here can be considered pay television—Bravo, PRISM, and Gala Vision—but the others are provided by operators to cable subscribers for a subscription fee along with other services either as "basic" or "extended basic" so that the sum paid is not assigned to any one service in particular. Pay cable is a special category of satellite-delivered programming. It is the subject of the next chapter.

CABLE RADIO

In the rush to develop and market video services, cable radio has been somewhat neglected. Audio programming comes from the same sources as video: off the air from antennas mounted on the tower, through microwave relay stations, by satellite, and from audio origination facilities at the headend. Although not marketed aggressively by most cable systems, cable radio may be sold as part of the basic service, on other tiers, or added as a separate connection for $1.00 to $3.00.

Some audio services are put into the 88- to 108-mHz spectrum which can theoretically contain 50 channels with a 400-kHz separation. Systems usually carry fewer. A splitter connects the cable drop to an FM receiver in the home. As an alternative, or in addition to the FM band, audio services may accompany silent video services such as weather, news, stock market, and shopping channels.

Cable radio also provides the capability of simulcasting pay TV movies or concerts in stereo improving on the sound quality of the television receiver. The newer franchise applications and a few older systems are including this innovation. MTV, the rock music video channel, encourages cable systems to simulcast the stereo audio signal on the FM band and use it to help sell the FM radio service to subscribers.

Off-Air Radio

More than half the U.S. cable systems provide retransmission of local and distant AM and FM stations that can be received from atop the CATV antenna.[21] Since FM broadcasts are line of sight, the high antenna picks up FM signals that would ordinarily be blocked by the horizon. In smaller towns with only a few types of radio programming available, mostly middle-of-the-road music, cable can offer the full range of radio formats. In some of the bigger towns with more radio broadcasters, cable radio may still be valuable in bringing in stations received inadequately because of blockage by the terrain or man-made structures. In other metropolitan areas, cable radio is difficult to sell because people already have access to stations covering most listening interests. Many of these systems do not even offer the service.

Some cable systems have done well with AM and FM retransmission. One-third of the subscribers to the UA-Columbia San Antonio, Texas system opt for the FM connection; the figure is 27 percent for Gill Cable in San Jose, California.[22] These are far higher than the industry average, but they indicate the potential.

Satellite-Delivered Audio

Audio can be transmitted on a subcarrier frequency along with a primary video service on satellites. The radio service is completely independent of the video signal and its audio, and does not interfere. The technology can provide stereo. At the moment, plenty of subcarriers are available for audio service. In 1982 seven satellite subcarrier audio services were available to cable systems. WFMT, the Chicago-based FM broadcast station, is now a radio superstation distributed by United Video, Inc., the company that distributes WGN-TV. (April 1982 system/subscriber count: 126/813,671.) WFMT is a classical music station with low-key advertising and some news. The others are Satellite Radio Network (religion and gospel music), Bonneville Beautiful Music (easy listening), Seeburg Lifestyle Music ("upbeat" music for graphics channels), Satellite Music Network (modern country, pop adult), Moody Broadcast Network (religious music, drama, education, and phone-in), CNN Radio Net (news updated in 30-minute cycles).

One plan for satellite audio is noncommercial instruction. KPBF-FM, a National Public Radio (NPR) station associated with San Diego State University, offers full-credit courses on the San Diego cable system. The courses will be distributed nationally by satellite, if successful in San Diego. NPR has a Satellite Program Development Fund to encourage noncommercial uses of the available NPR satellite capacity.

Audio Origination

A few cable systems originate audio services. These may be college or high school stations and public access radio or commercial stations.

Some college stations have taken to cable because the FCC has deleted 10-watt noncommercial FM. Cable radio has similarly substituted for college carrier-current stations. Cable eliminates the need for transmitters and dealing with the FCC and is capable of stereo. *TVC* magazine found college cable radio stations in Bloomington, Indiana; Athens and Toledo, Ohio; Wayne, New Jersey; DeKalb and Carbondale, Illinois; and Columbus, Ohio.[23]

Community stations may be developed to serve minority interests and minority tastes. An example is WRKB, owned and operated by the Knoxville, Tennessee Communications Cooperative and programmed with jazz, gospel, soul, African, and Latin music. The station is an audio complement to a video channel.[24] FM access stations may duplicate the audio of public access television stations or serve as an alternative access outlet which is faster, cheaper, and easier than video.

Commercial stations have operated on cable for years. One is the Coaxial Communications station in Columbus, Ohio, which is run by a paid manager and volunteer announcers. The station takes requests, which come frequently, mainly from young people. It will accept advertising, but it does not actively sell time. The breaks are filled mostly with promotional announcements for the pay TV services.

In Meridian, Mississippi, a daytimer radio station, which must go off the air at night, became a full-time operation by moving over to the cable system after sundown. Local residents asked for the service, preferring their local "beautiful music" format station to Muzak and three other easy-listening stations brought in from out of town.[25]

KBLE, an album-oriented rock format on the Hawkeye cable system in Des Moines, Iowa, has survived as a commercial station since 1975 by selling advertising at lower rates than broadcasters with a wider reach.[26] (A detailed discussion of cable radio is found in the three-part *TVC* magazine series referenced in this section, notes 21, 22 and 23.)

NOTES

[1]"Satellite Line Up," *Cablevision,* January 25, 1982, p. 88.

[2]"Cable Services Subscriber Counts—1981 Review" *Cablevision,* January 18, 1982, p. 79. "Cable Stats," *Cablevision,* June 14, 1982, p. 93.

[3]"New Era for Superstations, Part II, " *Cablevision,* August 11, 1980, p. 30.

[4]Yale M. Braunstein, "Recent Trends in Cable Television Related to the Prospects for New Television Networks," submitted to the FCC Network Inquiry Special Staff, Washington, D.C., August 1979, p. 131.

[5]"Newswire," *Cablevision,* October 20, 1980, p. 1.

[6]"Newswire," *Cablevision,* November 10, 1980, p. 12.

[7]"CNN Attractive to Advertisers," *Broadcasting,* July 28, 1980, p. 86.

[8]"C-SPAN: Carrying Out a New Programming Niche," *Broadcasting,* November 3, 1980, pp. 48–52.

[9]Harry F. Waters and George Hackett, "Cable's Culture Splurge," *Newsweek,* December 22, 1980, p. 58.

[10]Ibid.

[11]"Networking," *Access,* January 12, 1981, p. 4.

[12]"WGBH Forms Program Company," *Cablevision,* December 1, 1980, p. 18.

[13]"Cable-PBS Relationship: Opportunities for Both," *TVC,* August 1, 1980, pp. 48–50.

[14]Waters and Hackett, "Cable's Culture Splurge," p. 58.

[15]"Will Ecumenism Find a Home in Cable?" *Cablevision,* November 24, 1980, pp. 24–27.

[16]Ibid.

[17]Ibid.

[18]Ibid., p. 25.

[19]"Parting Words," *Cablevision,* January 12, 1981, p. 162.

[20]Ibid.

[21]"Hidden Treasure: Cable FM," *TVC*, December 15, 1980, pp. 163–172.

[22]Ned Mountain, "Cable Audio Services: The (Hi-Fi) Sky's the Limit," *TVC*, February 15, 1981, p. 61.

[23]Janet Quigley, "Cable FM: Unlocking the Door to More Radio in the Community," *TVC*, February 1, 1981, p. 73.

[24]Ibid., p. 74.

[25]"How One Daytimer Became a Full-Time Operation," *Broadcasting,* July 28, 1980, p. 90.

[26]Quigley, "Cable FM," p. 76.

8

Pay Television

Program supervisors and technical director monitor east and west coast transmission feeds at the Cinemax master control in New York City. Photograph by Lou Manna, courtesy of HBO, Incorporated.

Pay TV is the term applied to services for which the subscriber pays an additional amount, usually by the channel, sometimes by the program. In the early days of pay TV, it was a simple enough concept. The subscriber paid about $6.95 for some off-air channels, a few automated channels, and access channels. Then, for another $7.95 or so, the subscriber could have one more channel with no advertising, uncut movies, some sports events, and a few specials, mainly night club acts. Now there are "minipay," "maxipay," "dual maxis," "tiered," "specialized," and "bundled" pay services. These different pay options reflect the industry's experimentation with various pay packages in an area of booming but undefined consumer demand. Pay TV is very important to the cable industry and cable consumers. Pay cable has been responsible for expansion of cable into the urban markets and the mushrooming of earth stations, which, in turn, have opened up cable to all the other satellite services described earlier. Pay cable is a fascinating topic because of the incredible growth, the battles between Hollywood and pay cable distributors, the programming strategy games, and the sometimes surprising consumer appetites.

BACKGROUND

Seeking a cable system for its new pay TV service in 1972, the Home Box Office (HBO) Company signed cable pioneer John Walson who owned the Service Electric Cable Company in Pennsylvania.[1] Walson was the first to agree to try the pay service which took on other affiliates in the Northeast. Tapes of movies supplied to the cable system were played and repeated several times and then returned to HBO. Walson charged $6 per month and supplied a mimeographed program guide.

A per-program pay TV service called Telecinema started in 1973 in Columbus, Ohio on the Coaxial Communications system. Subscribers were permitted a few minutes of viewing of each film and then were billed for the film at about $2.50 if they viewed further. A two-way system monitored the set tuning so that viewing in each household could be ascertained. The headend computer automatically added each viewed movie, at the correct price, to the subscriber's monthly bill. (This system was designed and patented by one of the authors, McVoy. The two-way system developed for Telecinema has also been used, with modifications, in Rockford, Illinois; Syracuse, New York; Portland, Oregon; and Temple Terrace, Florida.) The Telecinema system was abandoned when it became apparent that much greater subscriber penetration and revenues would result from per-channel pay television. Four years later, in a different part of the same city, Warner initiated the Qube system with the pay TV offerings on a per-program basis. Programs are still available to those who subscribe to the Qube part of the Warner Amex Columbus service, but after a trial period with per-program pay only, Warner Amex also made pay TV available on a per-channel basis. Nonetheless, it is still expected that per-program pay TV may work well for special offerings. This will be discussed later in the chapter.

In 1975, HBO began transmitting by satellite to earth receiving stations owned by cable systems. Since the receiving stations cost about $100,000, only the big systems with 5,000 subscribers or more could make the capital investment. Others, large and small, continued to operate "stand-alone" pay services by videotape.[2]

Another event in the development of pay cable was the 1977 U.S. Court of Appeals decision overturning the FCC's pay cable rules which had, in essence, prohibited pay cable use of movies older than three years and sports events that had been shown on conventional television during the previous five years.[3]

Early pay cable entrepreneurs were plagued by problems with *churn*. The basic cable subscribers would take the service for a month or two and then quit; others would be persuaded to sign up and then do the same, so that there was a constant churning or turnover of pay subscribers. To calculate the churn percentage, some operators use this formula:

$$\text{Percentage churn} = \frac{\text{current month's disconnects}}{\text{last month's end subscriber base}} \times 100$$

The best that pay cable could do would be to hold about 25 percent of the basic subscribers, but these retained subscribers came at the high cost of installation, usually provided free as an incentive to subscribe, and disconnection for those who tried the service and did not stay with it.

Several problems accounted for the churn and low subscriber penetration. Pay cable was almost always oversold. The blockbuster film titles would be featured in advertising and promotion. The subscriber would realize only after the service started that there were not many blockbusters and that the "B" pictures used as filler were disappointing. The movie industry does not produce enough quality film to fill a daily schedule. Furthermore, Americans were not accustomed to *paying* for television. It took several years to establish the idea that television was something of value and that unedited, uninterrupted movies, even just a couple a month, were worth $7.00 or more. And, of course, promoting the unfortunate name "pay cable" played into the hands of TV network competitors who labeled their own service "free" TV. Also, the pay TV system, where subscribers buy the channel and everything on it, violated most consumer codes; there was so much waste, no one consumed anything near what was available.

One unsatisfied subscriber wrote to HBO's president: "I hope that

King Kong ascends the Time & Life building and passes gas into your office. Then maybe you will get the drift of what I think of your schedule."[4]

Many cable operators just as vehemently rejected pay TV, making it difficult for pay suppliers (networks) to build a cable subscriber base. These operators felt that their business was delivering over-the-air television—a business that was already doing nicely. Some were afraid to get mixed up with Hollywood and were afraid of uncut movies. Only gradually did the concept of the value of pay TV register. Pay cable subscribers rose to a national average of 53 percent of basic subscribers.[5]

A major boost to pay cable came with the FCC's reduction of the required size of the earth station receiving dish from 9 meters to 4.5 meters. The price dropped to as low as $6,000 for antenna and preamps, with an additional cost of $2,500 in receiving equipment for each channel. At $8,500 for a single channel this put almost every operator in the pay TV business. Each dish was capable of receiving not only pay channels but several other network services from the same satellite as well, further justifying the capital investment.

The pay networks had to learn to program. At first it seemed random; the subscriber was unable to perceive a pattern. But programming plans did emerge, with some rationale for the scheduling of premieres, repeats, specials, and R-rated films.

At the end of 1980 there were almost 8 million pay cable households.[6] The growth of subscribers is charted in Figure 8-1. Since 1980 the count of pay cable subscribers has been complicated by the increasing number of subscribers to more than one service. It is no longer possible simply to add up the number of subscribers to each pay service. The figure commonly used now is number of pay units, the unit being a subscription to one pay service. For April-May 1982 *Cablevision* reported 16,336,921 pay TV units.[7] The number of pay TV households would be somewhat less.

Three pay TV suppliers accounted for most of the systems/pay units in April-May 1982: HBO, 3,600/9,000,000; Showtime, 1,500/3,000,000; and The Movie Channel, 2,150/2,200,000. Others at that date were Cinemax, 900/1,500,000; Escapade/Playboy, 137/232,332; Home Theater Network, 275/155,000; Eros, 9/90,000; and Bravo, 28/59,589.[8]

Pay Suppliers

At first, some large cable systems, and some too small to construct a receive antenna, ran *stand-alone* pay channels. That is, the system would negotiate its own movie rights, generally through an agent, and secure videotapes for play on the system. This required a major administrative effort, staffing and equipment for playback, and the production

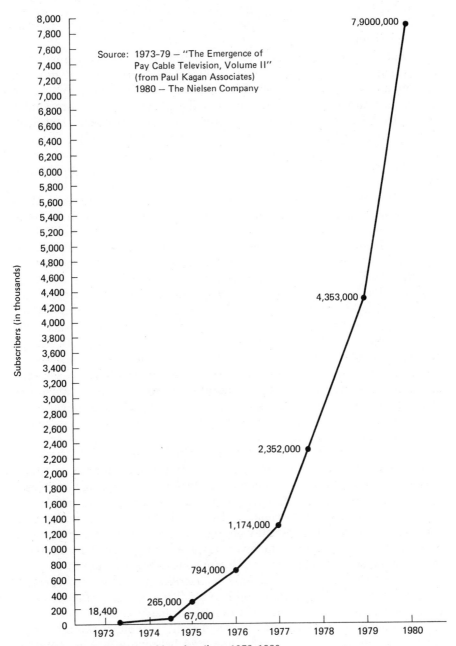

Figure 8-1. Growth of pay cable subscribers 1973–1980.

Subscribers (in thousands)

Source: 1973–79 — "The Emergence of Pay Cable Television, Volume II" (from Paul Kagan Associates) 1980 — The Nielsen Company

7,9000,000

4,353,000

2,352,000

1,174,000

794,000

265,000

18,400

67,000

of a program guide. Most of these systems eventually joined one of the networks, but custom pay TV packages from pay network suppliers or independent bookers are available to cable systems wanting to tailor the service to community tastes.

Each of the bigger pay channel suppliers is jointly owned by firms that are also multiple system operators (MSOs); therefore, they have an instant market for the service. Time, Inc. owns HBO and ATC, one of the largest cable MSOs. Showtime and The Movie Channel are jointly owned by MCA, Inc., Paramount Pictures, Warner Brothers, American Express and Viacom International. Times-Mirror, Storer, Cox, TCI, and Cablevision Systems are partners in Spotlight, a pay service that is predicted to be very big because of the number of subscribers to the five MSOs.[9]

A momentous discovery for the cable industry was made in 1978 when a Wometco cable system in Thibodaux, Louisiana, with no ownership ties to a pay cable supplier, offered *both* HBO and Showtime, presumably to give the subscribers a choice. Instead, many subscribers took both.[10] Somewhat incredulous, but afraid to miss the boat, other systems tried dual-pay offerings with the same result. Some systems took the supermarket approach, offering every available pay cable service and most of the other satellite-delivered networks as well. Showtime began to promote itself as a second service to those systems already receiving HBO. In response, HBO created a second service of its own, Cinemax, deliberately *counterprogrammed* to HBO. That is, offerings opposite each other were designed to appeal to different tastes. Since all the pay services draw on the same pool of movies, there is a clear subscriber perception of the duplication across pay services, but as long as the duplication is not in the same time period, the multipay subscriber may be satisfied.

The multipay systems have spawned a new lexicon of terms to identify the various types of pay services. *Duplication* refers to the same titles carried by two or more pay services in the same month (or other period). *Differentiation* is the degree of difference among pay services. *Foundation service* is the original or basic pay service—the anchor service (in most cases HBO, Showtime, or The Movie Channel are foundation services); other pay services may be tiered above the foundation service. *Specialized services* are narrowly targeted to particular interests (e.g., GalaVision, in Spanish, or Escapade/Playboy, for adults, are examples). Other terms in use include *maxiservice,* which is a full service, usually 24 hours, with G, PG-, and R-rated films. Systems offering more than one maxiservice are referred to as *dual* or *triple maxis.* A *miniservice* is a smaller package with fewer titles, usually without R-rated films to satisfy communities where such films may be generally unacceptable. Some MSOs have their own limited movie services that would qualify as minis. Cable operators offering more than one pay television service are called *multipay* systems. A few cable companies now combine pay services with other channels delivered by satellite, ordinarily a part of the basic service, to help sell the pay service.

PROGRAMMING

Programming of the pay networks has been a problem. The most fundamental of the difficulties is the lack of *product*. Product means programming, particularly the output of Hollywood. Hollywood produces about 300 or 400 movies per year. Of these, only about 50 get national attention and play in theaters in every city and town. (Examples of these films for 1980 are *Rough Cut, The Nude Bomb, The Elephant Man,* and *The Last Married Couple in America.*) Still fewer, perhaps 20 per year, are "blockbusters" that are highly publicized and gross over $20 million at the theater box office. (Examples for 1980 are *The Empire Strikes Back, The Jerk, The Electric Horseman,* and *All That Jazz.*) These blockbusters are the foundation of the pay cable offering, scheduled so that there are about one or two per month. Other nationally distributed films support the blockbusters, or the main attractions, and the rest of the Hollywood production available to the pay supplier is used as fill. As an example of the latter, in 1980 HBO secured exclusive exhibition and distribution rights for pay TV to such "lower-end" films as *Old Boyfriends, Roller Boogie, Bloodfiend,* and *Shame, Shame on the Bixby Boys.*[11]

The pay suppliers use theater box office success as an index of which films to feature (and also as an index of how much to pay). But sometimes a film that has failed at the theater box office will play well to pay cable homes. This may not be too surprising, since the principal theater audience is under 24 years of age and the pay cable audience spans the whole spectrum (still weighted at the young end).[12] In at least one instance, success on cable has caused the movie producer to re-release a film to theaters. In another case, a film, *The Great Santini,* was released first to pay cable and then circulated in theaters, perhaps helping to promote the theater run.

Faced with limited product, pay suppliers must repeat what they have available to fill time. Repeats, of course, are a convenience to subscribers. The subscriber can look at a month's schedule and pick the most convenient time to view. Or, for those who do not plan ahead, if a film is missed on one occasion, another time will come. Tony Cox of HBO says a big challenge of cable marketing is "in learning how to sell the asset of repeat programming and to overcome the kind of historical ingrained television viewing habits in which the consumer presumes the repeats are a bad buy." He speaks of "positive" and "negative" repeats saying that experience suggests that repeats are positive up to a point, perhaps six or seven in prime viewing time within a month, where audience accumulates with each play. Up to that point, all the people who have wanted to see the program have had their chance and repeats thereafter become negative in value. Few new viewers are added, and subscribers get irritated that the title continues to fill time that might be given to new titles. Excessive repeats are the most common complaint of pay subscribers and probably the most frequently stated reason for canceling (along with the concomitant, limited-product-related problem of not enough good films). The most popular movies are *encored* (repeated) in about six months.[13]

In economic terms, the first six showings can be said to increase total utility to the viewer although showings three to six increase utility at a decreasing rate (slope of graph decreases). The seventh and eighth showing give less total utility than do the fifth or sixth showing. There may be a number of showings which is so large and so disgusts the viewer that total utility approaches zero or falls below zero and he or she disconnects as illustrated in Figure 8-2.

The problems caused by repeats may actually get worse. The issue is less crucial now because pay TV is still subsidiary to commercial TV—an added service. As pay TV becomes more dominant (the principal reason for subscribing), the issue may become more important and the threshold of viewer tolerance altered.

One solution to the limited-product problem is to go outside the Hollywood theatrical film industry for programs. The two biggest pay suppliers (HBO and Showtime) do this, producing their own "specials." These are mainly night club acts or concerts, but may also be Broadway shows, documentaries, or consumer information programs. In the month of January 1981, HBO featured "Elton John Plays Central Park," "Kris

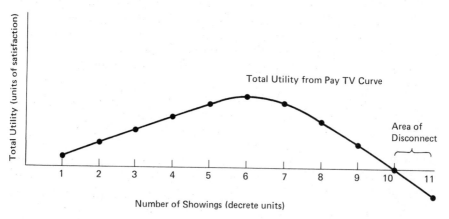

Figure 8-2. Effects of repeat showings on viewer utility.

Kristofferson and Anne Murray," "The Candid Candid Camera" (racier than the commercial television version), and "Consumer Reports Presents." The same month Showtime presented "Showtime Looks at 1980," "David Sheehan's Showtime in Hollywood," "Gabe Kaplan," "Eubie!" (the Broadway musical review), and "Celebration," a concert salute to song writer Dorsey Burnett.

The original programs were not very well received by subscribers at first. They perceived them to be detractions from the movies that were the reason for subscribing in the first place and perhaps they sensed correctly that some of the specials were only fill. But the specials had at least one appeal; they were novel to television. The night club acts were uncut. The two pay supply services also began to learn how to program the specials and, as the subscriber base grew, could spend more money for top-line talent. Of the Broadway material, both HBO and Showtime think comedies to be most successful. For other specials, one hour is considered the limit. The audience seems to accept the "performer performing" without gratutious guest stars and skits. Promotion between programs and in the program guide is crucial. The specials and marginal movies need the promotional attention because the audience knows so little about them.[14]

Since pay distributors like HBO and Showtime will both carry the box office hit movies at about the same time, unless HBO has an exclusive, the original specials and the quality and quantity of the "B" movie packages will help to differentiate one service from another. Differentiation is especially important to the pay suppliers where cable systems offer multipay services.

Most recently the pay suppliers have entered into co-production agreements with public broadcasting stations. Pay TV would get the first run, then public TV stations. The pay suppliers have also begun to participate in the financing of feature films—called "prebuys." By so doing, they are guaranteed access to the film at a favorable price, but they take the risk of investing in a box office dud that will not attract cable viewers. There are also a few made-for-pay-cable films.'

RELATIONSHIPS WITH HOLLYWOOD

Hollywood has been a somewhat reluctant partner to cable. Unused to being in a buyer's market, the major producers in Hollywood have rebelled against cable and, particularly, the domination of pay cable by HBO. At first Hollywood could play hard to get. Cable revenues were insignificant. Now, with pay cable serving millions of homes, it provides millions in revenues to the major production houses.

The movie distributors want more money for their product and would prefer compensation on a per-subscriber basis. The share of the revenues for the producer is now about 20 percent. The distributors would like to get closer to the 40 percent they get in theater distribution.[15] HBO books most films on a negotiated flat-fee basis for specified periods of time. The movie industry would like to book by "day and date" with all pay suppliers rather than for exclusive periods with one pay supplier.

The major industry thrust against the pay suppliers has failed for the time being. Four of the producers—20th Century-Fox, Paramount, MCA, and Columbia—joined to form a pay cable network called Premiere. According to the plan, films produced by the four companies would be run on Premiere and be withheld from the other pay cable networks until nine months after the Premiere run. The four companies accounted for more than half of HBO's best films. A U.S. District Court, on an action brought by the Justice Department, decided that withholding films to the competitive advantage of Premiere was a violation of the Sherman Act. The judge ruled that Premiere was guilty of a group boycott by refusing to release films simultaneously to other pay suppliers.[16]

Movie producer-distributors need to set up a release date scheme which maximizes profits from all four markets (theater, cable, videocassette/disc, and network TV). They have to consider what would be optimal playdates and *separations* (clearances) between these markets. This is difficult because cable and videocassette/disc markets are new and are changing their relative shares of the total market rapidly.

The movie industry cannot rationally turn its back on the pay industry, although some producers have threatened to make earlier release to the commercial networks, for a higher price, and then go directly to the sale of videocassettes or videodiscs, bypassing pay cable entirely. But network broadcast television is already paying about as much as is economically feasible for movies and is finding that series and miniseries are better audience producers anyway. Movies made for theaters, which bank on scenes that earn R ratings, may not be suitable for broadcast network TV. The pay cable business is growing. Even a small piece of a very big pie is better than none.

The cable industry, particularly the pay cable suppliers, argue that Hollywood is compensated fairly. They note that they take almost the entire production, even the big losers, not just the best titles. And they don't sell popcorn to add to revenues as the theaters do.[17]

The two industries still need each other. Pay cable suppliers are desperate for product. Movie producers need the increasing revenues from pay cable to help offset the high costs of film production. As Frank Biondi of HBO says, "There is a lot of money for both parties in the pay television business."[18]

"ADULT" CONTENT

Send the kids to bed. The kind of R-rated movies your customers want to see . . . when they want to see them. This stuff is explosive! Look at the trends in videocassette sales. Check the popularity of the "jiggle" and action shows on network programming. Think about the failure of pay TV channels without adult-oriented fare. America wants . . . and will pay for . . . action-packed, revealing movie entertainment in prime time (trade ad for Escapade).[19]

Adult programming is a good business opportunity but a difficult issue for the cable industry. It has always been accepted that uncut, R-rated movies are a major appeal of the big pay networks. They account for a substantial number of cable subscribers. Audience data seem to confirm this, although it is possible that violence, adult situations and language, and the more mature themes of the R movies contribute to the appeal. In the old Telecinema pay-per-view system, adult movies were the biggest draw.[20] It is widely assumed by industry people that the principal attraction of the Warner Amex Qube two-way system is the adult, pay-per-view channel with such titles and descriptions as

PASSIONS OF PLEASURE. When a man dreams about a beautiful blonde, it leads to the ultimate fantasy—a man, his wife and his mistress. $3.50
MUSTANG, HOUSE OF PLEASURE. A unique look at the infamous Mustang Ranch, Nevada's legal brothel. $3.50.[21]

R-rated movies have kept pay television out of some conservative communities. In others, the pay channels have been included against protests. Cable systems and the pay suppliers have been discreet in handling adult content. The channels may be locked out, so that adults can be assured that children do not have access. The MPAA rating and the reasons for the rating are always indicated in the printed program guides (helping to attract audience as well as warning them off, of course). On some pay networks, the R films are run at late hours. Qube requires special signed request to order the adult channel, and the channel is not advertised except in the guide.

The Home Theater Network supplies a package of only G and PG films in HTN *Plus*. It may be used as an alternative to the services that carry R films. The Disney Channel also serves a family audience. On the other hand, there are now specialized pay networks catering to "mature" tastes. Sex is the principal attraction. These services do not attempt to hide it, using mainly R-rated or unrated films (Escapade/Playboy, Private Screenings). Others offer toned-down softcore X films (Quality Cable

Network). One organization (RCH Cable Marketing) plans to have nude female announcers introduce the programs. RCH and Las Vegas Live are programming risqué night club acts from Atlantic City and Las Vegas. Some of the adult services program *Screw* magazine's "Midnight Blue," the video sex magazine. *Playboy* magazine has initiated a programming service, in association with Escapade, based on the magazine which will include "selected nudity consistent with the *Playboy* life-style."[22] *Penthouse* has also announced adult channel plans.

While most cable entrepreneurs would like to satisfy the demand for "adult" material, MSOs seeking future franchises must tread carefully in this market. In some cable systems, particularly rural ones, the pay service is coupled with a Christian channel to counterbalance the effect of the R movies. Warner Amex has had to explain its Qube adult channel as a result of awareness raised by competitive bidders. Cox, joined with Cablevision Systems, Daniels, and Comcast in ownership of Escapade, has also had trouble. For these companies, the original pairing of lowbrow Escapade with highbrow Bravo, the cultural program service, may have been designed partly as a response to questions of taste likely to be raised by franchising authorities.

PER-PROGRAM PAY TV

Although pay-per-view (PPV) cable has not been a notable success so far, except in advancing two-way technology, there are some clear applications in special events. The Don King Sports and Entertainment Network reported a live cable audience of more than one million households for the Holmes-Cooney heavyweight championship fight in June, 1982. Fifty cable systems used notch filters and ten systems used addressable. Charges were about twenty dollars per household.

Per-view charges would be preferred by the movie industry. It would put pay TV on a box office basis like theaters and closed-circuit television. Pay per program may also be economically sound. It permits a reflection of intensity of demand which could open up television to almost any kind of programming that people would be willing to pay enough for. A per-program system would also deal handily with the problem of repeats and scheduling. As demand falls off, programs are dropped or the price is lowered. Under the per-channel pay system, pay suppliers or cable systems must constantly survey audiences to determine demand, information that is received automatically in a per-program system. With per-program pay, reimbursement to the producer is a share of the gross per program. There is no need to make assumption about the relationship of cable viewing to theater box office success to negotiate fees.[23]

Twentieth Century-Fox Chairman and chief Executive Officer Alan

J. Hirshfield, sees the following film industry pattern of release: "The sequence will probably be an exclusive pay-per-view run, followed by a non-exclusive pay cable run, followed by a network run, followed by an ad-sponsored basic cable run, and finally traditional TV."[24]

ECONOMIC FUTURE

Pay TV has brought new life to the cable industry and obviously satisfied a strong consumer demand. It has substantially increased revenues per cable household justifying expansion into urban markets and low-density rural areas as well. It has brought a diversity of content, previously unknown to television, through pay channels and the other services received on the earth stations constructed principally to receive pay networks.

Diversity in pay cable may be threatened, however, by several economic pressures according to a report for the National Telecommunications and Information Administration.[25] First, as channels fill up, especially in low-capacity systems, operators will look at the revenue-producing capability of each channel and may have to reject or bump some services. The number of orbital slots also limits the satellite capacity. Some services may be forced out of the bidding for the available transponders. A second factor is the dominance of HBO over the supply market. If HBO purchases exclusive rights to product as a result of its dominant market position, other suppliers and their subscribers are denied the product. The third concern is the vertical integration of the pay industry—the ownership of multiple cable systems by the pay suppliers. Because of these relationships, competing offerings may be foreclosed from systems owned by particular pay suppliers who follow a self-preference strategy. Finally, the desire of movie producers for a larger share of pay TV revenues may force prices up and exclude some consumers from the market.

There are trends pulling against these factors, in every instance, that may maintain or increase present levels of diversity. New cable systems are all large capacity, more than 50 channels, and older systems are rebuilding at a record rate.[26] The movie industry is trying to sell on a nonexclusive day and date basis so that all pay suppliers will be a part of the prime market for movie products. The growth of Showtime, TMC, and stand-alone pay systems has reduced HBO power. (However, what is emerging is a very strong triopoly which can collectively dominate the industry and under the proper circumstances act as a single monopolist.) The success of multipay systems has lessened the effect of vertical integration, and cable systems bidding new franchises include several pay services for fear of being outdone by others. Many ATC systems (HBO) now carry Showtime (Group W Cable and Viacom International), for example; but if Cinemax and HBO, which are jointly owned, succeed as *the* foundation package, as Time, Inc., hopes, other pay suppliers may be closed out of some markets and HBO will restore its dominating market power vis-à-vis Hollywood. The movie industry will be able to increase its pay cable revenues by simply waiting for cable to develop into the urban areas. Holding the line on prices may increase pay cable penetration.

As pay cable grows in total number of households, it will certainly affect network broadcast of theater movies, reducing their value to broadcasters and probably increasing the number of made-for-broadcast television movies. The networks are now thinking about reducing their bids on movies due to impact of pay TV. Theater-run movies on broadcast television may be offered only in syndication long after the theater and pay cable runs.

NOTES

[1]For a discussion of the earlier history of pay television and pay cable, see Barbara Ruger, "Will Baltin and Pay TV: The Thirty Years' War," *Cablevision,* September 22, 1980, pp. 40–49.

[2]"The Emergence of Pay Cable Television." Volume II. "Background Data and Final Report," prepared by Technology and Economics, Inc., for National Telecommunications and Information Administration, Washington, D.C., July 1980, p. 19.

[3]*Home Box Office* v. *FCC,* 567 F 2d 9, cert. denied 434 U.S. 829 (1977).

[4]Howard Polskin, "Inside Pay-Cable's Most Savage War," *Panorama,* March 1981, p. 57.

[5]"Cable Stats," *Cablevision,* April 26, 1982, p. 248.

[6]Dwight M. Cosner, "The Changing Audience of the '80's," Nielsen Media Research, presented at the BEA Faculty/Industry Programming Seminar, Washington, D.C., November 7, 1980.

[7]"Cable Stats," *Cablevision,* June 14, 1982, p. 93.

[8]"Cable Stats," *Cablevision,* June 14, 1982, p. 93.

[9]*The Pay TV Newsletter,* January 21, 1982, p. 1.

[10]"The Emergence of Pay Cable," p. 96.

[11]"HBO Increases Rights to Films," *Cablevision,* October 20, 1980, p. 17.

[12]"Analysts Disagree Whether Pay TV Will Hurt Box Office," *Cablevision,* December 15, 1980, p. 247.

[13]Barbara Ruger, "Pay Executives Weigh Value of Danger of Duplication," *Cablevision,* September 22, 1980, p. 28.

[14]"HBO, Showtime Refine Original Programming Policies," *Cablevision,* January 5, 1981, p. 17.

[15] Fred Dawson, "Pay After Premiere," *Cablevision,* January 19, 1981, p. 28.

[16]Jill Marks and Chuck Moozakis, "Premiere: Inside the Issues and Tactics," *TVC,* February 15, 1981.

[17]Dawson, "Pay After Premiere."

[18]Ibid, p. 28.

[19]Ad for Escapade in *Cablevision* magazine, January 26, 1981.

[20]Michael D. Wirth, Thomas F. Baldwin, and Jayne W. Zenaty, "Consumption Patterns in Pay TV," mimeo, Michigan State University, East Lansing 1981.

[21]Qube Edition, *Cable TV Program,* June 1–14, 1980, p. 7.

[22]*Cablevision,* December 15, 1980, p. 19.

[23]For further discussion, see Thomas F. Baldwin, Michael O. Wirth, and Jayne W. Zenaty, "The Economics of Per-Program Pay Cable Television," *Journal of Broadcasting,* Spring 1978, pp. 143–153.

[24]Patricia Goldstone, "Cablevision Plus Interviews Alan Hirshfield," *Cablevision,* March 1, 1982, p. cp 5.

[25]"The Emergence of Pay Cable Television." Volume I. "Overview," prepared by Technology and Economics, Inc., for National Telecommunications and Information Administration, Washington, D.C. July 1980, p. 28.

[26]Fred Dawson, "The $1.5 Billion Sellers' Market," *Cablevision,* January 5, 1981, pp. 26–28.

9

Two-Way Services

Videotext Tree System Indexing. Photographs courtesy of Tocom, Incorporated.

The cable industry is still experimenting with the two-way technology and its applications. Skeptics in the cable industry and outsiders can point to some challenging technical problems and economic issues yet to be addressed fully. Few of the two-way services, mainly field trials, can be considered in themselves, a "business," the term used in the industry to label a service that has crossed the line from research and development to profit contributor.

The cable industry has been forced into experimenting with two-way services by the demands of franchising authorities and competition for franchises. Only the most committed of these companies are likely to sustain the efforts in the absence of early realization of a demand that can be met economically. In the meantime, the cost of experimentation in two-way may be well worth the value of a franchise.

Still, the promise of two-way cable excites the imagination: interaction with television after all these years of passive viewing, home alarm systems, automated meter reading, electric utility control and conservation systems, armchair shopping, electronic text reference and information services, prizefights and other special sports events, electronic funds transfer, and so on.

In the end, it may be two-way services that distinguish cable from other communication services and provide the competitive edge.

One of the great problems in two-way cable is the need to aggregate services to justify the capital investment and operating costs in the home terminal, distribution plant, and headend hardware and software. Development of cost-effective two-way systems may also require a large population of subscribers within the service area. The demand for any one service among a relatively small number of subscribers served may be insufficient, but the demand for several two-way services, however infrequent or limited, over a large body of subscribers may support the cost. Many different services can use the same hardware on a time-sharing basis.

We take up the two-way services one at a time, describe experiments that have taken place or are proposed, and attempt to assess the potential. The two-way services are ordered more or less from the most advanced to the least advanced in terms of industry experimentation.

PER-PROGRAM PAY TV

This application on the two-way cable technology has been described in the pay TV chapter. The Telecinema movie service and its area multiplexing technology proved to be a profitable business. The problem, however, was that there was more money to be made in per-channel pay TV that did not require the two-way technology. This presumably also motivated the Warner Amex Qube switch from an exclusive per-view system to the per-channel pay TV option. It remains to be seen whether the per-program options such as boxing, football games, and perhaps first-run movies, released on pay TV early after the theater openings, can justify the capital investment in the two-way system.

Cable systems are looking for per-program revenues from special events. Two-way, or addressable converters make this possible. In the interim, one-way systems without addressable converters sometimes use *notch filters* to make these events available to cable subscribers who are interested. The subscriber calls the cable company asking for the event and is mailed the notch filter. The subscriber, him/herself, inserts the filter between the drop and the matching transformer. The notch blocks out an interfering carrier in the center of the channel removing the interference to produce a clear picture. The filter self-destructs 72 hours after the event. Subscribers without the notch filter see a garbled picture.

ALARM SERVICES

Several cable systems have offered alarm services. We describe two in detail, The Woodlands, Texas, and Syracuse, New York, representing different conditions and technologies. The idea of home alarm systems is appealing to homeowners and to some public safety people. The traditional security alarm business, using phone lines, has so far served mainly industry, business, and a few wealthy homeowners with a good deal to protect and the resources to do it—about three percent of the residential households.[1] If reasonably priced fire and burglar alarms along with medical alerts or ambulance call buttons could be offered to homeowners, life and property would be protected at an efficiency heretofore unknown. With 97 percent of the homes unprotected, the cable industry anticipates a major new business.

In general, the two-way cable alarm systems work like this. Smoke or heat detectors, and sensing devices at doors and windows, are usually hard wired into the cable terminal. Some systems are wireless. A medical alert button, probably located in a master bedroom, may also be wired into the cable. When the fire or burglar alarms are triggered, an audible alarm is heard in the household if it is occupied, and at the same time a signal is sent to alarm system operators or directly to police and fire department dispatchers. The signal to public safety officers may also include vital information, called up from computer storage, about the household such as location of handicapped persons, number of occupants, and placement of utility shutoffs. The medical alert is received by the proper medical authority or ambulance service. A medical history may be communicated along with the alert. It is also possible for respiration, heartbeat, and other vital signs to be monitored by the system. The status of the alarm is monitored continuously through the cable. Signals to the headend travel upstream in the cable distribution plant as described in Chapter 5. An active alarm would cause the computer at the dispatch office to print out the address and other information.

It is highly probable that a given signal is a false alarm. Various checks on the system, prior to responding to the call with people and equipment, are established to meet this difficulty. Some believe that the false alarms generated by such a system are a fatal flaw. False alarms can divert equipment and personnel from actual emergencies. It is one thing to build a one-way cable system for entertainment where a breakdown may mean missing an episode of "Happy Days" and quite another to build a two-way system where failure could mean loss of life or property. Cable systems haven't had much experience with the latter. As discussed in Chapter 5, a two-way cable system must be better designed and more carefully constructed and maintained. Some engineers are not certain that cable can ever overcome the problems of noise interfering with the return communication or generating false alarms. Further, devices to provide necessary redundancy and backup power in case of power failure may be too costly.[2]

The value of the alarm system to the household is clear. If the house or apartment is unoccupied, the alarm is still answered. In the case of a fire in the unoccupied home, it is usually the case that it is too late to save the structure by the time the fire has reached the point that it breaks through and is visible to the outside. When the home is occupied, the alarm communicated directly to dispatch offices improves response time significantly. Several minutes are lost in the time it takes for a householder, in an emergency, to phone the proper authorities. In the case of a fire, the victim may have to awaken neighbors to make the call. In these emergencies, people do not always function well, and it may be difficult to communicate accurate information. Response time and the difficulty in communicating is also reduced by the medical alert and police call buttons.

Insurance companies have reduced rates for households with cable alarm services. If alarms are effective, fire service personnel foresee a different structuring of the departments with lightweight, two-person trucks in many locations to meet the different demands of early-detected fires. The heavy equipment is located more centrally.

Telephone lines are capable of the same communication service except that the broadband capacity of cable is much greater. Present telephone systems can accommodate alarm systems but without the testing capability provided by the continuous monitoring of cable.

All the homes in The Woodlands, Texas, a planned urban development near Houston, are wired for cable when built. The builder must supply the minimum package of a smoke detector, two TV outlets, and two medical and two police alarm buttons. The buyer or builder can order additional alarms and detectors and an intrusion-detection system if desired. The equipment is supplied by Tocom, an original developer of two-way cable systems.

Every six seconds the central computer monitoring unit interrogates the connected homes. If an alarm is active, the computer prints the address, kind of alarm, and other information about the household. A dispatcher calls the home to verify the alarm. If the alarm turns out to be burnt toast, or a curious kid trying out the buttons, there is no further action. If the alarm is confirmed or if there is no answer to the dispatcher's call, the proper emergency units are dispatched. Smoke detectors are responsible for most of the false alarms (about half the alarms received). Very few prank alarms are received because they are traced immediately to the perpetrator.

A story told by *Fire Engineering* magazine describes The Woodlands system at work:

Late in the afternoon, the alarm system's high-speed teleprinter sounded a warning. Five seconds later, the message was complete—a smoke alarm at a residential address. Following procedures, the department dispatcher immediately dialed the homeowner. Getting no answer after five or six tries, she gave Neill [the Fire Chief] and the department's two 1000-gpm pumpers a go signal . . . a housewife had put a skillet of grease on to heat at just the moment her husband wheeled a brand new camper/van into their driveway. In her excitement, she forgot the grease, and her kitchen was now on fire.

"The first inkling these people had that anything was wrong was when our trucks rolled up in their driveway," Neill recalls.

Inside, the cabinets were in flames, but what could have been a disastrous fire for the family was quickly extinguished and kept to a few thousand dollars in damages.[3]

In the first three years of service, no protected home had suffered a loss of more than $10,000. In 1977, the total fire loss for The Woodlands was $40,000. These are very good figures for a town of 4,500 homes. Although not too many homes are signed up for the intrusion alarms, there were *no* successful burglaries in the first two years of service compared to 12 in homes not on the system. The emergency medical team averages only three minutes to the home from the moment the alarm button is punched.[4]

Insurance companies have recognized The Woodlands security system by giving discounts of 15 to 36 percent on premiums to alarm service subscribers. The deduction is greater than the monthly cost of the service.

In Syracuse, New York the security concept is somewhat different. According to Robert Clasen, vice president of Rogers Cablesystems, owner of the Syracuse system, the "intent was to develop a system that would be marketed at a low cost."[5] A limited security system (smoke detectors on each sleeping level and a manual police-medical emergency button) initially cost $49.95 for installation and $3.95 per month for the service. After the experimental period a price of about $8.00 was anticipated. In most systems the home equipment and installation is about $300 and the monthly monitoring fee about $17.00.[6]

Syracuse is beginning with a 1,000 home test which was required by the franchise at the request of the fire department. It employs the area multiplexing concept for two-way communication described in Chapter 5. In the event of an alarm, the condition (fire or security), time of day, resident's name, address, and subscriber number, police beat and reporting area, and fire vehicle dispatch pattern are communicated directly to printers in the police and fire departments. The computer automatically links the alarm household by telephone with the public safety dispatcher. The dispatcher determines the nature of the emergency (fire, ambulance, police). If no answer, an emergency vehicle is sent immediately. In other systems, alarms are monitored by the cable company or alarm service, which, in turn, transfers the information, after checking, to the appropriate public safety unit. Major manufacturers of cable alarm systems are Tocom, Pioneer, Warner Amex (DTI Security), Jerrold, CableBus, and Control-Com.

Public safety officials and the cable operators expect to have to deal with problems of power outages, interference, and false alarms, but Syracuse Fire Chief Thomas Hanlon is optimistic: "Reducing the time span between detection and the arrival of firefighters will be the greatest advance in life safety in this century."[7]

Harry Shaw, director of technology development for the National Fire Prevention and Control Administration, also praises cable alarms:

These systems can have a hell of an impact. The more of these systems that are out there, the less time a firefighter will have to spend on the job. If he gets there while a fire is small, it takes less time to put it out and clean it up. If he spends less time there, it means he has more time to do something else. Home inspection, fire prevention. And with these kinds of campaigns, there has to be fewer fires. It's a kind of cycle, once you get the ball rolling.[8]

POLLING

The term *interactive* is used here to indicate a system in which individuals make responses on a home terminal keyboard of some sort (Figure 9-1). The responses could be in a polling, instructional, shopping, games, or other situation.

Polling has some interesting prospects. A television viewer can par-

Figure 9-1. Two-way response and channel selection keyboard. Photograph courtesy of Pioneer Communications of America.

ticipate in the programming with a sense of the other viewers as he or she receives feedback on the aggregated responses. Certain kinds of television are, no doubt, improved by this option. The entertainment value of sports events is enhanced where viewers are given the chance to predict the plays, suggest game strategies, and judge boxing matches, round by round. Some people may like to hit the gong, figuratively, in a talent show. Meetings where the home viewer enters opinions or "votes" probably are more interesting and hold attention better.

Polling is seldom representative of a meaningful group. The sample is distorted. First, it is limited to the people who have cable television and then to those who subscribe to the two-way service. Finally, the users of the two-way system in response to any program are only a small portion of that already narrow group. But public officials can probably safely assume that people in a cable audience, responding to issues raised at a public meeting, are among the most interested in the issues. As two-way cable grows, as an inevitable result of the current franchising practices, the proportion of the public with access to the response system will also grow. And, for certain subgroups, it is possible to imagine a meeting via cable television, where polling or voting would take place among a quorum of members.

In addition to sampling problems in polling, there is the danger of inadvertent or deliberate *leading* questions that draw out a particular answer. For example, the apparently simple question, "How many times a week do you watch television news?" suggests that everyone watches news; it is only a matter of how much news. Since attending to public affairs information is considered a socially desirable activity, the question topic exacerbates the problem. A politician, intending to show dramatic support for certain positions, may lead out the desired response. For example, "Do you want the historic character and economic survival of the downtown area in your city destroyed by unfavorable tax policies?" It would be hard to answer "yes," whatever the merits of the tax policies.

Town meetings were conducted on cable in The Woodlands, Texas. The Woodlands cable subscribers responded to the proceedings with different code numbers meaning "approve," "disapprove," talk louder," "go faster," "go slower," and "change the subject."[9] The Qube system of Warner Amex in Columbus, Ohio has been used extensively for polling on local and national issues, attracting significant subscriber interest and national attention.

Polling is principally a programming service to subscribers, but time could be sold to companies for market research. They could use the system to explore markets for products or services, get reactions to use of products, and secure sales leads.

VIDEOTEXT

As a mullet wrapper, the newspaper of the future is doomed.[10]

Videotext is information presented on the home television screen or computer terminal in text or simple graphic forms. Several terms have been applied to this kind of service, which may be provided by telephone lines and broadcast television as well as cable. They are distinguished by the communication carrier employed, and the nature of the storage and retrieval system.

In the next paragraphs, we define the four major categories of electronic text information systems. The definitions conform to conventional usage, but there are frequent variants in meaning for most of the terms. "Videotext" is used here as the generic term. Videotext should not be confused with videotex (without the "t"), which is a specific category.

Teletext is the term used for transmitting print over a few lines of the vertical blanking interval of television signals. The information does not affect the regular picture and is not visible without a special decoder in the receiver which recognizes and extracts the signals from the television waveform and gathers them into a store. They are then used to activate an electronic character generator in the receiver to display whatever page the viewer has selected. The viewer with a specially adapted television set and decoder keyboard can select normal television reception, teletext, or both superimposed. Because the information is transmitted in cycles, the viewer must wait until the desired page is transmitted in the cycle before it appears on the screen. This severely limits the amount of information which may be transmitted, assuming that users would not want to wait too long. The same system could be adapted to cable television as the transmission medium, particularly when channel capacity is scarce. Teletext is used for the Southern Satellite Systems news service. In this case a single decoder at the headend converts the signal avoiding the expense of a character generator.

Teletext over cable has a significantly higher information capability than over broadcast television. First, all 30, 50, or 100 channels can be used for teletext, thereby providing several thousand pages of information. Second, if a whole television channel is dedicated to teletext, instead of a few lines of a signal used for other purposes, several thousand pages can be carried in a cycle time of only a few seconds.

Videotex (narrowband interactive) is an interactive, on-demand data retrieval system that usually employs the switched telephone network as a transmission medium. The viewer makes a call to the data bank. Then, coded signals come back through the line. A *modem* (modulator-demodulator) in the television set converts the signals into digital coding. This feeds through an input processor and memory directly into the video circuit of the television receiver. Using the same type of decoder keyboard that is used with teletext, the viewer selects information by the *tree method* or accesses information directly using a printed catalog or a complete video table of contents. Using an alphanumeric keyboard, the user may enter key words or phrases to search the data base for related information.

One-way cable text is the term used here to describe text information transmitted over cable lines, usually by character generator. The information is recycled frequently and is updated periodically. The viewer simply tunes to the channel and accepts whatever text information is being presented without having the option of selection as in teletext or videotex. The alphanumeric or automated channels discussed in Chapter 6 are one-way cable text channels.

Two-way cable text (wideband interactive) is videotex via cable. Here the communication carrier is cable instead of telephone lines. Many of the tests of cable text are still in the planning stages. Warner Amex cable has started a 15-household test with the CompuServe System in Columbus, Ohio using cable lines instead of telephone. A significant advantage of two-way cable text over videotex (phone lines) is the much greater bandwidth of cable which transmits a page in a shorter time. Further, videotex ties up phone lines. Unless a separate line is ordered, the household is without telephone service for other purposes while the line is being used for videotex. Widespread development of videotex within a community would overtax existing telephone switching systems.

A disadvantage of cable is its lower penetration. The director of the Knight-Ridder experiments in videotex has acknowledged that he considered cable but rejected it because not enough cable systems are now actually capable of two-way communication. Telephone serves a higher percentage of homes in most communities among the higher income prospects for cable text. As cable adds services and attracts more subscribers, however, the difference may be reduced or even reversed.

At this date, consumer videotext must be considered experimental. Even in Europe (Prestel, Antiope), Canada (Telidon) and Japan (Captain) where government-funded videotext services are far ahead of development in the United States, the home market for videotext services has not been established. Aside from the relatively unexplored consumer demand, there are obvious problems in resolution and graphic presentation that may prove to be perceptually uncomfortable for consumers.

Newspaper, telephone, data-base, and cable companies are all interested in interactive electronic information retrieval systems for a number of reasons. Newspapers feel that this is a logical extension of their information-gathering business and are concerned that other organizations with new distribution technologies will move into the field. For instance, newspaper classified advertising, a nearly $5 billion annual business in the United States, could be offered competitively by cable systems. Newspapers also have cost and efficiency problems with their present printing and distribution systems.

Telephone companies see new business opportunities in using their lines for information retrieval. Electronic distribution of directory information (White and Yellow Pages) may also be effective. France intends to convert its entire directory service to videotex, eliminating the conventional phone book. If telephone companies do not move into this area, other businesses may encroach on the profitable Yellow Pages service, delivering the same information electronically.

Data-base companies (e.g., The Source, CompuServe) see cable as another means of accessing their service. Cable may prove to be a less expensive, higher-capacity distribution system than telephone when tied into satellite networks.

For the cable industry, information systems are another application of the two-way technology that would help justify its cost. Cable systems could compete with newspapers and telephone companies in some services or, at least in the case of newspapers, cooperate through joint efforts or channel leasing arrangements.

This is how cable would work in the interactive electronic text mode, using a classified advertising example. The user would tune to a particular channel that would display an index or table of contents. From a listing which might also include airline schedules, restaurants, several categories of news, weather, crop information, encyclopedia or atlas-type information, financial reports, sports statistics and scores, supermarket specials, and so on, the user would select the index number for classified ads. This number would be entered into a terminal similar to the one illustrated on page 146 and a listing of classified advertising categories would then appear on the television receiver. From this list the user might enter the index number for automobiles. A listing of automobile makes would appear with an index number for each make. If the user selected Chevrolet, another index to Chevrolet models would appear. A selection of Caprice would bring the user finally to the ads for the desired car. The ads could take several "pages" of the text. (See the example on the chapter title page.) This is called a *menu* or *tree* system for accessing information. Alternate indexing approaches using the same database might be important to the consumer. In the automobile classified ads, for instance, the user might opt for classifieds, then automobiles, then a particular price range.

If the user selected airline reservations from the index or contents, the display might then produce locations, for example, northeast, southeast, central, southwest, west in the United States and Canada, Mexico, Central America, and the Carribean as well as the other continents. Once the destination index had been entered, the user would make a choice among all the flights to that destination from his or her city. Then the month and day would be entered and the number of persons. If the desired flight were available, the screen would show a confirmation. The terminal would identify the user and the ticket price would be added to the monthly bill or put on a credit card account.

How would the customer be billed for the other services? Several possibilities exist. For services such as a daily, one-way cable version of the weekly newspaper, the subscriber might be billed by the channel. For some services (e.g., supermarket specials, classified advertising), the advertiser might be billed and the consumer would pay nothing. For news or reference services, the user would be billed by the page used or by the minute.

Text on a television screen would be about 40 characters per line. This is about the same as the character count of a single column in a six-column newspaper. The screen would hold about 16 short lines, or about the equivalent of two-and-three-quarters column inches of a newspaper.

The text on the screen at any given time is referred to as a *page*. The page may appear all at once and remain on the screen until most readers have had adequate time to read the material or to make notes, if that is appropriate. The page may also develop a line at a time. The graphic capability of videotext systems is crude, but simple drawings (e.g., floor plans in classified real estate ads), charts, and symbols may be used to enhance communication and break the monotony of text. Use of different colors for background, text, and graphics may serve similar purposes.

At least two different system designs are planned for cable text. One limits simultaneous access to the data; the other provides unlimited simultaneous access. In the first design, being tested in Portland, Oregon, the decoding equipment is out in the cable distribution plant to be shared by several households (see Chapter 5). One or more decoders are located at each bridger amplifier. The bridger amplifiers are located between the main trunk lines of the cable system and the feeder lines that serve residential streets. At maximum, 300 households are served by each bridger amplifier. If 50 percent of the households subscribe to cable, then a single decoder would serve 150 households. Two decoders, one for each of two separate television channels, would probably accommodate the demand for the service, assuming that people would seek access at a variety of times of day for only short periods. If one channel were occupied, the system would automatically switch to the other. Under this system, any subscriber associated with a particular bridger-decoder would be able to see the information requested by any other subscriber in the same bridger-decoder area. In this design, the decoders at the bridger amplifiers are the same as the home decoder except for weatherproofing. The advantage of this design is entirely in the cost. Decoders, now costing $320 to $1,000, while perhaps not practical for a single household, may be practical if shared at least until decoder prices come down.

The second design, with the decoder in each household, has the clear advantage of unlimited access—the one-party line—for those households with a need for this level of service.

Reference to the *need* for the videotext service gives rise to some unanswered questions. Is there a consumer demand? Even in the most advanced electronic text systems, for example, Prestel and Antiope in Europe, no clear consumer demand beyond business use has been established. Eighty-seven percent of the Prestel customers are commercial.[11] What kinds of information will the people use? What price will suppliers and users pay for information delivered through cable? How much electronic text, with its low resolution, can people tolerate? What format and speed of delivery is most comfortable? Will consumers overcome fears of uncontrollable monthly fees because of *usage-sensitive* billing systems?[12]

The answers to these questions in the next few years will determine the viability of cable text.

╳ INTERACTIVE TWO-WAY INSTRUCTION

There are many applications of cable television to education and training. In communicating, television may appear to be as efficient or more efficient than the conventional live classroom, but however stimulating the visuals and the presentation, students generally find it difficult to maintain interest and attention.

A study of television used in the training of firefighters, funded by the National Science Foundation, demonstrates the use of two-way cable in instruction.[13]

In creating the interactive system, several assumptions were made about the value of the interaction. These assumptions dealt with specific learning and administrative components, as follows:

Attention and participation. Interactive items, spaced throughout the instructional programs, would force participation and help to keep the trainees alert and attentive.

Motivation. Awareness that each response would be fed back individually and in aggregate scores at the end of the lessons, and that hard copy records would be made, would serve to keep trainees motivated to create a good record.

Feedback. Reinforcement would be provided by the feedback at each step of the instruction.

Competition. Since small group or individual scores could be compared, competition would maintain interest and motivation.

Teasing. On occasion, interactive items could be used as teasers to lead into a new segment of instruction. Participants would have to guess or rely on previous experience. This technique would heighten interest in learning the material.

Pacing. The interactive question format would serve to break up the television lecture-demonstration format and revive interest.

Drill. Frequent repetition of symbols and other material would aid recall. Quizzes would provide a summary and review.

Administration. The interactive system, including a log-in procedure, frequent interactive questions, and computer printout of results, would improve training system administration and reduce administrative costs.

The firefighter training research was conducted by the Michigan State University Department of Telecommunication, Rockford Cablevision, Inc., Coaxial Scientific, Inc., and the Rockford Fire Department. Firefighters were trained in their station houses.

The entire instructional system, including attendance taking, video instruction and questions, feedback, and individualized reports, was automated. Firefighters responded by punching buttons on a modified cable channel converter. The system was also used in Rockford for teacher development and was demonstrated by one of the hospitals for continuing medical education. (See Chapter 5 opening photograph.)

The initial experiment was a 12-lesson series on "prefire planning" for firefighters. In the two-way version of the training experiment, the firefighters "logged in" by entering a three-letter code in the response terminal. As soon as the last letter was transmitted, the code letters appeared opposite the fire station number displayed on the television screen by a character generator. The instructional programs, on three-quarter-inch videocassettes, were conventional instructional television with the exception that every two to five minutes a question was asked about the content. In this respect the tapes were much like a programmed instructional sequence. The firefighters responded by selecting and transmitting one of four answer options. The videotape was paused until all the firefighters who were logged in had responded.

As soon as all responses were received, each response was displayed on the screen for each individual by code letter or the responses were aggregated indicating the percentage responding to each of the options. The videotape then proceeded.

At the end of each lesson, after several questions and responses like the one just described, a "quick quiz" appeared. The quiz reviewed all the previous material and presented a drill on the identification of prefire planning symbols that were in the early part of the videotape and previously viewed tapes. The quick quiz was different from the interactive questions in the body of the lesson in that the tape ran continuously through the quiz, allowing the firefighters only five seconds to respond to each quiz question. At the end of the quick quiz, the percentage score for each participating individual was displayed on the screen. This was followed by a display of the overall score, combining the quick quiz with all the other interactive questions. Finally, each individual's score on the instructional series to date was presented.

Immediately after the instructional tape concluded, a computer printout was provided which listed each individual's item-by-item and total score. A second printout reported scores by individuals in each lesson in the series. Blanks in the report indicated that an individual missed a lesson, because of sick leave, vacation, or a fire emergency during the lesson. This printout was used for scheduling makeups.

The training experiment compared one-way television with the two-way instructional system. In both experimental conditions, firefighters received the same videotape materials, including all the questions. The 100 firefighters in the two-way television version learned more from the

12-lesson series than did the 100 firefighters in the one-way, no-feedback version. The firefighters were generally favorable toward instructional television with those in the two-way version of the experiment considerably more favorable. After six months, both groups retained most of the information, with the two-way interactive participants still superior to the one-way learning group. The cost of the instruction, using rates published in Rockford Cablevision's lease plan, was about $5.00 per lesson per person assuming that the videotape materials could be purchased from an outside source. This was about twice the cost of one-way television but substantially less than the cost of lectures at the training academy or lectures at the station houses by academy personnel. The costs are reduced somewhat if the series is repeated for refresher training and new recruits.

While the Rockford two-way experiment was entirely automated, using prepackaged instructional materials, in other circumstances it might be desirable to present the instruction over television *live*. In a live situation, the instructor is in touch with the students through the interactive system and can adjust to student feedback. There is a real contact between instructor and student. Another National Science Foundation–supported experiment took this approach.

The research was conducted in Spartanburg, South Carolina in a program to prepare people for high school General Equivalency Development exams. Students attended interactive television classes at home, three hours a day, four days a week for fifteen weeks. As in Rockford they answered questions in the multiple-choice format. But here the teacher could respond to the students' performance on these questions, knowing each student's answer. The teachers would often address students by name, correcting or praising. The system also permitted the students to send messages to the teacher such as "slow down" and "repeat."

The interactive television students in Spartanburg were compared with students who took the same instruction in the conventional face-to-face classroom. The two-way television students did just as well as those in the classroom, which the directors of the experiment considered to be a real achievement. The report indicates that there were some strengths to the two-way television instruction that offset its weaknesses. In observing the conventional classes, they noted that the average class did not necessarily engage in "lively dialogue." Only infrequently did the teachers address open-ended questions to the class and then only one or two students would respond. In the cable class it was necessary for every student to "focus on, select an answer and actively respond" to all the questions.[14] (An 11-minute film, describing the Rockford and Spartanburg experiments in two-way cable along with a cable teleconferencing demonstration in Reading, Pennsylvania, entitled "Television: Testing the Future," is available through the National Science Foundation, Washington, D.C. 20550.)

Warner Amex has experimented with interactive instruction in Columbus, Ohio. The system's chief executive officer says "when you ask which new services come next in video two-way, I think education services have to be important."[15] But an important question at this juncture is, "Who will buy it?" Certain groups such as doctors and nurses must participate in continuing education to maintain certification. Thus, two-way television might serve the needs of people with legal or economic reasons for continuing education. Some adult education courses that would lend themselves to television could also attract paying viewers. These courses would no doubt have to be very attractive, perhaps responding to fashionable interests or having direct utility (e.g., family finance). Families with children who need remedial academic work might be willing to pay for interactive programs in the appropriate areas. Many educators believe that these programs are most effective with parent involvement—involvement that perhaps could be obtained most easily using interactive home television. Two-way cable instruction might be subsidized by educational institutions with obligations to homebound people or preschoolers. For example, the Traverse Bay Area Intermediate School District covering a large part of northern Michigan is required to make two contacts per week with some children who are handicapped. Among other technologies, they are considering cable as a more efficient means of serving some of the needs of these families.[16] In fields such as firefighting and elementary and secondary education, where needs and the tradition for continuous in-service training have been well-established and where people are widely dispersed geographically, for some purposes interactive instruction by cable has a natural application.

HOME SHOPPING

The high price of travel and the high value of time is causing consumers to supplement traditional retail distribution systems with new methods of choosing, buying and obtaining merchandise.[17]

Americans are depending more and more on mail orders and 800 phone numbers for buying. This is the fastest-growing element of retail sales. Shopping by cable is a logical extension of this trend. Two-way cable has the unique capability to demonstrate products and services, respond to inquiries, consummate the sale, transmit the invoice, and transfer funds for payment.[18] Furthermore, in *transaction services*, the vendor, not the customer pays for access to the system.

A videotext system may be used by consumers to obtain product information including price. This information might be prepared "objectively" by organizations independent of manufacturers and sales agencies or by the marketer as part of the sales effort. In this kind of system, the consumer with a particular type of product in mind enters the index to find the category number and, by transmitting the number through the home terminal, calls to the home television screen all the product information in that category. When a choice has been made, the order can be placed by transmitting an item number and a password (for security). Since the transmitting household code is already stored in the computer, along with a credit card number, no further information is needed at the time of purchase. In this example, the article ordered would probably be delivered by mail or UPS.

Local consumer staples found in supermarkets and drugstores could be ordered through the same system and delivered on a route along with other orders from the neighborhood. This might well be efficient for households where all adult members are working or where transportation to the stores is more costly than the delivery. People without an automobile or adequate transportation might find the service desirable.

When the product is complex and has a high price ticket, the full video might be important to the decision process. This is possible, but very few people could use the system at any given time. A full 6mHz video channel would be needed for this purpose, whereas in videotext much less bandwidth is consumed and a great many people could be served simultaneously. An alternative is slow-scan television where a still picture wipes on the screen slowly using as little as 4kHz.

Warner Amex and Cox are both planning to institute pilot projects for interactive cable shopping. Warner Amex calls its service "Touch 'n Buy."

In the meantime, several one-way shopping services are developing which could eventually be adapted to interactive systems. The "Home Shopping Show," distributed by Modern Satellite Network to cable systems, is a one-hour program which gives advertisers (e.g., Maytag, Mr. Coffee, Encyclopaedia Britannica, Amoco, and *Better Homes and Gardens*) a chance to demonstrate their products in a talk-show format.[19] Articles may be ordered through direct-mailing addresses or 800 numbers. WOR-TV, one of the superstations used by cable systems, has a daily hour called "Shopping at Home." The "electronic catalog" will have service information programming and direct-response advertising for items that may be ordered by phone.[20] Comp-U-Card, a telephone merchandising company intends to experiment with cable. The subscribers would familiarize themselves with prices and products by shopping in local stores. Shoppers would then look for the product on the cable channel at a specifically scheduled time for that product category. Price and product information would be available. If the Comp-U-Card price is cheaper, the shopper can dial a toll-free number and order it. Cable operators would share in the sales revenues. The service is on CBN every day for six hours.[21]

The Compustar company operates a home shopping service using dial-up telephone lines and home microcomputers. It has contracted with cable companies to test the service over cable.

Banking, or electronic funds transfer (EFT), by cable is another interactive service. The householder can pay bills, transfer money from one account to another, find out the current balance, borrow, and so on. Cox Cable is testing a "bank-at-home" service in a few homes in San Diego.

GAMES

Computer video games may be played by interactive television. Firefighters in Rockford, Illinois played blackjack against the computer between the lessons described earlier. After being dealt two cards, which appeared on the screen, they could "hit" or "stay." When one player punched the "stay" button, the computer would go on to the next player. Firefighters from several different fire stations could play at once. (The fire chief assumed that no money was changing hands.)

Video games can be adapted to two-way cable so that the game program is at the headend computer, not in the hands of the player (at $20 per cartridge). A list of available games would appear on a game channel. The player would simply order the desired game, indicate whether or not instructions are needed, punch in the number of players, and commence play. The game channel could be made available at a monthly rate with unlimited playing time, or if addicts clogged the system capacity, at a per-minute-of-play rate.

Warner Amex, which has an ownership interest in Atari, is now pilot testing computer video games.[22] "PlayCable" by Jerrold and Mattel is available on one-way systems. A noninteractive game "TV Powww" is now being made available to cable systems. The game is activated by a telephone call. Viewers play for a prescribed time for prizes. Cable companies can lease the system.[23]

AUTOMATED METER READING

Two-way cable systems can be used to read utility meters. The difficulty in making this application of the two-way technology has been in the cost. If this were the only service of the two-way system, the cable companies would have to charge far more than the cost of persons going house to house, which may be less than $10 per year per household. Another problem is in the cost of interfacing the cable to current meters. However, there are other values of automated meter reading and connection to the cable system. A major advantage of automated metering is the immediate signal that is communicated if the meter is damaged or if theft is attempted. Large electric utilities lose millions annually through theft of service and unrecorded consumption due to faulty meters.

ENERGY CONSERVATION

Energy costs and shortages have forced consideration of electric power conservation measures.[24] Some of these measures require specialized communication systems for load control, rate incentives, and consumer information. Cable is one of the communication systems under consideration.

To understand this application of two-way cable, some background on the electric utility industry is necessary. Electrical utilities must adjust the output of the generating facilities to varying load levels as determined by consumer demand. In general, two types of generating units are utilized to accommodate these variations: baseload units and auxiliary peaking units. The baseload units (hydro, coal, nuclear) operate at essentially constant output and relatively high efficiencies. Peaking units, on the other hand, operate on varying load levels and must be brought on line as required during high demand periods to augment the baseload production. Peaking units in general have lower thermal efficiencies than do baseload units and require high-grade fuels (usually gas or oil) to accommodate fast start-up and shutdown capability. For this reason, electrical energy generated during the peak periods is more expensive than that during off-peak periods as measured both in cost and in fuel consumption per unit of energy generated.

Furthermore, if the construction of peaking plants could be deferred or rendered unnecessary by better control of peaks, the industry would save immense costs and untold anguish in the political battles necessary to build new capacity.

One way in which to reduce peak consumption of electricity is to control certain household utilities, with permission of the customer. The consumer who accepts the plan may have a monthly reduction in the bill. Electric water heaters and air conditioners can be shut off automatically for short periods without noticeable effect. The hot water in the insulated tank does not lose much heat before the power comes on again. With improved technology, air conditioners could be cycled on and off every 15 minutes with no more than a one-degree fluctuation in temperature under most conditions. Cable may be used as the communication system to control the appliance under this plan. And, if the power company needs to reduce load quickly in emergencies, to avoid a brownout or a blackout, this system could respond very quickly to save the day. The electric utility might also use cable to control distribution on the power grid. This task becomes more complex if households generate their own energy by solar and wind devices and contribute the excess to the system.

A second means of limiting peak consumption is to employ price incentives to encourage consumers to defer electricity use to off-peak periods. If rates are lower at certain times, the use of dishwashers, washing machines, clothes dryers, vacuum cleaners, and other appliances may be shifted to those times. This requires a dual rate and a means of metering by time of day. If meter reading is automated by cable, this can be accomplished conveniently. Peak periods can be changed seasonally without difficulty to reflect seasonal differences in demand.

For incentives to work well, householders must be well informed about the cost savings and, of course, know the off-peak periods. Cable can be used to communicate this information to the consumer in a variety of ways. In emergencies, consumers may be alerted to reduce consumption and remove some electrical utilities from service.

Some of the applications of cable to automated metering and energy conservation use the downstream (headend to household) communication channels and some the upstream (household to headend) system. In summary, the downstream and upstream communications are as follows:

Downstream communication channels include

1. Load control. The downstream channel could accommodate the control commands for a number of load control devices (e.g., water heater switches, air conditioning cycling switches).
2. Rate information. Because consumers' cooperation is necessary to a load management program, communication is essential. Most simply, the communication would be through the use of light emitting diode (LED) indicator lights or other alert devices to remind the customer of peak and off-peak periods. The same LED device or the television screen could be used to inform the consumer of the price of energy per kilowatt-hour at the moment. More elaborate information could also be communicated to make the consumer more conscious of conservation and the cost of energy. This could include the energy, in dollars, consumed by the household during the peak and off-peak periods, a comparison of this month's consumption to the same month a year ago, and so on.
3. Emergency alert. Overloads on the electrical network can result in reduced voltage to the consumer, or transformer failures. Therefore, when load on the network is excessive, an alarm (buzzer) could be activated to advise the customer to disengage motors that might be damaged due to low voltage.
4. Power distribution monitoring and control. The power company can use the same scanning technique employed in signaling the consumer about time-of-day rate structures or per-kilowatt price. In this case, however,

the command will be initiated from the utility to some other utility network device instead of the customer hardware. This provides the power company with the capacity to remotely control or read on-line equipment.

5. Emergency control. This is the essential capability to dump all unnecessary load during extreme emergencies to avoid extensive damage to utility generating and network trunk line equipment.

Upstream communication channels include

1. Metering and load study. During computer scanning, the upstream channel has the capability of accommodating the retrieval of digital utility meter information for billing purposes and also individual load study. The latter is important to electric utilities to determine the effects of various price incentives and other policies under these new circumstances.
2. Power distribution monitoring and control. The upstream channel will allow necessary feedback from utility system management devices to permit the monitoring of sectional switches, reclosers, and other similar devices to maintain a central management of the electric utility network.
3. System security. The continuous-scanning computer system ensures that each meter is connected and functioning. Microswitches, voltage sensors, and logic circuits are incorporated to guard against tampering and theft of energy. Likewise, each home terminal is protected to prevent attempts to disconnect meters from the encoding circuitry.

While electric utilities have been used as the example here, metering and other services for gas and water utilities are also possible. Cable control might be used as a quick means of gas shutoff in emergencies. And gas-sensing devices, similar to smoke detectors, could be tied into cable.

It would not be necessary for utility customers to be cable subscribers. The utility customer could be connected to cable without receiving other services of the cable company. There would be problems, however, in any mismatch between the cable service areas and the utility service areas. Further, utilities would be reluctant to have an intermediate party involved in such crucial functions as distibution monitoring, control, and metering. The cable industry has certainly not yet established credibility for such services. It is likely that a number of experiments will be conducted in this area before cable is treated as a major potential communication system for utilities along with telephone, radio, and power lines themselves. Load management equipment has been installed in Monroe, Georgia; Alton, Iowa; Orange City, Iowa; and Grosse Pointe, Michigan.

OTHER TWO-WAY APPLICATIONS

Two-way cable systems are very useful for market research. Questionnaires can be administered automatically by computer at the participant's convenience. Exposure to television advertising and programming can be determined with far greater reliability than with other methods, a capability that is valuable in marketing and audience research.

Two-way cable systems are also used for traffic signal control, automatic vehicle location, video surveillance of high-crime-rate areas, and interconnection of remote fire-police callboxes. (For two-way institutional and business data communication services see institutional networks in Chapter 6.)

NOTES

[1]Brad Metz, "Cable Home Security Battles Restraints, Criticisms," *Cable Age,* June 29, 1981, p. 10.

[2]For a full discussion of these questions see, William Greer, "The Technical History of Cable Security." Part 1. "Early Failures," *Alarm Signal,* November–December 1980, pp. 10–14, and "The Technical History of Cable Security." Part 2. "Ready or Not, Here It Comes," *Alarm Signal,* January–February 1981, pp. 20–31.

[3]Dudley Lynch, "Cable TV System Detects, Reports Fires in Homes," *Fire Engineering,* September 1978, pp. 35–36.

[4]Ibid.

[5]Jill Marks, "Security in Syracuse," *TVC,* September 15, 1980, p. 75.

[6]Metz, "Cable Home Security."

[7]Marks, "Security in Syracuse."

[8]Dudley Lynch, "Cable TV System Watches the House When No One's Home: It Even Reports Fires," *Western Fire Journal,* July 1978, p. 27.

[9]Louis Alexander, "The Vote Is in on Two-Way TV," *TV Guide,* August 13, 1977, pp. 31–32.

[10]Steve Piacente, staffwriter for the *Tampa Tribune* (quoted in *Cablevision,* February 16, 1981, p. 58).

[11]*Communications Daily,* February 20, 1981, p. 1.

[12]For a discussion of a research program to address the issues in adapting to videotext, see Richard V. Ducey and Robert E. Yadon, "A Human Factors Research Program for Videotex Technology," *IEEE Transactions on Broadcasting,* Vol. BC-28, No. 1, March 1982, pp. 8-19.

[13]One of the authors, Baldwin, directed the study and the other, McVoy, designed the basic two-way system employed. The study is reported in four volumes: Thomas F. Baldwin, Bradley S. Greenberg, Martin P. Block, John B. Eulenberg, and Thomas A. Muth, "Volume I: Summary, Michigan State University-Rockford Two-Way Cable Project: System Design, Application Experiments and Public Policy Issues" (June 1978); "Volume II: System Design, Application Experiments and Public Policy Issues" (full report, June 1978); "Volume III: Minicomputer System Software" (June 1978); "Volume IV: Dissemination Report" (June 1980), Department of Telecommunication, Michigan State University, East Lansing 48824. The reports are available at this address. Other reports of the study are found in the following journals: J. B. Wright, M. P. Block, and D. S. McVoy, "An Evolutionary Approach to the Development of Two-Way Cable Communication Technology," *IEEE Transaction on Cable Television,* CATV-2, Institute of Electrical and Electronics Engineers, Inc., January 1977, pp. 52–61; Thomas Baldwin, Bradley Greenberg, Martin Block, and Nick Stoyanoff,

"Cognitive and Affective Outcomes of a Telecommunication Interaction System: The MSU/Rockford Two-Way Cable Project," *Journal of Communication,* Spring 1978, pp. 180–194; Thomas F. Baldwin, Thomas A. Muth, and Judith E. Saxton, "Public Policy in Two-Way Cable: Difficult Issues for a Developing Technology," *Telecommunications Policy,* June 1979, pp. 126–133; Jayne W. Zenaty, Martin P. Block, John B. Eulenberg, and Eric S. Smith, "A Minicomputer Software System for Administering Instructional Programs via Two-Way Cable Television," *Journal of Computer-Based Instruction,* May 1979, pp. 96–108.

[14]William A. Lucas, "Spartanburg, S.C.: Testing the Effectiveness of Video, Voice and Data Feedback," *Journal of Communication,* Spring 1978, pp. 168–179.

[15]Fred Dawson and Barbara Ruger, "Two-Way: Cable's Race Against Competing Industries," *Cablevision,* November 3, 1980, p. 37.

[16]Thomas F. Baldwin, "Traverse Bay Area Cable Communication Services Available to Schools," report to Traverse Bay Area Intermediate School District, Charles D. Mayer, assistant superintendent, E. Lansing, Michigan, March 1980.

[17]Edward L. Niner, "Marketing in the 80's," address to the 1980 Annual Meeting, Food Distribution Research Society, October 14, 1980, p. 3.

[18]Ibid., p. 7.

[19]"Shopping Program Showcases Product," *Cablevision,* October 27, 1980, p. 26.

[20]"Arm-Chair Shopping," *Broadcasting,* January 19, 1981, p. 7.

[21]"Shop at Home via Cable, and Satellite," *Broadcasting,* December 15, 1980, p. 31.

[22]Niner, "Marketing in the 80's."

[23]"Cable TV Powww," *Cablevision,* January 19, 1981, p. 9.

[24]This section is based on a series of papers: Thomas Baldwin, Martin Block, and Robert Yadon, "Application of Two-Way Broadband Cable Communication Technology to Energy Conservation for Consumers and Electric Utilities," *Proceedings of the International Conference on Energy Use Management,* Los Angeles, California, 1979; Frank Whitney and Thomas Baldwin, "Using CATV for Load Research, Automatic Meter Reading and Load Management," Rate Committee Workshop, American Public Power Association, Washington, D.C., January 23, 1978; T. F. Baldwin, "Two-Way Broadband Cable Communication and Power System Load Management," report to the Load Management Roundtable, Engineering and Operations Workshop, American Public Power Association, San Francisco, California, March 2, 1978.

PART III

PUBLIC POLICY

10

Federal and State Policy

Federal Communication Commission Meeting. Photograph courtesy of the FCC.

Public policy governing cable television is formulated at several levels. The Congress sets communication policy through legislation and oversight of the Federal Communications Commission. The FCC acts for the Congress in carrying out the details of the Communications Act. The FCC holds jurisdiction over microwave relays and satellite transponders used to bring in distant signals and has established rules for cable systems on the grounds that cable is ancillary to the broadcasting system for which it is specifically responsible. The executive branch of the federal government is represented by the National Telecommunications and Information Administration in the Department of Commerce. The White House may also have an advisor on communication matters. Local governments franchise cable systems because they use public rights-of-way in wiring a community. State governments have asserted authority where it has not been granted to local authorities and have offered assistance to local governments in dealing with the complex matters of franchising and regulating cable systems. The courts have frequently had to step into conflicts created by the development of this new medium in its relationships with the federal government and competitive media.

FEDERAL POLICY

The Congress and FCC

Two subcommittees of the Congress concern themselves with cable: the Subcommittee on Telecommunications, Consumer Protection, and Finance of the House Committee on Energy and Commerce; and the Subcommittee on Communications of the Senate Committee on Commerce, Science, and Transportation. Communication policy resides in the Commerce Committees of both houses because communication is considered interstate and foreign commerce, the regulation of which is specifically assigned to the Congress by the Constitution. Both subcommittees are staffed with specialists in communication.

The FCC is an agency of the Congress assigned to carry out the broad policies of the Communication Act of 1934, lending its accumulated technical expertise to the task. More congressional input to the FCC is made through oversight—the review of FCC actions and plans—than through legislation. The oversight hearings before each subcommittee, at least once per year, instruct the commission on congressional intent and provide reaction to the agency plans. One of the difficulties of this procedure is the mixed messages to the FCC that come from the various personal and political interests of committee members. On occasion, in cable matters, the FCC has asked, without success, for more direct guidance in the form of legislation. The Congress has been in the process of rewriting the Communications Act for the past several years.

The FCC is composed of seven commissioners appointed by the president with the approval of the Senate. No more than four of the seven shall be members of the same political party. The commission administers (e.g., registers cable systems), legislates (e.g., sets technical standards), and adjudicates (e.g., hears a petition of a cable system to waive rules). The Cable Bureau, one of several divisions of the FCC, administers the cable rules and advises the commissioners on cable issues. The Cable Bureau has never had the status or power of the more established Broadcast and Common Carrier Bureaus, and with the deregulation of cable over recent years, Cable Bureau personnel have been reduced to a small cadre. Through most of its history, the FCC has been ruled by attorneys and engineers. Only recently have economists been employed in greater numbers in influential positions. This has led to an attempt to structure the communications industries so that workable competition in the market substitutes for regulation. This trend has been abetted by new communication technologies, including cable, which have offered alternatives and have forced new thinking.

NTIA

The National Telecommunications and Information Administration is a new agency combining functions of the White House Office of Telecommunications Policy and the Communications units of the Department of Commerce. In the early 1970s, its predecessor, the Office of Telecommunications Policy, played a major role in bringing together broadcasting and cable industry interests in a compromise that allowed cable to develop into the larger markets. NTIA has been involved most notably in cable through its advocacy of the concept of retransmission consent, to be discussed in this chapter under the copyright section, and the Public Telecommunications Facilities Program. NTIA makes planning and construction grants to "noncommercial, nonbroadcast public telecommunication entities," which include government or nonprofit organizations operating publicly oriented cable channels. The grants have been awarded to organizations as diverse as the Junior League of Summit, New Jersey, the Eastern Band of Cherokee Indians, and cities and universities, mainly to develop government, educational, and community access cable services. The nonbroadcast telecommunications program has been added to the public broadcasting facilities grants program in recognition of the potential role of the new technologies.[1]

As would be expected, several special interest professional groups have also played a major role in the evolution of cable policy: National Cable Television Association and the Community Antenna Television Association, National Association of Broadcasters, Association of Maximum Service Telecasters, National League of Cities, Motion Picture Producers Association of America, National Association of Theater Owners, and others.

In this chapter, we discuss public policy as it has developed in cable television and the contribution of the several interests that have shaped policy. Rather than a detailed history of government regulation in cable, much of which is not now applicable, we identify the main currents for purposes of perspective and concentrate on present policies. A good history of FCC regulation of cable is in two articles by George H. Shapiro.[2]

Fortunately, the FCC rules and federal-state-local jurisdictions seem to be fairly well stabilized at this point, having been accommodated frequently over the years to court rulings and changes in the character of the industry. Certain aspects of the federal rules are covered more appropriately in other sections of this book.

Technical performance requirements and rules governing microwave facilities are in Chapter 3. Signal carriage rules and the rules relating to local origination on community channels, cablecasts by candidates for public office, the Fairness Doctrine, lotteries, sponsorship identification, and cablecasting of obscene or indecent material are in Chapter 6. The rules on franchise fees and rates are in Chapter 11. Rules on cable system ownership are in the section on ownership in Chapter 12. The other FCC rules are included in this chapter along with copyright, privacy, and state regulation of cable.

Background

From the beginning, local governments granted franchises, licenses, and permits to community antenna television systems (CATV), although many systems emerged without any government authorization or attention. A few governments themselves, organized or actually built CATV systems in the absence of entrepreneurial interest. It seemed purely a local matter with no significant bearing on television broadcasting. Most of the early systems were outside the defined television markets, and broadcasters were happy to have their signals extended. In 1959 the FCC ruled that it did not have jurisdiction over CATV. A Senate bill authorizing the FCC to license CATV systems failed.

Some of the cable systems were bringing in distant TV signals by microwave relay. The FCC had always licensed microwave relay systems and issued rules in 1965 governing certain functions of the microwave-relay-served CATV systems.[3] By this time, in addition to serving places without any broadcast TV, CATV was moving into communities with one or more broadcast stations in the vicinity. The broadcast industry became alarmed. By bringing several more stations into a television market, audiences would be diluted and the price of advertising, held up by the scarcity of channels, would fall. In the smallest towns, barely able to sustain a single station by advertising sales, the stations might be so injured economically as to be forced off the air, leaving those communities with no local service. This concern was expressed as early as 1959 when the FCC heard arguments by a television station protesting the award of microwave transmission licenses to bring distant television stations into its market.[4]

Furthermore, the FCC had just gotten fully behind UHF broadcasting. All TV sets built after 1964, by statute, would have built-in UHF receiving capability. The FCC was now committed to UHF as a solution to the television station scarcity problem. But none of the UHF stations was financially healthy at this time. If audiences were siphoned off by cable in the bigger markets where UHF was beginning to gain a foothold, then the whole UHF policy might falter.

In 1966 the FCC extended its authority over all CATV systems, arguing that CATV, which at that time was only a community antenna service for delivering off-air broadcast signals, was "ancillary" to broadcasting. Since, under the Communications Act, the FCC must regulate broadcasting, it must therefore have jurisdiction over services derived from broadcasting and affecting the broadcast service. Anxious to protect the UHF stations, the FCC prohibited CATV in the top 100 broadcast markets if a UHF station, or even some group intending to build a UHF station, objected to CATV.[5] The Supreme Court upheld the FCC against several challenges of its authority to regulate cable as long as its regulation was "reasonably ancillary" to its regulations of television broadcasting.[6] Actually, it was suspected by economists at the time that cable would help UHF stations by equalizing signal quality and dial position (UHF stations were converted by the CATV system to a channel between 2 and 13) and extending the reach of UHF stations into distant communities. The real beneficiaries of the FCC policy were to be the big city VHF stations, and indeed the Association of Maximum Service Telecasters, representing these stations, was strongly behind the FCC position.

In 1968 the FCC began to develop a comprehensive set of cable rules. Three years later an outline of the proposed rules was presented to Congress in a "letter of intent." The rules presented in the letter were modified on the basis of a consensus agreement, on distant signal importation and signal exclusivity, among broadcasters, the cable industry, and program producers. The rules went into effect March 31, 1972.[7] The 1972 rules required cable systems to obtain an FCC Certificate of Compliance and set out franchising standards, limited carriage of distant signals and required carriage of local signals, protected program exclusivity, required program origination and applied broadcast-type rules, required access channels, required 20 channels and two-way capacity, limited cross-ownership, and set technical standards. The rules were so detailed and complex that cable operators, franchising authorities, the public, and the FCC itself had difficulty comprehending them. After some experience with the rules, the FCC issued a "reconsideration"[8] and a "clarification."[9]

The FCC's fears of "economic impact" of cable on local broadcasting service never did materialize. Cable did not enter many UHF markets in the 1960s and 1970s because it did not have a service to offer. These markets already had a full complement of stations available off-air with household antennas. It was not until pay television was "discovered" that cable became viable for these markets. The small stations have also survived. Of 12 stations that petitioned the Congress for protection in 1958, all were still in business in 1970.[10]

Under the growing political power of the cable industry, the awareness of consumer demand, better knowledge of economic impacts, and the deregulatory climate in Washington, the FCC has now reversed its position on signal carriage. The limits on signal carriage and syndicated program exclusivity have now been lifted.[11] The only carriage rules remaining are the "must-carry" rules designed to protect consumers from being denied their own local stations. This is a generally noncontroversial policy, although even it has been challenged (see Chapter 7).

The FCC policy on program origination has a similar history. At first, looking at CATV as ancillary to broadcasting, the FCC was opposed to cable origination. Later it seemed like a good idea, following out of the FCC's sustained interest in local program service. The commission also realized that cable was earning the fruits of broadcast efforts without any of the obligations for service. So the 1972 cable rules required origination by systems of over 3,500 subscribers, those thought to be big enough to support a studio and its operating expense. This rule was challenged in the federal courts on the grounds that it went beyond the FCC's authority. The FCC was upheld by the Supreme Court,[12] but by the time of the final verdict the commission had decided to abandon the rule anyway. Today, the FCC does not require cable origination, but some franchising authorities do. In other places, without any government requirement, cable companies originate programming to win franchises elsewhere and to attract subscribers and advertisers.

Although the federal rules have undergone significant changes, it is well to remember that the FCC created the rules in *anticipation* of the industry development, without guidance from Congress. At the beginning, *local* authorities had little experience with communications matters, an area mainly preempted by the federal establishment or shared by federal and state agencies. In many ways the FCC helped to launch the industry and contributed several concepts that, although resisted by various special interests at first, are now integral elements of the modern service (e.g., access channels, local origination, two-way).

The remaining FCC cable rules not covered in other sections of the book follow.

Registration

In place of "Certificates of Compliance," which under the 1972 rules required FCC approval of ordinances, franchise agreements, and signal carriage plans, the FCC has substituted a much simpler and less time-consuming *registration* procedure. Before beginning operation or adding any television broadcast signals to existing systems, the operator must register each *system community unit* with the FCC. A system community unit is a "cable system or portion of a cable system, operating within a separate and distinct community or municipal entity, including unincorporated areas."[13] This is to distinguish a community unit from a *cable television system,* which is an entire physical system served by a single headend and capable of covering several political units.

To register the cable system, the operator need only provide the owner's name, the name of the business, address, date of service to 50 or more subscribers, name of community and county, television broadcast signals to be carried (not previously certified or registered), and, for a new cable system with five or more employees, a statement of the community unit's equal employment opportunity program. As soon as the statement is filed, the community unit is registered. Registration does not mean FCC approval of the unit.

Pole attachment. Under the Communications Act Amendments of 1978, the FCC is required to regulate rates, terms, and conditions of cable television's use of poles, conduits, ducts, and rights-of-way in privately owned telephone and electric utilities.[14] The FCC exercises this responsibility only if the states do not do so. States that have certified to the commission that they have taken the *pole attachment* regulation under their jurisdiction are Alaska, California, Connecticut, Hawaii, Idaho, Illinois, Indiana, Louisiana, Massachusetts, Michigan, Nebraska, Nevada, New Jersey, New York, Oregon, Pennsylvania, Vermont, Washington, and Wisconsin.

The object of pole attachment regulation is to prevent discrimination against cable companies and cable consumers in rates charged and the conditions of use. The legislation gives cable companies and utilities a forum for adjudication of conflicts.

Historically, delays in the granting of *pole rights* and *make-ready* (pole preparation for cable) and struggles over the charges have been the bane of cable operators. Utilities may have higher priorities related to their own interests, may overvalue the cost of pole use, and, in the case of telephone companies, may even have selfish interests in deterring a competing communication system.

The state may preempt the FCC pole attachment jurisdiction only if it shows that it "has the authority to consider and does consider the *interests of subscribers of cable television services,* as well as the interests of the consumer of the utility services" (emphasis added).

To determine the fairness of pole attachment rates, the FCC establishes a zone of reasonableness with the *minimum,* the additional costs to accommodate cable system users such as special maintenance and administrative costs, and at the *maximum,* the cable system share of the fully allocated costs. The latter is based on the original cost of poles and the maintenance cost. The cable system share might be calculated by determining the portion of the usable space (the amount of pole above the required ground clearance) occupied by the cable.

The FCC has recently issued a number of rulings which bring the pole rates down dramatically in nonregulated states. For example, in Winter Haven, Florida, Tampa Electric Company wanted to raise the rate paid by Warner Amex from $4.50 to $9.24 per pole. The cable company challenged the rate before the FCC. The FCC ruled that a reasonable yearly rate would be $1.36 per pole.[15]

Generally, the states that regulate pole attachment rates have not been as favorable to the cable companies as the FCC. In some of those states, the cable industry has been successfully challenging the jurisdiction of public utility commissions to regulate pole rates under the existing state statutes.

Reports to the FCC. The commission requires a general "Annual Report of Cable Television Systems" (Form 325), which asks for number of homes passed, number of miles of cable, number of subscribers and the population of the community, broadcast signals carried, nonbroadcast signals carried for a specified week, ownership, and other media interests.

The FCC "Cable Television Annual Financial Report" (Form 326) reports installation and subscriber fees, expenses, revenues, profits, assets, and liabilities for each cable operating entity. The annual report and the annual financial report provide information on the cable industry, available in aggregated form from the commission.

An "Annual Employment Report" (Form 395A) is also required by the FCC. The form requires listing of the number of full-time *males* and *females* in each of several *racial or ethnic categories*—American Indian, Alaskan native; Asian, Pacific Islander; black; Hispanic; white—and each of several *job categories*—officials and managers, professionals, technicians, sales workers, office and clerical, craftsmen [sic] (skilled), operatives (semiskilled), laborers (unskilled), and service workers.

Operators of cable systems and cable relay stations are prohibited from discrimination in employment because of race, color, religion, national origin, or sex. Programs must be maintained to assure equal opportunity in recruitment, selection, training, placement, promotion, pay, working conditions, demotion, layoff, and termination. A cable system must keep an up-to-date statement of the equal opportunity program on file with the FCC and report any *changes* annually on or before May 31. An annual report of equal employment opportunity complaints and their resolution, in summary narrative form, must also be filed. It may be submitted along with the Form 395A.

Public File

A public inspection file, available to the public during business hours, must be kept by all cable systems. The file must contain the equal employment opportunity plan and annual, technical performance test records for the past five years. Records of origination cablecasts by candidates for public office and lists of sponsors of originated programming are to be kept in the file for two years. Records on network program nonduplication private agreements must be maintained for the life of the agreement. The public file must also contain a copy of the franchise, applications or special petitions to the FCC, and the FCC annual reports (325, 326, 395A). Systems with under 1,000 subscribers are not required to provide nonduplication protection or conduct performance tests.[16]

A current copy of the FCC's cable rules must be on hand at the system office, although not a part of the public file.

Fines

For violation of its rules, the FCC may levy fines of $2,000 up to a maximum per offense of $20,000 on cable operators and $5,000 on cable television relay service licensees. The FCC initiates the proceeding by issuing a notice of a hearing or a notice of apparent liability.

Cable Systems Under 1,000 Subscribers

Cable systems with fewer than 1,000 subscribers are exempted from most of the cable rules. The *only rules that do apply* are (1) registration, (2) carriage of local television stations if requested by the television stations, (3) compliance with technical standards (the annual proof of performance tests are not required), and (4) completion of the first two parts of the annual report (Form 325), the annual financial report (Form 326), and the annual employment report (Form 395A) without the statistics portion. Systems with fewer than five employees do not need to file a statement of their equal opportunity program with the FCC.

FCC Preemptions

Although jurisdiction over cable is shared with state and local governments, the FCC has preempted certain areas. In some cases, this means that the FCC has *taken action* itself; in other cases, it means that the FCC is *preventing action* by state and local governments and intends the area to be unregulated, at least for the time being. The preempted areas are (1) technical standards—the FCC has set minimum standards and prescribes performance tests; local standards are not permitted unless a waiver is obtained; (2) origination programming—state and local governments *may not prohibit* cable systems from originating or carrying programs; the FCC intends to keep the programming options open for cable and prevent censorship; (3) signal carriage—the FCC will specify "must-carry" signals, require nonduplication, and reserves for itself other rules on signal carriage; (4) pay cable and other nonbroadcast rates— state and local authorities cannot regulate these rates; the FCC intends to free these rates from regulation at any level so that in the developmental stages, at least, nonbroadcast services will not be encumbered; and (5) franchise fees.[17]

STATE POLICY

The FCC, having asserted jurisdiction over cable television, also acknowledged concurrent jurisdiction with state and local governments— "a deliberately structured dualism."[18] Originally, the FCC clearly intended to play the major role in policy that would direct the development of the cable industry and establish its position *vis-à-vis* other telecommunication media. And the FCC, somewhat nervous about a nontraditional state and local government role in a medium protected by the First Amendment, took precautions to maintain federal rules pertinent to that area (rules governing community origination programming) and to prevent local interference with public access. The state and local roles were to be in the field of franchising and rate making. The FCC, not to mention the cable business, was very much concerned about a trilevel regulatory system that would burden the new industry with three layers of regulation, perhaps duplicative. The FCC and the cable industry would have preferred state *or* local authority in cable, not both.

State Positions on Cable

As it is, states have taken every possible posture toward cable. Some have ignored cable or have studied it without taking action. Other states have given municipal or county governments exclusive jurisdiction in the nonfederal aspects of regulation.[19] Five states have preempted franchising. Many have assumed responsibility only for narrowly defined areas such as pole attachment or theft of service. Eleven states have comprehensive regulatory commissions established independently for cable television or as part of public utility commissions. These states are

Alaska, Connecticut, Delaware, Hawaii, Nevada, New Jersey, Rhode Island, and Vermont, which regulate cable through preexisting utility commissions or other agencies, and Massachusetts, Minnesota and New York, which have set up independent commissions for regulating cable.[20]

Franchising

The five states that have preempted franchising are Alaska, Connecticut, Hawaii, Rhode Island, and Vermont. These states set the conditions for cable franchises and issue certificates. Massachusetts, Minnesota, and New York set franchise standards, meaning that they may set the term for initial and renewal franchise periods, prescribe the procedures for granting franchises, and prescribe items to be included in the franchise. Some states (e.g. Kansas, New York) do not allow landlords to refuse to allow cable access to tenants.

Rate Regulation

Some states regulate cable rates in lieu of local authorities; others serve in an appeals capacity where there is an impasse between local authorities and the cable operation. In California, under certain conditions, rates are deregulated. The state has taken away the local option to set rates if the operators meet those conditions. This is discussed fully in Chapter 11. The cable industry is actively seeking rate deregulation at both state and local levels. The cable companies have been willing to trade off additional services for deregulation. In California, in a *competitive community* (where other media are available in sufficient abundance to provide an alternative), a cable company may opt for deregulation if it is willing to provide community channels and contribute funds for their support. A similar agreement was reached by the City of Lansing, Michigan and the franchisee, Continental Cablevision.

Most states involved in rates use a form of rate-of-return regulation with the acceptable return set at about 18 percent. A major issue in rate proceedings has been the degree of "competition" in the community. If there is an alternative to cable, that is, good availability of off-air signals, the cable company does not have a firm hold on the consumer. Presumably in this case the cable rate is elastic; if the rate goes too high, subscriptions will fall off. An index of competitiveness is the level of penetration. If only half the households in a community subscribe to cable, there is apparently less need for cable, and the price of the service, in theory, would be adjusted to those market conditions. In these places, cable television and available off-air television are reasonably close substitutes. On the other hand, if almost all households in the community subscribe to cable, it is assumed to be noncompetitive and rates requires regulation.

New Jersey has an innovative system called *common tariff* rate regulation. Cable systems may choose either the common tariff method or the more traditional procedures. The majority have chosen common tariff. Under this approach, cable systems are assigned to one of six rate categories, depending on competition (as described), the density of subscribers per cable mile, and number of channels (12 or under, more than 12). A maximum level is established for each category. The company is permitted to raise prices up to the maximum in incremental steps, once per year. This scheme has significantly lowered the cost of ratemaking in New Jersey.[21]

Does state regulation of cable, particularly rates, result in a net social benefit? The acid test is whether or not rates are higher or lower in the regulating states. If regulation protects the consumer from inefficient (higher) rates resulting from monopoly pricing by cable companies, the regulated states would have lower rates. A study by Braunstein, et al., found that rates were slightly higher in the regulating states and that penetration levels were about the same as in nonregulating states.[22] This is not a clear negative answer to the question, however. Rates are difficult to compare because the services offered under each rate vary greatly and the regulated state may have higher cost-of-living indices. Nevertheless, these are the measures that should be used ultimately to judge the effect of rate regulation and bear watching. The rates charged for comparable services in rate-regulated states should be lower when adjustments are made to accommodate differences in construction and operating costs.

Ownership

Massachusetts, Rhode Island, and Connecticut have concerns about newspaper ownership of cable systems. The Connecticut public utility commission decided that newspaper ownership of a cable system in the same town would have a negative impact on the cable franchise and instructed the Times Mirror Company to divest either *The Hartford Courant* or two of its cable companies serving the circulation area of the *Courant*. Connecticut also ruled that the General Electric Company could not sell television sets and also own cable systems in the state. The Massachusetts statute prohibits common newspaper and cable ownership in a major circulation area. Rhode Island penalizes newspaper ownership in comparative hearings on franchises.

Maine, Massachusetts, Montana, and North Carolina all have laws designed to facilitate cable construction in rural areas. In Maine, municipalities are specifically authorized to operate telecommunications systems. Massachusetts permits municipal electric plants to operate cable systems. Montana and North Carolina authorize rural telephone cooperatives to offer cable service.[23]

Development

A developmental function has been assumed by some states. This function is discussed in Chapter 11. Briefly, the idea is to stimulate development of programming, public service channels, interconnection, line extension, and so on. For example, the Minnesota Cable Communications Board is required by statute to "develop and maintain a state-wide plan for development of cable communications services." The plan was completed in 1977.[24]

Minnesota, New York, Rhode Island, Connecticut, and North Carolina either support access or community programming in some way or are contemplating the means by which to do so. The withdrawal of federal rules on access and local origination has encouraged state interest. Interconnection, to facilitate regional shared interests, is of concern to some states. This appears to be a logical role for the states, since coordination may be necessary to bridge communities. Minnesota has started a videotape-sharing network in advance of physical interconnection. New Jersey has plans for microwave interconnection of all cable systems in the state.

COPYRIGHT LAW

Background

Cable systems carry responsibilities and are granted special privileges under federal copyright law. The objectives of copyright law are well stated in the 1976 Copyright Act statement of purposes for the Copyright Royalty Tribunal, the body that collects royalty fees for cable system retransmission of certain broadcast signals.[25] The first purpose is "to maximize the availability of creative works to the public." The copyright act grants monopoly property rights in the production and publication of literary, musical, artistic, and dramatic works. It is assumed that these rights are necessary incentives to creators. But also, the ability to avail oneself of creative work is a public benefit that must be facilitated. Copyright law provides an administrative procedure by which original material may be shared.

The second purpose is "to afford the copyright owner a fair return for his creative work and the copyright user a fair income under existing economic conditions." The Copyright Act attempts to protect the livelihood of the copyright owner and at the same time offer fair incentives to the user of copyrighted materials (e.g., a cable company) so that they may be disseminated fully.

A third purpose is "to reflect the relative roles of the copyright user in the product made available to the public with respect to relative creative contribution, technological contribution, capital investment, cost, risk, and contribution to the opening of new markets for creative expression and media for their communication." This acknowledges the complexities of the modern creative process and the role and costs of communication technology in making original work available.

The final purpose is "to minimize any disruptive impact on the structure of the industries involved and on generally prevailing industry practices." The implementation of the copyright law is a delicate task. As new communication technologies emerge and royalty rates are established and adjusted, the Copyright Royalty Tribunal must be cautious not to upset or restructure communications industries to the detriment of copyright owners, disseminators, or the public.

Broadcasting and cable of course were not covered expressly by the 1909 Copyright Act which was still in force at the time CATV systems began capturing and redistributing television and radio broadcast signals. Attempts by motion picture copyright owners[26] and broadcasters[27] to apply the Copyright Act to cable transmission of broadcast signals failed in the Supreme Court. According to the Court, CATV carried broadcast signals without alteration, thereby only enhancing the viewer's ability to use the signal. Technically, under the 1909 law, cable systems did not "perform" the copyrighted work.

Copyright owners were originally protected somewhat by the FCC signal importation limits and the program exclusivity rules. The program exclusivity rules preserved the contract between the syndicator and television station that grants program rights to the television market. The rule prevented the cable system from bringing in a syndicated program from a distant station that was already in the market. It was presumed that this would erode the value of the program property to the television station serving the market in which the cable system lies.

Copyright Act of 1976

In the early 1970s, much of the cable industry had conceded a copyright liability. The National Cable Television Association and Motion Picture Producers Association of America worked out a compromise that was incorporated in the 1976 Copyright Act. Under this law, cable systems are entitled to obtain a compulsory license for retransmission of all television and radio signals which they may carry under the FCC rules. In return, the cable systems pay for the *distant, nonnetwork* television programs carried. If the cable system is not licensed or does not report fully the distant, nonnetwork programs carried, it is liable to those copyright owners. Since the blanket fee paid under the compulsory license is lower than that which would be assessed by each copyright owner separately, it is in the best interests of the cable system to participate.

The compulsory license arrangement covers *secondary transmissions,* meaning the simultaneous retransmission of signals originating from another source. The definition is extended to include nonsimultaneous transmission in off-shore areas (e.g., Hawaii, Alaska, Puerto Rico) to permit the customary delayed transmission of programs due to time differentials. The compulsory license applies only to secondary transmissions. But cable systems have full liability for (the responsibility to pay for or clear) secondary transmissions not intended for the public at large but directed to *controlled* groups. This would exclude from coverage by the compulsory license privilege subscription television stations, pay cable, background music services, closed-circuit broadcasts, and other programming intended solely for a specially qualified audience (qualified, usually, by paying for the service).

The secondary transmissions must not be altered in any way by the cable system. For example, the cable system could not substitute its own commercials for those broadcast except under specified conditions during market research. The compulsory licensing arrangement also covers Canadian and Mexican broadcast stations that might be imported by cable system near the borders.

Copyright Royalty Tribunal

The compulsory licensing system is administered by the Copyright Royalty Tribunal (CRT). The tribunal is composed of five commissioners appointed by the President for seven-year terms. The duties of the CRT are to (1) adjust royalty rates in accordance with inflation or deflation and changes in rates to subscribers and (2) to distribute royalty fees to claimant copyright owners after administrative costs have been deducted. Adjustments in the royalty rates are made every five years, starting in 1980. Copyright holders claiming distant, nonnetwork, secondary transmission of their works may file individual claims with the CRT or participate in joint claims.

The computation of the royalty fee to be paid by cable systems semiannually is complex. A *statement of account* covering a six-month period is submitted. The statement lists the total number of subscribers and gross amounts paid to the system for basic service. The cable system must list all nonnetwork programming carried from beyond the local service area and distant, nonnetwork television programming on a substituted basis. The latter requires the cable system to keep a log of the substituted programs. The substituted programming does not figure in the royalty fee owed, but it aids the CRT in distributing the funds collected.

The calculation of royalty payments is dependent on semiannual basic subscriber revenue. This includes the basic service and second connection revenues but excludes installation fees and pay cable. The CRT makes a distinction between smaller systems, which pay royalties based solely on revenue, and larger systems, which pay a percentage of revenue determined by the number of distant signals carried. The 1980 adjustment was to go into effect January 1, 1981 but has been delayed as a result of court appeals by both parties, the cable industry, and the copyright owners.[28]

The Copyright Act states specifically that, if the FCC changes the signal carriage, syndicated exclusivity, and sports exclusivity rules, then the CRT may make reasonable adjustments in the rates. In the wake of the FCC elimination of the signal carriage and syndicated exclusivity rules, copyright owners are arguing that the CRT rate adjustment mechanism is not sufficient to accommodate a change of such magnitude and are requesting that Congress review the entire question of cable's copyright liability.[29]

An alternative to the compulsory licensing procedure that has frequently been proposed is to eliminate the compulsory license altogether and require cable systems to obtain *retransmission consent* to carry broadcast signals. This would have the effect of placing cable systems in a position of negotiating the rights to use broadcast material with broadcasters or copyright owners. The cable industry fears both the cost and complexity of this plan. Proponents, however, argue that it would more realistically reflect the value of the signals carried; in other words, the market rather than the CRT would set the price for copyrighted works. An FCC notice of inquiry that included the retransmission consent proposal and an experiment that permitted a cable system to carry distant signals on a consent basis resulted in a rejection of the concept.[30] Opponents of retransmission consent believe that this was a conclusive action.

A middle-ground proposal is to retain the compulsory licensing system but determine royalty payments by bargaining between the parties with arbitration as a backup.

Distant broadcast signals may play a lesser and lesser role in cable, but the transition to satellite-delivered, made-for-cable programming will be difficult for small town, older systems because they now rely on these very inexpensive off-air signals.

It should be noted that the compulsory licensing arrangement discussed here relates only to *secondary transmissions*. Cable system originations (fed into the system from the headend or elsewhere in the distribution system, whatever the source—original production, videotape, records, printed material, photographs, etc.) bear full copyright liability, meaning that use of copyrighted material is an infringement unless permission to use, or rights, have been negotiated with the owner. The law does permit limited "fair use" of copyrighted work for criticism, comment, news reporting, and teaching.

PRIVACY

Both one-way and two-way cable present risks to individual privacy. A tremendous variety of programming is "hosted" by the cable home. If the two-way cable services now contemplated are fully realized, the home terminal could yield the household financial condition, details of business transactions, travel plans, energy consumption, medical records, entertainment and information appetites, opinions, and scholastic achievement. Most of this information could now be compiled from other sources, but not from a *single* source. Similar risks are taken by business and institutional users of cable for data transmission. The cable industry itself may not realize the potential of its investment in two-way equipment if threats to privacy diminish business.

Intrusion of Unwanted Information

One type of privacy violation can be called *intrusion of unwanted information.* As unwanted "junk" may come through the mailbox, undesired information may come in by cable. The cable subscriber cannot always be properly warned of what to expect from 30 or more cable channels. The offending communication might be obscenity, hard-sell advertising, radical politics, unsolicited advice, religious evangelism, or even certain topics of instruction.

With the cooperation of the cable operator, the consumer may develop a self-defense against unwanted content. Cable programmers should give each channel a recognizable character that is consistent. For example, a movie channel such as Home Theater Network is identified as family viewing; the viewer will expect not to be exposed to heavy violence, sexual themes, or nudity. A lockout device can be supplied where the system carries some channels that may be deemed inappropriate for some members of the household. R-rated product may be shown only late at night. Certain channels may be made available selectively; that is, the subscriber must order and pay for particular channels. Any channel that might be undesirable to a large number of subscribers should probably not be programmed as part of the basic service or extended basic service.

Cable systems may also have to develop an internal code of practice in accepting programs and advertising similar to the old NAB Codes for radio and television. These codes treated broadcasting as a "guest" in the home and thereby disavow any content that would be a breach of conventional taste or manners.[31] While it is a major advantage of cable to treat mature themes in appropriately designated channels, it might be useful for cable to follow the broadcaster lead for basic services.

Unauthorized Access to Information

Perhaps a more serious form of privacy invasion is *unauthorized access* to information stored in the terminal or transmitted through the system. A two-way cable system continuously monitors the status of the home terminal, receiving a variety of information to determine channels viewed, alarm condition, personal health, polling responses, shopping orders, responses to instructional materials, utility consumption, banking transactions, and so on. All this information is communicated for a specific purpose to authorized persons. Unauthorized persons might also desire the information. (Because of the party-line nature of cable, and the ease with which signals can be intercepted at almost any point on the cable system, cable is more easily tapped than is the phone network, where tapping requires access to the individual telephone line.) Governments might seek information related to tax and law enforcement; advertisers and direct marketing companies, data on viewing habits and purchases; and thieves, evidence of assets.

In an obscenity case in Columbus, Ohio against an adult movie theater operator, the defense sought to prove that the content of the films was widely accepted within the community by using the records of viewing of such films on the Warner Amex adult pay TV channel. Confronted with a subpoena, Warner Amex revealed viewing information about the film in question and general patterns of adult movie consumption. At the time, Warner Amex said that it would resist court attempts to secure *individual* viewer records all the way to the Supreme Court.[32]

If all the communication in the cable to and from a single home were *aggregated*, a comprehensive picture of the household would emerge. Now, without two-way cable, bits and pieces of the same information are given up to a variety of organizations for very specific purposes. Nowhere is there the single source for a composite view of a household as might be accessible through two-way cable.

The cable company itself could sell information about users or capitulate to government requests for information. Or individual cable employees might do the same for personal profit in violation of company policy. Still others may tap into the cable, intercepting the data in transmission or calling it up from storage in the household terminal.

What are the consumer protections against unauthorized access to data? The data may be encrypted. This makes it more difficult and more expensive to access. Encrypting the data, and frequently changing the codes, is possible and now more practical under advances in microcomputer technology and digital communication. Another safeguard is to establish very strict rules governing access to be enforced by the cable operator. The cable operator has an economic incentive to preserve the integrity of the system. Consumers would not patronize the services if privacy could not be promised and reports of violations surfaced.

Warner Amex, one of the pioneers in two-way cable, has published a "Code of Privacy" which asserts that the company will explain its information gathering functions to subscribers; maintain physical security and confidentiality; use *individual* viewing records only for billing or service purposes; aggregate data never identifying individuals; deny requests for individual subscriber data unless legally required; allow subscribers to review and copy data about themselves; correct inaccurate information about subscribers; keep information only as long as necessary; make subscriber mailing lists available only with the permission of subscribers; comply with all federal, state, local and industry privacy codes; and require adherence to the Code of Privacy by third parties involved in the provision of service.[33]

The cable system security precautions can be buttressed by state laws penalizing electronic surveillance and unauthorized use of personal data banks. These are suggestions made by Nash and Smith in a paper prepared for the Federal Trade Commission. They believe that the Omnibus Crime Control Act, which sets controls on accessing private information about individuals or groups by electronic surveillance or other means, "might well be extended to cover the interception of data and messages from computer terminals within a public information utility system" (household).[34]

Legislation similar to the Privacy Act of 1974 would help to protect against some abuses of privacy. The law gives individuals the right to know what information about them is held in information banks. Inaccurate information may be corrected. The law also specifies the kind of information that may be collected and how it may be aggregated. Both civil and criminal remedies are available to those who have had their files administered improperly. Nash and Smith argue that this kind of law could be applied to use of data banks created by cable system services.

State or local governments might enact laws prohibiting unauthorized interception or divulgence of cable transmissions or knowing use of such illegally obtained transmissions. The federal Communications Act, Section 605, applies such a prohibition to interstate or foreign communication by wire or radio.[35]

The cable operator should inform the subscriber of exactly what information is collected through the two-way system, how it is used, and who is authorized access. A subscriber agreement form, which the subscriber signs, authorizes the specified use of the data. The subscriber agreement is valuable if the subscriber reads the form. The salesperson, anxious to close the sale, will not want to emphasize the information collection aspect of the two-way cable service and perhaps alarm the subscriber. Nonetheless, it might be good cable system policy to have the salesperson present the information orally so that it is certain that the subscriber is aware of the procedures and cable system policies. Since subscribers to two-way services are likely to be adding services one at a time as they become available, they may not be sensitive to the accumulation of information they are communicating about themselves. It would be well for the operator to periodically *remind* subscribers about the data that are being gathered and their use. This might be done through bill stuffers, notices in the program guide, or a special communication. The most certain device for reminding the subscriber of the data being collected from the household would be to have a terminal date on the subscriber's agreement form after which the agreement would have to be *renewed*.

The information collected *separately* from each subscribing household should be used only for billing (e.g., per-program entertainment) and servicing (e.g., automated meter reading, alarms, scoring instructional tests). Results from polling subscribers should be aggregated immediately with other respondents and never reported by individual household.

Economics of Privacy

Privacy of communication is costly. An FCC working paper on the economics of telecommunications privacy, by Brown and Gordon, points out that privacy "may be analyzed as an economic good insofar as resources devoted to the protection of privacy must be taken from elsewhere."[36] For the cable consumer, the cost of privacy is in the price of the protected service. Cable operators will pass on the cost of equipment and computer software to encrypt and decode information as well as the personnel costs to monitor the security system. The more complex and secure the system, the more it costs the subscriber. It is possible for security measures to price some services out of their potential market. At the other extreme, lack of security could exclude persons from the service who are not willing to take the risk. Some households would sacrifice privacy for a savings in the service charge, others would not. A compromise must be found so that the greatest number of people can be served without unreasonable risks.

Brown and Gordon prefer judicial enforcement of privacy rights to administrative enforcement.[37] In essence, competition and industry self-regulation protect against loss of privacy to the extent that is most efficient for consumers and the industry. Where individual rights of privacy are abused, on occasion, the remedy is in common law. If someone is injured by unauthorized use of information, damages may be awarded by the court. Brown and Gordon argue that the judicial redress "is highly empirical, in that it generally takes action only upon presentation of factual evidence that some offense has truly occurred." The authors believe this is superior to legislation covering a whole "catalogue of hypothetically possible abuses" and continuous regulation at public expense.[38]

At this point, the privacy problem of cable companies is not as serious as the problem for telephone companies. The phone companies have access to whom and when calls are made and can actually record conversations as well as intercept data. The cable systems have access to far less information, at least for the present and near future. A privacy problem arises with each technology used to deliver the potentially convenient and efficient new communication services. Essentially, privacy is not a cable or telephone problem but, more generally, a social problem.

A good general reference to communication and cable law is *Broadcast Law and Regulation* by John Bittner.[39]

NOTES

[1]Public Telecommunications Financing Act of 1978; Public Telecommunications Facilities Program, Report and Order, National Telecommunications and Information Administration, Department of Commerce, 15 CFR Part 2301, Docket No. 78-1.

[2]George H. Shapiro, "Federal Regulation of Cable TV—History and Outlook," in *The Cable/Broadband Communications Book, 1977–1978,* Mary Louise Hollowell, ed. (Washington, D.C.: Communications Press, 1977), pp. 3–20; George H. Shapiro, "Up the Hill and Down: Perspectives on Federal Regulation," in *The Cable/Broadband Communications Book,* Vol. 2, *1980–1981,* Mary Louise Hollowell, ed. (Washington, D.C.: Communications Press, 1980), pp. 20–34.

[3]*First Report and Order in Docket Nos. 14895 and 15233,* 38 FCC 683, 4 RR 2d 1725 (1965).

[4]*Carter Mountain Transmission Corp.* 32 FCC 459, 22 RR 193 (1962), affirmed *Carter Mountain Transmission Corp.* vs. *FCC,* 321 F2d 359 (D.C. Cir. 1963), cert. denied 375 U.S. 951 (1963).

[5]*Second Report and Order in Docket Nos. 14895, 15233 and 15971,* 2 FCC 2d 725, 6 RR 1717 (1966).

[6]*United States* v. *Southwestern Cable Co.,* 392 U.S. 157 (1968).

[7]*Cable Television Report and Order,* 36 FCC 2d 143 (1972).

[8]*Memorandum Opinion and Order on Reconsideration of the Cable Television Report and Order,* 36 FCC 2d 326, 25 RR 2d 1501 (1972).

[9]*Clarification of Rules and Notice of Proposed Rule Making,* 46 FCC 2d 175, 29 RR 2d 1621 (1974).

[10]Ralph Lee Smith, *The Wired Nation* (New York: Harper & Row, 1970), p. 46.

[11]*Report and Order* adopted July 22, 1980, FCC 80-443, 45 *Fed. Reg.* 60186, September 11, 1980.

[12]*FCC* v. *Midwest Video Corp.,* 440 U.S. 689 (1979).

[13]FCC Information Bulletin 00867, "Cable Television," Washington, D.C., October 1980, p. 5.

[14]47 U.S.C.A. 224.

[15]*Warner Amex Cable Communications Company* v. *Tampa Electric Company,* file No. PA-80-0019, released June 26, 1981.

[16]FCC Information Bulletin 00867, p. 15.

[17]The FCC action in pay TV preemption was supported by *Brookhaven Cable TV, Inc.* v. *Kelly,* 428 F. Supp. 1216 (N.D.N.Y. 1977), affirmed 573 F 2d 765 (2d Circ. March 29, 1978), cert. denied 99 S. Ct. 1991 (2d Cir. 1979).

[18]*Cable Television Report and Order,* 36 FCC 2d 143, 24 RR 2d 1501 (1972).

[19]Thomas A. Muth, *State Interest in Cable Communications* (New York: Arno Press, 1979).

[20]A table identifying the functions of all 50 of the states in cable television regulation is found in Sharon A. Briley, "State Involvement in Cable TV and Other Communications Services: A Current Review," in *The Cable/Broadband Communications Book,* Vol. 2., *1980–1981,* Mary Louis Hollowell, ed., (Washington, D.C.: Communication Press, 1980), pp. 46–48. The article is a thorough 1980 update on state regulation of cable.

[21]Ibid., p. 61.

[22]Yale M. Braunstein, Konrad K. Kalba, and Larry S. Levine, *The Economic Impact of State Cable TV Regulation,* The Harvard Program on Information Resources Policy, P-78-7, Cambridge, Mass., October 1978.

[23]Hollowell, *The Cable/Broadband Communications Book,* pp. 52–53.

[24]Minnesota Cable Communications Board, *Statewide Development Plan: Planning and Development Guide for Cable and Related Telecommunications Facilities and Services in Minnesota,* St. Paul, Minnesota, April 1977.

[25]17 U.S,C.A. Sec. 1, *et seq.*

[26]*Fortnightly Corporation* v. *United Artists Television, Inc.,* 392 U.S. 390 (1968).

[27]*Teleprompter Corp.* v. *Columbia Broadcasting System, Inc.,* 415 U.S. 394 (1974).

[28]In 1983, operators were paying the following fees. Systems with semiannual revenues of under $55,500 pay a flat $20. Systems with revenues between $55,500 and $107,000 pay 0.5 percent of "adjusted revenue." Adjusted revenue is calculated by subtracting the actual revenue from $107,000. The result is subtracted from actual revenue to get adjusted revenue. Example: $107,000 − $87,000 (hypothetical actual revenue) = $20,000; $87,000 (actual revenue) − $20,000 (result of first step) = $67,000; $67,000 (adjusted revenue) × 0.005 = $335 (semiannual royalty payment). Cable systems with revenues from $107,000 to $214,000 pay 0.5 percent of gross subscriber revenues up to $107,000 plus 1 percent of gross subscriber revenue between $107,000 and $214,000. Example: hypothetical revenue $200,000; 0.005 × $107,000 = $535; 0.01 × $93,000 (amount of revenue over $107,000) = $930; $535 (from step 1) + $930 (from step 2) = $1,465 (semiannual royalty payment). Cable systems with revenues of more than $214,000 pay royalties based on the number of distant signal equivalents (DSE) carried. To calculate DSEs, independent stations are counted as one and a distant network affiliated stations are counted as one-quarter. The one-quarter represents a rough proportion of the network affiliate stations' nonnetwork programming, which is what counts for this purpose, as noted earlier. Programs that are substituted for required deletions do not count unless they are "live," in which case they count as one-three-hundred-sixty-fifth of a DSE for each day. A station carried part time (e.g., after sign-off of another station) would be counted for that portion of the day (e.g., 1–7 A.M. would be one-third DSE). Translator stations and Canadian, Mexican, specialty, and religious stations all count as DSEs if they qualify as distant, nonnetwork stations. Cable systems pay a percentage of gross receipts for the first DSE, a lesser percentage for the next three, and a still smaller percentage for DSEs over four. Example: hypothetical revenue $700,000 and DSE 4.25; $700,000 × 0.00799 (1980 CRT rate) × 1 (first DSE) = $5,593; $700,000 × 0.00503 (1980 CRT rate) × 3 (DSEs between 1 and 4) = $10,563; $700,000 × 0.00237 (1980 CRT rate) × 0.5 (DSEs over 4) = $830; $5,593 (from step 1) + $10,563 (from step 2) + $830 (from step 3) = $16,986 (semiannual royalty payment).

[29]See Stuart F. Feldstein, "Program Rights and Copyright Issues in Broadcast Signals," in *Current Developments in CATV 1981,* George H. Shapiro, ed. (New York: Practising Law Institute, 1981), pp. 141–176.

[30]*Cable Television Report and Order,* 36 FCC 2d 143, 24 RR 2d 1501 (1972).

[31]NAB Radio Code, NAB Television Code, reprinted in Frank & Kahn, *Documents of American Broadcasting,* 2nd ed. (New York: Appleton-Century-Crofts, 1973), pp. 329–353.

[32]Deanna Collingwood Nash and John B. Smith, *Interactive Home Media and Privacy Issues,* prepared by Collingwood Associates, Inc. for the Federal Trade Commission, Washington, D.C., February 1981.

[33]"Code of Privacy," Warner Amex Cable Communications, 75 Rockefeller Plaza, New York, NY 10019, October 10, 1981.

[34]Collingwood and Nash, *Interactive Home Media and Privacy Issues.*

[35]47 U.S.C.A. 605.

[36]James A. Brown, Jr. and Kenneth Gordon, "Economics and Telecommunication Privacy: A Framework for Analysis," Office of Plans and Policy, Federal Communications Commission, Washington, D.C., December 1980, p. ii.

[37]Ibid., p. 41.

[38]Ibid., p. 42.

[39]John R. Bittner, *Broadcast Law and Regulation* (Englewood Cliffs, N.J.: Prentice-Hall, Inc., 1982). Chapter 9, "Cable," pp. 290–311.

11

Franchising

Franchise applicant conducts seminar on cable for community leaders. Photograph, Christopher Wright Ramsey.

THE OWNERSHIP DECISION

Cable systems may be (1) owned and operated by the city, (2) owned by the city and operated by a cable company, (3) owned and operated by a public, nonprofit corporation, cooperative or power company, (4) a private, profit-making corporation, or (5) a private company sharing a minority interest with the franchising authority. Therefore, a basic decision prior to establishing a community cable system is to decide the most appropriate ownership structure. Almost all cable systems are in the private, profit-making corporation category. But several systems are operated by cities or public corporations chartered to operate the system without profit. Most of these systems are in very small towns that did not initially attract private entrepreneurs. In many cases, people got together, assessed each other a sum that covered the construction, and began operating, forming some institutional structure that would manage and perpetuate the system in their behalf. These organizations function well as community antenna television systems. Since they are older systems, none has been tested as a modern, two-way, multipurpose broadband cable system.

Many larger cities, under quite different circumstances, have considered a publicly owned cable system, most currently, Minneapolis, St. Paul, Cleveland and St. Louis. A variety of private corporation-municipal ownership plans have surfaced recently. For example, Rogers Cablesystems offered the city of St. Paul an option of buying back half the system at two-thirds its market value after five years.[1]

There are features of cable that suggest municipal or public ownership. Many of the newer services are *public* services or vital utilities—government, education, library, and public access channels; home security systems; automated meter reading and power-load management; and polling. A municipal system, funded by revenue bonds where permissible, would have a low debt service cost. These bonds, because of tax advantages, pay low rates of interest. Revenue bonds do not put the city or taxpayer at risk, since they may draw only on the revenues of the cable system. Since most cable systems are a monopoly, the franchising authorities have responsibilities to the community and consumers that, as we shall see, are not always effectively discharged by the regulatory system. A municipal system would be more likely to extend service to low-density and low-income neighborhoods.

On the other hand, there are some difficulties with municipal or public corporation ownership of a cable system. The tradition in the United States, of separating news media and other communication systems from government, is long standing. It would be difficult to insulate a government communication system from political influence, although a public corporation, completely independent of the political system, might suffice for this purpose. It may also be difficult to build in management incentives for efficient and innovative operation, although for this purpose an operating company might be permitted to increase its revenues as a reward for service development and efficiency. Then, there is the greater possibility that a municipal or publicly owned system would develop public or social services, at the expense of subscribers, that most subscribers do not want. Finally, because the growth of entertainment television requires substantial promotion and flexibility in packaging programs, it would be awkward to lease out channels to many different entertainment services. A single successful bidder for entertainment and commercial information channels might be able to function effectively but, of course, at the risks to consumers generally associated with monopoly. Avoiding the latter was a principal reason for public ownership in the first place.

Since all but a handful of cable systems are franchised to privately owned, profit-making companies, the remainder of this chapter treats the franchising and regulation of such systems. Much of what is said, however, would apply to the selection of an operating company for a municipal system, for those municipal systems where that is appropriate, and to the monitoring of system performance which would be much the same whatever the structure of ownership.

FRANCHISES

Local governments in most states grant franchises to cable systems under state-granted home rule powers. The franchise permits use of public land in wiring the community with aerial and buried cable. It provides a collective representation of the consumers. Franchises are usually granted "nonexclusively," but for practical purposes, under the present economics of the cable industry, the franchise is a monopoly. Only one applicant is accepted. Once a franchise is granted to one cable company, no other cable company could *overbuild* (build another system over the same territory) until the system became obsolete. There is not enough revenue to support the capital investment of two or more companies, and the service of one company could not be differentiated significantly from another. This may change. In the past, the lion's share of the investment has been in the cable plant. With two-way services, a much greater percentage of the investment is going into the home. It therefore becomes more feasible for two plants to be built, since the in-home investment is made only as the customer subscribes to the service. In the future we may also see some rival cable companies seeking franchises in communities with old cable systems—5 or 12 channels—that have not been rebuilt to keep pace with the state of the art.

The granting of franchises in cable communications raises several issues. A report of Technology and Economics, Inc. to the National Telecommunications and Information Administration (NTIA) notes the risk of municipal liability for antitrust violations in granting exclusive franchises, or selecting a single "nonexclusive" franchisee.[2] The Louisiana Supreme Court ruled that a city is immune from such liability if the state has "a comprehensive and actively supported . . . policy permitting regulation to displace competition."[3] Does a state have such a regulatory system for cable, or is such power assumed by the municipality under privileges granted by the state? If not, it may be necessary to allow competition.

More recently, the Supreme Court has decided that the City of Boulder, Colorado is not necessarily exempt from antitrust liability on the strength of the state exemption.[4] This may open up competition for franchises or force states to adopt legislation specifically dealing with the franchising authority.

Questions about the exclusivity of franchises are likely to surface more strongly when all the major franchises have been awarded. Then cable companies may try to overbuild weak or outdated systems.

Exclusive franchises, either by franchise agreement or *de facto*, have also been attacked on First Amendment grounds. An attorney for Palo Mesa Cablevision, in defending the company against a lawsuit charging it with violation of an exclusive Times Mirror cable franchise in Vista, California, says that exclusivity in cable is "no different than if you granted a franchise to the *Los Angeles Times* to be the sole distributor of newspapers in Vista."[5]

FRANCHISE COMPETITION

The value of a cable franchise is immense. Cable systems franchised before 1980 were built for $500 or less per subscriber. Those franchised after 1980 may cost $800 to $1,000 per subscriber. They are being sold for $1,000 to $1,500 per subscriber, with expectations of even higher market values. The difference between the construction price per subscriber and the market value is a rough index to the value of a franchise. Under these circumstances it is obvious that competition for franchises is intense. There are several applicants for each new franchise. The franchise bidding process has forced companies into business and lobbying practices which are an embarrassment to the industry and to city officials.

The franchise bidding wars, painful and distasteful as they can be, may nonetheless benefit the communities, the consumers, and ultimately the industry itself. As we have said several times earlier, the most advanced services and technologies are bid in each new franchise application. The technology has been stretched from 300-mHz to 400-mHz and from one-way to two-way. In attempting to outbid each other, cable companies are accelerating the development of new services, for example, videotext. Cable companies are attempting to ascertain the communication needs of each city and are finding new ways to serve those needs through institutional networks, interactive services, and new programming. If only a small proportion of the plans turn out to be practical, there should be a net gain socially and economically. Each franchise is somewhat unique as the bidders attempt to come up with something new. The successes in one place will be imitated in others.

There are those who fear, with some justification, that franchise bidding has gotten out of hand—that cities are taking advantage of the situation and are demanding too much and that cable companies are making potentially ruinous capital commitments and promises of service. Concerned about the supersystems proposed as a result of the "demand-and-promise spiral in urban franchising contests," one large cable MSO president, John Malone of Tele-Communication, Inc., says, "In our judgment, there's no major market in franchising today that is economic as bid. We think the bidders are depending upon changes in the franchise, the rates, or the development of services not yet surfaced."[6] It is highly probable that many cable companies will default on commitments or be delayed in their delivery on franchise promises while capital and the technology catch up. Cities now in the franchising process or working with the supersystems now under construction will have to recognize the sugar plums for what they are. The hopes of franchise authorities may be raised falsely by the agreements they sign. If the technology lags or if the services promised are not cost feasible, there is little to be done. The franchising authority cannot, itself, force the technology and may be unwilling or unable to subsidize services. And, in this frantic developmental stage, the technology is changing rapidly. A risk to cable companies is to be caught with a large capital investment in nonfunctional or impractical equipment. There is a recent trend toward cable company drop out when the bidding gets too high.

What is needed at this point is a rational approach by franchising authorities and cable companies alike. The companies must be honest with franchising authorities about the state of the art, and the franchising authorities must be realistic in their expectations. This is easy to say, but so much is unknown and so much is at stake that an orderly, rational franchising process will be difficult to achieve. Nonetheless, we attempt to lay out such a procedure here, describe the major steps, and provide some anecdotal illustration of the process and the pitfalls. The steps usually followed include (1) writing a cable ordinance, (2) publishing a request for proposal, (3) evaluating applicants and making a selection, and (4) negotiating a franchise agreement with the successful applicant.

Once the franchise is settled, the franchising authority monitors construction and later the performance of the franchisee in accordance with the agreement and may attempt to stimulate and coordinate development of public services, regulate the rates for service, handle complaints that cannot be resolved, and eventually determine if the franchise is to be renewed.

(Note: While most communities have already awarded franchises, a few remain. New suburbs are continuously developing outside franchised areas. Furthermore, hundreds of communities must renew or renegotiate franchises each year. Generally, the earliest cable systems were built under ordinances and franchise agreements that are inadequate for today's cable technology and services. These communities must now go through a refranchising and upgrading process essentially the same as the original franchising described below.)

CABLE ORDINANCES

Not all jurisdictions require an ordinance preparatory to franchising a cable system. Under general authority, a license may be granted or a franchise agreement signed. An ordinance and franchise agreement may be combined. A separate ordinance, however, fills several purposes and has advantages over a franchise agreement standing alone. The ordinance sets out the procedures for obtaining a franchise and may outline some basic and specific requirements of a cable franchisee. Since the ordinance is prior to the franchising process, it is not negotiated as is the franchise agreement.

These are the common provisions of an ordinance.

Definitions

An ordinance begins with definitions of key terms that are fundamental to the ordinance, for example, "cable communications system," "city," "franchisee," "franchise agreement," "subscriber," "public channels." Other terms may be defined when they appear. A number of concepts such as "two-way communication" and "institutional network" could have many different meanings and, therefore, should be described carefully in the ordinance or franchise agreement.

Procedure for Application

This section of the ordinance describes the process of soliciting applicants and, in general, the kind of information desired from applicants. The "request for proposal," to be discussed, prescribes the content and the format of the application and sets a deadline for application.

Procedures for Selection of Applicants and Franchising

Often the procedures for franchising are prescribed under state law or more general ordinances. Appropriate state and local law should be identified and summarized here. The ordinance may require public access to applications and other relevant documents, a public hearing on the applications, and a public hearing on the franchise agreement.

Certain criteria are important in the evaluation of a franchise, and these criteria should be stated in the ordinance—among them financial capability, record of performance, character of the owner, engineering design, services, and initial rates. Weights given to these criteria may also be stated. We believe this to be important. Many cities tend to look at each criterion equally so that an applicant that is weak in one or more of the most crucial areas may secure a franchise because of strength in lesser important areas. We believe that the engineering design, because of its permanence, is most important. Program and two-way services are also important, not so much because cable companies differ in services, but because specification of interest in particular areas of service will bring out creative responses among applicants which, in the franchise agreement, become obligations. Whatever the interests of the community, it is useful for these interests to be represented in the criteria and weighted properly so that the most vital interests get the most attention during evaluation of applications.

How does a city determine its own interests in cable? An attempt should be made to systematically ascertain the community needs. There are several approaches. A convenient method is to call one or more meetings of groups of community leaders and government officials. The meeting might start with a discussion of general communication problems and later focus on the potential of cable in addressing the problems. A procedure and format for such meetings is included in Appendix D.[7] A helpful booklet entitled "Minnesota Cable Communications and Local Self-Determination" was produced by the Minnesota Cable Communications Board in 1979.[8]

As noted earlier, the fire chief in Syracuse, New York was very much interested in alarm systems. As a result, the Syracuse franchise required a 1,000-home cable experiment with smoke detectors and other alarms. Members of the ACLU may push strongly for a public access channel. Educators may seek a means for distributing audiovisual materials. Through a systematic assessment process, most of these needs would be discovered. They can be reflected in the ordinance, and a "statement of communication needs" can be included with the request for proposals.

An alternative is to ask the applicants to ascertain community needs. This is certainly easier for the city, but it seems backward to ask the applicant to tell the city what it needs—an abdication of the city's responsibility. It is also a major burden on community leaders to have several cable applicants contacting them independently in an attempt to ascertain needs.

This section of the ordinance should indicate how applicants are to be evaluated. Because selection from among several applicants is a complex task, city council members are not likely to have time themselves for the basic work. A committee of citizens or citizen and government representatives may be organized to perform an advisory function. This committee can be charged to receive input from the entire community.

Citizens and community institutions should play a role in determining the nature of the city's cable service. The city, in addition to assessment of needs and public hearings, should make an effort to educate the community about cable. It is surprising what misinformation and limited knowledge people have about cable before it has actually been experienced in the community—the distinction from commercial broadcast and subscription television, the extent of services, and the pricing structure are all confusing. The local media will probably do the best advance job of backgrounding people as long as the city government assures that all steps in the process are open so that there is something for media to report and there are some news pegs for background material.

Monitoring Franchisee Performance

In granting the franchise, the city takes responsibility for the performance of the franchisee. Some mechanism is necessary to oversee construction of the system, hoping to hold it on schedule, to review service in accordance with the franchise agreement, and to arbitrate complaints from subscribers and system users that cannot be settled with the company. If the city regulates rates, rate increase requests must be evaluated. The city may want periodic reports on community programming, access channel and institutional network use, interactive services, and so on. Again, it is not likely that a city council itself, would have time to do justice to this function.

The ordinance can create the mechanism for performing these monitoring functions. If a commission is established, it will indicate how it is composed and its responsibilities. An excerpt from the East Lansing, Michigan ordinance serves as an example:

Commission Established. Before any franchise is granted, there shall be appointed a commission, to be known as the East Lansing Cable Communications Commission.
Commission Composition. The Commission shall consist of seven residents

of the City, representative of its population characteristics, appointed by the City Council. Each member shall serve a term of three years; provided, however, that appointments to the first Commission, shall be for such terms as follows: Three members for a term of three years; two members for a term of two years; and two members for a term of one year. Any vacancy in the office shall be filled by the City Council for the remainder of the term. No employee or person with ownership interest in a cable television franchise granted pursuant to this ordinance shall be eligible for membership on the Commission. *Commission Functions.* The Commission in addition to any functions assigned to it elsewhere in this ordinance, shall have the following functions:

(1) Advise the Council on applications for franchises.
(2) Advise the Council on matters which might constitute grounds for revocation of the franchise in accordance with this ordinance.
(3) Resolve disagreements among franchisees, subscribers and public and private users of the system; such decisions of the Commission shall be appealable to the City Council.
(4) Advise the Council on the regulation of rates in accordance with this ordinance.
(5) Coordinate the franchisee's consultant services for best use of public facilities and channels of the system.
(6) Determine general policy relating to the service provided subscribers and the operation and use of public channels, with a view to maximizing the diversity of programs and services to subscribers. The use of public channels shall be allocated on a first come, first served basis, subject to limitations on monopolization of system time, or prime times.
(7) Encourage use of public channels among the widest range of institutions, groups and individuals within the City. This endeavor shall be conducted with a view toward establishing different categories of uses, and the annual reports by the Commission, to the City Council, shall be by such categories, defined as follows:

(a) Local educational uses including library, public schools, Lansing Community College, Michigan State University.
(b) Public access for local programming under public control with guaranteed access for students and minority groups.
(c) Public agency access (including fire, police, burglar alarms, and public announcements).
(d) Off-the-air network and independent entertainment programs.
(e) Off-the-air educational programs.
(f) Availability of channel time for lease or pay TV.
(g) Availability of channel time for lease for business uses, including telemetry of information.
(h) Information retrieval and professional communication.

(8) Cooperate with other systems, and supervise interconnection of systems.
(9) Disburse all City revenues from franchisees for the development of the use of public channels, including production grants to users and the

purchase and maintenance of equipment not required to be provided by the franchisee.

(10) Audit all franchisee records required by this ordinance and, in the Commission's discretion, require the preparation and filing of information additional to that required herein.

(11) Make an annual report to the Council, including: an account of franchise fees received and distributed, the total number of hours of utilization of public channels, and hourly subtotals for various programming categories, and a review of any plans submitted during the year by franchisees for development of new services.

(12) Conduct evaluations of the system at least every 3 years, with the franchisee, and pursuant thereto, make recommendations to the Council for amendments to this ordinance or the franchise agreement.

Action by Majority. Any action of the Commission shall require the concurrence of four members.[9]

Franchise Fee

The ordinance establishes the franchise fee within the FCC-established maximum of 3 percent (5 percent with special permission). The franchise fee is most commonly a percentage of a gross revenue base. The base may be basic subscriber revenues, total subscriber revenues (basic and all other tiers including pay channel options), or total revenues (including advertising, leased channel, and data communication revenues).

It is in the best interests of cable system development, for consumers and cable operator alike, that the franchise fee cover only regulatory costs and perhaps certain expenses of the public channels. High franchise fees contributing to the general fund to defer more direct and visible taxes are indeed taxes, but are applied only to cable subscribers and users since they are passed through. The franchise fee is added into the expenses justifying rates. The franchise fee was once a major factor in franchise competition, with some companies offering as high as 20 percent. This is a prospect again if the FCC deregulates the franchise fee area.

The plan for distribution of franchise fee revenues may be included in this section. A percentage may be reserved for regulatory costs. Another percentage may be turned over to the cable commission, if one is set up by the ordinance, to be used for the public channels (e.g., purchase and maintenance of equipment, supplies). The portion of the franchise fee for this latter purpose should go directly to the commission, *not* into the general fund to be appropriated annually. The latter would tie the operation of the public channels directly to the political process. This would be particularly inappropriate for public access, which, if it is to function as an outlet for free expression, should not be required to satisfy city council members for its existence.

The ordinance may need to be amended to adjust distribution of the franchise fee revenues periodically. Over time, the revenues may change dramatically (e.g., when the franchise fee is based on all cable system revenues and a new service is added such as alarm systems), or the costs for regulatory activity could increase (e.g., in a major rate case).

Rates

Most ordinances specify that the city must approve rate changes. Recently, the FCC has given franchising authorities the option of *not* regulating rates, however, and some cities will take that option. In a sense, the market for services can regulate the rates. The consumer will reject the service if rates are too high. Still, the monopoly prices may be higher than necessary.

In writing this section of the ordinance, provision must be made for the city to obtain sufficient financial information to make sound judgments. In the case of multiple system operators, information must be obtained on the overhead listed for the home office and other centralized services. In multiple system operations, there is a danger to the community of too much being drained off existing systems to obtain new franchises and build new systems elsewhere.

Because rate regulation is very difficult, expensive, and perhaps even hopeless, some communities permit automatic, periodic inflation adjustments in the rates. San Diego County provides an example of such a clause. It is quoted in part.

Sec. 21.1626. RATE REGULATION—COST OF LIVING PASS THROUGH. Subscriber rates for cable television services shall be set and maintained pursuant to the provisions of this section.

(a) Subject to the provisions of [paragraphs b, c, d, relating to good performance], the licensee may adjust its rates and charges not more than once in any 12-month period, as follows:

(1) If the cost of living, as defined by the Consumer Price Index for "all Items, Urban Wage Earner," for San Diego, California, has increased from the previous year, the licensee may elect to increase its service charges by sixty percent (60%) of said cost of living increase. Should the licensee elect not to take advantage of said increase, the amount of the increase to which the licensee is entitled may be carried forward to a future year; provided, however, rights to an increase for any one year shall be waived permanently if not implemented in an increase by the licensee pursuant to this within a four-year period from the date of publication of the Consumer Price Index for the quarter which is carried forward. In no event may any increase pursuant to paragraph (a), including accumulated increases, exceed fifteen percent (15%) of the rate or charge existing at the time the rate increase is being sought.

(2) If the aforesaid Consumer Price Index decreases from one year to the next, a licensee shall, if it has elected to take advantage of a Consumer Price Index increase or increases, decrease its rates and charges by sixty percent (60%) of the decrease of the Index. To the extent that a licensee has not taken advantage of past or current Consumer Price Index increases, the rights the licensee has to increase its rates through the cumulation of past or current increases in said Index shall be reduced by the decrease in the Consumer Price Index.

(3) Any licensee may petition the Commission, at any time, for an increase in rates greater than that permitted pursuant to paragraph (a)(1).[10]

A full, general discussion of the controversial automatic adjustment clause is contained in Michael Schmidt, *Automatic Adjustment Clauses: Theory and Application.*[11]

Transfer

A city could go through a painstaking process of selecting a franchisee, only to have the system sold to another party which might not meet the standards the city had set. To prevent this, the ordinance usually provides for a transfer of ownership process that is essentially identical to the original franchise award procedure except that new applicants may not be solicited. The prospective transferee must go through all steps in the evaluation process, including the appropriate public hearings.

Franchise Term

This is usually set at 10 or 15 years and is renewable for period of 5, 7 or 10 years. Franchise periods of less than 10 years are generally not acceptable to cable companies and their lending institutions. A shorter period would not be likely to attract applicants. Franchise periods of longer than 15 years constitute a commitment that most cities are unwilling to make.

Forfeiture

This section contains a listing of the sins for which a franchise may be revoked or the franchisee fined. Since revocation is a harsh penalty for minor failures, more recent ordinances have attempted to establish lesser penalties in the form of a schedule of fines.

State of the Art

Out of concern that a cable company may become obsolete before the end of the franchise term, some ordinances include a clause requiring the franchisee to maintain the system at the current state of the art. This would protect the community from being stuck with a system that is hopelessly out of date. It doubtless could not be used to require every minor advance in the technology or the complete rebuilding of a system that was state of the art when originally built, but it would demand reasonable upgrading as technical advances occur.

Free Drops

Almost all cable ordinances specify free connections and at least free *basic* service to every fire station, school, and college in the service area. The obligation may be either to bring cable to a single designated room or to wire the whole building.

Public Channels and Institutional Networks

Since public channels are no longer required by the FCC, if a community wants such channels, they should be required by the ordinance or franchise agreement. Conventionally, one or more channels are reserved for the public schools and one or more channels for community colleges and universities. There is a government channel, a public access channel, and sometimes a library channel. The new 100-channel systems may have many more. It is important for the ordinance to say who is responsible for administering each channel, especially when one is shared: two colleges on the same channel, for example, or parochial schools that are intended to benefit from the public school system channel.

Many cable systems build a separate trunk line interconnecting schools, government offices, library branches, police and fire stations, and other community institutions. As discussed in Chapter 6, this institutional network can be used for internal communication or as a means of sending information from out in the institutional network to the headend and subsequently downstream on the trunk and feeder system serving all the subscriber homes. If a community desires an institutional network, it should be written into the ordinance specifying the institutions to be served and how the network will be administered.

Interconnection

The franchising authority may wish to require interconnection of the cable system with adjacent systems. For example, an entire county may support and use a community college located within one cable system. The college may have its own channel on that system or share time on a channel. Other communities may also wish to have access to the channel. The cable systems may be interconnected to form a network to carry the community college programming. Another example is the government-sponsored channel in Columbus, Ohio, which feeds programming to four cable systems interconnected for that purpose.

Complaints

As the franchising authority, the city has a responsibility to consumers of the service. The ordinance may establish a procedure for handling complaints or unresolved disputes between the franchisee and users of the service. (Until just a few years ago, the FCC required franchising authorities to "specify procedures for the investigation and resolution of all complaints.") A cable commission may have authority to act for the city with the city council hearing only appeals. New subscribers should each receive a notice of the complaint procedures and, perhaps, be reminded of the procedures periodically with bill stuffers or some other device.

Buyback

Ordinances often reserve the right of the city to buy back the cable system at the termination of the franchise—expiration of the term, revocation, bankruptcy, or in lieu of transfer. If this is to occur, cable companies want the system to be valued at fair *market* value. Cities, in recognition of the fact that a substantial part of the market value of a cable system is in the value of the franchise itself, are reluctant to pay for what they have usually granted without fee. One solution is to refer to the purchase price as "fair and reasonable" with a provision for arbitration.

Other Provisions

Other routine items in the ordinance attempt to assure that the franchisee will meet accepted engineering standards and follow safe procedures in construction, will be prompt in connecting and disconnecting subscribers, will be properly bonded and insured, will not discriminate in the hiring of personnel and in the provision of service, and will make the services of the system available in emergencies.

REQUEST FOR PROPOSAL

Once an ordinance has been adopted, the city prepares a request for proposal (RFP). The RFP must be written carefully to itemize all interests of the city and elicit conveniently comparable responses from all applicants. The RFP describes the city for the prospective applicant, for example, square miles, street miles, number of households, household income, population and major industry. The object is to give enough information to help in the initial decision on whether or not to apply; it need not be complete, since the applicants will make detailed analyses of the community on their own.

It is desirable for the city to attract as many proposals as possible. The requirements for responding to the RFP and the specification of the system desired, therefore, should be well reasoned and not too different from what the industry provides in similar communities. This is not to discourage innovative plans in an attempt to create a unique system for the community. But, if the city demands too much, few if any applications will be received.

The size of the community is a major factor in what can be asked. A large population can generally support more capital investment and service than can a smaller population. The bigger city also has more bargaining power. This is why some suburban areas, with many adjacent small towns, have united for purposes of granting a franchise. The loss of autonomy may be acceptable if some provision is made to retain community identity on the system. This may be achieved by reserving channels for specific communities within the group and requiring a commitment to community programming for each of the geographic subunits. In joint franchising arrangements, the cities involved should agree in advance on a procedure for making a single choice. Split decisions could mean that the process would have to begin all over again with expectations scaled down.

RFPs usually require a filing fee which can be used to defray the cost of evaluating the applications. A deadline must be stated. A single source for information about the community and the franchise is given. In some cities, the response to a question by one applicant is addressed to all others. Now, after serious accusations of attempts at improper influence, conspiracy cases, and FBI investigations of the franchising process, most RFPs urge the applicants to refrain from contact with elected officials and government personnel other than the designated contact. This may even be strengthened by a provision to automatically disqualify an applicant making such contacts.

Ethics

The city of Southfield, Michigan developed a "Code of Ethics" for the CATV Committee:

> The only contact with cable companies or their representatives that will be allowed is in the research of CATV or the attendance at a bonafide cable conference or seminar which is open to the general public.

Members shall refuse any gratuities from cable companies or their representatives.

If any member shall benefit in any monetary way from any decision made by this Committee, that person should resign.

Any contact made with cable companies or their representatives shall be reported to the Chairperson. The Chairperson will discuss contact with the remainder of the CATV Committee at the next meeting.

Any member with a direct interest (i.e., stocks, bonds, partnership, etc.) in a cable company shall resign from the Committee.

Failure to disclose possible conflicts of interest will be cause for dismissal from the Committee.

If a member should discover a conflict of interest during the proceedings or if that person's vote could be affected by this conflict, that person shall abstain from voting and/or resign from the Committee.

Any member found to have violated this code shall be dismissed from the Committee.[12]

The National League of Cities has developed a "Code of Good Cable Television Franchising Conduct." It is included as Appendix E.

The RFP may also require a lump sum against future franchise fees to be paid by the successful applicant. In some cases this sum is left open ended so that the applicants can, in effect, make an offer. This practice may generate badly needed funds for the city, but it introduces an element into the evaluation that has nothing to do with the quality of the system design and service offered.

RFP Format

For comparability among applicants, a rigid format should be prescribed for the application. This forces the applicant to address the specific interests of the city. The format may be a list of expected contents or, at the other extreme, a set of standard forms to be filled out without opportunity to deviate. The latter may be a good idea since it puts all applicants on an equal footing; they can then be compared page by page.

The City of Sterling Heights, Michigan used a series of forms for the RFP. The city was quite firm in requiring adherence to the application form:

All applicants must use only the pages of the official application forms (or identical extension of these pages if, for example, more space is needed to list equipment or provide manufacturer's specifications). Alternative proposal forms are neither desired nor will they be considered. Any attempt to merely use the official forms as an "index" to voluminous "boiler-plate" may disqualify the applicant from consideration.[13]

Each of the Sterling Heights application forms is described and discussed here.

There is a temptation to ask for too much in an RFP. Unnecessary detail encumbers the evaluation process and obscures the principle criteria on which the franchise decision should be made. The Sterling Heights RFP forms are a good example. In a highly systematized way, they ask all the important questions. But the forms also provide illustration of some commonly required unnecessary details as we have noted in those sections.

"Identification of Applicant" and "Applicant's Affidavit"

These two forms simply identify the applicant and the principal to whom inquiries would be addressed, binds the applicant to the representations in the application, and gives consent to the city to make inquiries into the legal, character, technical, financial, and other qualifications of the applicant.

"Cable Communications Franchise Applicant Expense Disclosure"

This form asks the applicant to list all expenses incurred in seeking the franchise by the following categories: salaries, contracted services (consultants, attorneys, local spokespersons, lobbyists, etc.), advertising and public relations (media ads, audiovisual presentations, etc.), printing, studies and surveys, travel, and other. The form also asks the applicant, on a separate sheet, to "provide information regarding any existing contingency agreement or bonus plans relevant to the franchising process including, but not limited to, cash, property, stock or stock options."

It is difficult to see what purpose the categorical expense disclosure serves; however, the separate statement on "contingency agreements and bonus plans" indicates ownership interests related to the franchising process. This is important and will be discussed in some detail under Form A: "Ownership and Control Information."

"Cable Communications Franchise Applicant Personnel"

This is a listing of all persons ("locally and nationally based employees, attorneys, consultants, spokespersons, lobbyists, public relations counsel, local owner, etc.") who speak for the company. This informs the city of the people authorized to act for the applicant.

"Overview and Summary of Proposal"

This is in effect an abstract of the proposal to give the evaluators an overview of the application, unencumbered with the details. It may be useful for preliminary screening. The topics requested are overview of proposal, ownership and management of system, financial commitments, system design and construction (including bidirectional capability), signal carriage and channel allocations, local origination and access, rates and rate guarantees, and instructional services.

"Summary of Channel Allocations"

This is just a convenient listing of programming to be carried, channel by channel. The form asks that divisions between "tiers" be indicated clearly.

Form A: "Ownership and Control Information"

A separate form is to be filled out by all principals, officers, and directors and all individuals, corporations, partnerships, joint ventures, and unincorporated associations that have 1 percent or more of ownership.

Another part of the form requires a listing of principals, officers, corporate directors, and owners of 3 percent or more of all corporations or organizations that are listed in the first section. These two parts of the form serve the purpose of identifying all people, companies, and organizations with an interest in the applying company. These are the people who are investigated for "character" and other purposes that may be of interest to the franchising authority such as race and sex balance.

A third section of this form requests an important disclosure:

> Applicants, including all shareholders and parties with any financial interest in the applicant, must fully disclose all agreements and understandings with any person, firm, group, association or corporation with respect to the franchise and the proposed system. This includes agreements between local investors and national companies. Failure to reveal such agreements will be considered cause to withhold or revoke award of the franchise.

This part of the form addresses a problem in the franchising process referred to as "rent-a-citizen" or "rent-an-institution." Many cable companies have attempted to influence the franchise award by offering an ownership position in the company, often without significant financial investment, to prominent local citizens who would then lobby for the application. Local ownership may be highly desirable, if that ownership is active. People living in the franchise city will be more sensitive to the community needs and could exercise some control over an absentee MSO owner. But, where the ownership is silent or bought out soon after the franchise is awarded, another irrelevant element is added to the franchise decision process, and another cost is passed through to the consumer.

In Omaha, Nebraska, influential citizen-investors were solicited with this letter, quoted in part:

> Specifically [a company, that eventually became one of the six finalists] is prepared to support up to 20 percent local investment on a carried interest basis; that is, these investors are required only to subscribe for their stock at a nominal par value, with parent company advancing all necessary funds for the construction and operation of the franchise. . . .
>
> Aside from financing, however, we view the local investors as full partners, particularly with regard to developing the strategy to obtain the favorable vote of the city for award of the franchise.
>
> Finally, the winning of a cable franchise is essentially a political campaign . . . The ability of local investors to take the political temperature, make introductions and appointments on a timely basis, and to lend their personal credibility to our formal business proposal is vitally important to the success of our proposal.[14]

The successful applicant in Omaha was Cox (not the letter writer), a major multiple system operator. Cox gave a 20 percent interest in the profits of the system to a group of eight investors who put up a total of $200 of the $36,879,000 investment. Cox estimated the 20 percent interest would have a value of $12 million in ten years, "roughly, a six million percent gain" on the investment. Or, if the profits were not as hoped, the eight investors would sell out in five years for a guaranteed $1 million.[15]

Once "rent-a-citizen" became exposed, "rent-an-institution" became the vogue. This plan worked for Warner Amex in Pittsburgh and again in Cincinnati while its competitors were being embarrassed by rent-a-citizen publicity. In this case, the local equity (usually 20 percent) is given, or sold at a token sum, to community institutions or groups presumed to have political power in the community. In Pittsburgh, it was minority groups; in Cincinnati, it was educational institutions. The Fairfax County Council on the Arts accepted a 1 percent interest in the Storer cable subsidiary applying for the Fairfax County, Virginia franchise. In return, the council would advise on arts programming.[16]

These community institutions should be evaluating all the applications and advising the city in their areas of interest. But, by becoming ownership participants, they are in conflict of interest and must forego this role.

Sterling Heights warned against token local ownership in its instructions to applicants:

> The ownership structure of the applicant is a matter to be determined by the applicant, but the City strongly discourages the solicitation and/or use of local citizens or affiliations for the purpose of influencing the award of the franchise. If local participation is a component of the ownership structure of an applicant, then the City desires that such local interests have a bonafide investment in that company.

A final section of this form requires a description of the capitalization of the firm—class of stock, shares authorized, shares subscribed, and so on.

Form B: "Ownership Qualifications"

The first section of this form asks for disclosure of media cross-ownership, that is, ownership of a television network, television broadcast station, television translator, telephone company, newspaper with local circulation within the community, radio station, or cable program service. The first of these is unnecessary, since television networks cannot own cable systems. (CBS has successfully petitioned the FCC for waiver of the rule in one instance.) The others are important to the franchising authority if there is a concern for conglomerated media power within the community or potential anticompetitive practices. Ownership of cable program services might help to explain the particular line-up of program services proposed and suggest future influences on program choices.

The remainder of the form asks citizenship information, past and present ownership by elected officials of Sterling Heights, and details of any pre-RFP communication with council members.

Form C: "Character Qualifications"

This form asks for details of any criminal conviction for fraud, embezzlement, tax evasion, bribery, extortion, jury tampering, obstruction of justice, false and misleading advertising, perjury, antitrust violations, violations of FCC regulations, and conspiracy to commit any of the foregoing. The applicant is also asked about civil proceedings for which it was held liable—unfair or anticompetitive business practices, violations of securities laws, false and misleading advertising, and violations of FCC regulations. There is a question about whether a business license had ever been revoked. The form also asks details about any violation of a cable franchise agreement and whether or not the company has ever initiated litigation against a franchising authority.

The Sterling Heights form leaves out violations of fair employment practices and the National Labor Relations Board Code. These might be important questions for some cities. Violations of state and federal civil rights laws should also be considered.

Form D: "Experience—Current Cable Holdings"

This form asks for a listing of each franchise or system owned and a few details about each: date of acquisition, plant miles, date first subscribers served, date construction completed, current subscriber rate, date rate approved, and name and address of local government officials responsible for cable operations. (The form probably should break subscriber rates into the various tiers of service.)

Although the form would run to hundreds of pages for big MSOs, it provides useful information. The franchising authority could investigate the company's comparable systems, choosing those systems *on its own* rather than looking at a showcase system selected by the applicant. The city is perhaps more interested in comparable systems operated by the applicant (in terms of recency of franchising and size of city). A look at the rates charged elsewhere by the applicant is perhaps a better indication of the company's rate structure than are the initial rates proposed for the new franchise. The time between the date of franchise award and the date construction was completed could also be important. Some companies are slower than others in building cable systems. Their management or capital may be spread too thinly, they may have difficulty with contractors, they may not have a good relationship with suppliers, and so on. Whatever the reason, these data would be a clue to potential problems.

Form E: "Former Franchises"

Here the applicant is required to list any formerly held franchises and indicate the reason and manner of disposition. These dispositions may tell something about the company. The franchising authority may choose to make an independent inquiry about the performance of the applicant in these locations.

Form F: "Financial Resources, Existing Capital Commitments, and Potential Building Commitments"

This form makes inquiry about source and terms of financing, in substantial detail, and requires documentation of financial viability for constructing and operating the Sterling Heights cable system. This would include letters of commitment from financial institutions, uncommited lines of credit, cash, and so on. The rest of the form is devoted to building commitments for new plant, commitments to rebuild in old plants, and the capital costs involved in each. This would be reported for every community including Sterling Heights.

The capital structure of the applicant is not too important to the franchising authority. In the present economic climate for the cable industry, any company holding a franchise will be able to find adequate funding if the company management is capable. Whether or not the company has large cash reserves is of little importance. If the cash is invested in a new cable system, it is at the sacrifice of the interest it is earning, which is about identical to the rate that would be paid by another company that is funded by outside lenders. In other words, the money costs each company about the same. In one case, it is a real cost; in the other, it is an opportunity cost.

The building commitments are more important, but the franchising authority must go *beyond* the listing of commitments and costs to learn anything of value. A company with only a few commitments may be overcommitted compared with a company with many commitments, depending on the company's management and engineering staff, commitments from suppliers, contracts with construction companies, and so forth. The information derived from the form is useful only as a basis for these further questions that must be pursued through other channels, perhaps at a public hearing or through investigation of construction programs in other cities.

Form G: "Financial Pro Forma"

Because a pro forma statement is conventionally required by RFPs, we describe it in detail. It asks for anticipated growth year by year over a 15-year period in the following categories: households in franchise area, average basic subscribers, average second-set subscribers, average pay cable subscribers, and percentage penetration of homes passed for basic and pay subscribers. A second part of the form asks, for the same years, the anticipated revenue per subscriber and the annual total for basic, second-set, pay, installation, and other services.

Another page of the form requests a narrative description of how the figures are obtained. This is followed by an income statement, projected for each of the 15 years, with these column headings: revenue, less operating expenses, equals operating income, less interest, less depreciation, equals pretax income, less income taxes, equals net income, plus depreciation, equals cash flow. The next section of the form requires a narrative statement of the applicant's financial goals and asks how income taxes are computed.

Another page reports a projection of sources and uses of funds each year for 15 years. The sources of funds include beginning cash balance, equity funds, loans, revenue, and total sources. Uses of funds include capital expenditures, operating expenses, interest payments, income taxes, loan repayment, dividends, and total.

The next part details annual loan information year by year with the average loan balance and average interest rates for the year. A form on anticipated capital expenditures, for each of the 15 years, asks expenditures for antenna(s) and towers, microwave, headend, earth station, aerial distribution, underground distribution, pole arrangement, institutional network, drops, converters, buildings, leasehold improvements, land, studios, mobile vans, origination equipment, test equipment and spare parts, vehicles, preoperating, engineering, pay-cable-related equipment, capitalized overhead and equipment, other, and total. Next is an itemization of construction costs, separated by aerial and underground: distribution cost per mile—make-ready, engineering, labor, hardware and strand, cable, electronics, other, and total cost per mile; cost per drop—drop material, labor, converter, and total cost per drop. Then depreciation for each of the capital items is listed for the 15 years. On a separate form, depreciation is justified by indicating the depreciation life of each item in years.

The next page of the pro forma is the itemization of the payroll for years 3, 5, and 10. Salaries are listed under plant, origination, and general and administrative personnel. A projection of expenses for years 3, 5, and 10 is asked, for several categories of expenses, under each of these main headings: plant, origination expenses, and general, selling, and administrative expenses.

For cable companies with more than one system, a special form itemizes services purchased from the parent organization, again by year for 15 years, under these column headings: management services, legal, accounting, customer billing, programming, other, and total.

The final page in the pro forma is a summary of expenses under several categories for each of the years. These are simply totals from other parts of the form.

To repeat, we have described these financial pro forma statements in detail because cities usually ask for the information. We do not believe that the figures have much meaning, nor are they important in discriminating among applicants. Fifteen-year projections of penetration and revenues from new and developing services are not reliable. Financial goals, especially rate of return, will be stated very conservatively so that they do not strike the evaluators as extravagant. As a matter of fact, in most applications the rate of return on investment is listed at below the rate of interest that would be earned in the current money market, which leads one to question why the company makes this more difficult investment. Actually cable systems are most concerned about growth in the market value of the system or growth in the price of its stock as a result of increase in the value of its assets and discounted potential of the company. Whatever the case, cable franchise applicants are not going to disclose their real goals.

We believe that the pro forma should include a statement of expected capital investment and operating expenses for the year in which the system is completed, along with expected revenues. The principal purpose of these figures would be to evaluate the rates to be charged. Low service charges might be attractive, but would not mean much in the long run if based on unrealistic estimates of costs and revenues.

The 15-year projection of the cost of services purchased from the parent organization (MSO) is important. Applicants can be compared on these costs. Only reasonable sums should be taken out of the community for the parent company. These should be in line with the actual value of services provided. The figures can be retained for use in subsequent rate hearings. An established company should not make substantial changes in the proportion of expenses attributed to the parent company. Harold Horn, president of the consulting firm Cable Television Information Center, told the 1980 National Cable Television Association convention:

> It is ironic, and not going unnoticed by local officials in existing cabled cities, that MSOs that built their cities are taking their profits . . . and using them to build or at least promise to build super-duper systems in other major cities in another part of the country. . . . Why haven't you chosen one of these financially viable high-subscriber existing systems to try out your promises on before taking on the unknown risks of a major city?[17]

Within the industry these "financially viable high-subscriber existing systems" are sometimes called "cash cows."

Form H: "Initial Service Area and Line Extensions"

If the city does not actually prescribe the initial service area, it is very interested in the information provided in this form. In a community of varied housing density, the city probably should *not* specify the initial service area since cable company policies vary and a fairly detailed survey of the community is necessary before decisions can be made. An applicant who proposes to build initially the smallest proportion of the city, or leaves out certain sections of the city (e.g., low-income areas) would raise questions. If there are some areas of the city which cannot be constructed economically at the time of the franchise grant, then the *line extension policy* determines when those areas would be constructed, as the housing density increases. A liberal line extension policy benefits new housing areas but disadvantages other subscribers who will have to subsidize it.

The form asks for a map indicating the initial service area, the line extension policy, and the rationale for the policy. It also asks if there are cost-sharing or other arrangements that can be made for subscribers who do not qualify for service under the general policy. It requires specification of the construction schedule by census tract and by plant mileage, aerial and underground, year by year. The form also asks if construction will be done by a contractor and, if so, the identity of the contractor. The availability of work crews and the arrangements with contractors are to be disclosed along with safety standards and reliability.

The construction schedule is, of course, necessary to monitor progress once the franchise is awarded. It is only important as a means of discriminating among applicants if the time to complete the construction is open ended.

Form I: "Channel Capacity and System Design"

For Sterling Heights, this was a multifaceted, 32-page form. It asks for mileage of plant in the subscriber network and the institutional network and a brief verbal description of the type of layout. Another item asks for manufacturer and type and model number for the major equipment under each of three categories: cable, active electronics, and passive electronics.

The form inquires whether or not converters will be provided to all subscribers and, if not, under what conditions they will be made available. The plans to operate or contract for transmission services must be detailed under common carrier, cable television relay service (CARS), multipoint distribution service (MDS), and "other." The applicant is asked to describe satellite earth station equipment contemplated and the headend design. It asks whether or when a home security service will be available and what equipment will be used. There is a question about whether a *status monitoring* system will be employed and, if so, to describe it. A status monitoring system is an electronic system which receives continuous signals from all points in the system to locate trouble spots.

Other parts of the form request descriptions of the emergency alert system, standby power at the headend, hubs and satellite terminal, the equipment used to program automated channels, and kind of interconnection between headend and hubs and with other cable systems.

The form asks channel capacity for upstream and downstream channels in the subscriber and institutional networks and a justification of the capacity in terms of the plans. Where upstream capacity is not to be activated immediately, the applicant is to indicate when and in which parts of the system the upstream capacity will be activated. The applicant must declare which institutions the institutional network will serve, which will be actually connected (as opposed to passed), and the policies on provision of terminal equipment. At this point, the applicant is to describe the anticipated use of the institutional network. (It would seem that this should appear elsewhere. Form I is technical. This is the only item within the form that would be reviewed by nontechnical people.)

Then the applicant is asked about technical standards, the amplifier cascade, technical performance test procedures, and the equipment to be used in performance tests. There is another section on preventive maintenance and the technical staff and service facility. The applicant is asked how technical complaints are handled.

Finally, the form requests a system map and a headend block diagram.

All these items seem to be of major importance. The section of this chapter on evaluation will provide more detail.

Form J: "Proposed Signal Carriage and Channel Allocations"

Form J identifies the services on each channel, separated by tiers, if multiple tiers are offered. The first page lists local broadcast television channels carried full time by network affiliation, city, call letters, broadcast channel, cable channel, and proposed activation date. The following page provides the same information for *imported* television broadcast signals carried full-time. This information is also asked for television broadcast stations carried part-time.

Another page of the form asks the following information about automated programming: service, source, cable channel, hours per day, and proposed activation date. The same information is requested for nonautomated programming, excluding pay cable, received by satellite (on one page), and system-originated programming (on another page). Still under the nonbroadcast category, the designated access channels are identified by type, cable channel, hours per day available, and the proposed activation date. Similar information is required for pay cable service, reported separately for per-channel services and per-program service. All the television services are repeated on a summary form.

The remaining pages in the signal carriage form require listings of audio services: broadcast radio stations (AM, FM, shortwave, and other frequencies) and nonbroadcast audio services.

Form K: "Local Programming"

The proposed local programming section begins with a detailing of local program production equipment and facilities. The first form indicates location and size of the local origination studio followed by the local origination equipment list with approximate itemized cost. This is reported separately for company origination and access channels with notations where facilities and equipment are to be shared (with indication of which service has priority of access).

The operating budget for local origination and access is estimated for the first, third, fifth, and tenth years and the full- and part-time staff for local origination and access for the same years. The form asks "How many part-time positions equal one full person year?" so that the numbers of the part-timers can be evaluated properly.

The form asks the number of original (not repeated) hours of programming to be produced locally by the operator and, separately, programming obtained from other sources. The percentage of the operating budget devoted to assistance for access users is requested. The local programming philosophy and objectives must be discussed along with the names of local organizations and individuals contacted to assess needs.

A complete set of rules and procedures for operation of public, educational, government, and leased access channels must be presented, including availability of channels to various users; availability of equipment and rules governing use of equipment; scheduling procedures for reserving equipment and channel time; any rates to be charged, including deposits; copies of contract forms and application forms; and availability of production assistance.

Form L: "Proposed Rates"

This form lists the proposed rate schedule for basic subscribers, commercial rates, multiple dwellings, and separate tiers, with installation fee and monthly service rate for each service. The applicant is asked if any guarantee of the rates (for a particular period of time) is offered. If a deposit is required from the subscriber for a converter, the amount and terms must be stated. The rates for pay cable are listed separately with plans and charges for channel lockout devices, if any.

The form also asks studio and equipment usage rates for commercial and noncommercial users, installation fees and monthly rates to educational and governmental facilities, and a description of advertising policies.

Form M: "Employment Practices"

Applicants are requested to "familiarize themselves with all federal, state and local laws pertaining to discrimination, equal opportunity employment programs, and affirmative action programs" and then present plans to comply with the regulations.

Once the RFP has been prepared, it should be circulated with a copy of the ordinance and a statement of community needs (if one has been prepared). The package might also include promotional and market information about the city. The package should go to all cable firms that have made inquiries. Announcements of the availability of the franchise should be made through publicity and classified advertisements. Trade periodicals used commonly are *Cablevision, TVC, Multichannel News,* and *Broadcasting.* A direct-mail announcement to cable MSOs and companies serving the immediate region would also be useful. The deadline should be set at least three months from the date of the announcement so that interested parties have adequate time to prepare.

In the interest of fairness and an orderly selection process, applicants should not be permitted to amend the applications after the deadline. Some cities have opened the applications and, once they are public, have allowed amendments, thus encouraging applicants to make more competitive bids in the knowledge of other submissions. This delays the procedure and raises ethical questions. The original application should represent the best judgment of each applicant on the system design and services most appropriate to the community.

EVALUATION AND SELECTION

In this section we discuss the general process of evaluation and the use of consultants now playing an increasingly important role in franchising. The evaluation is complex and technical.

It should be said at this point that *too much* can be made of the franchisee selection. Most, if not all, of the applicants will be reputable multiple system operators. Each has access to the most advanced technology. Each will propose essentially the same services. In fact, in terms of the entertainment services, for which there is the greatest level of awareness and highest demand among consumers, the applicants may not differ at all. They will differ subtly on the engineering design, management capability, and the nonentertainment services proposed. It is, therefore, these subtleties that must be detected and evaluated. Furthermore, although one applicant may be as good as another, the city has an obligation to the applicants, who have at this point made a major investment in the application, to be careful and objective in the analysis. The city wants to protect itself from litigation which will prolong completion of the system. Some cities are very systematic in the evaluation process, establishing elaborate point systems for review of applications. If the city assigns more importance to some criteria than to others, the point system can reflect the weights.

The evaluation may be done in stages. Phase 1 might be the preliminary screening to make sure that applications are complete and in compliance with the instructions. The remaining applicants would be reviewed on the criteria most important to the community. All the applicants having met minimal standards on those criteria might then be subjected to a thorough scrutiny in all areas.

Engineering Design

As we have stated, the engineering of a system is quite permanent. Cable systems are built to last at least 15 years without major design modification. The system must be designed to accommodate advances in technology and expansion in services (see Chapters 2–5). The design of the system must also conform to the social and geographic subdivisions of the city. In other words, the hubs of the system, which may be programmed separately, should fit the principal neighborhoods. The two-way cable design should be studied. Cable companies do vary in this area. Experience with two-way engineering and operation should also be a factor in the evaluation. The system that has a status monitoring feature may be able to prevent malfunctions more effectively and, when they occur, isolate the problem more quickly. The application should also indicate the quality of the equipment proposed.

Service

The other most important area for evaluation is the service proposed. Entertainment services will be very much alike but perhaps packaged differently. Does the consumer have all the options available, or is there a structuring of the entertainment package that appears to favor program suppliers in which the applicant has a financial interest?

An important part of the service evaluation is an assessment of the manner in which services are packaged. Are the tiers of service structured in a logical manner so that consumers can get what they want at the least cost? For example, is an automated shopping guide service, which gives the lowest weekly marketbasket prices, a service that might be highly desirable at the basic subscription level to low-income subscribers, placed out of reach in another tier? Does another applicant put the shopping basket service in the basic subscription price, even though that price is slightly higher? Which makes best sense for the consumer? These are typical of the questions that should arise about the packaging of service. The city must look at the rationale presented for the tiering of services, and the pricing scheme, to make the judgment.

The institutional network service is important. Does the application reflect the city's statement of needs and/or an independent study of community communication needs? Since the institutional network is a novel service in the community, is the system structured and staffed to facilitate its use? Are the institutions with the greatest interest connected or passed?

Access channels—government, educational, and public—are likely to be proposed. Is the cable company staffed to provide assistance to users? Do the rules governing use seem reasonable and designed to encourage maximum use? Are there service and production charges? Do the rules governing public access encourage all elements of the population assuring the greatest degree of freedom of expression? Do the channels provided meet the needs of the community as stated in the RFP or determined by the applicant?

The commitment to community programming should also be studied. Crucial is whether or not the company plans to staff specific programs fully or to rely on some volunteers. If the volunteers do not materialize or if the interest of volunteers flags, does the program remain? One of the most important kinds of community programming, in our judgment, is local news. This serves a community or neighborhood that is likely to be buried in the broadcast television news aimed at a much larger metropolitan area. Is local news proposed? Is it designed to serve the distinct neighborhoods of the community? Is the news staffed by full-time professionals from within the cable company or outside (e.g., the local newspaper)? How specific are community program plans?

Not enough, or not the right kind of local programming, is one problem. Too much local progamming is also possible. Recent proposals commit 20 or 30 percent of operating expenses to local programming. This would mean that roughly 10 to 15 percent of the subscriber fee is devoted to local programming. Will consumers value the programming that highly?

It is difficult to state how two-way services should be evaluated. The applicant should probably propose experiments, at least, in alarm systems. The evaluators might also look for tests of interactive electronic text. In the evaluation, a distinction should be made between two-way capability and operational two-way systems. "Two-way capability" is likely to mean that the amplifier housings are built to accommodate return amplifiers. The headend and the home terminals may not have the equipment for two-way communication. An operational two-way system may have return amplifiers in place with some two-way equipment in homes and community institutions and at the cable headend. The system would have to be "deingressed" to reduce electronic noise. The evaluators need to know how much of the distribution and feeder system is to be served by the two-way system and, if not the entire system, under what conditions the system would be completed. A more thorough discussion of the activation of two-way systems appears under the heading "Monitoring System Performance and Development" in this chapter.

A *flexible* plan of service that lets the system evolve in directions where there is the most need and the greatest community interest may be most effective, as opposed to an entirely preplanned and inflexible system.

Proposed Rates and Guarantees

Obviously the franchise authority wants to get the most service for the least money for city institutions and consumers. This will not be an easy quantitative comparison, however. The services offered at each price will not be directly comparable. As suggested earlier, the tiers of service should be analyzed to determine the optimum package and price. For two-way services, the price should be within reach of the greatest number of potential users. Impressive, elaborate services that are out of reach for the average consumer are not very meaningful.

The rates charged to consumers will subsidize all the free services, whether or not this is made plain in the application. Therefore, the number of free drops, the extent of the institutional channels, the amount of community programming, the number of access channels, and so on, come as part of the price to the consumer. Does the community want these services and is the price paid by the consumer a fair subsidy? Or is it better for the community to accept less institutional service for a lower price to consumers?

Guarantees of rates should not be used as a means of discriminating among applicants. Cities should probably ask for a one- or two-year guarantee from all applicants. If none is asked, then the lowest initial rates must be the major consideration, not the projected rates over a long-term period as these are not commitments.

Experience and Ownership

If applicants operate multiple systems, visits or phone inquiries should be made to several cities to determine the quality of service and management provided by the company. There seem to be major differences in MSOs in management quality. A judgment of management capability is, therefore, a principal function of the city in making the evaluation. As suggested earlier, the city should make the selection of sites to be studied rather than leave the choice to the applicants who would, of course, identify one or two showcase systems where the relations with the city and consumers have been most favorable. More than one system should be selected for each multiple system applicant to avoid a chance bias. The information provided by the investigation of other systems, for MSO applicants, is added to the information provided in the application for making the evaluation.

The character of the owner is disclosed by the information gathered in the application and through independent investigation about criminal convictions and civil liabilities of the applicant, company and personnel. Cable and communication law cases may be weighted most heavily (e.g., false and misleading advertising, violation of a cable franchise agreement).

The franchising authority should use the ownership information provided in the application to know who the applicant really is. The applicant may be a huge MSO, a local independent company, a national media conglomerate, a major regional media owner, or a cross-owner of local media (e.g., local newspaper cable applicant). All these characteristics may be evaluated negatively or positively by the franchise authority, depending on philosophy and the other applicants. A big MSO may have experience and home office services of value to the local franchise; it may also take money out of the community to build its next franchise. The local independent company may be more accessible and responsible to the community but will lack the resources of a bigger concern. A national media conglomerate brings important resources to the franchise even though it is bound to be an absentee owner. A regional media owner may have great strength in its nearby operations to benefit the system but could be too strong a regional monopoly for some evaluators. The same could be said for the local cross-ownership situation. More will be said about these matters in Chapter 12, on cable industry ownership patterns.

Construction Schedule

This should be a factor in the evaluation if the ordinance or RFP does not state that the system is to be built within a specified time after the franchise agreement. The ability of the company to maintain its commitment should be considered, although this is difficult. The company may be affected by parts and construction personnel shortages now plaguing the industry. We have suggested earlier some of the information to be asked in the RFP that might help to make this evaluation. Perhaps the most useful for the evaluation of MSO applicants would be to make inquiries about the status of the construction schedule in systems now under construction or just recently completed. Much depends on the size and commitment of the engineering staff and the relationship with the major equipment suppliers.

Other Factors

There will probably be key members of the city government with an interest in employment practices related to women, minorities, and unionization. The applicants should be expected to present a well-designed affirmative action policy or statement of personnel policies. The best indication of the company's performance in this area, however, is not plans but previous record. The annual Equal Employment Opportunity forms are available for review at the FCC and in each cable system's public file (see Chapter 10). Some communities may also want to look at the labor practices of the applicants.

Applicants could also differ on automated services offered. Some of the automated services may be put in additional tiers instead of in the basic service. Therefore, it is important that applicants be compared on automated services offered and the costs of the services.

Comportment of the applicants during the franchising process must be considered. In fairness, behavior that will be considered "improper" should be identified in the RFP or other documents. In Sterling Heights, Michigan, one individual was designated as the contact. Contact with any other was considered improper. The Southfield, Michigan Code of Ethics, presented earlier, or the National League of Cities Code, would provide excellent guidelines for applicants and cities. If applicants are duly informed of the expected conduct, then a breach of conduct should be disqualifying.

Weighing the Elements

Franchise authorities may labor over some information provided by applicants that is relatively unimportant. If these elements of the application are weighed equally with engineering design and services, which we consider to be most important, then the evaluation is distorted. It is critical that the most important criteria in the evaluation emerge strongly. If the franchising authority has not made clear how the various elements of the application have been weighted, or if each is weighted equally, then it becomes the burden of the cable applicants to attempt to place emphasis on the most significant areas. But, for the city's point of view, this is not the ideal time to be deciding what is important. It then becomes a post hoc decision and is dependent on strength of the persuasion of the applicants under conditions which might not be fair.

David Korte, a consultant to cities on franchising warns the evaluators to ignore vague promises cued by phrases like "when there is sufficient public demand," "when economically feasible," or simply "may" as a preface to a promise. He says "a particular applicant should not be favored simply because it offered the longest laundry list of possible future services."[18]

We emphasize again that long-term pro forma statements are not significant discriminators. These are entirely hypothetical figures. They are based on projections for a dynamic industry which does not know, at this point, how to estimate revenues and expenses for various entertainment packages, not to mention the presently experimental two-way services. One cable company staffer says, "this whole pro forma business is a lot of flim-flam, anyway, since nobody knows what these systems are going to do and what people will buy."[19] The figures will reflect what the applicant believes to be impressive to the business-naïve evaluator and politically acceptable to all. The figures will not be anything like the solid pro forma statements presented to the bank. The projections of cable applicants may differ significantly, only because they take relatively conservative or liberal approaches. In reality, the capital investment, expenses, and the revenues will be about the same for each applicant. The need for return on investment will be essentially the same for each company. The city is not going to "luck onto" a cable applicant that, through errors in calculation, is giving away the service.

Information on the capital structure of the company is not too important. The cost of money is essentially the same for every company, whether the cost is a direct cost or an opportunity cost (foregone interest on alternative investments). The decision on a franchise should not come down to details of finance as it did in Fairfield, Connecticut. There, the hearing examiner reported, "The financial provisions of UA-Columbia were not as firm as those of Fairfield County Cable Communication (Storer)."[20] It is unfortunate to have to make this kind of distinction between two such solidly financed companies.

The franchising authority should be assured that the applicants have good credit records and available lines of credit if needed. However, the franchise in hand may be sufficient for any reputable organization to get funds necessary to build a well-planned system.

Some cities in financial difficulty have asked for, or accepted, cash advances on franchise fees as high as $4 million.[21] This amounts to an interest-free loan. If a specified amount of this "up-front money" is not asked, then applicants make offers. The size of the offer may then influence the decision on the franchise instead of issues of longer-term significance. If the amount of front money is specified, then at least each applicant comes in equal in that respect. Whatever the case, the money is likely to go into some immediate city need, lost forever to applications of the funds that might benefit the public interest development of the cable system and the subscriber who will eventually pay.

Once the finalists have been chosen, it is customary to have a public hearing in which the applicants can make an oral presentation and respond to questions. It is useful if the preliminary evaluation, described earlier, has already been made so that the principal participants in the evaluation process are well prepared to assimilate the new information and ask relevant questions. This is a good opportunity for the cable company applicants to supplement their restricted initial proposal and attempt to ascertain the perceived response to the application. The kinds of questions asked should give a fairly clear picture. The people in the city who must make the final decision on the franchise must use the hearing to get some feelings for community reaction to the applicants and a sense of what seems to be of major interest. The public reaction at the hearing must not be overvalued, however, since such a hearing rarely draws many people.

CONSULTANTS

Because there are so many applicants and because the applications are so voluminous and technical, most cities hire consultants to help with the evaluation. There are now about five consulting organizations that do the bulk of the work: Cable Television Information Center, Washington, D.C.; Telecommunications Management Corporation (Carl Pilnick), Los Angeles; Malarkey, Taylor, Washington, D.C.; Kalba Bowen, Cambridge, Massachusetts; Michael Botein, New York. The point at which to engage the consultant is perhaps the first issue. The consultant can help to write the ordinance, prepare the RFP, and make the preliminary evaluation (leaving the final judgment to the client). Consultants like to be on board at the time the RFP is written because it provides the information they must work with during the evaluation. There are cases where consultants have refused to step in at the evaluation stage because the information solicited from applicants was not obtained systematically and is difficult to compare.

We see three major contributions of consultants. First, if they have a good engineering resource, they are able to make assessments of the system design. This is probably outside the capability of most city staff and other local persons. Second, the consulting organization is up to date on the services being offered in other cities. In other words, the consultant will know about what should be expected for the city. Finally, and perhaps most important, consultants will recognize applicant innovations and subtle differences between applicants. As we have said, applications and applicants will be quite similar. It will be the subtleties that distinguish among them.

There is some merit in a city not officially disclosing the consulting firm until after the application deadline. (This is impossible if the consultant advises on the RFP since it would be immediately recognizable to most applicants.) MSOs keep a "book" on each consultant. In fact, there is even a consultant to cable companies who makes a business of providing systematic analyses, "profiles," of the consultants. The result of knowing the consultant in advance is a proposal that is tailored more to the consultant than to the city. The city is likely to get more honest and innovative proposals if it does not name the consultant early.

Cable companies sometimes get trapped by catering to the consultants. In several cities, for instance, Cable Television Information Center (CTIC), the largest-volume consultant, did not comment on several applications for different cities proposing *universal service*—certain channels available free to all homes passed. So, in an effort to be competitive, some applicants in Dallas, where CTIC was the consultant, included universal service, only to be criticized with the suggestion that such a costly service might force up prices for the paying subscribers.[22]

These are evidences of the power of the consultants. It is a power, no doubt, that the consultants do not want. They would prefer clear statements of the community's preferences and needs as well as more independent behavior by the applicants. But, as a practical matter, this is not to be. Too little is known at the outset by most franchising authorities, and too much is at stake for the cable companies.

It is important that the consultants be paid enough to do a thorough job. The cable industry generally believes that consultants are spread too thinly and are underfunded for adequate analysis. A vice president of one MSO says, "The cities get what they pay for. The consulting reports today are quick and dirty."[23] The city should probably ask for intensive analysis *in the areas of major interest* and be prepared to pay for it. The consultant fee can be built into the application charge and should be worth it, in the long run, to the consumer who will subsequently pay.

After all the evaluations have been made—the reports from consultants, reviews by citizens, advisories by commissions—the city council must make a choice. The next step is to negotiate a franchise agreement with the successful applicant.

FRANCHISE AGREEMENT

The franchise agreement sets the terms of the franchise; it is, in effect, a contract between the city and cable company. All the details of the application should be written into the franchise agreement including the engineering design, programming and other services, initial rates, access channel rules, description of local production facilities, location of public access studios, job description of access coordinator, construction schedule, line extension policy, and specification of periodic reports to the city.

Because the franchise agreement, along with the ordinance, will be the principal documents against which the performance of the cable company will be judged, the specifications for the cable plant and the description of services must be stated in the franchise agreement so that both parties have a mutual understanding of the meaning. Where the application is unclear, or there is insufficient detail, the clarification should be provided in the translation to the franchise agreement. The initiation date for community programs and services should be stated so that both parties know when the obligation is to be in effect. It may not be practical for *all* programs and services to be ready at the date of completion of construction and testing. Some may be projected for later dates. On the other hand, certain programming and services should be ready at the time the first section of the system is turned on.

The nature of two-way cable communication is now clear enough so that some guidelines may be suggested for franchising authorities and cable companies anticipating a two-way system.[24]

If it is the intent to write a two-way communication requirement into a franchise agreement, the nature of the two-way communication technology demands that the communication service or services to be provided be specified carefully. Each type of service makes unique demands on the character and technical capacity of the system—at the home terminal, in the distribution plant equipment, and at the headend. (To the extent that the household terminal and the headend equipment can be made modular, new services may be added to those specified with minimum cost.)

At this point it is useful to discuss the categories of service that might be provided by a two-way system. Some services may be wholly the province of private enterprise such as per-view pay programs for entertainment. Services such as training firefighters and other civil employees are associated with government and are of predominant concern to public health, safety, and welfare. Services such as fire, burglar, and medical alarms represent consumer *and* public benefits. The distinctions might be made according to the following scheme.

Consumer services would be defined as entertainment, education, alarms, and so on that are consumed directly by individuals. *Institutional services* are those that are used by private institutions (e.g., interbranch communication by banks and department stores) and by government (e.g., internal communication and training in public safety departments).

These definitions require further refinement in terms of the source of support. Are the services associated primarily with the public or private sector? Where two-way services are associated primarily with the private sector, as is the case with per-view pay entertainment, advertising and electronic games, they may be defined as *consumer-private two-way services*. Where associated with private sector institutions, such as business data transfers, they may be defined as *institutional-private two-way services*.

Services that are supported principally by government may also be divided into consumer and institutional categories. *Consumer-public two-way services* may be defined as those used by the public but involving the government. These might include fire alarms, education, electronic mail, and public recreation. *Institutional-public two-way services* would include those services used internally by the government such as firefighter training or civil service education.

	Private	*Public*
Consumer	Electronic games, etc.	Alarm systems, etc.
Institutional	Data transfer between bank branches, etc.	Firefighter training, etc.

If a franchise authority wished to develop particular two-way services, specification of such services could enter the agreement with the franchisee in at least two ways. One way would be the simple requirement that such a service be available on completion of the construction schedule (or as the system is turned on after each stage of construction). Such a franchise clause would seem to be appropriate for consumer- or institutional-private services, where the service specified has been tested operationally and where market experience or projections would assure sufficient revenues to keep the two-way service from becoming a burden to the system or its subscribers.

If a two-way system were required exclusively for government services (institutional-public), the capital cost of the two-way system also could be viewed as socially desirable for the community and treated as a cost of acquiring the privileges in a franchise or as a direct cost to the government. In either case, the potential public benefit of the service would still be weighed against the costs, wherever assessed, in determining whether to include the service in the franchise.

The consumer-public category of two-way service presents special problems. In alarm communication, for example, the general public welfare is enhanced and the cost of government service reduced if alarm communication is available through two-way cable. At the same time, the consumer realizes personal benefits. If the alarm communication service is mandated by the government, the franchise or ordinance must contain the two-way provision so that cable is one of the options. If the desire is only to make the service available to those citizens who wish it, then the questions of marketability, cost, and general public benefit all weigh in the decision to require a particular two-way system.

If investigation by the franchising authority indicates a consumer benefit, greater public welfare, and/or increased government efficiency, writing a two-way service clause into the franchise would be appropriate. On the other hand, in the absence of strong evidence of the benefits of a service, the franchise could stipulate a field test. This would provide an opportunity for both the operator and the franchising authority to evaluate the benefit of the service without the high cost of completing a particular two-way system configuration. Although many of the head-end costs for a two-way system are fixed, distribution plants in many systems have been built to accommodate a two-way retrofit. The necessary switching hardware and amplifiers within the distribution plant can be added after construction. Thus, a field test would require modification of only a part of the cable system.

Although a minimum-cost field test could not provide a random sample of households or geographically dispersed institutional sites, the test area could be designed to provide an economically feasible representation of a potential universe of users. Such a field test was written into the Syracuse, New York franchise.[25]

The Syracuse franchise appears to leave the decision to extend the service to the entire franchise territory to the franchising authority, although the franchisee will certainly provide a major input to the evaluation process.[26] To be most cautious, an arbitration arrangement could be specified to resolve differences in interpretation of field test results.

MONITORING SYSTEM PERFORMANCE AND DEVELOPMENT

Once the franchise agreement has been signed, the cable company and the franchising authority are partners. They share responsibility for, and interest in, the consumer welfare. If the access channels and institutional services are to work, the cable company must be enthusiastic and supportive and the city institutions imaginative and effective in the development. For the company, there is a disincentive to develop most of the institutional side. Many of the services are to be provided as a tax for the franchise privilege and are not directly revenue producing. The city and the users of these services must take the leadership in *development*. This is the major positive role of the franchising authority, and we deal with it first. The second major function is *regulatory*: to monitor the performance of the franchisee against the franchise agreement and ordinance.

Development Role

The city wastes the resources it has bargained for in the franchising process if it does not aggressively pursue the use of government and education access channels and the institutional network.

A local government will have to assume some special burdens as it takes up the issue of cable development. As well as determining the kind of specific services it requires, the community may find it in the public interest to encourage development of community communication services on access and institutional network channels that require advanced technology, a function similar to the FCC responsibility to "study new uses for radio [telecommunications], provide for experimental uses for frequencies and generally encourage the larger and more effective use of radio [telecommunication] in the public interest."[27] A continuous assessment of communication needs is useful for these purposes.

Perhaps the best approach is to identify quickly the agencies that have the greatest interest in using cable and get them started as models. These groups will have emerged in needs assessment by the city or cable applicants or in other ways during the franchising. If the fire department has expressed a strong interest in training by cable, the department of social services wants to prepare and evaluate foster parents by cable, and the director of the science resource center in the public schools sees merit in teleconferencing between the center and user schools, then these services should be encouraged and perhaps funded from franchise fee revenues. These services become models for other uses if they are communicated through demonstrations, newsletters, and meetings.

A city employee responsible for coordination of cable uses along with a coordinator for the cable company can initially play a promotional role to initiate service. This later becomes more a consulting and administrative function as uses develop. The enthusiasm and energy of these individuals in the initial promotional role is probably as important as knowledge.

A major issue that will face most older cable companies and their franchising authorities in the next few years is the development of two-way cable.

If a franchise authority is reluctant to impose even an experimental field test on a cable franchisee, as discussed in the previous section on franchise agreements, it might treat two-way cable under a "state of the art" clause in the ordinance. Criteria by which state of the art technology and service are judged may be hard to come by; however, the burden of establishing two-way cable technology as the state of the art has been eased somewhat by the 1972 FCC rules requirement that systems have two-way capacity and the consequent manufacturers' modular design of amplifers. This FCC rule, although now defunct, suggested that two-way service is important and imminent enough to warrant system design to accommodate it. Practical demonstrations of a two-way service in other systems should provide impetus for suggesting the activation of the existing capability.

It is possible to set forth conditions which would lead to implementation of two-way service. The aggregation of a particular number of users for various types of two-way service would be an important condition. In aggregating users, the franchising authority may play a developmental role. This role could be particularly important for government because operators may not, on their own initiative, seek to develop applications of the technology which involve additional and unique public responsibility.

Whether a franchising authority can require activation of two-way capacity during the term of a franchise agreement, where activation is opposed by a cable system, varies from one jurisdiction to another. It seems that, if the ordinance or legislative action which authorizes the franchise includes a provision for amendment of the franchise, the courts would support reasonable change. If the franchise agreement stands alone without adequate supporting legislation, it may be looked upon as a contractual relationship, and change may be more difficult, absent franchisee concurrence.[28]

Two-way cable is inherently a local service. The services to be supplied by such a system may involve agencies of local government (e.g., fire and police departments), entities endowed with a public interest (e.g., educational institutions), or local businesses.

A unique responsibility for the local authority stems from the fact that, in two-way cable, a variety of public and private services may eventually compete for upstream spectrum space. How the spectrum is allocated to these services is important to all users and potential users. Careful and conservative allocation is more critical as new services are developed and users increase.

At the present stage of development of two-way cable, it is possible to make only a tentative apportionment of spectrum to services. This initial allocation can be flexible, particularly if the transmitting-receiving equipment remains in the hands of the cable system. While the cable system may be in the best position to make the initial spectrum decisions in the developmental period, the franchising authority should reserve the opportunity to review the spectrum plan and lease rates to protect certain public interest users (e.g., in firefighter training, alarm systems, electric power system communication). This is particularly important as competition for upstream spectrum increases.

Finally, the franchise authority and cable system must face the problem of adding new capacity as initial upstream spectrum is fully utilized. This matter is complicated by the high capital cost of changing the split between downstream and upstream signals or adding another cable. In these circumstances, a cable monopolist might forestall the capital cost of adding capacity by controlling demand through the lease rate structure.

The major problem for local authority is how to represent the public interest. On the upstream spectrum allocation and two-way rate issues, perhaps the appropriate procedure is to exercise a right of approval so that a mechanism exists for the franchising authority to become informed of system development and to have the opportunity to express a judgment of public and user interest.

Of the functions for a cable television commission suggested in the section on ordinances, the developmental functions, repeated here briefly, are policy making related to maximizing the diversity of programs and services to subscribers; encouragement of the widest use of public channels; coordination of consultant services for best use of public facilities; supervision of interconnection; coordinating institutional network users; and disbursement of funds for development.

Regulatory Role

The function of the franchise authority in regulating the franchisee and overseeing service development is derived from the responsibility to the users of the system who are relatively powerless as individuals to act in their own best interests, and from the belief that monopolies have certain defects—among them, an artificially high rate structure which is not adjusted to optimum levels by competition and a lack of incentive for development of the most efficient and advanced services and technology, because competition does not exist to provide the incentives. Regulation substitutes for competition.

Generally, regulated firms are intended to have rights and duties:

Rights. (1) They are entitled to "reasonable" prices and profits. (2) They are given complete or partial protection from competition [via a franchise]. (3) They can exercise eminent domain in acquiring property, even by coercion. (4) Rules governing them must be reasonable.

Duties. (1) Prices and profits are to be no more than "reasonable." (2) At those prices, all demand must be met, even at peak times. Service must be adequate in quantity and quality. (3) All changes in services [adding *or* dropping them] must be approved in advance [not clearly applicable to cable because of the First Amendment]. (4) The safety of the public is to be protected.[29]

The First Amendment protection of a free press has been used to deny that cities have the power to regulate cable. The previously mentioned report of the NTIA points out that franchising cable is significantly different from franchising taxi services in two ways. As communications media, cable systems come under special constitutional guarantees. And cable systems are "intrinsically interstate." That is, by retransmission of broadcast signals and use of satellite networks, they interchange a variety of regional and national communication material. Cape Cod Cablevision disputes the Massachusetts cable television commission's authority to regulate rates, comparing it with a "newspaper commission" that would set newspaper rates.[30] In a dissenting opinion in the Boulder, Colorado case, Federal Judge Markey labeled cable systems "electronic newspapers":

When, as studies show, the majority of our people get their news from television, I cannot, in First Amendment jurisprudence, . . . distinguish the dissemination of news and information by cable TV from that of newspapers. Surely, an attempt by a city to use control of its streets and ways as a bludgeon to deny delivery of a newspaper . . . would be rapidly struck down on First Amendment grounds.[31]

The NTIA report sees implications of the "electronic newspaper" concept in all aspects of cable: "the cable operator, as publisher of the 'newspaper' would have exclusive control over all of his channels, and no requirement for public access or leasing could be placed upon these systems."[32]

Under general authority to promote the health, safety, and welfare of the citizens, a city may set standards relating to the practices of franchisees. The limits of this power have not really been tested. In *Simpson v. North Platte,* the Nebraska Supreme Court, in reference to access channels, stated that "A city may not, under the guise of its police power, require a property owner to dedicate private property for some future public purpose as a condition of obtaining a building permit without paying the property owner just compensation."[33] It is not clear whether the access channels would be equally confiscatory if the cable system volunteered them in a franchise application. The voluntary nature of the offer could certainly be questioned if the RFP specifically invited the applicant to discuss access channels in the proposal.

Despite these questions and dissents to cable franchising authority, most cities assume some regulatory responsibility for the reasons stated at the outset of this section.

As noted in the discussion of ordinances, the city council itself will not have time to deal with the details of development and regulation. The principal responsibilities of the city council should be in approving rates, and oversight to determine if the city's objectives for the system have been met. A commission or committee takes over the detail with some independent decision-making authority, and serves in an advisory capacity. Usually the commission is served by a paid ex officio member of the city government staff in an executive role. This person is the liaison with the city government and city council and is the "staff" resource for the cable commission.

There are two main functions in the regulatory role of the franchising authority. One is enforcing the franchise agreement; the other is rate regulation.

If the franchise agreement is thorough and complete, it should contain every obligation of the franchisee. Therefore, it is a convenient checklist against which to evaluate the performance of the franchisee. The city should periodically review the franchise agreement to assure conformance. Representatives of the city, usually the cable commission and city staffers, should meet regularly with the cable company, first to monitor construction progress and later programming and development of other services. If the franchise agreement has deadlines for the initiation of local programs and services, progress toward meeting these commitments is discussed.

If the cable company fails to perform in accordance with the city's interpretation of the ordinance and franchise agreement, the city has the burden of enforcement. The procedures will be spelled out in the ordinance. If fines can be levied by the city, the offenses and associated fines will be in the ordinance. Where there is no fine system, or the performance of the company is seriously inadequate, the enforcement action is revocation. This, of course, is a drastic step which would be time consuming and costly for the city and the company. There have been few such cases. Most of them have been for failure to construct a system after the franchise has been awarded, where companies have been simply warehousing franchises awaiting the most opportune time in which to build. Since franchises are not exclusive, another approach to dealing with an inadequately performing system, without the cost and legal difficulties of revocation, is to grant a second franchise. This has happened in Pickerington and Canal Winchester, Ohio and Hillsborough County, Florida.

The city sits in an appellate capacity for disputes between subscribers and users of the cable system and the company. Most of these issues should be settled without city intervention, but some may reach an impasse. When major issues come up, the action of the city establishes policy, and future cases are then settled more efficiently. In an active cable system, this function is likely to require a monthly meeting of the cable commission or smaller subcommittees that hear various categories of cases. If an intermediate body such as the cable commission makes the initial decision, there is usually an option to appeal to the city council.

Rate regulation is the most complex of the regulatory functions if done properly. In simplest terms, the object of the regulator is to control the "rate of return" to the cable company, thus keeping a "fair ceiling" on prices. The conventional mechanism is to apply this formula:

$$\text{Rate of return} = \frac{\text{total revenue} - \text{total operating cost}}{\text{capital}}$$

The rate of return is supposed to include the return to both equity and debt investors. A *fair* rate of return is defined as "the criterion regulators are supposed to meet: avoids confiscation of owner's value while not gouging consumers."[34] The means used to regulate the rate of return by the franchising authority is to control prices. Ideally, the regulator is interested in the structure of prices, that is, a pricing scheme for each of the services to each of the consumers and the relationship of the prices to the cost of providing the service. For example, the price of basic cable to its subscribers, a pay movie channel to its subscribers, and automated meter reading to the electric company would each be priced in accordance with the true cost so that no class of customers is subsidizing another. The structure of prices cannot be controlled by the city because the FCC does not permit the franchising authority to regulate anything but "regular subscriber service." Advertising, pay service, digital services, alarm systems, two-way experiments, and so on are preempted by the FCC on the grounds that imposing rate regulation on services not yet developed is "premature" and might have a "chilling effect on anticipated development."[35]

The regulator is also in difficulty because the revenue, capital, and cost figures are in the control of the cable system. The city can argue over these numbers (e.g., attempt to disallow some costs), but it is impossible to make the case without substantial knowledge of the industry and access to a great deal of information.

The success of rate regulation of monopolies in the United States—in energy, transportation, and communication—in terms of price and performance efficiency has been very limited. If the state and federal commissions, with professional staffs, are unable to regulate rates, can a cable commission of volunteer citizens and limited or nonexistent staff do so? In larger cities, where government resources may be greater, paid staff and consultants, if available, might make some impact. The literature and research on cable rate regulation is very thin. It will be several years before we know how the industry functions and how well regulation or deregulation of rates works. In reality, cable rate regulation becomes a political and power contest between the cable company and elected or appointed officials. The resulting rate scheme is *negotiated*.

Certain market forces can also serve to regulate cable rates. A number of services, while not perfectly substitutable, can compete—theater movies, over-the-air television, newspapers, magazines, videodiscs, subscription television, MDS, SMATV, DBS, LPTV, for example. (See MDS section of Chapter 16.) Since much of what cable television now offers is a luxury (compared with natural gas in cold climates), cable television prices may be quite elastic; if they go too high, demand will fall.

For all these reasons—the great difficulty of rate regulation with its questionable results and the other forces that act on price levels—rate regulation in cable may be of marginal significance. Deregulation and automatic adjustment clauses have been the answers for some communities.

The State of California has a rate deregulation scheme which allows cable systems meeting certain conditions, at their option, to operate without rate regulation. Eligible systems must be more than 20 channels, have an earth station, and be located in a county that has three significantly viewed stations. The deregulated system must participate in a community channel service program that requires up to three channels, depending on channel capacity, set aside for community use. The system must also contribute $0.50 per subscriber per year to a foundation established by the industry itself to promote community service channels.[36]

The National Cable Television Association has published a manual to aid cable systems in obtaining rate deregulation which contains the California law.[37]

In rate regulating communities, the periodic rate hearings may serve best in restraining rate increases. A rate hearing can also function to raise pertinent issues about the quality of the service. In the give and take of the rate hearing, problems in service may come up, and corrections promised by the cable system in return for the rate increase will be implemented.

Renewals

After the initial franchise period, the franchise may be renewed for periods of five to ten years or longer. At this point, the franchising authority should review the performance of the franchisee for the entire period of the franchise and look at a detailed plan for future development of the system based on a thorough assessment of communication need. If the system has lagged behind the state of the art in technology or service, the city has the most leverage and justification at this time to require change. Some ordinances or franchise agreements may permit a reopening of the bidding process at the end of the franchise period. In others, some preference is given to the incumbent with an option to renew for another period of years.

The renewal process should begin as much as three years before the end of the initial franchise term. With this much time, the process can be completed before expiration, and, in the case of a poorly performing company or a company without plans for future development, a new operator could be selected without interruption in service. This is important. If the renewal is not considered until the expiration of the franchise, the company can threaten to abandon the franchise and leave the city without service for a period of many months—perhaps as long as three years, the time it would take to select a new franchisee and construct a new system or modify the old one. Therefore, a late renewal proceeding puts the city in a very bad bargaining position.

The renewal period need not be as long as the initial franchise. However, if a major retrofit is contemplated as a condition of renewal, then the company is entitled to ask for a longer term. The situation, under these conditions, is more like the original grant of the franchise where a long term protects the capital investment. In any case, the renewal is an ideal time for the city and the operator to review the system in terms of the state of the art in both equipment and services. The city can certainly ask the franchisee for a renewal proposal that would go through most of the steps of the original RFP.

A franchise may be renewed well before the expiration in return for the cable operator's agreement to upgrade the facilities. The cable company may argue that it cannot commit to a rebuild with only a short term left on the franchise. Lending institutions may require a longer term. Most franchises may be renegotiated at any time to change the terms of the agreement.

A new franchise agreement should be negotiated at the time of renewal. It should have the full detail of the first one and again be used as the principal document for determining the obligations and rights of the franchisee.

NOTES

[1]"Municipal Cable Ownership Reconsidered in St. Paul," *Cablevision,* February 2, 1981, p. 37.

[2]"The Emergence of Pay Cable Television," Volume IV, "The Urban Franchising Context," Technology and Economics, Inc., Cambridge, Massachusetts, prepared for the National Telecommunications and Information Administration, Washington, D.C., August 1980, p. 49.

[3]*City of Lafayette* v. *Louisiana Power and Light,* 435 U.S. 389 (1978).

[4]*Community Communications Co.* v. *City of Boulder,* et. al., Case No. 80-1350 argued October 13, 1981, decided January 13, 1982. Certiorari to the U.S. Court of Appeals for the 10th Circuit.

[5]John Andrew, "Courts Ponder Status of Cable TV, To Rule on Legality of Regulation," *The Wall Street Journal,* December 29, 1980.

[6]"The Emergence of Pay Cable Television," p. 44.

[7]From Thomas F. Baldwin, Thomas A. Muth, and Michael O. Wirth, "Assessment of Communication Needs: Meeting with Informed Citizens," *Cable Communications in Minnesota: Suggestions for Systematic Development,* Minnesota Cable Communications Board, Bloomington, Minnesota, August 1975.

[8]"Minnesota Cable Communications and Local Self-Determination: A Practical Guide for Communities That Want to Announce Their Own Communication Needs and Plan Their Own Cable Communication Services," The Cable Communications Board, State of Minnesota, St. Paul, Minnesota, 1979.

[9]Article IX, Sections 7.280–7.283, Ordinance 311, City of East Lansing, Michigan, September 5, 1972.

[10]Section 21.1626, Ordinance 5576 (new series), County of San Diego, California, September 7, 1979.

[11]Michael Schmidt, *Automatic Adjustment Clauses: Theory and Application,* Division of Research, Graduate School of Business Administration, Michigan State University, East Lansing, 1981.

[12]Minutes of the regular meeting of the Southfield CATV Committee, November 22, 1980.

[13]"Request for Proposals, Providing Cable Television Service to the City of Sterling Heights, Michigan, Instructions to Applicants." All subsequent references to Sterling Heights are from this document.

[14]Warren Buffett, "How Cable Franchises Are Bought (Not Won)," *Access,* October 6, 1980, p. 1. The letter was received by the publisher of the Sun Newspapers in Omaha, of which Mr. Buffet is board chairman.

[15]Ibid.

[16]"The Emergence of Pay Cable Television," p. 43.

[17]Harold Horn, address to National Cable Television Association Convention, Dallas, Texas, May 1980.

[18]David Owen Korte, "Cable Franchising—The Preferred Approach," *Public Management*, June 1980, p. 17. (Cable Television Information Center *Cablebooks* that are useful in planning for franchising and renewal are "Volume I, The Community Medium," explaining various cable services, and "Volume II, A Guide to Local Policy.")

[19]Fred Dawson, "The Franchise Story," *Cablevision*, May 19, 1980, p. 83.

[20]Hugh Panero, "Connecticut Examiner Ranks Storer First in Fairfield Franchise Competition," *Cablevision*, February 16, 1981, p. 38.

[21]"The Emergence of Pay Cable Television," p. 35.

[22]Hugh Panero and Fred Dawson, "The Cable Consultants: Are They Doing the Job?" *Cablevision*, December 8, 1980, p. 38.

[23]Ibid., p. 40.

[24]This discussion is based on Thomas F. Baldwin et al., "Public Policy in Two-Way Cable," in Volume II, Final Report, Michigan State University-Rockford Two-Way Cable Project, National Science Foundation Grant No. APR 75-14286, Michigan State University, East Lansing, June 1978, pp. 77–94.

[25]City of Syracuse Franchise Agreement, 1977, Section VI, "Alarm Systems," Section 6.2, "Pilot Programs," Syracuse, New York.

[26]Ibid., Section 6.5(a), "Alarm System Testing."

[27]47 U.S.C.A. 303(g).

[28]41 *ALR 3rd* 384, 6, pp. 400–404; *City of Liberal* v. *Teleprompter Cable Service, Inc.* 544 p. 2d 330, 1975.

[29]Clair Wilcox and William G. Shepherd, *Public Policies Toward Business*, 5th ed. (Homewood, Ill.: Irwin, 1975), p. 333. A thorough discussion of regulation is found in chaps. 13–15.

[30]"The Emergence of Pay Cable Television."

[31]*Community Communications Co.* v. *City of Boulder.*

[32]"The Emergence of Pay Cable Television," p. 54.

[33]*Simpson* v. *North Platte*, 292 NW 2d 297 (Neb. 1980).

[34]Wilcox and Sheperd, *Public Policies Toward Business*, p. 344.

[35]*Clarification of the Cable Television Rules*, supra, 46 FCC 2d at 199–200.

[36]California Assembly Bill No. 699, March 1, 1979.

[37]"Strategies for Rate Deregulation," National Cable Television Association, Washington, D.C., October 1979.

PART IV

ORGANIZATION
AND
OPERATIONS

12

Ownership

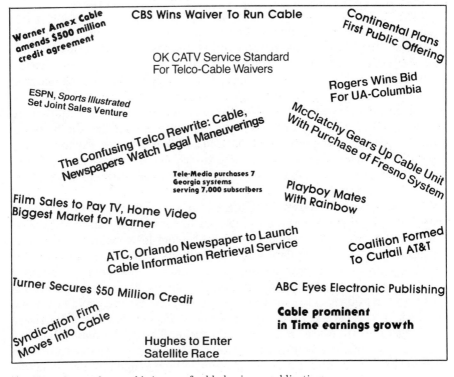

Headlines from a few week's issues of cable business publications.

Part 4 describes the organization and operation of the cable communication industry. Chapter 12 is a discussion of the emerging ownership patterns in the industry. The remaining chapters follow the organizational chart of a typical cable company. Chapter 13 treats the cable television audience and the functions of a programming department. Chapter 14 is about marketing department functions and also includes advertising, although as advertising in cable grows, it will no doubt become a separate department, as the marketing of cable services and advertising are so different. Chapter 15 covers the accounting, customer service, field operations, and engineering departments.

LOCAL MONOPOLY

The transition from isolated, small-town community antenna systems to urban broadband cable systems has brought an entirely new ownership pattern to the cable industry. The original, independent "mom and pop" CATV operations are now dwarfed by conglomerates, and questions arise about monopoly and horizontal and vertical integration.[1]

Perhaps the most pressing ownership question is that of *local monopoly*. Some of the issues concerning monopoly ownership have already been discussed, but they bear revisitation here. It is generally considered that direct competition in the capital-intensive cable industry would be inefficient. *One* cable, 30 to 54 channels, even today with dual-cable systems in the new urban areas, is presently sufficient for the most attractive programming now available and two-way services. Further, cable operators believe that it is necessary to achieve a critical mass of subscribers in any area to make major investments in program origination and two-way service.

Theoretically, there are significant dangers in the local cable monopolies. The service may be overpriced to consumers, channel lessors, and advertisers. The monopoly pricing problem for consumers has been discussed under rate regulation in the previous chapter. The problem for lessors is similar. Those who would seek channel time for independently produced programs, shopping services, data transmission, and so on cannot negotiate effectively over price with a monopolist and could be forced, by lack of competing suppliers, to accept inferior service. Advertisers seeking cable time are in the same position. The cable monopolist ties up whole television advertising markets. Increasingly, as cable television penetrates higher and higher proportions of households in a city, advertisers *must* include cable in balanced marketing plans. The local advertiser has only one *entré* to this medium.

Monopoly may also affect the quality of the cable output. The response time to service calls, picture quality, local origination, and initiation of new services could all suffer from the limited incentives of a monopolist.

There are a number of proposed resolutions to the problems that monopoly theoretically creates. Cable franchising authorities or federal regulations might require nondiscriminatory leased access channels, under regulated rates, with a provision that new channels be added as the originals approach capacity. Others would then always have the opportunity to lease channels at fair rates if they desired to compete with the cable operator. The lessor would have to have access to more than just a channel—headend computers and production equipment, household terminals, and so on—but this could be arranged. Lease prices would have to be regulated so that potential users were not eliminated by exclusionary charges; however, prices should be high enough to compensate the cable operator for the initial risk in building the system. It would be unfortunate for the cable entrepreneur to build the system and then be forced to turn over parts of it to others at unfairly low rates. On the other hand, services competing with cable fear that cable systems, with their many different sources of revenue, might cross subsidize some services and compete unfairly in pricing.

A similar, but more dramatic, approach is known as the "separations" policy, which was proposed by a cabinet committee to the president in 1974.[2] The report suggested that, at some transitional point, perhaps at the 50 percent level of national cable penetration, cable operators be separated from all programming of cable channels and henceforth serve only as a common carrier of programming materials under a price-regulated channel-leasing scheme. Under this plan, no entity would be excluded from cable programming, and programmers would compete for audience attention and dollars. With the present 50 to 100 channel systems, there would be sufficient space for programming competitors. Perfect competition, with its theoretical advantages, is approached, and very little regulation of any kind would be necessary. The policy, however, would be difficult to implement. Forcing cable systems to give up the programming services at some arbitrary point would be considered confiscatory and unfair by the cable companies, and certain management difficulties are likely. Centralized marketing and billing would be necessary. A marketing program that would have to accommodate all programmers, on a first-come, first-served basis, would be a challenge to the operator in its administration and to the subscriber in its interpretation.

A means of lessening the effect of local monopoly is to district the community and parcel out the districts to different companies, thus creating side-by-side comparison. If two or more franchises are serving the same community and not colluding, the quality of service and state of the art technology of one would probably have to be matched by the other. Some cities have divided the territory, as in Columbus, Ohio. In Columbus the companies have cooperated in a government-community channel, available on all four of the systems, and pursued different approaches to programming and service. Most cable operators would argue, however, that the pie cannot be divided too many times; customers must be aggregated in large numbers to justify some of the technologically advanced services.

With a 100-channel, *dual*-cable system contemplated for a community, it would be possible to put an upper limit on the number of *channels* franchised to a single operator. In the 400-mHz technology, the limit might be placed at 54 (one cable). Two or more companies receiving franchises, at the same time could share costs of building the distribution plant. The cost of the two headends spread over a large number of subscribers would not be significantly greater *per subscriber* than the single headend. Scale economies in administrative costs per subscriber would not be greatly different with the two operator system. To our knowledge this approach has never been taken, but as the number of available new franchises diminishes, and available programming expands, cable operators would be likely to bid on such a system if proposed by a city.

Another solution to private monopoly is a public monopoly. This is contemplated at one point or another in almost every recent franchise and renewal. A publicly owned cable system might be structured to meet public-oriented needs (alarm systems, education, and other institutional communication) and control prices in the interest of consumer welfare. No large municipality has yet been willing to carry through on the massive organization and political effort necessary to launch such a system and raise the capital. The utility of cable in the public sector has not been demonstrated fully, and communication freedom would have to be assured, a difficult and uncertain task.

For the time being, it appears that local cable monopoly will be regulated by the franchise-granting authority, city or state, rather than imposing new structures. At the federal level, efforts are being made to encourage a wide variety of communication media in addition to conventional broadcasting—direct broadcast satellite, subscription TV, multipoint distribution services, low-power TV, additional radio frequencies—all lessening the market power of a single distribution system (see Chapter 16). As noted in the Chapter 11 discussion of rate regulation, the penetration level of cable in a given community is a major indicator of the impact of these substitute services.

MULTIPLE SYSTEM OPERATORS

Another characteristic of the cable industry is its horizontal integration or, more accurately, *concentration of ownership* across communities. The top 15 multiple system operators (MSOs) serve a majority of the cable subscribers. This proportion will increase dramatically since these are the companies that are bidding and building the urban systems. The big MSOs have managerial finesse and centralized management resources, which, if not necessary to operate cable systems, seem to have been necessary in bidding for the big franchises. The research and development of technology and service applications is easier for the larger MSOs since they may capitalize to a greater extent, and more quickly, on the research and development endeavors. And, as is customary in the U.S. economy, the large operator fares better in the capital market.

The number of broadcast stations permitted any group owner is limited by the FCC. Similar limits have been considered for cable but are based on an upper limit for the subscriber count, the number of cable systems being meaningless, given the radical variation in the size of systems. The FCC concern about concentration dates back to an inquiry in 1968.[3] The issue is still alive, but action has always been deferred. For the present, the FCC must approve most mergers since cable television relay services (CARS) are licensed by the FCC.[4] These licenses are used by cable MSOs and cannot be transferred without approval. The FCC generally approves the mergers. The Justice Department and the Federal Trade Commission also look at mergers under the antitrust laws.[5] The Justice Department filed suit against the ATC and Cox merger proposal in 1972, and the two parties withdrew. In addition to surviving FCC, FTC, and Justice Department scrutiny, merger plans must be cleared by all the individual franchising authorities that, by ordinance or franchise agreement, reserve the right of approval for transfer of ownership.

The reason for concern about the growing concentration in cable is the *economic* and *intellectual* power that is vested in the industry. Cable MSOs will control access to many markets for advertisers. Program producers may also need the large block of cable systems controlled by single operators for survival of particular programming ventures. Furthermore, it is of serious concern that a major MSO can control the content of television and other information into a great many communities, often concentrated regionally. The concern is heightened by the development of home communication centers using cable for access to entertainment, electronic text information, instruction, and public affairs programming.

Despite the consolidation of cable MSOs and the large MSO dominance of the urban markets, no single operator has a very high share of the total cable households, and 15 or more companies are sharing in the new franchise awards. There may be constraints on the size of most MSOs arising from the massive capital requirements and the crushing managerial burdens of obtaining franchises and building the new systems, all of which will take place within a short span of years.

INDEPENDENTS AND SINGLE SYSTEM OPERATORS

Single system operators and small MSOs, sometimes called independents because they are not affiliated with major corporations and are exclusively in the cable operation business, are still important in the industry. Although most of these companies concede franchise bidding to less conservative and bigger MSOs, they serve a major industry function in developing small population pockets that would be neglected, for the time being, by the bigger operators. Once developed, the systems may be sold to a nearby MSO, but often the independents run systems on the 5,000 to 10,000 subscriber scale with the same services as most major MSOs, including some local origination and all but the most experimental technology.[6] As noted elsewhere, economies of scale in system construction and operation are only important in the most advanced two-way systems. The principal capital expense is based on a per-mile cable cost and the household terminal or converter. These costs do not vary significantly as the scale increases. Therefore, the small-scale operator can continue to survive in the milieu of corporate conglomerates.

VERTICAL INTEGRATION

Historical experience in the telephone industry, with a strong integration of equipment manufacturing and operating companies, and in the film industry, with integration of producers and distributors, has created some reservations about the *vertical integration* of the cable industry. Jerrold Electronics, once the dominant force in the supply of cable industry electronic components, serviced the systems and was also an MSO. Jerrold sold complete cable systems (*turnkey* construction) to other operators and threatened to overbuild and operate its own systems in communities where other operators did not purchase Jerrold equipment.[7] Justice Department suits ended the service contracts and temporarily halted the acquisition of new operating systems. Eventually, Jerrold sold the operating systems to Sammons. Other equipment manufacturers operate systems, for example, General Electric, and Westinghouse. Cable MSOs with equipment-manufacturing arms could have an effect on competition in the industry, but since the separation of the Jerrold equipment and operating units, no problems have surfaced.

Cable operators, program suppliers, and equipment manufacturers are also owners of signal distribution networks either in common carrier microwave systems or satellite resale common carriers. Microwave system ownership and ownership of cable systems do not currently represent an antitrust problem, although the combination might offer advantages in new bidding for small town franchises as the original terms expire.

The limited number of satellite transponders, and the high demand, has created several problems in satellite service to cable. The FCC has not chosen to regulate rates, allowing the market to determine rates. Although satellite transponders available to cable are increasing, the supply is still limited; therefore, it remains a seller's market. Additional satellites require additional earth stations so that transponders on an established satellite may be more valuable to program suppliers and to cable operators than on a newly launched satellite. Some cable program suppliers have contracts that monopolize transponder time, no doubt as a result of accurate foresight. But this squeezes out other program services.

Vertical integration in program supply and system operation without the transmission link is quite common. Cable operating companies are in an advantageous position to experiment with programming and market the successes. Risk and investment in programming for cable may be most likely to occur among MSOs with empty channels and substantial incentives to provide services to attract subscribers. The problems this creates for independent producers and distributors and other cable operators, as well as the effects it might have on the diversity of programming available to subscribers, have been discussed in Chapter 8 on pay cable. As suggested there, subscriber willingness to buy multiple tiers of pay programming has dictated a cable programming policy of accepting competing services. The vertically integrated MSOs and program distributors market each other's program services—for example, Warner Amex cable systems offer HBO (associated with ATC cable) along with their own, The Movie Channel. ATC markets The Movie Channel as well as HBO. Until available programming services begin to fill available channels, it is probable that every program distributor will have a fair chance in the market, although big operators may have the upper hand in negotiating the terms of the agreement. If channel space becomes tight, the Justice Department may become more active in this field. Of course, a leased channel or separations policy, described in the local monopoly discussion, addresses this issue also.

Program producers may be integrated with pay program distributors and cable operators. Warner Communications, Inc., with films, TMC, Showtime, records, MTV (The Music Television satellite network supplier), and Warner Amex (the cable MSO) is a good example of corporate integration of this type. Several other ties between producers and the cable distribution systems have been formalized. In made-for-cable productions and "prebuys," the cable industry finances, or helps to finance, specials and feature movies. These associations give the cable industry a measure of control over the production industry and may restrict competition.

It should be noted here that some cable operators are concerned that their own identities may be swallowed up by the foundation pay service. This is likely in markets in which pay is the principal attraction to cable and the pay service is promoted heavily with the logo of the distributor. Independently establishing and marketing new services of the local cable company may be made more difficult as a result.

CROSS-MEDIA OWNERSHIP

A pattern of *cross-media ownership* that has developed over the years was extended quickly to cable. Other media are early to recognize the potential of a new medium, have complementary professional and management expertise, and can add a measure of security by investing as a hedge against possible restructuring of the media industries through new technologies. Cable has attracted interest and capital from all the other media since present or future cable services relate to each.

Newspapers own cable systems. Newspaper executives are now prone to say "We are in the information distribution business, not the printing business." Many of the newspaper services can be provided more currently by cable through alphanumeric and graphic displays on a television screen or printed in the home. Newspapers do not want to give up these functions or lose the business. They believe that they are experienced and staffed appropriately for some of the new cable services if they develop as anticipated. Furthermore, cable offers new opportunities for entry into the more conventional television services. Newspapers can use their resources to enter television news and public affairs programming or add to their line-up of stations, if they have not already done so. Cable offers the opportunity for flexibility and depth in television news that is perhaps more akin to the function of a newspaper than a television station.

Some state governments discourage or prevent newspaper ownership of cable systems (see Chapter 10).

Cable is a natural extension of a broadcasting business. The cable industry will need the acquired knowledge of broadcasters as advertising and program production become greater factors. The entry of broadcasters in the cable business has been slowed somewhat by a competitive antipathy and the attempt to stave off cable encroachment. Now that the future role of cable is more clear, broadcasters can protect their businesses best by buying into the cable industry. (There is also a need for broadcasters to develop broadcast programming along lines that will capitalize on their strengths vis-à-vis the new cable and cable newspaper services. This is presumed to be in local program production.)

Broadcasters have been urged to negotiate long-term leases on their local cable channels for program origination. Alan Bennett of Katz Programming, a unit of the television station sales representative firm, has proposed that stations take on two channels, programming one with classic films, presumably from the station library, and the other with news and sports. The news-sports channel, he suggests, should be programmed with 15-minute news blocks hourly in anticipation of the time when CNN or some other all-news service will break away for local feeds. He also encouraged the stations to "aggressively go after" television rights, local professional sports franchises, and college and high school sports events for use on the channel.[8] Local television stations have a leg up on other competitors in the same service area because of existing production facilities and personnel and the contact with advertisers.

Several media conglomerates have extensive holdings in cable. Under the Time, Inc. umbrella are HBO; Time-Life Books; Book-of-the-Month Club; Little, Brown and Company; New York Graphic Society; Pioneer Press; *Time, Life, People, Sports Illustrated, Fortune, Money, Discover;* WOTV, Grand Rapids; a paper mill and over a million acres of forest land; American Television and Communication, one of the biggest cable MSOs; and the USA Cable Network. The Times Mirror Corporation is another with television stations, several magazines and major newspapers, book publishers, forests and paper mills, and now several cable systems. The New York Times Company, in addition to the *Times,* owns several other newspapers, magazines, television stations, book publishers, educational resource companies, the New York Times Information Bank, and cable systems. Other cable MSOs with various interests in radio, television, publishing, and motion picture exhibition include Capital Cities, Cox, Dow Jones, General Electric, Harte-Hanks, Knight-Ridder, Midwest Video, McClachety, Newhouse, Plains TV, Storer, The (Chicago) Tribune, Viacom International, Westinghouse Electric, Warner Amex, and Wometco.

Some media conglomerates have no principal ownership of cable system operating companies but do have divisions to develop specialized programming to serve the cable industry. ABC, CBS, NBC, Hearst, *Playboy, Readers' Digest* and Twentieth Century-Fox are examples.

The FCC has limited cross-media ownership. The television networks are not permitted to own cable systems. CBS was forced to divest its systems (which became Viacom). With support of the other networks, in 1981, CBS asked for *waiver* of the rule to permit experimentation with programming in a small system. The FCC granted the waiver. At the time of the petition, there were strong arguments for and against the rule itself. The FCC also forbids broadcast station ownership of cable systems serving subscribers in the same local service area, defined by the Grade B signal contour, which is about a 70-mile radius from the transmitter. Television translator stations and cable systems may not be co-owned in the same community. This rule prevents formation of local cable-broadcast television combinations and required divestiture of existing combinations. Later the divestiture requirement was amended to require separation in only the "egregious" cases—those where the combination would represent a significant television monopoly.[9]

There are three major concerns arising from cross-media ownership. Most critical is the possibility of a complete media monopoly in a community. The FCC has taken steps to ban or break up radio, television, and newspaper monopolies through its regulation of radio and television, especially where there is only a single entity of each type. Such a combination, should it also include cable, would give inordinate control of a community's information resources to a single owner. Apart from the media monopoly of a single owner, the FCC and others concerned with media policy value maximum diversity of media ownership in any community. In this theory, it is better to have three media owners than two, better to have four than three, and so on. Finally, there is a fear of too much media power, regionally or nationally, with its political, economic, and intellectual consequences.

An issue related to ownership diversity is the special question of minority ownership of media. Most newspapers were founded, television and radio stations licensed, and many cable systems franchised before minorities had the economic and managerial resources to participate in ownership. Limiting the holdings of established owners to accommodate new owners is, therefore, prerequisite to including minorities among them.

The Justice Department can look at media cross-ownership on a case-by-case basis. The Congress or FCC can create policy that is more general, but the First Amendment rights of communication media stand in the way. If media are looked upon as the "press," then one's right to acquire channels is protected, as media conglomerates have argued in court (see Chapter 11). It is in this area, however, where the accumulated power of media conglomerates is of the greatest social interest. If media are looked upon as competing businesses, affecting one another in accordance with the structure of the whole media complex, limitation of ownership depends upon the interpretation of antitrust laws.

Whatever the case, it is much easier to theorize the effect of media cross-ownership than to provide empirical demonstrations. If cross-owned media are compared with independent media, whether the performance to be analyzed is journalistic (i.e., expenditures for news presentation) or competitive (i.e., advertising space or time prices), the evidence does not clearly favor one side or the other.

The FCC has studied cross-media ownership and media concentration for several years. "Multiple ownership and radio-television-newspaper cross-ownership of cable systems," "television station-cable television system cross-ownership," and "multiple ownership of any FM and TV stations and CATV systems" are all pending investigations in separate rulemaking proceedings.[10]

CONGLOMERATE OWNERSHIP OF CABLE

Getty Oil, Chris-Craft, American Express, and the Orkin Exterminating Company are all in the cable business. The cable industry is now looking to unrelated industries as a source of capital, and many companies in mature industries are looking at cable as a promising opportunity for entry into the growing information economy.

ALIEN OWNERSHIP

The FCC has refused to prevent alien ownership of cable systems. Therefore, the issue is open for franchising authorities to decide. U.S. cable companies have been concerned mainly with the success of Canadian applicants for U.S. franchises. The Canadian companies, principally Rogers and MacLean-Hunter, are fully matured MSOs in Canada until recently precluded from pay television services in their own country. Expansion south into the United States is a logical option. Their U.S.-owned competitors for franchises, of course, make the franchising authorities well aware of the Canadian affiliation.

TELCOS AND CABLE

The cable industry and the related media organizations (i.e., newspapers) have an almost pathological fear of American Telephone & Telegraph (AT&T) and its operating companies. AT&T has several overwhelming characteristics: (1) command of vast capital resources, (2) a presumed ability to cross-subsidize new ventures, (3) an enormous, well-disciplined and well-paid staff, (4) unmatched communications research and development facilities, and (5) the political power of an organization with thousands of stockholders that serves almost every household in the United States. For many years AT&T was prevented from entering the cable business by a consent decree resulting from an antitrust action,[11] although in the early years, Bell companies built distribution plants and leased them to cable companies. In a new consent decree, announced January 8, 1982, AT&T will no longer be restricted from entering cable television, teletext/videotex, data processing and communications or other information providing activities. The company is to divest the 22 Bell Operating Companies.

The Bell Operating Companies are still foreclosed from cable in most of the nation by an FCC rule that prohibits telephone companies from owning cable companies in their own exchange areas.[12] The object of the rule was to "deter anticompetitive and discriminatory practices that evolved from the local telephone company's monopoly position in the community and its ownership of the utility poles, which usually carry the distribution cables."[13] The FCC considers waiver of this rule for low-population-density areas (fewer than 30 homes per mile) where the conditions make it more practical for telephone companies to operate cable systems than separate organizations.[14]

In the meantime, AT&T is developing high-capacity fiber optic communication systems, which could be installed in competition with cable. The company has tested videotext in several locations for an electronic Yellow Pages and general information service. These consumer services will be marketed by a new subsidiary nicknamed "Baby Bell." Before the most recent consent decree AT&T, as a result of the FCC Computer I and II inquiries, was permitted to *enhance* services—use computer processing to transform or interact with subscribers' transmissions rather than simply providing a transmission path as a common carrier.[15] AT&T's entry into these areas has cable and newspaper people looking over their shoulders as they develop their own plans to become information utilities.

TELEVISION RECEIVER SALES AND SERVICES

Some of the earliest CATV businesses were established by appliance dealers and radio repair shops as a means of getting into the television sales or service business. As the cable industry grew, some ordinances and franchises specifically prohibited the cable franchisee from entering the sales or repair business. This was to protect the existing businesses and prevent anticompetitive situations where the cable system might use its position to dominate the market. To avoid conflicts, the bigger cable operators have stayed out of sales and receiver service, even where not denied the opportunity.

Actually, some economies might be realized in combination of receiver service and cable service. The cable company is almost always called first on a service problem because the service is free. Operators screen the calls to try to avoid house calls where the problem is clearly the receiver, but often the difficulty is not clear cut or the customer is insistent on a cable service call. It would be more efficient to take the call and perform the necessary service be it cable system or receiver.

SUMMARY

Despite local monopoly and increasing concentration within the cable industry and across media, diversity of ownership of media and the diversity of media content is increasing exponentially, principally as a *result* of cable. Under the present circumstances, we should not expect much change in ownership controls. According to Christopher Sterling,

Further controls over cable system ownership do not appear likely as long as: (1) there is generally adequate channel capacity to allow for expansion of programming "voices" reaching the public; (2) there are sufficient separate firms providing program material to cable systems; (3) there are sufficient different means of cable networking (satellites, microwave lines, etc.) available; (4) examples of outright system abuse of the community monopoly position are absent; and (5) competing systems of pay cable are available for local carriage.[16]

NOTES

[1]Detailed discussion of these issues may be found in Benjamin M. Compaine, ed. *Who Owns the Media: Concentration of Ownership in the Mass Communications Industry* (White Plains, N.Y.: Knowledge Industry Publications, 1972); William H. Johnson, "Structure and Ownership of the Cable TV Industry," in *The Cable/Broadband Communication Book,* Mary Louise Hollowell, ed. (Washington, D.C.: Communications Press, 1980), pp. 1–10; Yale M. Braunstein, "Recent Trends in Cable Television Related to the Prospects for New Television Networks," paper submitted to the Federal Communications Commission, Network Inquiry Special Staff, Washington, D.C., August 1979. For current information on industry structure see the annual issues of *Television Factbook,* 1836 Jefferson Place, N.W., Washington, D.C. 20036.

[2]The Cabinet Committee on Cable Communications, *Cable: Report to the President* (Washington, D.C.: G.P.O., 1974).

[3]*Notice of Proposed Rule Making and Notice of Inquiry in Docket No. 18397,* 15 FCC 2d 417 (1968).

[4]*Cable Television Report and Order,* 36 FCC 2d 143, 24 RR 2d 1501 (1972).

[5]15 U.S.C.A. 4, 18, 21.

[6]Victoria Gits, "A Thriving Band of Small Independents Is Keeping Doldrums and MSOs at Bay," *Cablevision,* May 4, 1981, pp. 36–41.

[7]William H. Johnson, "Structure and Ownership of the Cable TV Industry," in *The Cable/Broadband Communications Book,* p. 12.

[8]"Bennett Urges Broadcasters to Program Leased-Channels," *Cablevision,* March 30, 1981, pp. 117–119.

[9]*Second Report and Order in Docket 18110,* FCC 75–104, 50 FCC 2d 1046 (1975). (An extensive discussion of the topic is found in "FCC Staff Report on Cable TV Cross Ownership Policies," FCC, November 17, 1981, pp. 202.)

[10]*Notice of Proposed Rule Making and Inquiry in Docket 18891,* FCC 70–674, 23 FCC 2d 833, 35 *Fed. Reg.* 11042 (1970); *Further Notice of Proposed Rule Making in Docket 20423,* FCC 80–355, _____FCC 2d _____(1980), 45 *Fed. Reg.* 47445 (June 15, 1980); *Notice of Inquiry and Notice of Proposed Rule Making in BC Docket 78–239,* FCC 78–555, 68 FCC 2d 1302 (1978), 43 *Fed Reg.* 36978 (August 21, 1978).

[11]*U.S.* v. *Western Electric Co.,* 1956 Trade Case 71,134 (D.N.J.).

[12]*Cable Television Report and Order,* 36 FCC 2d 143, 24 RR 2d 1501 (1972).

[13]FCC, "Information Bulletin, Cable Television," 00867, October, 1980.

[14]*Report and Order in CC Docket 78–219,* FCC 79–775, 44 *Fed. Reg.* 75156 (December 19, 1979).

[15]*Memorandum Opinion and Order in Docket 20828* (Second Computer Inquiry), FCC 80–628, October 28, 1980.

[16]Christopher H. Sterling, "Cable and Pay Television," *Who Owns the Media?: Concentration of Ownership in the Mass Communications Industry,* Benjamin M. Compaine, ed. (White Plains, N.Y.: Knowledge Industry Publications, 1979), p. 308.

13

Audiences and Programming

Source of Household Viewing—Prime Time (Mon.-Sun. 8-11pm)
Pay Cable, Basic Cable and Non-cable Households

	July 1980			Nov. 1980			Feb. 1981		
% TV Usage*	58.4	51.8	47.9	73.2	65.6	62.2	71.8	67.5	63.7
Viewing To . . .									
Pay Cable	13.2			10.9			11.8		
Cable Originated Programming	2.8	2.0		2.9	2.2		2.8	1.7	
Other On-Air Stations	12.8	10.7	8.2	12.1	11.4	8.7	11.6	11.9	9.2
Network Affiliate Stations	32.5	40.2	40.4	50.9	53.8	54.7	49.7	55.3	55.7
Network Share**	(53)	(76)	(83)	(66)	(80)	(86)	(65)	(80)	(86)
	Pay Cable	Basic Cable	Non– Cable	Pay Cable	Basic Cable	Non– Cable	Pay Cable	Basic Cable	Non– Cable

*May be less than sum of reception sources because of simultaneous viewing
**% network/sum of sources

Broadcast and cable television viewing statistics. Courtesy of A.C. Nielsen Company.

AUDIENCES

Knowledge of audience interests and behavior is important to programming of cable channels, marketing the services, and more generally, assessing the social impact of cable communication. Cable audience data are limited, often only partially released because of proprietary interests, and always dependent on the television environment of a particular community. For example, cable television has different values for an individual in Liberal, Kansas, where the nearest television station is 60 miles away, than an individual in Cincinnati, Ohio, where there are several television stations in town. The two cable system services in these two places are also vastly different.

Information on cable audiences comes from several sources. Cable systems report basic information on number of subscribers and penetration levels annually to the FCC (see Chapter 10). Nielsen and Arbitron, television audience measurement services, report on cable audiences included in their market-by-market surveys and do special surveys to assist the broadcast, cable, and advertising industries in determining audience trends. Other polling services are commissioned occasionally to study cable, and gradually, a body of academic research literature is developing. From these sources, using findings that appear consistently, a composite picture of the cable audience may be drawn. Each finding reported here has been confirmed by at least one other study.[1]

In communities with few good quality broadcast signals available, almost all television households are cable subscribers. As the number of available, clear broadcast television signals increases, the number of cable subscribers decreases. In a community served fully by broadcast television—three network affiliates, one or more independents, and a PBS affiliate—cable television penetration hovers around 40 or 50 percent. In communities where the penetration is relatively low, it might be said that subscription to cable television is clearly optional; a substantial proportion of the television households are electing *not* to subscribe. What distinguishes the subscriber from the nonsubscriber?

Nonsubscribers

The nonsubscriber is likely to be satisfied with the television available without cable. Television is television. A small increment in television diversity, or even a big one, at whatever the cost, is superfluous. For others, cost is a factor. The marginal increase in satisfaction is not sufficient to warrant the monthly charge. A subset of these cost-conscious people is offended by the very idea of paying for television. It violates a 30-year tradition of "free" television. A very small percentage of people have so little interest in television that cable cannot make a difference.

The group of nonsubscribers is older, on the average, has fewer children in the household, and has lower income than subscribers. All these differences are slight, however, in the neighborhood of a few percentage points.

Basic Subscribers

The fundamental reasons for subscribing to cable television are to obtain clear television signals and a diversity of programs. A good picture, even if only on a few channels, is crucial in towns on the fringes of major television markets. In the major markets, where several broadcast television transmitters are close at hand, the opportunity to receive still more programs is the attraction to subscribers. In the abundant broadcast markets, a substantial proportion of the basic subscribers takes basic principally as a means of access to pay movie channels. In only a few places is pay available separately from basic.

Subscribers spend a greater proportion of their time viewing stations from other cities than do nonsubscribers. The difference between subscribers and nonsubscribers in this respect is dependent on the number of local stations available in town. For example, in New York, with 16 local stations in the television market, nonsubscribing homes spend 97 percent of their time with local stations; in cable homes, 89 percent of the viewing is to local stations. In Des Moines, 96 percent of the viewing time in the noncable homes is spent with the five local stations; 70 percent in cable homes. In Meridian, Mississippi, where there are only four stations and only two of those are commercial, noncable households spend 81 percent of their time with the local stations; cabled households spend 51 percent of their viewing time with the local stations.[2] All this is probably obvious, but the point is that *cable diverts audience from local stations*. The smaller the market, the greater the diversion. This has some social significance, in terms of the commonality of media experience within a community, and is discussed in Chapter 16.

As might be expected from the smaller audiences for local stations on cable, the availability of distant stations seems to draw some audience away from *local news*.[3] The audience for local news may be several ratings points lower for cable homes. In many communities, households without cable have very few options except local news at certain time periods. There is also evidence that people with cable may view local, nonnetwork news from a distant larger city rather than view the hometown news.[4] Local television news in the bigger cities may be somewhat more dramatic, faster paced, and have more attractive "news personalities" and slick production.

The audience for local cable origination is generally very low by commercial television standards, but audience shares which are competitive with commercial network affiliates have been reported for community news originating on cable.[5] About one-third of the basic and pay subscribers use automated channels more than once a week, some quite frequently.

The average cable household views about 44 hours of television weekly; the noncable home 41 hours. The figures are total hours of weekly viewing for the whole *household*, not weekly hours by the average *individual*, which are considerably less. Since cable homes average slightly more people, this may not necessarily mean that the viewing per individual is greater in the cable home. Interestingly, the lower the cable penetration in a community, the higher the total household hours viewed. This suggests that the cable household in the community with many over-the-air stations (hence the low penetration) is *very* interested in television.[6]

The typical basic cable household "adds on" cable programs to the diet of television available over the air. Viewing of distant independent television stations and the superstations is the major distinction between basic cable and noncable homes for the time being. Increasing national penetration of pay and greater prominence of nonbroadcast satellite channels will probably change this, since these are the main reasons for buying cable in urban areas. Basic subscribers are somewhat less tolerant of unrestricted R-rated movies than are other cable subscribers who take pay services, but the main reason stated for rejecting pay is the cost and the low quality of movies available. Most basic-only cable subscribers are at intermediate levels between noncable households and pay households in age of household head (lower than noncable, higher than pay), average size of family (larger than noncable, smaller than pay), and education and income (higher than noncable, lower than pay).

Pay Subscribers

Almost all subscribers to pay cable sign up to receive movies. Substantial proportions of these people appreciate the fact that the films are uninterrupted by commercials or other material, unedited and adult. For some pay subscribers, it is also important to have an opportunity to see movies that were missed during theater runs and to see movies that are not shown on broadcast television. Finally, some subscribers acknowledge the economy of viewing films at home, saving the cost of tickets, perhaps a baby-sitter, and paying only a fraction of the theater cost for popcorn, snacks, and drinks. Although theater viewing of a large screen, with audience reaction, is not exactly the same experience, the monthly cost of a pay cable channel is roughly equivalent to a single movie at a theater for a couple.

Fall and winter viewing of the top-rated broadcast network programs among pay cable households is the same as basic and noncable households. During the spring and summer, when the top broadcast network shows are in reruns, and throughout the year against the less popular network programs, pay cable has an increased share of audience. It is generally believed that pay cable is not subject to the seasonal dips of broadcast television. Pay cable audiences hold steady across all seasons, thus the higher spring and summer share when broadcast network audiences are in decline. In fall and winter, prime time, pay cable programs get about a 14 percent share of the pay cable households using television. In the summer, the share is about 21 percent.

When well-known R-rated movies "premiere" (are shown on cable for the first time), the share of audience among pay cable subscribers is greater than the shares for any of the broadcast network shows, even though there will be multiple opportunities to view. For example, on the night *Saturday Night Fever* premiered on HBO, it earned a 54 percent share of the HBO household television viewers.[7] G and PG pictures do not get such high shares on premiere nights.[8] Pay cable may also cut into the share of audience for public affairs programming. During the Republican convention in 1980, for instance, the pay cable viewing share was up to 38 percent compared with the average summer nonconvention weeks of 24 percent. The audience lost to pay television by other programming is of a higher income and younger. This fact has caused alarm among advertisers and has generated interest in advertising on pay cable. Researchers have determined that advertising between pay cable programs would not be objectionable to most people, and some would welcome intermissions within programs. These ideas would be received more favorably if adoption were to reduce the cost of the service.

Despite some erosion of network viewing during prime time, the average pay cable household views almost as much of the prime-time television that is available over the air as the noncable and basic-only cable subscriber; watches more prime-time programs available only on cable; and then "adds on" the pay cable viewing. During the daytime hours, the average pay cable household views more television that is available over the air; watches more cable-only programming than both basic-only and noncable homes; and then adds some pay cable programming.[9]

Attitudinal studies find pay cable subscribers to be more permissive about sex on television. For example, a survey by Dean Krugman and Donald Eckrich found pay cable users much less likely to agree with the statements "there is too much sex in prime-time television" and "television commercials place too much emphasis on sex." Incidentally, the Krugman–Eckrich study also found 6 percent of a large sample (523 pay cable and 662 basic-only subscribers in four cities served by the TeleCable Corporation) of pay cable subscribers also subscribing to *Penthouse* magazine and 13 percent taking *Playboy*. This compares with 1 percent and 7 percent subscribers to the same magazines among the basic-cable-only users.[10]

Research reports indicate that the household viewing of pay cable is around five or six hours per week. As noted earlier, the pay cable household is of a higher income, better educated, younger and has more people.

Functions of Cable for the User

Broadband cable broadens the functions of television for the user. The new functions are somewhat slow to emerge, and the cable household takes time to *integrate* new programs and services, that is, to first accept and then make regular or habitual use of the services. Television becomes more of a utility that can be turned to for reference as well as for entertainment. This is true of the automated channels, two-way electronic text services, and the all-news channel.

Conventional broadcast television is used by many people as background while they are in and out of the room where the television set is on or as accompaniment for other activities (e.g., conversation, dressing, meals, housework, homework). Attention to television comes into and out of focus depending on the primacy of other activities, moment by moment. Cable programming enhances the value of television as a background medium with more programs that are meaningful in very short segments such as the all-news channel, video music, and night club acts. Conversely, many people who are accustomed to the use of television as background for intermittent short periods of time between other activities find it difficult to view the long, uninterrupted movies of pay cable. Some of these people do not subscribe to pay cable because they "don't have time" for that kind of viewing.

PROGRAMMING

Program Planning

Programming is used in this context to mean planning and organizing program content. There are three basic areas for decision in programming cable systems. One is to determine which channels or programs to carry, beyond the must-carry signals, from among available broadcast or satellite services. The second is to establish the local origination channels. The third is to package all the programming into levels or tiers of service that fit the needs of subscribers and make sense in marketing. At least one MSO, Tele-Communications, Inc. (TCI), is putting together *national* basic and pay packages for all of its systems. The national packages will facilitate the use of a national programming guide in addition to giving the huge MSO considerable leverage in negotiating affiliation agreements, including volume discounts, and selling advertising.

Programming from external sources is least difficult for the 40 or more channel systems. Here, the philosophy is generally to offer practically everything that is available. The principal issues may be the redundancy in religious channels, the number of pay channels (really a marketing question), the value of an additional earth station to receive more of the satellite-delivered services, and whether to include an adult pay option. For systems with a high subscriber count, the per-subscriber cost for the equipment necessary to receive, process, and distribute signals is marginal, particularly if addressable converters are used, when considered against the value of attracting or keeping (maintaining) even a few subscribers. But the increasing number of program services and satellite transponders will complicate the programming of even the high-capacity cable systems in the future, presenting problems similar to those facing the 12- and 30-channel systems now.

The value of multiple pay services has been established, at least for the bigger systems. Subscribers will communicate their interest in new pay channels while the service is being introduced. The number of pay channels thus becomes a marketing matter. Do enough homes subscribe to warrant the marketing cost? Do second, third, and more pay channels undermine existing pay channels over the long run so that there is a net loss when marketing costs are included?

The lower capacity systems, particularly the 12s, must choose a few channels from among a large pool available. The operator who knows the community may be able to make intuitive selections of services that satisfy the greatest number. For example, the operator should know the sports teams that are followed in the city and what stations or satellite services cover those teams. The operator may also know what program interests are underserved in the community. Filling these needs is a different matter from attempting to serve the greatest number of subscribers. In this case there may be a strong minority audience interest that is not satisfied by television. The numbers may not be great, but the need may be sufficient to attract them as subscribers, perhaps a Spanish-language channel where there is an Hispanic minority. Experience in selling cable subscriptions also tells the operator what program types are most attractive.

Formal surveys of subscribers and nonsubscribers may aid in programming. If available services are described carefully, with concrete examples of programs, respondents should be able to make a decision about which would make a marginal and which would make a significant contribution to their satisfaction if they are already subscribing, or to their willingness to subscribe to cable if they are not. The surveys should have a high response rate (the proportion of actual replies to the total in the original sample). Surveys that do not get a high response rate should not be used to project to the whole community or make comparisons of the relative value of various options. They could be used to project the percentage of the population from which they are drawn and may be sufficient to indicate if there are enough people, just within that population, to make a program service viable. When initially surveying a community, or nonsubscribers in a mature system, the level of interest expressed by households surveyed should be discounted substantially, the nonsubscribers most because of their previous resistance to cable.

The professional trade magazines and people at regional and national professional meetings share information about the relative "lift" provided by the different program options. Experience in other, similar communities is perhaps the best indication of the merit of programming, but care must be taken to sort out good evidence from casual use of a few phone calls praising or objecting to a program service. Satellite-delivered network affiliate relations representatives aggressively promote their programming and, in the case of the 12-channel systems, attempt to present evidence that would lead to substitutions, their only hope in the limited-channel situation.

A solid basis for program decision making is also important to franchising authorities and cable commissions where there is a tendency to react to a limited number of personal requests for program types, in the absence of other information.

Local Origination

Experience with local origination on cable is quite limited. What we have seems to be different from community to community. Public, education, and government access as well as community channels have been discussed in Chapter 6. Programming strategy is important to all these channels. The operator must decide what to put on community channels, although this may be prescribed in part by the franchise agreement. News and sports are dominant features of most such channels. Furthermore, the operator must determine who will program the channels. Most are programmed by the cable operators themselves, but newspapers alone or jointly with cable operators program some channels. The government and the schools take programming responsibility for their channels and the access coordinator for the public access channel (to the extent that it can be "programmed" with its diversity of content). Local broadcasters have been encouraged to lease cable channels for newscasts and other programming. Joint cable-broadcaster efforts might arise here also. In joint operations with either newspapers or broadcasters, the cable company takes advantage of an existing news-gathering staff *and* an existing advertising sales staff. In joint ventures or channel leasing, however, the cable company gives up autonomy and potential profit.

Some cable companies book their own movies and syndicated programming. These *stand-alone* channels select from catalogs available from film and television program syndicators. (Lists of distributors are available in most cable directories.) In the case of films, cable systems usually book classics or older, lesser known titles with recognizable actors. They may pay a flat rate of about $70 per week or a per-subscriber fee of 10 to 70 cents per month. Syndicated television programming for basic cable is leased on a flat-fee basis which is negotiated. In addition to the rental fees, systems may be asked to pay shipping and duplication costs. The programs and films are supplied on videocassettes.

Aside from content, the cable operators and access channel users must develop scheduling strategies. A first principle, unique to cable, is program redundancy. Cable systems may repeat programs far more often within a short period than may commercial and public broadcasters. This maximizes opportunities for viewing and, since programming other than news and sports on origination channels may not be sufficiently attractive to draw an audience to a single viewing time, may reach substantial cumulative audiences with repeat showings. A broadcast television station leasing a cable channel might repeat its latest newscast over and over again until the next update, providing a valuable service to viewers who cannot arrange schedules to suit the broadcast and extending the value of the commercial announcements to advertisers.

It is unlikely that repetition would be a negative factor to viewers of local origination as in the pay channels where consumers relate their satisfaction to the cost of the service or the availability of fresh material. But local origination viewers would have to be able to learn a programming pattern for each channel.

Cable Journalism

Much of the local origination by cable systems themselves, on community channels and through one-way and interactive electronic text systems, is *journalism*. This is a new function in the cable industry that carries serious responsibilities and important privileges.

The responsibilities are to be accurate, fair, complete, and comprehensible. Since cable news operations started on shoestring budgets, frequently staffed by volunteers, these responsibilities were difficult to meet. A new kind of journalist is required for cable—one steeped in the professional traditions of journalism through education and experience in newspapers and broadcasting, but adventuresome enough to look for new opportunities in cable, with its higher capacities, to permit (1) in-depth reporting and beginning-to-end transmission of events, (2) scheduling flexibilities to suit user schedules, (3) interactive retrieval systems to allow subscribers to reference information and order news tailored to specific interests, and (4) narrowcasting to address neglected audiences within a metropolitan media environment.

Local cable origination journalism can be integrated with the national services (CNN, CNN2, Satellite News Channels, Financial News Network, UPI Cable News, Reuters News View, Associated Press, Dow Jones Cable News, C-SPAN, The Cable Health Network, The Weather Channel, etc., and videotext reference and news services) to form a well-rounded household information budget never before available on television. The packaging and promotion of both local and national information services is a new challenge for cable operators.

In the bigger cable systems, there are likely to be economic incentives and resources to fulfill these journalistic responsibilities and opportunities. Of all local programming in television broadcasting, news is by far the most popular. Advertisers—including retailers foreclosed from metropolitan broadcast television covering a 70-mile radius because of wasted circulation—will support cable news. Subscriber fees may also be adjusted to provide operating expenses for news. (The need for the journalistic independence of cable from city government, incidentally, is a strong argument against rate regulation.)

On the other hand, exercise of these responsibilities is subject to two major disincentives. One is the monopoly position of cable systems. Competition, on cable, is excluded and competition from other news media, in cable systems or hubs which serve only part of large metropolitan markets, is very limited. The second disincentive is the subordinate position of the journalistic function of cable in relation to the other services. Cable journalism will have a low priority in management attention because it will produce only a small portion of the total revenue.

The privileges of journalism under U.S. law are equally important to cable. As the newest of the news media, cable may have difficulty in establishing these rights. The struggle of CNN to participate fully in Washington news pools on a parity with the broadcast television networks is an illustration of the difficulties to be faced.

Cable journalists must be aware of and assert rights of reporter access to public proceedings and records under the Freedom of Information Act[11] and comparable state laws. Cable journalists should be partners with broadcasters and news photographers in seeking access for their reporting tools to courts and other public proceedings. The cable journalist must protect his or her news sources and resist being used by law enforcement agencies at the risk of undermining future performance and credibility. Cable journalists responsible for videotext and conventional television news have a good argument for treatment as newspapers,

under the First Amendment, against the application of the Fairness Doctrine, particularly where leased and public access channels are operable.
Cable systems should contribute to, and join, journalistic organizations
such as Sigma Delta Chi that seek to preserve news media freedoms.

Packaging

In describing cable services in Chapter 6, we identified the *packages*
of cable services conventionally made available to consumers. It will be
recalled that there is a major distinction between basic and pay channels.
Some operators also insert a level in between the two, expanded basic,
made up of satellite-delivered channels at a small charge beyond basic.
This charge helps to recover the cost of a converter, the monthly fee to
the program supplier, if any, satellite-receive dishes, and promotion as
well as to provide revenue. The satellite services and advertisers are
insistent, now, that they be included as a part of basic cable since that
assures them of the largest audience penetration. Unfortunately, insufficient experimentation in packaging cable programs has taken place to
assess the value of deviations from these packages. New services have
become available gradually. Once a subscriber becomes familiar with one
packaging scheme, it may be poor programming or marketing strategy
to make major modifications. The technology, before addressable converters, did not permit the offering of uniquely tailored services to each
household. With the new addressable technology and more opportunities
to experiment as the industry matures, greater attention and more imagination may be applied to the programming task.

PROGRAM GUIDES

The number of channels offered by cable systems makes program
guides essential. There are several program guide options available to
serve this consumer and cable system need.

Alphanumeric

Many cable systems devote a full channel to program listings for
the other channels. Programs are listed by channel and program title,
usually by the half hour for the whole day, or at any given time, the
remainder of the day, automatically dropping off the hours as they pass.
The character-generated listings recycle as soon as the day's listings are
complete. Alphanumeric listings may be provided by an outside source,
customized to a particular cable system. These logs include program descriptions.

The program channel can have space for advertising messages crawling across the bottom. When not sold to local businesses, the crawl may be used to promote locally originated programs or pay services.

Printed Guides

Most printed guides are custom printed by specialized TV guide publishers, of which there are several. The guide publishers will do as much or as little as the cable system desires. Some will take over the selling of advertising. Program descriptions for all broadcast stations and all basic and premium cable networks are collected by the publisher from the stations and networks. The cable system need only provide program information for local origination channels. They are sold to the cable system and then sold or given to subscribers. Some are sold directly to subscribers by the publisher, with the operator providing mailing lists.

The guides may be bill stuffers. To save postage, including the guide and the bill under the minimum first-class postage rate, a bill stuffer guide must be under one ounce. The guide must be monthly to go along with the monthly bill which further limits the content.

Some guides cover only the major cable basic and premium networks (e.g., USA, ESPN, CNN, HBO, Showtime, TMC) and are published nationally with the same content except for time zone differences. Newspaper guides do the same thing for their circulation regions.

Full-sized guides are usually not mailed with the bill. They may be weekly, bimonthly, or monthly. Since weight and size is not an issue, particularly for weeklies and bimonthlies, the full-sized guide can contain full listings for all channels.

Program logs (rolling logs) list programs with times chronologically in three formats: (1) *title only,* for monthlies or bill stuffers; (2) *partial descriptions,* with titles for series and descriptions for movies, talk shows, and specials; and (3) *full description,* with every program titled and described. Generally, the more frequent the publication, the more descriptive the guide.

Guides may also have programs presented in a *grid* format, where the hours of the day are listed down the grid on the left and the channels across the top. Because only titles are used in the grid, program highlights are usually added with descriptions of movies, sports, specials, and talk shows.

All guides may have *breakouts,* separate listings of each day's programs in particular categories such as sports, movies, and specials. And, of course, guides may include picture and text features on programs and performers. Most of the full-sized guides sell advertising space.

There are several significant problems in publishing guides. With as many channels as are available in a dual 400-mHz system, it is difficult to present the listings in a comprehensible, usable format. Television stations, and the cable systems themselves, are not very good at keeping the publisher (whether in-house or outside) informed of program changes. If the guide is intended to cover a fairly large geographic area, there are so many cable systems involved that channel alignment becomes a problem. Each system assigns program services to channels independently, and most are different.

Value of Guides

The consumer is not likely to value the cable subscription fully unless a complete guide is made available. Cable systems offer far too much for the subscriber to commit the television schedule to memory as was once done with the three-network schedule. Systematically switching channels is even too cumbersome and time consuming for a 30-plus channel system. With so many program options, the viewer may need descriptions to help make choices.

The cable system benefits in several ways from the guides. It provides a company identity, ever present in the home. The cornucopia of programs listed in the guide keeps people aware of all they are getting by cable and discourages turnoffs. To those who are not subscribers to the full service, a listing of *all* programs and channels available on the system is a constant reminder of what they are missing. A single guide covering all programs and channels replaces several separate guides that are necessary for a multipay system. Finally, the guides themselves may be another cable "profit center" through sale of the guides, sale of advertising space, or both. Advertisers may be offered a five-way impact through print ads in cable guides; ads on alphanumeric, local origination, and cable network channels; and bill stuffers. Unsold advertising space in the guides can be used to promote pay channels and in maintenance marketing programs (discussed later).

NOTES

[1]Sources are Video Probe Index five-market survey reported in *Cablevision,* May 21, 1979, pp. 84–104; Hart Survey, "System Operating Series," National Cable Television Association, July 1979; Arbitron, "New Electronic Media Study," reported in *CPB News Briefs,* December 5, 1980; Young & Rubicam pay impact study, reported in *Cablevision,* July 21, 1980, pp. 10–12; Benton & Bowles new media report, in *Broadcasting,* April 27, 1981, p. 86; "The Changing Audience of the '80s," address by Dwight M. Cosner, A.C. Nielsen Company, to BEA Faculty/Industry Programming Seminar, Washington, D.C., November 7, 1980; A. C. Nielsen pay cable report for July 1980, reported in *Cablevision,* November 10, 1980; *Panorama* survey by Stanley Marcus, "The Viewers' Verdict—So Far—on Cable TV," *Panorama,* October 1980, pp. 40–45; Stuart J. Kaplan, "The Impact of Cable Television Services on the Use of Competing Media," *Journal of Broadcasting,* Spring 1978, pp. 155–165; Leo W. Jeffres, "Cable TV and Viewer Selectivity," *Journal of Broadcasting,*

Spring 1978, pp. 168–177. A. C. Nielsen Company, Northbrook, Illinois, "Nielsen Report on Television 1981," "Beyond the Ratings," Arbitron, Beltsville, Maryland (several issues, 1980); Dean M. Krugman and Donald Eckrich, "The Cable Television Market," mimeo, Michigan State University, East Lansing, 1981; A.C. Nielsen Company, Northbrook, Illinois, "1982 Nielsen Report on Television."

[2]"The Changing Audience of the '80s," Address by Dwight M. Cosner, A. C. Nielsen Company, to BEA Faculty/Industry Programming Seminar, Washington, D.C., November 7, 1980.

[3]Ibid.

[4]David B. Hill and James A. Dyer, "Extent of Diversion to Newscasts from Distant Stations by Cable Viewers," *Journalism Quarterly,* Winter 1981, pp. 552-555.

[5]Cosner, A. C. Nielsen Company.

[6]"Cable Viewing Facts," *Beyond the Ratings,* Arbitron, May 1979, p. 5.

[7]"Y & R Releases Pay Impact Study," *Cablevision,* July 12, 1980.

[8]Cosner, A. C. Nielsen Company.

[9]A. C. Nielsen Company, "Nielsen Report on Television 1981," A. C. Nielsen Company, Northbrook, Illinois, pp. 13–14. See illustration at the opening of this chapter.

[10]Dean M. Krugman and Donald Eckrich, "Differences in Cable and Pay Cable Audiences," *Journal of Advertising Research,* August 1982.

[11]5 U.S.C.A. 552.

14

Marketing and Advertising

Cable salesperson makes presentation to a family, United Cable, East Lansing, Michigan.

MARKETING

The marketing of cable system services is of interest to the consumer and franchising authority as well as to the system operator. The cost of service to the consumer is a function of the number of subscribers who use the service. If the system is not marketed aggressively, the monthly charge to subscribers will be high, and the profits to the operator will be low. Furthermore, the market value of the cable system itself—the index that is often used to assess the return on investment rather than the earnings—is usually stated in terms of a dollar figure for each subscriber. That value is currently as high as $1,500 per subscriber. The homes passed (not subscribing) are valued at about $150. This clearly indicates the significance of signing and retaining a single subscriber.

Marketing will be subdivided into four areas: (1) marketing in new construction areas, (2) launching new pay services, (3) remarketing to established cable service areas, and (4) maintaining subscribers (preventing attrition).

Marketing New Construction

Selling cable subscriptions in new systems or areas of new construction, called *new-builds* in the cable industry, follows an established pattern with variations from one operator to another. This section describes the process of introducing cable to an area for the first time. The marketing of new construction which is an extension of an established system is somewhat different and much easier because people already know about cable and are anticipating its availability in their neighborhood.

In planning selling strategy, a knowledge of the diversity of consumer attitudes toward cable is essential. Some of these attitudes have been suggested in the audience section. They will be expanded here in an attempt to catalog consumer responses fully.

Positive responses: (1) Television is already a primary activity in the household, so even a marginal improvement in the quality of that activity is highly valued. (2) Television is not a dominant activity in the household. Programs are viewed selectively. Therefore, an increase in program choice is valued. (3) Movie fans want to see films before they are available on broadcast television or fill in, by pay television, the titles they did not get to see in theaters. (4) R-rated movies are attractive for their novelty on television and the stimulating content. (5) People who work odd hours need the 24-hour cable networks to satisfy viewing interests. (6) Children urge cable on the household because of the increase in programs, particularly outside of prime time. (7) People of modest income need inexpensive entertainment and escape. (8) Conscious of status and cable-stimulated topics of conversation, people may feel some pressure to be included among the group of subscribers. (9) A single intensely desired program category, such as a cultural channel for an intellectual, an ethnic channel for a member of that group, or a sports channel for the sports fan, will justify the subscription. (10) Innovators will be curious about cable and want to try it.

Negative responses: (1) Paying for television is an affront to one's value system. (2) The few channels already available are adequate. (3) The household has managed to get along for a long time without cable. (4) The content of some cable channels is offensive. (5) The children already watch too much television. (6) Cable would be nice to have but the household can't afford it now. (7) Older people, in particular, question the R-rated films, express lack of interest in today's movies, and seek the familiar content of broadcast television networks.

To address all these different motivations for subscribing to cable, or for rejecting it, the sales message must cover *all* the ground quickly and then focus on the perceived interests or circumstances of the individual consumer.

In new-builds, cable companies use a *top-down* approach, attempting to sell every available service—the top tier. Some operators do not even offer anything else in early advertising, direct-mail promotions, and sales contacts. The deliberate effort *not* to make distinctions among services in an effort to sell everything is called *smudging*. Eventually if the household rejects the top tier, the salesperson drops down to the next lower tier. Basic only is the last resort if all other levels fail to attract interest or are too expensive. Apart from the obvious revenue considerations, this approach is taken because, through experience in cable marketing, it has been demonstrated that it is much easier to sell the pay services initially to a new subscriber than to get them to *upgrade*—add a service later.

In almost all cable sales strategies, incentives are used to encourage subscription. In a new-build area, introductory offers are important to get people to try the service. The most common incentive is a reduction in the installation price. The household is urged to sign up *now* to get a special installation price or to have the installation charge waived entirely. Ostensibly this saves the subscriber $15 or more, although the operator does not plan on collecting many such fees because the installation fee is reduced in subsequent sales promotions as well as in the initial round. Another incentive is a period of free service as a trial ("risk-free service"). The household may cancel at the end of the period without paying or continue after that time at the regular cost. Premiums, such as canvas bags printed with the name of a pay channel supplier or the cable company, are also used. Often the pricing structure of cable is set up so that there is a discount for accepting the whole package. For example, basic might be $8.00 and two pay channels might be offered at

$9.00 each, but if the subscriber takes both pay services, the price might be $24.00, with a "value" of $26.00. Cable companies may hold one or two satellite networks out of basic and include them in the top tier as a bonus—another incentive for taking the top tier.

Some cable marketers disdain any kind of incentives on the theory that the subscriber won by such devices may be persuaded by the incentive rather than by the merit of the service. There is some evidence of a higher disconnect rate among subscribers gained by incentives as opposed to those signed up without any incentive. Nevertheless, most operators think that it is necessary to provide incentives to get subscribers to try cable.

Most cable operators now collect *front money* at the time of the sale. This may be one or two months' service charge in advance, an installation charge, if there is one, and a deposit on the converter. (It is difficult to determine how much of a converter deposit to take. On the one hand, converters are expensive and the theft or destruction of a converter is a significant loss. On the other hand, a substantial deposit will have a negative effect on sales.) Some front money is an assurance of the sincerity of interest on the part of the new subscriber. Through experience, cable operators learned that, if no money is collected in advance, if it is too easy to subscribe, then a substantial proportion of the subscribers would soon disconnect. Many operators now accept credit card purchases. Sales people carry lightweight, portable imprinters.

A few cable operators rely on contract sales organizations for marketing. Since most marketing efforts are concentrated in short periods of time (e.g., the initial marketing of a system or the launch of a new pay service), the contract sales company circumvents temporary in-house staffing. The outside sales company may bring in a single supervisor who hires and trains local people or come in with a full crew of experienced sales people. Most of the contract sales firms like to be involved in the decisions on pricing and incentive policies to maximize the subscription sales.

Promotion, publicity, advertising. During the franchising process, cable is publicized in a variety of ways. Ideally, news media, on their own initiative, cover each phase of the franchising and supplement that news with features about the cable technology and services. This, of course, contributes to informed decision making in the franchising, but it also serves to educate the consumer. The cable applicants, and the eventual awardee, make news releases and assist the media in reporting the news. Often advertising is used during the franchising period by applicants in an attempt to differentiate one application from another. After the award, *teaser* ads are used to hold interest and keep up anticipation during the slow process of construction. Marketing services from program suppliers include all the direct sales and advertising materials discussed in this section with space for local imprint or tag as well as sales training materials. (Sometimes sales training programs are delivered by satellite.)

Cable systems are built a section at a time. As soon as a section is built and tested, cable subscriptions are sold in that section. Thus, the system begins to generate revenue as soon as the first section is built. The availability of cable in each additional neighborhood is announced to the news media along with the planned progress to the next section. Because only a small section of cable is being marketed at a time, television, radio, and daily newspaper advertising at this point is designed mainly to inform residents in unbuilt areas that construction is progressing. This type of advertising tapers off as the universe of unconstructed sections is reduced. Broadcast television, which of course is a good medium for selling television, may not be available since some broadcasters have a policy of not helping a potential rival.

Nonpersonal sales. Because the sales efforts are targeted directly to the neighborhoods where construction has just been completed, *direct mail* or *door hangers* with response cards or telephone ordering information are efficient devices for reaching the appropriate homes. The people who order cable this way are usually quite interested and have been waiting for cable to be available in their neighborhood. They have been *presold*. Taking their orders by the most inexpensive means possible is called *creaming*. The more expensive, personal sales methods are reserved for the more hesitant.

Direct mail pieces or door hangers may be most effective in a new section of cable that has been added onto an older system. The people already know about cable. Personal selling is not necessary to "educate" the consumer as in new cable markets. Direct mail and literature, along with advertising, serves to set the scene for later sales efforts, even if not actually making sales. It is sometimes called *preheating* the market.

Telephone. After direct mail, door hangers, and advertising have exhausted the first sales, some cable systems use the telephone to contact the remaining households. Some homes are more receptive to telephone than to door-to-door salespersons whom they may not trust. Commissions paid on telephone sales are lower than door-to-door sales. A battery of phones is installed, phone salespersons trained, and the calls made in the early evening or weekend hours. The phone salespersons have a prepared script, usually permitting some personalization, that they can use as the basis for their approach. The principal attractions of the service are described briefly, usually followed by the offer of an incentive to subscribe.

Door-to-door. The next step is to sell face to face, door-to-door. The salesperson has a credential that identifies the person with the company which may be presented or only held in case the identity is questioned. The approach is similar to the telephone with the brief service description covering all the major appeals and a special incentive to subscribe. The salesperson usually has a folder that illustrates the range of programming available and program guides. In this sales situation, the salesperson has more cues as to household interests than in telephone sales. The salesperson may ask a few questions about household television viewing and satisfaction with over-the-air television in an attempt to draw out some *dissatisfactions* that cable can address or *interests* that cable serves better. If the sale cannot be closed immediately, a brochure is left with the invitation to place the order later by order card, phone, or at the business office.

Most cable systems have a conveniently located business office, which encourages walk-in business. People can come in, sample the programming on television receivers in the lobby, talk to customer service people, place orders, and pay bills. One operator, in Tacoma, Washington, labels the business office "The Cable TV Store."

The approach to consumers and the particular sales method, whether by direct mail and advertising, telephone, or face to face, may depend on the demographics of the community. It is generally believed that lower-income households do not respond well to direct mail and advertising but do respond to personal, face to face presentations. The reverse seems to be true for higher-income households.

Launching pay services. Many cable systems were built and serving subscribers before the beginning of pay television. New pay networks are starting every year. The *launch* of a new pay service, to be added onto existing cable services, presents a different marketing problem. Almost everywhere a lower pay-to-basic ratio is achieved in these circumstances. The new pay service must be marketed to existing subscribers and to nonsubscribers as well since the new service may be desirable to those who have not previously been attracted to cable. The techniques for selling the two groups are different.

The marketing of multipay packages has the advantage of giving the household more than a choice of "Do you want it or don't you?" but rather "How many do you want?"[1] With competing pay services offered at once, the suppliers are likely to try to match each other in promotional advertising. There is some doubt within the industry, however, about going from double to triple and beyond in maxipay service where there is not much differentiation except for schedule because *switchovers* may create administrative costs without a net gain in pay units. The industry is now concerned about evidence of a falloff of multipay subscriptions. Some of the newer franchise bids are predicated on high multipay penetration.

A common approach to marketing a new pay service to existing subscribers is to allow a few free days of *preview* so the subscribers can sample the programming. This must be arranged in advance with the pay suppliers who, in turn, make an agreement with film distributors. The per-subscriber fee for the promotional period is negotiated with the supplier. Occasionally, a cable operator will offer a preview to all connected households without authorization, which is a violation of contractual agreements between pay supplier and film distributors.

The preview is advertised through one or more media—bill stuffers, billboards, radio, newspapers, television, and program guides. The advertising may be subsidized partly or in whole by the supplier. Radio and TV spots, newspaper art or mats, billboard sheets, and envelope stuffers will be supplied by the pay distributor as desired. Some cable companies would rather prepare their own materials to give a bigger play to the local cable system. During this period and thereafter, pay services are promoted on audio and video portions of alphanumeric channels, and promotional spots are inserted in satellite network channel local availabilities and local originations that are not sold to advertisers.

The preview is usually timed to include a blockbuster film or event. During breaks in the schedule, filler material is replaced with locally originated promotional material inviting subscription. Frequently, these are live *telethons* where the subscriber is urged to phone in an order or to order via the cable two-way system. Videotaped excerpts presenting a broader sample of the programming are also used in the breaks. Local and national celebrities and representatives of the premium service often appear. Contests, prizes, and live remote radio and television programs add some excitement.

Program guides for the new pay channel may be sent to subscribers and nonsubscribers to heighten interest. As noted earlier, program guides covering all the cable system programming are useful in marketing since they continuously remind lower-level subscribers of the other programming on the cable.

Subscribers who are not sold in the preview, and nonsubscribers are contacted by direct mail, door hangers, telephone, and door-to-door salespersons in much the same way as in the initial marketing. At this time all services of the cable system are sold, "lifting" all levels of service, although the new pay service may be emphasized to attract interest and take advantage of any advertising that has been placed. Salespersons must know what services the existing subscribers are getting so they know what is left to sell.

Adult pay channels may need special treatment. Some cable companies have succeeded with very direct advertising copy telling just exactly what the product is and making the obvious appeals. Others have been more subtle and understated, with and without advertising. At the extreme, some companies use only direct mail and then only to *Playboy* and *Penthouse* subscriber lists. This may be one reason why both *Playboy* and *Penthouse* have gone into the cable television programming business.

Some companies feel that making credit checks on pay subscribers is important because there is an out-of-pocket cost if the subscriber fails to pay. The per-subscriber fee to the pay suppliers is paid whether or not the cable operator is paid by the customer.

The cable industry is only beginning to learn how to market cable in competition with existing STV and MDS services. Cable people have underestimated the loyalty of some STV and MDS customers, and perhaps overvalued the multichannel capacity of cable. Competition through major advertising media is not practical for cable since the areas marketed by cable, at any given time, are miniscule in relation to the market for STV and MDS. Cable marketers will need to develop literature and personal sales presentations that meet head on the comparative merits of competitors.

Remarketing

After cable and any of the subsequent add-on services have been launched, the services must be *remarketed*. This may be continuous cycling through the community with a permanent sales staff and through special campaigns using systemwide advertising and promotion. Subscriber incentives may be used for the special campaigns.

Remarketing in a mature system must be controlled carefully. Since most people who have a real interest in cable have subscribed already, the *universe* of nonsubscribers is difficult to sell and retain. It may be that the number of retained subscribers resulting from a remarketing campaign is so small that the marketing costs are not justified. Furthermore, aggressive marketing in a mature system may produce a *supersaturated* system, where penetration goes above an equilibrium state with many of the new subscribers eventually disconnecting. This may be a result of overselling, premium offers, failure to collect front money or make credit checks, discounts, and other devices that induce the subscription sales for artificial reasons.

The most productive remarketing is with new arrivals. People in single-family dwellings move about once every five years and apartment dwellers much more frequently. Keeping in contact with these households is a major administrative problem. Real estate organizations, utilities, Welcome Wagons, and the cable operator's own disconnect reports may be used to identify new households in the community. When a cable subscriber moves, it may be the policy not to disconnect that household physically. The new occupants are informed that they are connected and are invited to subscribe. They may be offered a free introductory week of viewing everything that is available on the cable.

Apartments, with highest turnover, are most difficult. Some cable companies engage building supervisors to identify and present cable literature to new residents. They are paid a commission for all apartments that are hooked up or are given a discount on their own service. Many large apartment owners are attempting to take a share of cable revenues or establish a competing service. Service to the large apartment complexes is becoming difficult for cable systems to negotiate. As a result of the Supreme Court decision in *Loretto v. Teleprompter*, landlords may demand *fair compensation* for permitting installation of cable equipment. But, the court affirmed the right of states to make laws giving cable systems *access* to apartment tenants who order service.[2]

A major remarketing task is upgrading existing subscribers who are thought to be the best market for additional services. Some companies attempt to have a direct-mail piece in every monthly statement to those subscribers taking less than the full service, encouraging upgrading to one or another of the available services. The computer billing designates the subscribers not taking the particular service being promoted for the month, and only those subscribers receive the message.

Cable companies must *audit* the system periodically to discover illegal connections. Sometimes households are not disconnected when they are supposed to be or connected households are not paying for all the services they are receiving. Some people have actually made the connection themselves. Whatever the reason, they are politely informed of the situation by a salesperson and invited to become a paying subscriber. Since these people have been enjoying the service, a surprising number of the "illegals" become legal, paying subscribers.

Maintenance Marketing

The retention of a subscriber and prevention of a *downgrade* (dropping one or more of the services) is, of course, as important as adding a new subscriber. A part of the marketing program is designed to keep customers happy, reminding them of the benefits of the cable service. Each new service that is added to basic cable is promoted through advertising and mail announcements (bill stuffers). Occasional advertisements compare cable service to the cost of alternate entertainment (e.g., pay cable versus theater movies). A system operator can count on funds from pay and advertiser-supported networks to help with maintenance marketing. The program guide itself, with the extensive listings for each hour is a promotional vehicle and can also be used for advertisements and feature articles about cable and cable programs. Points for each month of subscriber longevity may be given to be applied by the subscriber to merchandise or travel. All of this is called *maintenance* marketing. A concentration of maintenance marketing effort may be necessary at the time of a rate increase to minimize disconnects. Cable systems frequently time the addition of new channels to coincide with a rate increase.

Probably the most important aspect of maintenance marketing is the quality of customer service personnel. They are trained to think of themselves as part of the marketing program. They must know the entire service well, be able to answer questions, handle problems pleasantly and efficiently, and discourage disconnects politely. It is essential that the customer service or business office have enough personnel and phone lines to accommodate the traffic.

Marketing Two-Way Services

Not too much is known about the marketing of two-way services. More experience is needed. At this point, two-way services are most always sold separately from the one-way entertainment and information packages, although the basic and pay salespersons may offer the two-way services and make uncomplicated sales or, more likely, get *leads* for follow-up by specialists. Incentives are seldom used because the sale is not triggered by impulse but by a well-developed, rational argument on the merits.

Direct mail, advertising, and telephone are used to produce leads for face-to-face sales calls. Most of the two-way services require demonstration, if not on line, through simulation with the equipment or on videotape. Time payment plans may be necessary for purchase of necessary hardware for security, videotext, and games.

In selling per-program pay services or any other usage-billed service, the cable operator is obligated to make a very careful credit check before making the installation, since the user is in effect given unlimited credit.

There has been a trend toward *third-party* sales of two-way services. A burglar and fire alarm company, for example, may take over the marketing and operation of alarm systems. Some cable companies are looking for an experienced buffer between themselves and consumers in this sensitive area where failures or mistakes could be disastrous. A newspaper may be associated with a cable company in a videotext venture. Modest goals are set for the initial marketing of most two-way services, generally five percent or fewer of the homes passed.

Sales Management

Administrative procedures. The sales effort is tied directly to construction and installation. As soon as the new construction is energized and satisfies performance tests, sales begin. The sales and installation staffs must be precisely the right size so that the sales people keep up with construction and the installers keep up with the sales. The installers should not get more than a week or two behind the sales staff so that the new subscribers do not lose enthusiasm. While not as big a logistic problem, installations must keep pace with sales in remarketing also.

Installers are company representatives. Cable operators do not consider the sale complete until the customer has been connected satisfactorily. The installer may have to explain the service and the converter and, in some circumstances (e.g., direct mail and phone sales), collect money and get signatures on an agreement. Because some members of a household may be absent during instruction on using the converter and the instructions are not always passed on adequately, a second visit may be necessary, or customer service people may be required to "talk" other members of the household through the procedures by telephone.

Every household passed by cable is stored in a computer or in files. Specific streets or sections are indexed so that they may be pulled out as needed. Streets, blocks, or sales packets of 50 or 100 contiguous homes are assigned to salespersons. After the initial mailings and sales, only the unsold households are drawn for the telephone selling, if used, and the door-to-door sales.

For each sales contact, the date and result are recorded. If the household refuses cable, it is helpful to record the reason and, perhaps more important, any signs of interest that may be developed later in remarketing. This is best entered into the computer by marking a list of preprinted reasons. For the new subscribers, of course, the level of service is also checked. Where the order is less than the full service, the salesperson may be asked to check the reasons for not subscribing to the rejected services.

A callback procedure for people not at home is prescribed for the sales staff, with sales people keeping records of the contacts and time of day so that return calls can be made at different times.

Training. Training is a continuing part of cable marketing because of the high turnover and frequent introduction of new services on which the sales and customer service staffs must be retrained. The first objective of the training is to acquaint the salesperson with the cable service. This is no simple matter in a modern, multitiered system. Any one of the channels may be an important attraction; therefore, the salesperson must be able to answer questions about each. The salesperson may be equipped with separate program guides for each of the channels.

The second objective is to teach sales technique. After some experience with hard-sell, high-pressure pitches, most cable companies concerned with the company image and long-term retention of subscribers now use a low-keyed, soft-sell approach. The training explains the use of sales aids such as a flip chart or full-color brochure. Sales aids may also graphically explain the pricing scheme, which is complicated in the multitier system. The salesperson must learn to communicate the price structure clearly.

One of the best training techniques for this work is role playing. The instructor plays the role of the consumer once or twice and then may break down the group into pairs with the trainees selling to each other. The training may be concluded by pairing each new salesperson with an experienced employee for a day or two of exposure to the real thing.

A third objective of the training is to detail the administrative procedures. The importance of record keeping is emphasized. The compensation scheme is outlined.

Finally, the salespersons must be motivated. While still keeping the expectations of eventual success high, they must be prepared for rejection and a short period of low productivity. The training program may also serve to shake out those people with a low aptitude for sales or insufficient motivation. Role playing and a thorough description of the task should give a fairly clear picture of the nature of the work.

Compensation. Salespersons are paid on a commission, with sales management personnel usually receiving an override. The commission plan is structured to provide several incentives. The most basic is, of course, to motivate sales, but higher commissions are paid for full-service sales to encourage sales of the maximum package of services to each household. Commission plans are also designed to pay a higher rate for sales over a particular number within any week to keep people working. Compensation plans may factor in penetration so that the commission is not only based on an absolute number of sales but on the percentage of sales within the territory—the higher the penetration, the higher the commission. This provides an incentive to deal with the tougher customers.

If the salesperson does not close the sale at the time of contact, the commission is still paid if the household orders the service within a specified time period. Door-to-door sales are compensated at a higher rate than are phone sales. Remarketing commissions may be higher than commissions in original marketing because the sales are more difficult and prospects scattered over a wider area.

Salespersons may be paid only for subscribers who are *retained* for a couple of months to discourage high pressure or overselling of the service that may result in quick disconnects. A part of the commission may be held so that the early disconnects can be written off against that reserve.

Pricing. The relationship between price and demand for cable services is not yet clear. Demand seems to be somewhat insensitive to price. Cable systems have been able to increase prices without serious attrition of subscribers, even in a period of economic recession. Estimates of the ceilings on average revenue per subscriber keep going up and are now way beyond expectations of just a few years ago.

Nonetheless, the cable operator must seek to set the optimum price. The following table is a simple example of the kind of projection that might be made for a tier of service.

Monthly Price	Estimated No. of Subscribers	Monthly Revenue
$5.00	600	$3,000
6.00	575	3,450
7.00	525	3,675
8.00	475	3,800
9.00	400	3,600

In this example the simple optimum price is $8.00 because it yields the greatest revenue. (Actually it is a bit more complicated. The $9.00 price might be optimum. If expenses were considered, the lower cost of servicing 400 subscribers versus 475 would probably mean a greater profit at the $9.00 price.)

The value of cable services to customers may vary somewhat according to the community. For instance, imported over-the-air broadcast stations are vital to the town with only one or two local stations, but relatively meaningless in a city with five or more stations.

Rate regulation and the monopoly circumstances for most franchises have prevented a natural market determination of prices. Cable prices have not kept pace with inflation over the past 20 years.

As mentioned earlier, a discounted price structure is used by some cable operators as an incentive to purchase a full service. Pay services may be priced less per unit in combination than independently.

Prices of basic cable may be static or increased at a slower rate than the pay services, as basic becomes more of an advertising-supported package of program services. Mass-consumption product advertisers will seek maximum circulation. Advertisers seeking narrowly defined audience targets will need a broad base of subscribers from which to aggregate a sufficient number in the target group. As advertising support develops, operators may be paying less per subscriber or even realize an income from advertiser-supported channels. In his Boston system, operator Chuck Dolan has experimented with an extremely low price for basic ($2.00). In some more recent franchises there is no charge at all for a large package of basic channels.

In other areas, operators have kept basic prices very high and pay cable low. The pay cable subscriber looks at the total price, not caring how it is split between basic and pay. Because HBO takes a proportional share of the pay price, it could be an advantage to the operator to keep that price low and basic high. The operator keeps all the basic fee.

Often in direct mail and advertising, price is not mentioned at all.

In a multitiered system, it is difficult to explain the pricing without a person-to-person exchange. The top-tier, or full-package price, may scare off the prospect. A better response rate is generally received with nonprice advertising.

Because the converter represents a substantial per-household capital cost, some operators, particularly those who offer the converter as an upgraded option to a 12-channel service, charge a monthly converter lease fee or a converter deposit. A few systems are experimenting with purchase plans for converters. This would, of course, eliminate the deposit and the company concern for theft or breakage. In Canada, converters have been sold through department and electronics stores for years. Still, in most U.S. systems the converter cost is buried in the general service charge.

Cost accounting. A number of figures are used as indices of sales productivity and for cost accounting. The universe of potential subscribers is *homes passed;* all homes that have access to cable, that is, where feeder lines actually go past the home either overhead or underground. *Basic penetration* is the percentage of households sold to households passed by cable. The *pay-to-basic* ratio indicates the proportion of basic subscriber households taking at least one pay service. *Pay-to-homes-passed* is the proportion of homes passed that take at least one pay service. Other ratios, or percentages, in use include *top-tier-to-basic* and *top-tier-to-homes-passed* indicating the proportions of households taking the full service. The figures are most meaningful in systems where there is only one pay tier. In multipay systems, pay penetration is usually indicated by the number of pay units sold. The pay-to-basic penetrations for each of the pay tiers are simply added together. If HBO is sold to 70 percent of the basic subscribers, Showtime to 40 percent, and The Movie Channel to 30 percent, the pay penetration is said to be 140 percent. This is sometimes called *percentage of all pay to basic.* Still another index is the number of *equivalent subscribers.* Here the total revenue of the system is divided by the basic rate to arrive at a figure that is comparable to a basic-only system. This latter figure is useful in comparing systems which may have a variety of different service packages.

The *retention rate* is also an important figure because cable systems fear *churn* or constant turnover of subscribers. It is expensive to make connections, particularly when a part of the installation charge is waived as an incentive to subscribe. The retention rate is the percentage of subscribers that remain connected for a specific period of time, perhaps two or three months. This is an index of satisfaction with the service and the quality of the sales campaign.

Cost per sale is the total marketing cost for a particular campaign divided by units of service sold, or retained units sold. *Cost per net unit* is the total number of units of service at the beginning of the year (or some other convenient period) subtracted from the number of units of service at the end of the year divided into the total marketing costs for the year. This is a cost-of-sales figure that reflects all marketing efforts, *including maintenance marketing.*

Cost analysis for direct-mail and coupon advertising is relatively simple. The response card or coupon is coded to indicate the particular mailing or advertisement from which it came. The response to the mailing or ad can be tabulated and the conversion to orders also recorded. The cost per unit sale can then be determined. When people phone in orders or come into the business office, the order taker can ask what prompted the order.

Keeping these cost figures permits comparison with company standards and gives a measure of control to marketing expenses. Because of higher costs in remarketing campaigns, cost analysis is critical. The value of maintenance marketing is most difficult to assess. If there is an attrition in subscribers, extra effort in maintenance marketing is necessary, but only enough to stem the tide and maintain long-term goodwill.

ADVERTISING

Advertising came to cable for one of the same reasons that it came to broadcasting and other media. Advertising was a means of supporting programming that could not be supported by subscription fees alone. Early CATV systems began selling advertising to help defray the costs of cablecasting local sports and other events. This was generally done on an ad hoc basis; when an event came up, the cable system staff would seek out one or two businesses that would put up some of the money, mainly as a community service contribution rather than as a marketing expenditure. A few companies, such as Palmer Communications in Naples, Florida, launched major programming efforts which attracted large audiences on a regular basis and discovered that advertising could not only cover costs but could develop as a new "profit center" for cable.

Automated alphanumeric channels also provided a medium for advertising, both audio and visual. Some cable companies sell sponsorship of weather and news services, with an identification heading the display or a bottom line that can crawl across the screen with an advertising message. The music which accompanies these alphanumeric channels can be programmed with audio advertising messages. Alphanumeric and audio channels provide a good medium for advertising that requires regular change: grocery specials, liquidation sale items, real estate, and so on. Trade-outs with radio stations are also common. Advertising of radio stations on alphanumeric channels is traded for radio advertising of cable services.

In the late 1970s the cable satellite networks, mainly CNN, ESPN, and USA, experienced some success selling spots and sponsorship to pioneering advertisers. These networks began operating like magazines or newspapers, earning revenues by both subscription and advertising. These networks make a few spots in each hour available for inserts of local announcements similar to the arrangement between broadcast networks and affiliates. Most of the local cable system availabilities are unused, but some operators have hired advertising salespersons to explore the market.

Advertisers are also anxious to exploit the potential of advertising at breaks between events in pay television services. Although pay cable is promoted as "uninterrupted," surveys of pay subscribers suggest that they would be amenable to commercials between the programs.

It is predicted that cable will get a fair share (about $2.25 billion) of over $100 billion in advertising expenditures by 1990.[3] Some advertising agencies are recommending that their clients shift five or six percent of their television advertising budgets to cable to compensate for broadcast network loss of audience.

For advertisers and agencies, cable has made the whole media buying process more complicated. To secure complete coverage of a mass market, it is no longer possible to buy one or two television networks. To reach specialized markets, several vertically programmed cable channels are available, as well as hundreds of narrowly targeted programs to consider along with magazines and the special sections of newspapers. Administrative costs in media buying, with more research necessary and more transactions, will rise.

Value to the Local Economy

Cable may be the only opportunity for television and radio advertising in some cable communities. Broadcast radio and television stations serving the community may serve other larger areas as well and, therefore, be too expensive and wasteful for localized retailers and other merchants. In small communities, with limited local radio and television outlets, cable becomes an alternate advertising medium, helps to break the monopoly lock on advertising time of the few stations, and opens the market to advertising competition.

Value to National and Regional Advertisers

National and regional advertisers are attracted to cable's young, *upscale* (high-income) subscribers with relatively large families. These people are difficult to reach without waste in other mass media. Furthermore, in a cable spot advertising campaign, the advertiser can pick the desired areas much more precisely than in broadcasting since cable systems cover smaller geographic areas which are often homogeneous demographically.[4]

Through specialized programming, advertisers can target particular demographic groups (e.g., businesspersons viewing a financial report on CNN). This opportunity has not been available in prime time to any extent in broadcast television.

The advertiser may test copy and various appeals at low cost in cable systems selected to represent the particular composition desired. Two-way technology facilitates the data collection.

Finally, cable offers a wide open opportunity to national and local advertisers to experiment with advertising forms. The advertiser is not restricted to 30 or 60 seconds. The message can be any length: 120 seconds, or half-hour "infomercials" or two-hour programs. Cable can serve as an electronic catalog. In two-way systems, ordering can take place instantly, perhaps impulsively, while interest is at its peak.

Some cable operators offer advertisers a package buy—cable advertising, space in the program guide, and bill stuffers.

Regional Interconnects

To be effective, advertising must generally reach a great many people with repeated impressions. Cable systems are small, in terms of the mass audiences that advertisers seek, and the number of persons viewing any one of the channels on which advertising time is available is even smaller. The administrative expense, in the advertising transaction between the advertiser (or advertising agency) and the several different cable systems that would be necessary for covering most areas, would be prohibitive. A further cost is in the equipment and staff to insert commercials in programming.

To address these problems, several *regional interconnections* have been organized. The interconnection aggregates enough cable subscribers to make the advertising buy of consequence to the advertiser. The interconnect may be either electronic or simulated. Only one negotiation is necessary for the whole group, which may include 20 or more cable companies. With an electronic, physical interconnection, only one playback facility is necessary to feed the entire group, and only one facility, acting as the headend, is necessary for the production of commercials. The same facility can be used for production of locally originated programming as long as the aggregated audience is of sufficient size to justify the production expense. The fixed costs are thus spread over a bigger subscriber base and several operators.

Automation is essential to success of cable advertising. Because of the small audience at any given time, cable ads require frequent repetition to make an impact. The price of a spot is so low that the cost of making the insertion manually could prevent a profit. To resolve this problem, equipment is available that puts a tone cue in program material about 5 seconds before a commercial is to begin. The tone starts the videocassette machine and, when it is up to speed, switches it into the program at just the right time. A tone on the commercial switches back to the program. The first tone can cue a character generator, slides, or a message wheel as well. Satellite networks that permit local advertising insertions carry the tones. Network filler material covers the time period if no local announcements are scheduled. The automatic insertion equipment can handle several channels at once. An operator simply puts the commercials on the tape in the right sequence and adds the tones; the proper insertion is automatic. Proof-of-performance recordings of commercials, run with time and date, can also be automated.

Interconnect groups or individual cable systems have rate cards that spell out the charges for time, which may vary by channel and day part. If there are production charges, these are presented. Most systems have significant frequency discounts. The more spots the advertiser buys within a time period, the lower the cost per spot.

A cable operator can get by without commercial production facilities by using advertiser-supplied materials, slides, message wheels, and a character generator, but eventually it will be necessary to develop a commercial production capability since many small local advertisers will not have their own ready-made spots.

Co-op advertising, where local advertising expenses for a manufacturer's product are shared with the retailer, is a good initial source of advertising for cable. Millions of dollars in available co-op advertising funds go unused each year. The manufacturer supplies the commercials. It is only necessary to supply the local dealer name and address by character generator or slide at the end of the commercial in the time provided.

Individual cable systems or even interconnected groups cannot sell spots to national advertisers on their own. The cost of making contacts with national advertisers and their advertising agencies in New York, Chicago, Los Angeles, and elsewhere would be too great for the amount of business that would be generated. Therefore, the cable system or group interconnect would engage a cable sales representative (rep) firm that would sell their time in the advertising market along with that of many other operators. The rep firms take a commission on the sales of about 15 percent. This practice developed in the newspaper and broadcasting business, where it is also impractical to be represented individually in all the cities where advertising time or space is purchased.

Some cable companies and advertiser-supported networks accept public service announcements (PSAs) from non-profit organizations to fill commercial availabilities that are not sold.

Audience Measurement

In some types of advertising, audience numbers are irrelevant. *Per-inquiry* advertising, where direct orders are taken by mail or telephone, is generally paid for by the advertiser as a percentage of sales. Interactive shopping channels may also sell merchandise directly. In both cases only the sales volume matters, not the size of the audience. But most advertisers, particularly national advertisers or large local advertisers with agencies, buy radio and television advertising on the basis of audience numbers. The audience for a program or station is surveyed by audience measurement companies (e.g., A. C. Nielsen, Arbitron). The cost of the time can then be assessed against the size of the audience. The index used is *cost per thousand* (CPM), as follows:

$$\text{CPM} = \frac{\text{cost of spot}}{\text{audience size}} \times 1,000$$

(If the spot on cable cost $40 and the audience at the time the spot was run were 2,000, the CPM would be $20—$40 divided by 2,000 and multiplied by 1,000. If a broadcast television spot cost $1,500 and were viewed by 100,000 people, the CPM would be $15. The cost of the two spots is not comparable, but the CPM is.)

All media can be compared on cost per thousand. The figure is particularly useful for comparing broadcast television with cable television advertising. Advertisers need to know how many people are being exposed to their messages. In the case of products and services that are sold to a narrow demographic group (e.g., OXY 10 to teenagers), the advertiser needs the number in that particular group. In this case, the CPM can be calculated for the *specific demographic category desired* if the audience is broken out in that category.

At this time, there are very few audience studies for cable television. Advertisers have been buying on the basis of subscriber counts and making guesses about the number of those subscribers watching a particular channel. Even the subscriber counts are undocumented. Eventually the cable industry is likely to have an independent organization that will audit subscribers similar to the Audit Bureau of Circulation (ABC) for newspapers and magazines. Of course, experience with cable advertising is also important. But it is rare that sales of a company that is advertising and promoting in a variety of ways can be traced to a single medium. A few of the satellite delivered, advertiser-supported cable networks qualify for metering by Nielsen (penetration of 15 percent of the U.S. television households).

Audience measurement in cable is much more difficult than it is in broadcasting. Cable may supply 30 or more channels of programming, whereas in broadcasting the number of stations in a market may be 4 or 5. A much larger sample is necessary to break out 30 channels than 4 because of sampling error. Furthermore, it is more difficult for people to recall or identify cable channels among many than it is to identify one broadcast station among a few. Finally, the upscale audience presumed to be using certain of the advertiser-supported cable channels is the least cooperative with, and least available for, audience surveys. They are generally considered to be underrepresented in audience surveys. A number of tests of audience measurement techniques addressing the unique problems in cable are being conducted.

Another different kind of difficulty in measuring the cable audience is economic. Broadcast rating services are supported principally by broadcasters rather than by advertisers who use the numbers. Several broadcasters share the cost of the surveys. In cable, there is only one company serving a given set of subscribers and no one with whom to share the cost of surveying that group. Therefore, the relatively higher cost of cable audience measurement would be a substantial proportion of the revenues that could be expected to be generated by advertising.

It is probably hopeless for cable to measure audience in the 15-minute blocks conventional in broadcasting. Cable should measure *cumulative* audiences. The cable audience "cume" is the number of people in an audience for a single channel (or several channels sold to advertisers as a package) over a period of time (a day or a week). The cable advertiser who buys a schedule of advertising spots disbursed frequently over that period of time knows roughly what he or she is getting.

The ultimate solution to cable audience measurement difficulties is two-way cable. In two-way, the customer agreement gives the cable operator permission to monitor channel tuning, *in aggregation* with other households. This provides a *census* of viewing behavior, which eliminates sampling error and does not rely on methods of determining viewing, such as interviews and diaries, which may be affected by faulty recall. Demographic characteristics of the viewing households may be determined by this method. The only shortcoming of the two-way monitoring system is the absence of information about the particular members of a household viewing.

When two-way cable is widespread, cable will have a far superior audience measurement system than will broadcast television or radio, newspapers, and magazines. It will eventually give a decided advantage over these other media. For the moment, the shoe is on the other foot.

In its infancy, the cable advertising business must first educate itself, and then advertisers and advertising agencies. The principal industry institution for this purpose is the Cabletelevision Advertising Bureau (CAB). The CAB runs advertising sales management meetings and seminars for the cable industry, is a cable management consulting resource, provides sales aids and materials, sponsors audience research methodology studies, promotes cable to advertisers and agencies, and is a resource on marketing and media information for prospective cable advertisers. The advertiser-supported cable networks also have representatives to assist cable operators in local advertising.

Questions of taste and ethics in advertising will face cable in the future as advertising in cable becomes more of a business. Does cable take commercials that are precluded from broadcast television or radio by the NAB codes or federal law (e.g., hard liquor, cigarettes)? Does cable take some ads only on specific channels (e.g., intimate products on adult channels)? Should there be self-regulation on the number of commercials per program hour? Does the average sound level on commercial announcements match the surrounding programming? Will the industry, federal agencies, or the courts police double billings on co-op advertising (to reduce the share of cost to the local retailer relative to the cost to the manufacturer)? Will cable advertising rate cards be applied equally to all buyers? Will sponsors be allowed to control program content?

These questions will be met and answered one way or another as the cable advertising business matures.

MARKETING/PROGRAMMING RESEARCH

Increasingly, as the growth of cable levels off and system operators have more time to maximize the potential of each system, market research will play a role. Programming research will also be important to serving subscribers and using the spectrum most effectively. Seemingly unlimited channel space, in the new systems, has made programming decisions too easy. Soon program availability may exceed capacity.

In-House, Basic Research

Perhaps the most productive and practical market research is that which is conducted in-house as a matter of routine within the marketing and customer service departments. This is not much more than specialized record keeping. Ideally, sales profiles are kept for every marketing district. Demographic characteristics of the district are determined and related to basic, pay-to-basic, and pay-to-homes-passed figures. These can be compared with systemwide standards and, in the case of an MSO, multiple system standards. For each phase of an original launch or remarketing effort, sales figures should be kept so that the productivity of each phase (e.g., direct mail, telephone, door-to-door) is known. These data should be broken out by meaningful demographic categories such as assumed neighborhood income level, so that it is known which sales techniques are most productive in particular categories of households.

The same records are kept for disconnects, upgrades, downgrades, and switchovers from one pay service to another. In the case of requests for disconnects and downgrades, subscribers are asked by the customer service representative if there were dissatisfactions with service, and why, as a part of the routine procedure for attempting to retain the subscriber at the existing level of service.

Survey Research

Through survey research, it is possible to determine subscriber and nonsubscriber attitudes toward services and potential services, packaging and programming plans, pricing, and reasons for disconnect, all for marketing purposes. Survey research may also generate important information for cable company use prior to rate increase requests or renewal proceedings.

Telephone and face-to-face personal interviews are most effective. Telephone is cheapest and effective if there is a high proportion of telephone households and few unlisted numbers. Random-digit dialing is a solution to the latter problem. Nontelephone homes may not be of serious concern in marketing research if it is assumed that most subscribers and the best prospective subscribers have telephone service.

Sampling

For survey purposes, a *sample* of the desired universe is sufficient. The necessary accuracy will determine the number in the sample. Other things being equal, the larger the sample, the lower the sampling error. But this is not a direct relationship. Because the size of the sample must be quadrupled to halve the error, there is a high cost to reducing error. For most purposes, a sample of about 400 is sufficient.

The sample is drawn from a *frame*. The frame is any listing of units in which one is interested. In cable, the desired frames should already be on hand and quite complete. The frames, or universes, that might be surveyed are all homes passed, nonsubscribers, basic subscribers, and pay subscribers (perhaps broken out by the various combinations or packages available).

Detailed Sampling Demonstration

For illustration here, we assume that the interest is in surveying nonsubscribers about their knowledge of cable and the appeal of specific new channels.

The system computer, or other record-keeping system, should be capable of producing a complete list of nonsubscribers. The computer may also be programmed to draw a sample, but for these purposes we assume a physical list of nonsubscribers. If there are 20,000 nonsubscribers, and we wish to sample 400, we divide 400 into 20,000 to determine that we need 1 household for every 50 households on the list. This number is known as the *skip interval*. We need to pick a random starting point within that interval. Use a table of random numbers in a statistics text or an almanac. In this case we enter the list blindly, land on a number, and use its last two digits. If the last two digits exceed 50, we keep dropping down the list until a number between 01 and 50 appears. If no table of random numbers is handy, we may use the numbers in a telephone book in the same way. Suppose that the number picked is 28. Thus we start at the head of the list, count to number 28, and select that household as the first of our sample. From that point, 50 households are counted off so that we take households 78, 128, 178 and so on until we get to 19,978, at which point we will have our 400-household sample. To avoid the tedium of counting, a template or rule may be used to measure off the space on the list taken by 50 households.

If the frame is mixed—for example, subscribers and nonsubscribers together, with the subscribers noted by a code of some sort—a similar procedure is used to obtain a sample of nonsubscribers. The total number in the list is known. If there are 44,000 total, we divide 400 into 44,000 to get a skip interval of 110. We select a number from 1 to 110 at random. When we enter the list and get to the randomly determined starting point, if that household is a nonsubscriber, we take it and count off 110 from that point. If any household we land on is not a nonsubscriber, we simply go down the list until we do reach a nonsubscriber and take that household, *but we must go back to the originally selected (but rejected household), to resume the counting.* Suppose that our starting point is household 61 and that it is a nonsubscriber. We take it. The next one would be household number 171. It is a subscriber and so is 172 and 173. Number 174 is not a subscriber, so household 174 becomes the second member of our sample. But, to count off the next 110, we return to 171 and start the counting from that point.

Sampling Error

What we have just described is a *systematic sample*. It is a *probability sample,* meaning that every household has had an equal chance of being selected. The laws of probability tell us that it is representative of the whole universe from which it is drawn; that is, the sample should have the same characteristics as the universe. In our example, the knowledge of cable and the interest in specific new channels would be about the same in the sample as in the whole group of nonsubscribers. They would not be *exactly* the same because of sampling error. There would be some difference because, in the luck of the draw, we may have gotten a few too many people who, in our knowledge of cable questions let us say, don't realize there are 24-hour movie channels on cable. Perhaps if we took a *census* of all 20,000 nonsubscribers, we might find 27 percent of the people who do not know about 24-hour movie channels and in our sample of 400 there are 29 percent. The difference can be attributed to sampling error. It may be calculated for a specific sample size and sampling procedure to give a plus or minus range of accuracy with a specific probability. For almost all purposes in marketing and programming research in cable, it can be assumed that the result actually obtained is a good estimate of the universe studied without actually calculating the sampling error.

Nonresponse Bias

In all surveys we can expect a certain amount of nonresponse. People are not home when contacted, even after a series of callbacks, or they refuse to cooperate, or in a telephone survey, the number has been disconnected. To have a sample that is representative of the whole, it is absolutely essential to keep the nonresponse to a minimum. The response rate should be 70 percent or better. The danger is in the probability that the nonrespondents will be somehow systematically different from the respondents. For example, if we are trying to judge how many nonsubscribers would be attracted to a particular new cable channel, and we project our estimate from a group of respondents who were home when we called, and 20 percent of the people in the sample were not home after the third callback, then we might have overestimated the likely "lift" that the new channel would provide. Why? Because the people who are not at home are less likely to be interested in the new cable service. They are not home very often to watch television. Our projection would be based on the stay-at-homes who have greater use for television. This is an example of a systematic nonresponse bias which will throw our results off a little. It is the reason for making several callbacks and trying to get absolutely as many people in the sample as possible.

If our original sample were 400 and we got 20 percent who are not home after the third callback and 10 percent refusals and disconnected phones, then we would have 280 people in our final tabulation. It does help to remove the nonresponse bias if we add additional members to the sample. We will get roughly the same nonresponse rate from the new households sampled, and so the *proportion* of those who are not at home much for television viewing will remain the same. *The point here is that nonresponse error cannot be corrected by increasing the sample, only by maximizing the likelihood of response by callbacks and proper interviewing techniques.*

Because of the very high nonresponse problem in mail surveys, they are not especially useful. A mail questionnaire, sent even to subscribers along with the bill, and an incentive to respond, is not likely to exceed a 30 percent response rate. This is too low to be reliable. There is a high probability that the other 70 percent is systematically different, in a number of unknown ways, from those who do respond.

Questionnaires

The purpose of the survey, along with another formal statement about how the information will be used, should be written out clearly before beginning to write the questionnaire. This focuses the questions and keeps the survey on track.

A survey questionnaire is introduced with a brief statement about its purpose. The sponsor is identified. Sometimes the real sponsor is disguised by using a research organization title. This could be an ambiguous research unit of the cable company in an in-house survey. The introduction does not ask cooperation (giving the respondent a chance to say no), but goes immediately to an easy or interesting question to get the respondent started and committed. ("Do you own a television set?")

The rest of the questionnaire should be simple and direct. The questions should not use words that a portion of the study population would not know. The respondent should not have to have a question repeated (a clue to an awkward question). Although it is a great temptation to ask everything that seems interesting, no question, other than perhaps an introductory throwaway question, should be in the questionnaire that does not relate directly to the prestated purpose of the survey and its specific use.

Simple surveys for internal use can be carried out by staff members, and it is important to develop that capability, internally. More complicated surveys might be contracted to one of several research firms, many with experience in cable. Listings are available in the *Broadcasting/Cablecasting Yearbook*.

Audience Count Research

Audience count research for individual television markets is usually done by telephone or by a combination of telephone and diary, and occasionally by personal interview. The objective of this kind of research is to find out how many people are viewing various channels and programs and how these audiences are demographically composed.

The best technique may be a telephone coincidental method whereby a sample of subscribers is interviewed by phone for each hour of the day in which audience data are desired. Subscribers are simply asked if they are presently viewing and, if so, what channel and program.

This might be asked for each member of the household, and it might be necessary to ask if the set being viewed is connected to the cable. Finally, there may be a question or two about household demographics. Because these interviews are very short, quite a few can be conducted. It would require several hundred people for each hour. A variation would be to ask people, rather than what they are viewing coincidentally, to recall their viewing for the day part immediately past (e.g., in the early afternoon for the morning).

Another method of audience research is to present the respondent with a list of channels or programs and ask if each had been viewed in some past period (usually the past week). This may be done by phone, if the list is not too long, for example, only the local origination programming or only the automated channels. For a longer list, perhaps covering all services on all channels, a personal interview with a checklist that is actually handed to the respondent and simultaneously read by the interviewer is most appropriate.

In the diary method, a sample of people is called by phone and asked to cooperate. This procedure is called *placement*. Those who agree are mailed a diary in which to record viewing, usually at 15-minute intervals throughout the day for seven days. Although this appears to be the most practical method of collecting audience information, it has some weaknesses. A substantial proportion of the sample is unwilling to keep the diary and, among those who say they will, there are many who do not follow through. Another difficulty is forgetting to keep up. Many people neglect the diary for several days and then try to recall a long period of previous viewing. Because there are so many channels on a cable system and the diaries so complex, recall of viewing is more difficult.

If audiences are being counted to determine the levels of interest in the various channel offerings for programming purposes (e.g., to make a decision about which channel to drop in order to add a pay service to a 12-channel system or to determine whether a local origination program is attracting enough viewers to justify the expense), then in-house research conducted by the cable system staff is adequate, probably through one of the telephone methods described earlier.

On the other hand, if the goal is to document audience for selling advertising time, then it is necessary to go outside. In-house staff research would not be credible to advertisers and advertising agencies. Furthermore, advertising agencies are habituated to Nielsen and Arbitron data for television, and it would be worth considering a custom survey by one of those companies. Some agencies will not use data from any other source. This would be most important if the goal is to use the data for selling national advertising. Local agencies might be willing to accept audience studies from a reputable local research agency.

If the object of the research is to attempt to change a programming plan that is written into the franchise agreement, again a credible outside research agency is necessary. The city council or cable commission would look upon in-house research as self-serving. (A bias in favor of a desired course of action could unintentionally creep in.)

Difficult Research Areas

It should be noted that certain types of survey research are not very successful in cable. It has been long established that program preference research does not produce very valid data. The results of questions about programs that viewers might like to watch, or would want more of, produce a *social desirability* response that may not predict behavior. People always seem to opt for educational and cultural programs that audience research indicates they do not watch even when available. Respondents know what's "good for them," but other motives often govern behavior.

It is also very difficult to do market research on the likely penetration of cable services *in advance* of any respondent experience with cable. If a community does not have cable, or if a cable service being introduced is quite novel, such as an alarm service or cabletext, people are unable to judge their own interest. They may accept the idea readily, when not faced with a decision that requires them to put cash on the line, or they may reject the service simply because they have gotten along without it in the past. Most people are unable to put themselves realistically in the hypothetical situations that this kind of research asks of them.

One way in which to address this problem is to offer the service free on a test basis to a limited number of subscribers and then to follow up with a questionnaire to get reactions and/or help plan sales and pricing strategies. The test group may be offered a continuation of the service for a monthly charge to estimate penetration for the whole system.

NOTES

[1]Alex Papagan, quoted in "Colony's New Marketing Effort," *Cable Marketing*, May 1981, p. 21.

[2]Lucy Huffman, "Supreme Court Rules Cable System Operators Must Pay Landlords for Access to Apartments," *Multichannel News*, July 5, 1982, p. 1.

[3]"The Kagan Report," quoted in "Cabletelevision Advertising Bureau," CAB, Inc., 575 Madison Ave., New York, N.Y. 10022, 1981.

[4]"And cable television, at this early stage at least, offers advertisers an affordable opportunity to take a more active role in programming.

Sponsors such as Kraft Inc., Bristol-Myers and Mobil Corp. already have seized this opportunity. This could produce a return to the good old days of early television, when sponsors enriched American culture with original drama.

Or it might be thrown back to the bad old days of early TV, when some of those same sponsors were accused of trying to control the content on the home video screen." ("Cable Television is Still in a Swirl," *Advertising Age*, November 16, 1981, pp. 5–22.)

15

Business Operations

Customer Service Representatives, Coaxial Communications, Columbus, Ohio.

This chapter covers the somewhat disparate business and operating departments and procedures of cable systems—first finance and accounting, then customer service, engineering and maintenance, security procedures, and, finally, personnel. The last section of this chapter identifies industry resources—professional associations and trade publications.

FINANCE

A continuous capital supply is necessary for the cable industry as new systems are built and existing systems expanded or rebuilt. Diverse sources are now available. Whereas the cable industry was once characterized by frantic entrepreneurs, trying to explain the cable business and make it credible and scrambling for money at any price, the game now is to weigh the wider options and manage equity and debt carefully.

Equity

Equity financing is still important in the cable industry, although some companies would rather not share ownership if it is avoidable. Venture capital was crucial in the formative years. The original cable developers relied on personal funds, friends, business acquaintances, and customers. It is interesting to note that many of the earliest cable systems were customer financed. A $100 to $150 connection fee was charged which completely covered the cost of building the system. Some venture capital investment companies seeking high returns took risks on the cable business. In recent years several major MSOs have made large stock offerings with very good success, drawing on the market enchantment with information technologies.

An important source of equity capital continues to be the limited partnership, a form of financing applied to cable television construction and acquisition by a leading proponent, Jones Intercable. In a public offering limited partnership interests are sold to qualified investors in small packages, as low as $1,000 per unit, who can take advantage of the tax write-off incentive of this particular investment vehicle. An amount equal to up to 100 percent or more of the limited partner's original investment can be sheltered from federal income tax, depending on the specific structure of the partnership agreement. Losses generated during the early years of the cable system development are "passed through" by the general partner to the nonvoting, limited investors who participate in a blind pool used to acquire the cable systems. Private limited partnerships are also used by the industry.[1]

Small business investment corporations (SBICs) are active in cable. These companies qualify for small business loans at below-market rates from the government and, in turn, invest in cable ventures.

Recent changes in the federal tax laws continue to promote cable television as an attractive investment. Under the provisions of the new 1981 Economic Recovery Tax Act, the Internal Revenue Code permits a cable firm an investment tax credit of ten percent of the cost of new tangible personal property, used in the business, with a life of five years or over, and six percent credit for property with a life of three years. The Act also provides for a special method of accelerated depreciation, called the Accelerated Cost Recovery System. The impact of the new law can best be demonstrated with an example. If a cable distribution plant (coaxial cable and electronics) costs $10 million to build, the investment tax credit will be $1 million (ten percent of $10 million). Using a five-year depreciation schedule (which permits depreciation expense equal to 15 percent of the cost of the equipment in the first year), the first year's depreciation is $1.5 million. The cable system is not likely to make a profit in the first year. If the investor is a business conglomerate in the 46 percent tax bracket, the depreciation and investment tax credit amount to a *tax savings* of $1.69 million in the first year on a $10 million investment ($1 million investment tax credit plus 46 percent of the $1.5 million depreciation allowance). When you add this to the benefits of *leveraging,* it is clear why cable is such a good tax shelter. In our example, if the investment is leveraged (money is borrowed), only a portion of the $10 million is equity. If it is 20 percent equity and 80 percent financed, then the first year's tax savings of $1.69 million would result from a $2 million investment.

To take advantage of the tax benefits, the investor in a cable system must consolidate the cable subsidiary and file a *consolidated return.* To do this, the parent company must own at least 80 percent of the voting stock. This is why American MSOs never give away more than 20 percent to local investors in applying for a new franchise. Canadian-based companies do not have this limitation because a different set of rules applies there.

Debt

The preferred method of financing for established cable companies is through borrowed money. Cable is said to be a heavily leveraged industry, where the debt-to-equity ratio is high. Robert Morris Associates reports the debt-to-worth ratio (calculated by dividing total liabilities by tangible net worth) at 14.7. This is an extremely high figure. The comparable ratio for television broadcasting stations is 2.1.[2]

Money is loaned for construction and operating costs with the system assets as security. There are three general types of lenders. The finance companies, or intermediate lenders, helped to finance the cable industry at a time when other money was not available. These companies (e.g., Barclays American/Aetna, Firstmark Financial, Heller-Oak Commercial Finance) have a proportionately lower share now that the industry is more established. Insurance companies (e.g., John Hancock Mutual Life Insurance, Teacher's Insurance and Annuity Association, Aetna Life and Casualty) were also involved in the early financing with longer-term loans. Banks (e.g., Chase Manhattan, First National Bank of Boston, Citibank), with typically shorter-term loans, have recently outdistanced insurance companies as the major lenders in cable. In 1980, banks had $1,184,000,000 in outstanding loans to cable; insurance companies, $835,000,000; and intermediate lenders, $142,000,000.[3] The distinction between the three types of lenders has been blurred as they compete to "sell" loans. Cable companies must shop the financial markets to obtain funds under the most favorable conditions that can be negotiated. In 1981, bank loans were short term of about five to eight years with *variable* interest rates about two and one-half to three percentage points over the prime lending rate. Variable interest rates are adjusted at fixed periods to reflect the market. Insurance company loans were longer term, of about 10 to 15 years at fixed interest rates of about 18 percent. The finance companies (intermediates) loan up to 10 years at 5 or 6 percent over the prime rates.

At least one cable company, Comcast, has used industrial development bonds. These are low-interest bonds issued by state or local governments to stimulate business. They might be used to encourage earlier cable expansion into areas that are marginal.[4]

Franchising authorities look carefully at the financial structure of cable applicants, apparently to protect themselves from subsequent criticism if the franchisee were to delay construction while arranging financing or struggling in bad times. Financial stability not only permits the company to ride out economic swings, which have so far not affected cable seriously, but also to absorb mistakes. This may be important in 100-plus channel, two-way systems now being built at high cost with uncertain revenue.

Senior cable creditors usually get a first lien on the cable plant, most operating equipment, accounts receivable, *and the franchise rights* of the borrower. In default, the bank, or other creditor, would take over all tangible and intangible rights of the franchise.

ACCOUNTING AND BOOKKEEPING

This section discusses some of the variables which must be accounted for in cable system management for purposes of control, and then describes factors that are peculiar to handling accounts receivable and keeping books in the cable industry.

Accounting Concepts

According to G. J. Hernandez, former vice president of Coaxial Communications,[5] it is useful to segregate the operating expenses of a cable system into manageable components typical of the industry. The "controllable" expenses include plant maintenance, customer service, local origination, sales and marketing, administrative, and general. In each of these categories, however, there is a minimum level of expense that is relatively fixed. The "noncontrollable" expenses are those that are imposed by outside forces such as franchise fees, fees paid to suppliers such as pay networks and superstations, and taxes.

It is advisable to establish an *operating budget* (a process by which estimates for all expense accounts are established in advance, are approved by management, and serve as a tool to measure performance) and to investigate discrepancies between actual results and budget. This is, of course, an important management function and one of the principal reasons that expense records are segmented into accounts.

Cable systems are subject to several taxes, depending on the location. These may include franchise fees to the franchise authority, and, in some cases, to the state; copyright fees; tangible personal property taxes on the cable plant as well as all other tangible personal property; intangible property taxes; and utility taxes in some jurisdictions. All the other normal business taxes and licenses are assessed against cable companies, such as federal and state income taxes. In addition, in some states cable service may be subject to sales tax which must be collected from the customers and passed on to the state.

Operating income and cash flow are important terms in the cable industry. *Operating income* is operating revenues minus operating expenses (cost of operations, depreciation, and amortization). *Operating cash flow* is operating income plus depreciation and amortization. *Net cash flow* is net income (loss) plus depreciation and amortization minus principal repayment on outstanding debt.

It is appropriate to point out that terms such as "operating income" and "cash flow" do not have a similar definition in all industries. Furthermore, these terms are not used consistently by all cable companies in their published financial information since many are subsidiaries of larger corporations, some of them conglomerates with operations in various industries. Consequently, the financial information of these cable companies may be presented in conformity with the practices of other lines of business in which the parent company operates.

Operating income is a figure that is useful in comparing one cable system with another because the figure is independent of capital structure (how the system is financed) and depreciation schedules (which are somewhat arbitrary accounting devices).

Cable is sometimes called a *cash flow business*. Since cable is a capital-intensive industry, big depreciation charges are generated each year. These charges are part of the cash flow and can be reinvested in the business for expansion (extending lines and buying or building new franchises) or capital improvement (retrofitting an older system). Limits on loans to established cable systems are often based on multiples of cash flow—up to about four and one-half times cash flow.

Charges by Pay TV Suppliers

Some of the pay services charge a flat fee per subscriber—about $3.50 per month. HBO has a graduated fee starting with a base rate and adding percentages depending on the cable system charge to subscribers. It amounts to about a 50:50 split of the cable system rate. For example, if the subscriber charge is $7.00 or less, the service charge is a flat $4.00; if the subscriber charge is $7.01 to $8.00, the service charge is $4.00 plus 50 percent of charges over $7.00; if the subscriber is charged $8.01 to $9.00, the service charge is $4.50 plus 20 percent of charges over $8.00; for a subscriber charge of $9.00 or more, the service charge is $4.70 plus 10 percent of charges over $9.00.[6] Pay services may give volume discounts for subscribers, for example, percentage reductions at various increments in absolute numbers of subscribers to the service: 10,000 or over, 2 percent; 25,000 or over, 3.5 percent; 40,000 or over, 5 percent; 75,000 or over, 15 percent; 100,000 or over, 20 percent.[7] Additional discounts may be offered for high levels of pay-to-basic penetration for a particular pay network, for example, for HBO service charges of $5.00 or more per subscriber, at 40 percent penetration of affiliates subscribers, 2 percent discount; at 60 percent, 4 percent; at 80 percent, 6 percent.[8]

Satellite Network Affiliate Business Practices

The advertiser-supported satellite networks prefer to be a part of the basic cable service of their affiliates. This provides the maximum subscriber count. Some of the networks charge a higher per-subscriber fee if the network is packaged in a tier that is above basic. This practice penalizes the system for not carrying the network in basic.

The per-subscriber fees charged by some of the advertiser-supported networks have become controversial. Most of the original networks made a monthly per-subscriber charge. As business increased some networks have reduced the charge or begun paying affiliates for each subscriber (a practice similar to broadcast television networks). The newer networks, forced to compete with existing line-ups, have generally offered the new service without charge.

Because some of the networks are on satellites for which few cable systems have earth receiver stations, the networks have been forced to supply the dishes or contribute to the cost. All of the networks on a particular satellite may join together to help affiliates equip headends to receive their services.

Many of the satellite networks will contribute about 25 cents per subscriber to help *launch* the service—to cover the costs of advertising and promotion when the service is introduced to subscribers. Some networks continue with 5 to 15 cents per year per subscriber, or some other assistance plan, for maintenance marketing after the launch.

The advertiser-supported networks make one-, two-, or three-minute local ad spots available per cablecast hour. These are unused by many systems, but are very important to the cable systems that have begun selling advertising. To this point the revenues from local advertising sales in network spot availabilities are far greater for most cable operators than from advertising sales in origination. The cable operators Affiliate Relations Board was organized to negotiate local spot availabilities and other compensation matters with the networks. The median length of the affiliation contract, which spells out the details of the affiliation business arrangements discussed above, is three years.

Accounts Receivable

Cable companies maintain an extraordinarily large number of open accounts receivable compared with an average business, and none are large accounts. This translates to high bookkeeping costs.

There are three kinds of cable billing systems in general use. Systems with under 1,000 subscribers may have a manual system. The subscriber is sent a book of coupons. One is returned every month (or every two months, or each quarter) with the payment.

Bigger systems may rely on batch processing, sending daily, or less often, by mail, subscriber information on specially provided forms to an organization which mails the bills and records collections. Most cable systems contract for this work with an independent data processing company that has service tailor-made for cable.

On-line, or *on-line shared-time* systems are used by the larger cable systems. In a shared-time system, the operator at the cable office enters information on a CRT which is connected to the central processing unit (CPU) of the data processing company by dedicated telephone line. In the on-line system, the computer is located at the cable system business office. The equipment itself is sold by a data management company which generally does not manufacture it, but which has developed programs, *software,* for this equipment and in turn licenses the programs and sells the equipment to the cable company. A monthly royalty is paid for the computer software, which is expanded and revised as necessary.

An operator enters all subscriber information, as soon as it is received, into the CRT—new orders of service, disconnects, switchovers, upgrades, downgrades. Bills are printed by the computer. They are added to the appropriate stuffers and guides, and mailed. When the bill is paid, the credit is entered in the computer. Special software programs print out dunning notices only for delinquent subscribers. If a customer calls to inquire about a statement, the operator need only enter the code into the CRT to call up the customer's history. The computer is also programmed to provide a series of summary reports and can be used for scheduling installations and routine maintenance, parts inventory, and so on.

The most advanced on-line system combines data processing with converter addressability. One entry on the system accomplishes both order taking and converter turn on or off.

The handling of overdue accounts varies with cable system and may be affected by provisions of the franchise that specify the conditions under which a subscriber can be disconnected. Most of these rules require formal notices before service may be cut off. These provisions will no doubt become more stringent where cable systems provide burglar and fire alarms, electronic funds transfer, and other two-way services.

The alert to overdue payments may be triggered by a prescribed number of days overdue or by a dollar amount overdue. The latter may be more appropriate for multipay services where the monthly bill per household may vary considerably. The first notice to the subscriber may be a printed notation of the overdue amount on the next month's bill or a special insert in the bill envelope with a mild admonition. If the overdue sum is not paid within a specified time, a special letter may be mailed taking a harder line and spelling out the consequences of nonpayment, including the charge to reconnect. The same notice accompanies the next billing. If this does not bring payment, a telephone call by a customer service representative may attempt to save the account. This failing, a disconnect notice is sent. The service is disconnected if the bill is not paid on a particular date (usually at about 65 days overdue). A technician collects the converter and may make a physical disconnect. In calling on the household, the technician may be instructed to make a last-ditch effort to collect the sum owed and save the account. To reconnect, the once-disconnected subscriber may have to repay the previous sum owed and make a higher than usual prepayment.

Collection agencies may be called in to clean up accounts that have not paid through the normal system follow-up procedures. Generally, they split the revenue with the cable operator. In some low income communities, "debit men" may be used to collect bills since the people are accustomed to that procedure.

CUSTOMER SERVICE

As a service business, particularly one in which the service is not necessarily essential, the cable industry considers customer service a very significant function. The term "customer service" is used here to mean the functions of dealing with customer installation orders, billing questions, and requests for repairs on the telephone or at the business office. In small cable companies, one or a few persons may handle all these areas. In the larger company, different groups of people in three departments specialize in installation, billing, and repair with separate phone listings for each.

Orders

The importance of customer service to the marketing function was emphasized in Chapter 14. Cable companies believe that there is a direct relationship between the quality of customer service and penetration levels. Taking requests for installations is a different type of sales from telephone solicitation or "cold" calling where the cable company calls the prospective customer. A softer sell is used, but the attempt is made to start the caller at the top in the "top-down" sales approach. Product knowledge is crucial for the customer service representative (CSR) taking orders. The composition of the tiers, pricing scheme, and billing procedures must all be explained. The CSR may be asked questions about public access, C-SPAN, CNN, R-rated movies, the content of the cultural channels, the shopping channel, payments at installation, the first billing, and so on. To keep work current, the CSR writes the order while the customer is on the line. Manuals and scripted protocols may help on billing procedures and installation but become outdated quickly on programming and pricing schemes.

CSRs taking orders may earn a "spiff," or small commission, on each sale—15 cents or more for each unit beyond basic, with a bonus amount for the full service to encourage emphasis on the top level of service. In some systems, the door-to-door salesperson may get credit for orders from people who have been contacted. Or the customer may only be entitled to a special rate on installation if the salesperson's name or number are mentioned. A salesperson, failing to close at the door, suggests that the individual think about the service and call in the order to take advantage of the special offer. The CSR records the salesperson's ID to give proper credit.

The CSR may schedule the installation at the time of the order and then make the credit check. If the customer does not clear a credit bureau check and the cable company's own records, then a letter is sent which may require a full deposit on the converter before installation.

The CSRs in this department also handle requests for downgrades or the ultimate downgrade, a disconnect. An attempt is made to save the customer, usually by asking why the downgrade or disconnect is wanted. (The CSR should be genuinely concerned that someone would not *want* the service or not *like* it.) Once the customers have aired some complaints about the cable service and heard some low-keyed, positive benefits, they may reconsider. A disconnect request for anything other than moving should be followed up prior to physical disconnection to encourage keeping the service.

Installers handle the installations and disconnects. They are sometimes independent contractors or when employed by the cable system may work on a per-installation fee, owning and maintaining their own vehicles. A commission may be paid for retention of disconnects or upgrading of orders. Usually installers are not radio dispatched; they pick up their orders for the day at the business office.

Billing

Customers call the Billing Department because they do not understand the bill (new subscribers have difficulty with partial month payments—prorating—and advance monthly charging), the handling of partial months, and installation charges with debit and credit entries to indicate waived charges. In batch-processed billings, in particular, there is a lag between the receipt of a payment and posting. The customer may be concerned that a check mailed several days ago does not appear to have been received by the cable company. Then, there are the inevitable mistakes on the bill. Inquiries come by phone, messages written on returned bills, or letters.

When the customer calls or writes, the CSR gets a microfiche record of the account or enters the customer ID into a computer terminal to call up the account. The CSR can then see all the transactions, current level of service, and account history.

If there are several billing cycles, or continuous billing throughout the month, the call load on billing CSRs is relatively even, and there is no problem with partial month billings. In the large customer service departments, a uniform call distribution telephone system distributes calls evenly among the several lines in use.

Repair

Dealing with technical faults in the cable system is now generally referred to as "repair" since "service" may also refer to the product offered. When the cable system receives a request for repair, the dispatcher first asks a series of questions about the exact nature of the problem reported. A clear understanding of the symptoms is the first step in determining the solution to the problem. A high percentage of the calls may be the result of an inability to tune the receiver, unplugging the set, or disconnecting the cable during a system outage. The customer is talked through a series of steps that may rectify the problem without an expensive service call. The customer is grateful, having been saved the embarrassment of having a repairperson call just to plug in or fine-tune the receiver. About 25 percent of the calls can be "cleared" on the telephone by talking customers through front-panel adjustment and other checks. This requires dispatchers who can relate various problems to the proper adjustments and have an awareness of the different types of receivers.

Before dispatching a repair call, the dispatcher checks billing status. The customer may have been disconnected for nonpayment, in which case, the bill must be paid before reconnection. If the account has not been disconnected but is in arrears, the dispatcher may ask for payment prior to repair work. The dispatcher then takes all appropriate data from the subscriber. It is important to record accurately the problem for the technician who must develop a priority for the calls. A loss of all signals is obviously a higher priority than a single impaired channel.

The dispatcher locates the repair call in an area or section of the system. This may be done by attaching an area or section designation code to each address in the subscriber data base. The code may have an electronic significance such as all households served by a particular bridger amplifier. If several calls are received with the same code, the technician has a good idea of where the trouble lies. If the cable company has a status monitoring system, the dispatcher may run a check to pinpoint the trouble. The dispatcher then enters the repair request on the appropriate dispatch log. Dispatch logs list all issued repair calls for each technician, the time they are issued, and the time they are completed. The log may also list the nature of the problem and other data. Many cable companies have computerized this function. The computer can keep the dispatch clerk informed of the status of the log at any moment and also generate reports on service problems in each electronic section of the system, the efficiency of technicians, and so on. If the dispatch log for a technician has too many calls, exceeding an established quota, an adjacent technician with fewer calls may be transferred temporarily into the territory. The technicians are in contact with the office by two-way radio.

CSRs working on the telephone in the order, billing, and repair departments take pride in their ability to deal with all types of customers and "turn" an irate caller into a satisfied customer. The CSR, approaching the task in the proper frame of mind, considers the unseen callers "my customers."

SYSTEMS MAINTENANCE AND ENGINEERING

A cable plant is maintained by the systems maintenance staff, consisting of the *chief technician* and *maintenance technicians* (who maintain the cable distribution system) and *service technicians* (who answer individual service complaints). In very small systems, there is usually no distinction between those categories, with a small number of technicians performing both tasks. Very large systems often have two or more *lead technicians* or *hub supervisors* who are responsible for the maintenance technicians within a particular hub or area of the system. Often, only the highest-level technicians maintain the trunk line and less experienced people maintain the feeder and individual drop lines.

Chief Technician

The chief technician in a cable system is both the manager of the field technical staff and the person called upon to deal with technical problems which are above the ability of the maintenance technicians. Frequently, chief technicians come up through the ranks of the field technical staff. They may have additional training and, in some cases, college degrees. They are familiar with use of various types of sophisticated test equipment. Often, the chief technician will also supervise a construction crew which makes system extentions and moves cable facilities.

Service Technicians

Service technicians are generally less technically qualified than maintenance technicians but must be presentable and courteous, since they are in constant contact with subscribers. Most subscriber complaints relate to problems with operation of their TV set or converter.

Cable service technicians must be capable of retuning television sets and of making minor adjustments to them. One of the service technician's main tools is a properly working TV set which is often brought into a subscriber's home to demonstrate that the problem is with the subscriber's television set rather than with the cable service.

Service technicians also troubleshoot problems in individual subscriber drop lines. Sometimes the cable will have been damaged or water may have entered one of the cable fittings, causing corrosion. If a service technician traces the problem back to the cable plant, a maintenance technician is notified to correct the problem.

Service technicians are often used to move cable outlets, add additional outlets within subscribers' homes, and install new equipment for new services.

Maintenance Technicians

Plant maintenance can be divided into two categories. First is preventive maintenance, which consists of routine inspection and testing of the system, particularly the trunks and supertrunks. In large cable systems, one or more people are often assigned solely to this task. A van is equipped with sophisticated test equipment, including frequency measuring equipment, spectrum analyzers, video monitors, and video test instruments. Usually, FCC testing and proof-of-performance testing is done by the preventive maintenance staff. Systems with status monitoring equipment require fewer preventive maintenance people, since many tests are performed automatically.

The second type of maintenance is demand maintenance which is performed in response to subscriber complaints. Status monitoring is of significant help in localizing faults. It is often difficult to distinguish between individual service complaints and plant problems. Status monitoring automatically pinpoints the exact location of a plant fault or informs the dispatch personnel that there is no system fault so that a service technician can be dispatched.

Most routine plant maintenance, such as failure of amplifier modules, blown fuses, or physically damaged cable, can be repaired by the maintenance technicians. Occasionally, however, faults occur which are difficult to isolate. Intermittent problems that come and go with different conditions or problems that are subtle in nature may require the services of a lead technician or even the chief technician.

Maintenance technicians usually drive small vans equipped with ladders, a stock of spare equipment, and a minimal amount of test equipment. Lead technicians and chief technicians have much more sophisticated test equipment and often have access to bucket trucks (vehicles with hoist equipment to lift a technician up to an amplifier or other piece of equipment to be serviced).

Maintenance technicians are assigned to a territory for long periods of time so that a particular area of the plant becomes their responsibility. Periodically the territory is changed to lend some variety to the work and to break up cliques of regional technicians who may begin to establish policies independent of the central office.

Technicians are issued tools for which they are responsible. At the termination of employment, they must turn in the tools or pay for them. Broken tools are replaced from inventory.

Parts inventory control is very rigid. The minimum levels must be set high enough to accommodate the worst periods of demand, usually after severe thunderstorms. Not all repairs are made in the field. Field technicians may bring electronic parts in for bench repair by another group of technicians. Once repaired, the parts are put back into inventory.

Cable company service hours vary greatly. Some companies provide around-the-clock maintenance staffs; others will respond to a problem only during normal working hours. Usually, after working hours a maintenance technician is on duty with a lead technician or a chief technician on call in case of an emergency.

System Faults

Cable system faults, even in a well-designed and well-managed system, are fairly frequent. The most common problems are as follows:

1. Electric power outage. Often, electrical service will be out in one part of town causing the cable system to be out not only in that area but also farther down the trunk. Newer systems, with standby power, will keep operating, but systems with normal power supplies will be out of service. If a power outage lasts for a significant period of time, a portable generator can be connected to the cable system to provide electric power temporarily.
2. Damage from lightning and electrical storms. Even the most modern cable amplifiers are subject to damage from high-intensity electrical discharges from lightning. In some areas of the country, particularly the South and Midwest, lightning damage is the main source of cable outages. Usually the damage is to amplifier modules, but sometimes passive devices and even cable can be damaged.
3. Physical damage. Aerial cables can be damaged by automobile accidents, wind, and ice. Underground cables can be damaged by new underground construction, installation of fences, mailboxes, and even flower gardens or by accidental or intentional damage to pedestals. In most cases, when physical damage occurs, a section of the cable must be replaced.
4. Failure of active equipment. Electronic components have a finite useful life. Although cable equipment has become more reliable over the years, amplifiers are still subject to occasional failure.
5. Connector problems. Over the years, connectors in cable systems can fail, allowing water to enter the cable. Often, signal ingress or egress and *flashing* (the presence of intermittent flashes in subscribers' television pictures) may occur. Many times these problems are difficult to find since they come and go with different weather or wind conditions. Two-way systems in particular are vulnerable to this type of problem.

The Engineering Department

In small- and medium-sized cable systems, the chief technician performs all the maintenance on the headend equipment and repairs of equipment which fail in the field. In larger systems, however, a separate

Engineering Department often exists, headed by the chief engineer. This department has responsibility for maintenance of all headend equipment, video equipment, computer systems, and defective amplifiers, passive devices, and converters. The Engineering Department is also responsible for preconstruction activities such as design, pole permits, easements, and the walkout. These functions are described in Chapter 3.

The Chief Engineer

The chief engineer frequently has a college degree and may even have an advanced degree. The chief engineer is usually familiar with television broadcast and production equipment in addition to cable equipment. In new systems offering two-way services, the chief engineer must have computer experience as well.

Bench Repair

Under the supervision of the chief engineer is usually the bench repair staff. In this area, defective cable TV equipment is repaired. The bench repair technicians have diagnostic test instruments and simulations of the cable system which allow them to repair and test cable equipment under conditions similar to those encountered in the field. Smaller cable companies may subcontract the repair of cable equipment and multiple system operators frequently centralize the repair of equipment on a regional basis.

Video, Microwave, Earth Stations, and Computer Equipment Maintenance

In small- and medium-sized systems, the chief engineer is often personally responsible for this type of maintenance. In larger, more sophisticated systems, one or more engineers or technicians may be required for these functions. Recent major market franchise proposals include elaborate studio facilities, microwave equipment, and a multitude of earth stations together with complex two-way and videotext computer systems. In these systems, several maintenance engineers and technicians may be required to keep all the equipment operating.

Headend Maintenance

The chief technician in smaller systems usually maintains the headend equipment. Larger systems with more than one headend or several hubs may require one or more people devoted entirely to headend maintenance and testing.

Technicians, installers, and dispatchers may have a weekly meeting. Part of the meeting is devoted to training: new procedures are outlined, new parts are described, and ways of meeting difficult problems are discussed. The meeting also serves to keep the technicians and installers in touch with the company, since they are otherwise occupied continuously in the field. Correspondence courses are encouraged by partial tuition reimbursement and pay increases on completion. Some investment of the employees' own money may be required to maintain a commitment to continuing the self-study.

SYSTEM SECURITY PROCEDURES

Technologies for dealing with the challenging problems of theft of service are discussed in Chapter 4. Theft of service may come from subscribers tampering with junction boxes or pedestals in apartment complexes or underground construction, dishonest employees or former employees hooking up their friends, and subscribers actually climbing poles to connect themselves, inserting splitters for additional connections, buying their own converters, or tampering with converters supplied by the operator.

Many people also get free cable service through administrative errors on the part of the cable company. Even a very small error rate (e.g., failure to disconnect when someone moves) will cause a large cummulative loss. Most cable systems conduct physical audits of their systems every 3 to 5 years. Typically, 2 to 5 percent illegal connections are discovered.

Theft of converters and descramblers is becoming serious because it is not feasible to ask for a deposit large enough to cover the cost and still sell the service at an attractive price. Cable companies have a variety of policies to protect themselves, including the following. Homeowners are given a converter with no deposit (saving the cost of a credit check). A credit check is run on the apartment dweller (at a cost of about $1). If the potential subscriber meets minimum credit standards, no deposit is required. If not, a substantial deposit is necessary. A customer with very poor credit will be refused the service entirely.

The subscriber must sign an agreement form that usually states the following: (1) the converter (terminal, console) is the property of the cable operator; (2) if the service is terminated, the converter must be returned promptly—the service representative is to be allowed to enter the premises to retrieve it; (3) the value of the converter is stated and the subscriber is obligated for that amount if it is not returned; and (4) if there is physical damage, beyond reasonable wear and tear, the subscriber is obligated for reasonable costs of repair. The subscriber is informed of the law on theft of cable television service and the penalties for violation.

The Ohio law reads, in part,

> Sec. 4933.42 (A) As used in this section and section 4933.99 of the revised code, "Cable Television Service" means any and all services provided by or through the facilities of any cable television system, or closed circuit coaxial cable communication system, or any microwave or similar transmission service used in connection with any cable television system or other similar closed circuit coaxial cable communications system.
>
> (B) No person shall knowingly obtain cable television service from another without the authorization of or compensation paid to the operator of said service. The existence, on property in the actual possession of the accused, of any connection, wire, conductor, or any device whatsoever, which effects the use of cable television service without the same being reported for payment as to service, or specifically authorized by the operator of the cable television service shall be prima-facie evidence of intent to violate and of the violation of this section by the accused.
>
> (C) No person shall knowingly assist or instruct any other person in obtaining any cable television service without authorization or payment to the operator of the cable television service.
>
> (D) No person shall willfully break, injure, or otherwise damage, destroy, or without lawful authority remove any equipment used by the operator of the cable television service.
>
> (E) No person shall knowingly sell, rent, lend, promote, offer, or advertise for sale, rental, or use any instrument, apparatus, equipment, device, or plans, specifications, or instructions for making or assembling the same to any person, with knowledge that the person intends to make unauthorized use of cable television service.
>
> Sec. 4933.99. (A) Whoever violates section 4933.16 or 4933.42 of the Revised Code is guilty of a misdeameanor of the third degree.[9]

About two-thirds of the states do have theft of service laws which protect cable. Cable operators may prosecute periodically to establish public awareness of the law as a deterrent to others or when the theft is especially serious (e.g., a person connects several neighbors or someone sells the service illegally).

PERSONNEL

Estimates of annual new employees in the cable industry for the early 1980s vary from 7,000 per year to 30,000.[10] Despite this broad range, there is universal agreement that a personnel shortage is an urgent problem of the 1980s. A survey of cable system managers concluded that recruiting and training is the highest-priority problem of the manager.[11]

Training

The greatest numbers of cable employees are in the technician and installer areas, at least while the cable industry is still in the construction stage. Several cable MSOs have their own training facilities where technical people learn basic electronics and cable system design, installation procedures, and line technology. These schools require outdoor facilities such as "wall laboratories" or "install houses" where aluminum, wood, brick, and asbestos walls present different installation problems; "pole farms" or "pole orchards" for line work; and earth stations.

Most companies, however, do not have training facilities. Training in the majority is a combination of correspondence courses and on-the-job experience. The National Cable Television Institute has a number of technical courses and single-subject short courses.[12]

Unions

Because the classic cable systems employed few people and were in small towns where the climate for unionization was not especially hospitable, few cable employees are unionized. This will change as cable moves into urban environments. Unions exert political pressure on franchising authorities to select applicants that plan construction with union personnel and have unions for installers and technicians. Big cable systems with hundreds of employees present a better opportunity for union organization. The most active unions in cable are the International Brotherhood of Electrical Workers (IBEW) and the Communications Workers of America (CWA).

Some managements have attempted to preempt union organization by offering regular cost-of-living increases and benefits packages that include profit sharing and stock options. These plans also help to prevent raiding of both technical and management personnel by other cable companies.

Equal Employment Opportunity

FCC data indicate that cable employment of women and minorities is far below the average proportion of these groups in the work force. The FCC is not aggressively forcing its standard of 50 percent of the proportion in the local labor force and 25 percent of the labor force in the top four job categories (officials and managers, professionals, technicians, sales workers) but uses these standards as a screening device for follow-up on affirmative action plans. If cable operators do not file the necessary EEO forms and affirmative action plans or fail to respond to FCC inquiries, the commission will send a notice of apparent liability, which is the first step in forfeiture (fine).[13]

PROFESSIONAL RESOURCES

Two major professional associations serve the cable industry. The largest is the National Cable Television Association (NCTA) with about 2,000 members serving 70 percent of the cable subscribers.[14] The association lobbies for the industry in Washington; advises members on business, public policy, and technical matters; sponsors an annual convention (approximately 16,500 attended in 1982) and other meetings on special topics; and attempts to educate the public and other businesses about the nature of the cable industry. A number of state cable associations are affiliated with NCTA.[15]

The Community Antenna Television Association (CATA) performs similar services for the smaller cable systems.[16]

The Cable Television Administration and Marketing Society (CTAM) is a forum for the exchange of ideas and information. The organization sponsors an annual meeting and regional and special-interest seminars on management topics.[17]

The Canadian industry association is Canadian Cable Television Association (CCTA).[18]

The work of the Cabletelevision Advertising Bureau (CAB) is discussed in Chapter 14.[19]

Public access, government, and education users of cable are served by the National Federation of Local Cable Programmers (NFLCP).[20] A comparable organization for cable company employees engaged in community channel programming is The Cable Programmers' Society.[21]

Cable programmers and program suppliers have recently been invited to participate in the National Association of Television Program Executives, a professional association for programming interests and a marketplace for program wares.[22]

Network Affiliates Board is an organization to represent cable operators before satellite networks.[23]

Minorities and women are served respectively by Minorities in Cable and New Technologies[24] and Women in Cable.[25] Franchising authority interests in cable are represented by the National Association of Telecommunications Officers and Advisors, an affiliate of the National League of Cities.[26]

There are several periodicals serving the cable industry. They are *Cablevision*,[27] *TVC*,[28] *Cable Age*,[29] *Cable Marketing*,[30] *Broadcasting*,[31] *CED* (*Communications Engineering Digest*, "The magazine of broadband technology"),[32] *View*,[33] and *Multichannel News*.[34] Many newsletters cover communications. Most specific to cable is a series by Paul Kagan Associates: *Cable TV Franchising, The Pay TV Newsletter, Cable TV Investor, Cable TV Advertising, Cable TV Programming, Cable TV Security, Cable TV Tax Letter, Cable TV Technology* and *Electronic Publisher*.[35] Another newsletter is titled *CableNews.*[36] Directed to public access, government, and education users of cable is *Community Television Review.*[37] Three directories for the industry include listings of all cable systems, the MSOs, suppliers, associations, and so on. They are *Cablefile,*[38] *Broadcasting Cablecasting Yearbook,*[39] and *Television Factbook.*[40]

NOTES

[1]Jeri Baker, "Financing the Cable Boom: Industry's Appeal to Lenders Sparks Effort Toward Anti-Inflationary Deals," *Cablevision,* April 6, 1981, pp. 44–53. Note: A "qualified" investor is determined by state and federal law.

[2]"Statement Studies," Robert Morris Associates, Philadelphia, Pennsylvania, 1980.

[3]Jeri Baker, "Financing the Cable Boom."

[4]Ibid.

[5]Interview with Thomas Baldwin, April 15, 1981.

[6]"Schedule of HBO Service Charge Rates," Home Box Office, Inc., New York, New York, January 1, 1982.

[7]Ibid.

[8]Ibid.

[9]Ohio Revised Code, Section 4933.42.

[10]*Cablevision,* June 15, 1981, p. 12; *TVC,* December 15, 1980, p. 105; *Cablevision,* January 19, 1981, p. 37.

[11]"Today's Cable System Manager: His Characteristics and Job Situation," *TVC,* October 15, 1980, pp. 42–54.

[12]National Cable Television Institute, P.O. Box 27277, Denver, Colorado 80227.

[13]Pat Gushman, "Cable and EEO," *Cablevision,* June 28, 1980, pp. 32–40.

[14]Interview with James McElveen, NCTA, August 24, 1981.

[15]National Cable Television Association, 1724 Massachusetts Avenue, Washington, D.C. 20036.

[16]Community Antenna Television Association, 1825 K Street, N.W., Washington, D.C. 20006.

[17]CTAM, 2033 M Street, N.W., Washington, D.C. 20036.

[18]Canadian Cable Television Association, 85 Albert Street, Suite 405, Ottawa KIP6A4.

[19]Cabletelevision Advertising Bureau, 575 Madison Avenue, New York, New York 10022.

[20]National Federation of Local Cable Programmers, 3700 Far Hills Avenue, Kettering, Ohio 45429.

[21]The Cable Programmers' Society, c/o Lauren Goldfarb, Adams-Russell Cable, 1380 Main Street, Waltham, Massachusetts 02154.

[22]National Association of Television Program Executives, 310 Madison Avenue, Suite 1207, New York, New York 10017.

[23]Network Affiliates Board, c/o William Gruber, Mission Cable TV, Inc., 6225 Federal Bldg., San Diego, California 92114.

[24]Minorities in Cable and New Technologies, c/o Will Horton, Columbia College, Chicago, Illinois 60611.

[25]Women in Cable, 2033 M Street, N.W., Suite 703, Washington, D.C. 20036.

[26]National League of Cities, 1301 Pennsylvania Ave., NW, Washington, D.C. 20004.

[27]*Cablevision,* 2500 Curtis Street, Denver, Colorado 80205.

[28]*TVC,* 6340 South Yosemite Street, Englewood, Colorado 80111.

[29]*Cable Age,* 1270 Avenue of the Americas, New York, New York 10020.

[30]*Cable Marketing,* 352 Park Avenue South, New York, New York 10010.

[31]*Broadcasting,* 1735 DeSales Street, N.W., Washington, D.C. 20036.

[32]*CED,* 2500 Curtis Street, Denver, Colorado 80205.

[33]*View: The Magazine of Cable TV Programming,* 150 E. 58th Street, N.Y., N.Y. 10022.

[34]*Multichannel News,* 300 South Jackson, Denver, Colorado 80209.

[35]Paul Kagan Associates, Inc., 26386 Carmel Rancho Lane, Carmel, California 93923.

[36]*Cable News,* 7315 Wisconsin Ave., #1200N, Bethesda, Maryland 20814.

[37]*Community Television Review,* 3700 Far Hills Ave., Kettering, Ohio 45429.

[38]*Cablefile,* 2500 Curtis Street, Denver, Colorado 80205.

[39]*Broadcasting Cablecasting Yearbook,* 1735 DeSales Street, N.W., Washington, D.C. 20036.

[40]*Television Factbook,* 1836 Jefferson Place, N.W., Washington, D.C. 20036.

PART V

THE FUTURE

16

Impact of New Communication Technologies

Home communications future.

Cable, along with other communication technologies, will have an impact on the media environment, telecommunication services, the economy, and perhaps human behavior. It is tempting to become overexcited by the possibilities of unlimited, broadband communication channels with two-way capability. One can envision a media environment perfectly suited to each individual's interests and needs, interactive communication with the rest of the world, and the home of the future where work, school, play, and home management resources are all efficiently available from within the household at a minimum expenditure of time and energy. Seeing the advantages and horrors of such a communication environment is barely a challenge to the imagination.

But fast as these new communication technologies seem to be coming, it will be argued here that the most immediate changes will be peripheral. Entertainment options will multiply quickly. The quality of television for both entertainment and information will be enhanced. Nevertheless, these are somewhat marginal increments in the usefulness of television. Major changes will evolve much more slowly. The benefits of two-way communication in a broadband context will be tested by trial and error over a long time as the technology, services, and marketing programs develop. The social change resulting from greater, more convenient access to information will certainly be slow as people accept, adapt to, and absorb information in new forms. Home management, working, and schooling, aided by broadband communication, may replace some earlier methods of approaching the same functions, but the force of habit and existing institutions will not submit easily and quickly. Human behavior, dependent on well-established family and institutional values, will not be suddenly corrupted or enlightened by new communication technologies.

The most important changes will be slow enough so that the impacts may be assessed and the communication systems adapted to desired goals. This is not to say that we will not institutionalize some undesirable characteristics of the new communication systems before we recognize more appropriate policies. But there will be time to contemplate, understand, and control the more profound aspects of our new communication environment as it develops.

In this chapter we look at cable and other communication technologies as they affect each other, the quality of telecommunications services, and the media environment. The results of the introduction of new communication technologies and services are not universal across the society. Rural, small town, urban, and suburban communities will realize different effects, both positive and negative.

MEDIA ENVIRONMENT

Some communities in the United States have no local mass media at all; others may have a weekly newspaper and faint signals from distant radio and television stations.[1] From this point, media availability ranges over a variety of combinations of radio, television, and newspapers up to the media-saturated metropolitan communities. Different media environments may be distinguished at one level by enumerating media— television stations, cable channels, radio stations, daily newspapers, and weekly newspapers. Of the mass media, only magazines are equally accessible, at least by mail, to all media environments. The character of mass media content and the relationship of media to individuals in the target audience also differs from community to community. It is essential to account for these differences in media environment in assessing mass-media service and impact. Communication technologies can be developed and structural changes made to remedy deficiencies in media service, where they exist, and approach a parity in access to media for all citizens.

News and the Media Environment

An important characteristic of the media environment is how it functions in *news dissemination.* Most of the differences in the news dissemination function of the media environment can be attributed to the size of the population served by these media. Although much more radio, television, and print news is available on a daily basis to people in the large population areas, only rarely does the news touch them personally. On the other hand, in the leaner news environment of small communities, local information is provided daily on the radio and at least weekly in the newspapers. Residents of small towns report regular exposure to news coverage of their friends, work associates, and neighborhoods through local news media. This is rare in bigger towns; the media are much less personal. People in the news are no closer, personally, than national and international figures.[2]

The central city metro newspaper reader suffers a further depersonalization in the news coverage. Researchers have found that some metro dailies emphasize suburban news at the expense of coverage of the central urban area which is not as valuable to the newspaper advertisers.[3] On the other hand, television news, with its limited time, covers mainly the central city.[4] With the exception of television news, the suburbanite is better off than the urban news consumer. The suburbanite is under the umbrella of the city media and is likely to have a weekly newspaper serving the suburb exclusively. These urban neighborhood and suburban weeklies generally serve much larger populations than small town rural weeklies but provide a detailed source of information on local government, schools, people, and community events.

The lack of personally relevant local news in central cities causes those consumers to focus attention on features and *soft* "human-interest" news and national and international news. There is likely to be greater consumption of *hard* local news in the smaller communities where that news is more relevant to the consumer. Thus, local news may be more useful to consumers in small communities than in the large, and the theoretical function of "a free press" in a democracy may have greater opportunity to work.

Because the news media for the small city residents are more personal, small town residents have a more positive feeling toward the local media and consider them supportive of the community. On the other hand, consumers of the more "psychologically distant" big city media perceive those media to be abrasive, powerful, and perhaps hypercritical. As the large city media keep watch over city institutions, in the process they may help to alienate news consumers from their communities. While the media-as-community-booster function in the small towns is probably socially important in some ways, the media functioning in this way do not easily accommodate the equally important surveillance function.

Having much less choice in media, the small town and rural residents all use the same media. Therefore, there is much more common media experience. The suburban-urban environment fractionates media audiences in so many ways that media experience is not universal, not a common, community binding experience.

The small town and rural people use imported media. In a media sense, they are much more cosmopolitan. They are exposed to newspapers, radio, and television stations from distant cities. The average big city resident is almost *never* exposed to media sources originating from outside the metro area.

Entertainment and Media Environments

In terms of general information and entertainment options, small town media environments, of course, offer least. Small town residents complain about radio because there is usually only one local radio station available that tries to satisfy "middle-of-the-road" tastes. No station is available with just the right format to suit special interests, at least not a station with a local identity. As radio environments grow larger, a differentiation in format takes place so that in the middle sized cities most information needs and musical tastes are satisfied. In the large media environments, not only is every taste well served but there is a choice within each format preference.

There is much greater diversity in newspaper entertainment features as we go from small town media environments to metropolitan areas. Although, in almost all small communities, metropolitan newspapers are available on the day of publication, the metropolitan resident has a choice of two or more daily newspapers and can choose the package of local and national entertainment features that best suits individual interests.

In terms of television service, the typical intermediate sized city is best off. Cable television is almost always available in these communities with the full range of services described in Chapters 6, 7, and 8. A 35-channel cable system provides ABC, CBS, NBC, and PBS, a couple of imported independent stations with a variety of syndicated programs, and satellite-delivered programming. These cable systems may also have local government and educational channels and a variety of automated text services. An option is a radio service that includes 20 or more FM stations, thus putting the intermediate sized towns on a parity with large metropolitan areas in radio format availability.

The full range of cable television service is not generally available in smaller towns where, if cable exists, it is likely to be an older, classic system of only 12 channels.

How valuable is diversity in entertainment? As everyone knows, Americans spend a good deal of time with radio and television. Such entertainment is cheap and probably necessary. Other forms of recreation are more expensive and less convenient. In communities where home entertainment options are limited, people are forced to make choices that might not be made under wider options. Furthermore, they are denied certain entertainment and information entirely. Wider choice may lead to more consumption than is "good for us," but it is nonetheless *liberating* to be able to build a more individually suited media menu from among the widest possible variety of options.

At the present stage of media development, as we have emphasized, major differences exist among communities in their access to media. "Relative deprivation" exists in every media environment, with different but equally significant deficiencies in the small town and rural areas at one extreme and the urban central city at another.

A combination of new communication technologies may serve to improve some media environments but in some cases widen the gap between the haves and the have nots. We discuss the technologies in relation to the impact on various media environments.

DIRECT BROADCAST SATELLITES

Definition

Direct broadcast satellite (DBS)[5] service has been defined as a "radio-communication service in which signals transmitted or retransmitted by space stations are intended for direct reception by the general public."[6] In the broadcasting-satellite service, two kinds of direct reception are possible: *individual reception* refers generally to simple domestic installations with small antennas, 1 meter or smaller; *community reception* involves a more complex system with larger antennas intended for use by a group at one location or through a distribution system such as cable covering a limited area.

Economic Future

As a new service, DBS has an unpredictable future. Some cost and revenue estimates are based upon services offered by industries which make use of similar technologies, such as multipoint distribution service (MDS). There is also some experience in other countries.

The Communications Satellite Corporation (COMSAT), through its subsidiary, Satellite Television Corporation, is hoping to provide the United States (contiguous states) with DBS service in the middle 1980s. Other companies are also planning to enter the market. Citing research results from a 1973 study,[7] the president of Scientific-Atlanta feels that there is a "significant market" for home dishes (receiving antennas) since 4 million homes in the United States receive one or no broadcast TV channels.[8] COMSAT plans to offer a subscription-supported service for about $25 per month. The receiving dish would cost about $200–300.[9] In Japan, the cost of a 1-meter home terminal is $395, approximately double the estimation made by COMSAT. An additional $100–150, based on MDS experience, would be required to *install* the rooftop receiving dish.[10] It is probably true, as COMSAT argues, that costs will decline in the coming years. Critics of the service do not believe that costs will fall as rapidly as COMSAT estimates.

The important cost variables are the satellite itself and the home terminals, including installation, security system, and decoding units. To receive an acceptable signal at the home using a small 1-meter dish, a high-powered and relatively concentrated signal needs to be broadcast by the satellite. This might require several satellites to serve the United States. Currently, most satellite-receiving stations use much larger dishes—4.5 meters and up. But the higher the power (signal strength) at the point of reception, the smaller the dish can be. Smaller dishes are, of course, cheaper.[11]

The success of the DBS venture proposed by COMSAT will depend to some extent on its marketing of the service. COMSAT believes that a base of 3–4 million subscribers will be required before the service can become commercially viable.[12]

The FCC has created a situation whereby multiple entry into the domestic satellite market is possible.[13] This could develop an industry structure for DBS that would encourage competition and result in desirable "technological advances and economic efficiency."[14]

Technology

DBS programming originates from some central point and is then beamed up to a satellite in the *uplink* portion of signal delivery. Most of the geostationary satellites serving the United States are relatively low powered, using about 5 watts per transponder. To transmit acceptable signals to small home antennas, DBS will have to use 100–200 watts per transponder. Because of this great increase in the power requirement, only 2 to 6 channels of TV programming will be available instead of the potential of 24 channels offered by present satellites. Total power is divided among transponders. To increase channel capacity at any given RF output wattage requires an increase in the diameter of the receiving earth station dish. DBS has been allocated to the KU band (12.3–12.7 gHz). The technical characteristics of this high frequency makes it unreliable because it is sensitive to atmospheric disturbances. The use of high-power, high-frequency transponders with new and less tested technology increases the risk of system failure.[15]

COMSAT plans to uplink signals to four satellites with two secondary satellites to serve as backup units in case of downtime on one of the primary satellites. Each satellite can broadcast to one time zone in the contiguous United States using a spot-beam transmission pattern. Depending on its position relative to the satellite's *footprint* (area of coverage), a few locations in the United States may be able to receive only two or three of the six channels COMSAT proposes. From the satellite then, the signals are amplified and retransmitted back to earth in the *downlink* segment. To receive the signals, one must be in the satellite's footprint and have a clear line of sight orientation between the satellite and the receiving terminal. In mountainous and urban areas, this can be a problem as natural or man-made obstructions interfere. Once the signal has been received at the home terminal, the high-frequency microwaves are converted to the lower, conventional TV channel frequencies. The home terminal includes a decoding system which unscrambles the programming. There may also be an "addressable box" with which a central office can communicate to turn the decoding system on or off. This is used to permit tiered services. To serve the entire country with DBS on a local time basis, it has been estimated that four or more channels could be provided across ten service areas; each area would serve about half a time zone.[16]

Programming

The service proposed by COMSAT is a subscription programming service with multiple channels and tiers of programming available. With the addressable boxes in the home terminals, the tiered programming is made possible. Marketers of the service could charge on a per-view basis or, in the multichannel system, per channel.

COMSAT envisions its offerings as including commercial-free, first-run movies, sports events, educational and cultural material, and data and text transmission. DBS could not serve local programming needs and interests. Audiences would be defined on the basis of interests and not geography. However, if DBS were to become a national service which threatened the economic survival of cable or broadcast services, local programming could be hurt. It has been suggested that the FCC require DBS operators to create programming relevant for their particular service areas. Thus, a programmer for the Central states might recognize the predominantly rural audiences.[17] While the DBS programmer might elect to do this, the FCC will not require it.

The experience of some other countries has indicated that a terrestrial television system may be more expensive than a satellite broadcasting system.[18] If this turns out to be the case in the United States development of DBS, it may be a cost-effective way in which to expand the availability television.

DBS and the Media Environment

In markets where cable is established, it is not likely that DBS would be competitive. Cable can provide more channels for about the same monthly cost and lower installation charges. In fact, COMSAT has suggested that it would provide its program service to cable for distribution like any other satellite program network. Assuming that cable beats DBS to the urban markets, overcoming franchising and construction delays, DBS is left with the sparsely populated countryside outside metropolitan areas, and the rural areas. It has been estimated that there are about 6 million such households. The 6 million homes could shrink considerably, however. Cable systems are at present wiring areas with under 30 homes per mile of density. In the future, cable may serve areas with as low as 5 homes per mile of density, if rates equivalent to those proposed by DBS could be charged. Telephone companies may also provide video service to very low density areas. Subscription and low-power television could reach some of these homes, but with fewer channels.

The programming service would be supported from the same sources that supply cable—the movie industry, sports, and independent producers. COMSAT speaks as if the DBS service would be original and exclusive, and of course this would be necessary if it were to supply programs to cable; but if COMSAT were satisfied to serve noncabled areas exclusively, it could *cherry pick* (take the best of) programs from all the cable suppliers. This would mean that the rural, low density areas would have access to the best of the national programs on cable. Localized interests would not be served, of course, although some special programs could be created to suit the interests of the rural audiences, for example, a television *Grit*.

It has been proposed that the FCC establish DBS as a high definition television distribution medium. (See discussion of HDTV in Chapter 5.) This would delay the initiation of service while the technology is developed, and increase the cost to consumers who would need a receiver designed to the new standard. HDTV via DBS could mean a different market for DBS among high income people anxious to improve television quality. Even here, there would be competitors, in cable systems and videocassettes and discs.

SUBSCRIPTION TELEVISION

Definition

Subscription television (STV) is a "system whereby subscription television broadcast programs . . . are transmitted and intended to be received in intelligible form by members of the public only for a fee or charge."[19] Each STV station is a commercially licensed broadcast facility which has received authorization from the FCC to operate a subscription service. The television signals are scrambled when transmitted so that only paying households with leased or purchased decoders may receive them. The programming is principally movies but may include sports events. The films are often somewhat racier (harder R) than pay cable. The FCC no longer requires that the stations broadcast for a part of each day without scrambling although some stations may still choose to do so.[20]

Economic Future

STV is a relatively new broadcast service. The first formally licensed STV station under the new rules began broadcasting in the Newark, N.J. area on March 1, 1977.[21] By the turn of the decade, several STV stations were on the air, with several more stations expected to begin operations.[22] STV is growing rapidly in number of subscribers. In some places where

STV has had a substantial lead it is quite competitive with cable. (See the discussion under MDS and the Media Environment, page 334.)

Present costs to the consumer for STV service include monthly subscriptions fees of about $20, installation fees of up to $90, and in some cases a deposit on the decoder unit. For this price, the subscriber typically receives 50 hours of premium television programming per week.[23] The unit cost of the decoder, which may be leased or sold to the subscriber, averages $150 but can range in price from under $100 to over $225. Prices vary depending on quantity discounts, number of channels (one or two), and addressability. Prices for the encoder range widely from $10,000 to $100,000.[24]

The FCC rules permit STV stations in any community where channel assignments are vacant or an existing station chooses to change to subscription service. (Until 1982 the Commission had limited STV to television markets with four or more non-pay stations.)[25] In some markets, two or more STV services may survive. The FCC does not require the use of compatible STV technologies or STV hardware within a given market.[26] If, as the FCC anticipates, a superior STV technology ultimately prevails in the marketplace, some cost savings would result. If compatible technologies were used within a given marketplace, the cost for decoders could be reduced by a substantial amount because the same decoder would be used to receive several STV services.

Depending on what kind of system is constructed and how much money is necessary for programming and marketing, the minimum break-even point can be as low as 35,000 subscribers. In practice, as many as 75,000 to 100,000 subscribers may be needed to reach the break-even point.[27] The New York and New Jersey STV services are approaching the break-even point with 75,000 subscribers; the Los Angeles station required 100,000 subscribers.

The FCC has assigned a UHF Task Force to study the problems impeding UHF development and to generate solutions and recommendations for improvement. The outcome of this activity could help STV in the UHF band to provide a technically improved service.

Operating expenses and capital costs increase as more subscribers are added to an STV system. Unlike conventional broadcast TV, STV operators need to install decoders in the homes of each new viewer. However, once a break-even point has been reached with a base of subscribers, costs per subscriber decrease as more subscribers enter the system. There is some feeling that, in the future, STV subscription prices will decline, making the service more attractive to those presently not subscribing.[28] Important cost variables which affect STV operations are the cost of the broadcasting facilities and the other costs associated with conventional broadcasting, the cost of encoders and decoders, and the costs of installations, maintenance, and marketing of the service.

As in the cable industry, theft of service is a problem. Legislation and court decisions have recently favored STV against theft of service, but the better resolution may be in improved technology. There is no way for the STV operator to know whether the signal is being received within a home; therefore policing the signal is very difficult.

Operating costs in STV are high. Since the coverage area is so broad, the customers for a given day's installations and maintenance may be many miles apart. Installing STV service is not as simple as sending a truck out and making the same installation at each home. Often the installer must experiment with different locations and heights for antennas and even different types of antennas. The construction of a high-rise building can create ghosting where it did not exist before.

Technology

The economic feasibility of STV is primarily a matter of how cheaply and reliably the service can be provided to subscribers while excluding nonsubscribers. By broadcasting a scrambled signal over a UHF frequency, the general public cannot receive an intelligible picture with the accompanying sound. Some kind of decoding device is needed.

STV technology is almost as old as conventional TV. The prototype technology for STV dates back to 1950 when WOR-TV tested the Skiatron system of scrambling. But in the first two decades of operation, no successful market was developed.[29] There are several possible ways in which to encode and subsequently decode a TV signal as a means for excluding nonsubscribers from receiving premium programming. The FCC has allowed at least eight systems to be used. Of the systems approved by the FCC, several are currently in use. Any STV system must meet certain technical criteria before the FCC will authorize its use. The FCC feels that the current state of STV technology is such that it would be inappropriate to single out any technology as the most satisfactory. All technologies are being improved. The best of the STV technologies should eventually emerge, precluding the need for an administrative decision by the FCC.[30]

The differences existing among the various STV technologies can be evaluated in terms of their capabilities regarding system security, billing, cost, and complexity. If the technology permits per-program billing rather than per-channel payment, a more complicated system will be used. In addition to excluding nonsubscribers in general from receiving the STV channel in a per-program billing system, a means for differentiating among subscribers must be used. One advantage of the per-program billing system is that the STV operator can cater to the intense preferences of very small audiences. Smaller audiences willing to pay the price can support relatively unpopular programming. In this sense an economic ideal of consumer sovereignty is realized. Presently however, STV stations use the technologically simpler per-channel billing system, which permits access in all programs at a single monthly rate.

Per-program billing may be accomplished by using telephone interfaces between the decoders and the STV operator's central computer or by using memory chips. The chip activates the decoder and records all programs watched. The subscriber mails in the chip once each month and is billed for the appropriate programs. A new chip is then issued. Systems with addressable decoders can instruct the central computer to provide unscrambled programming.

Although various STV technologies have been in use for 30 years, some problems remain. The frequency of consumer complaints has declined. Problems with individual decoder boxes include a flickering or slightly distorted picture or an occasional buzzing on the audio subcarrier channel.[31]

Since the operating STV stations are UHF, they are subject to the limitations of this service. UHF requires much more power than VHF to cover the same area. Signals are weaker from UHF stations which limits the Grade A contour (effective range) of the originating station. The descramblers used accentuate the problem since they operate properly under a more limited range of signals. The use of circularly polarized transmissions can improve reception of the outer limits by decreasing multipathing (ghosting).

The service area of an STV station is the same as that for any other UHF station. The quality of the signal received varies depending on the transmitting power, antenna height above average terrain, operating frequency, obstructions (natural or man-made), receiving antenna, TV set quality, and decoder. As with any conventional broadcasting station, STV stations must obtain licenses for three-year periods. Spectrum availabilities are predetermined according to the table of allocations for TV channels. If an applicant is granted a standard broadcast license, the licensee may operate the STV service.

Only those areas of the country which have available UHF or VHF channels can have the standard STV service. Any commercial television broadcast station licensee or holder of a construction permit for a new station may receive authorization to provide STV service. An STV license applicant need not ascertain community needs as does an applicant for a conventional broadcast television license.

Low power television stations may also provide subscription TV service. Since low power television requires much less capital, more areas will become accessible for STV service when the FCC plans for low-power TV stations are finalized.

Programming

No large amount of programming to date has been created expressly for the STV audience. Most of the fare is equally available through other media such as theaters or other pay TV services and, at a later date, broadcast television stations. The FCC Network Inquiry *Report on STV* noted that most of the "quality" programming predicted to appear on STV is actually available over public TV stations.[32]

There are some exceptions to this. Two STV stations in the Los Angeles area are able to cater to minority audiences with programming that is original. In some instances, revenues from the pay TV operation have been used to subsidize minority taste programming which is broadcast part of the day without scrambling.[33] Some STV services have exclusive contracts with local sports franchises.

There are no restrictions on the kind of programming that STV stations can offer other than those imposed on all broadcasters. The FCC removed all pay TV programming restrictions on STV (designed to protect broadcast TV) after a similar set of rules pertaining to pay cable was struck down by the D.C. Circuit Court of Appeals.[34]

Typically, STV offerings include movies, specials, sports, or other entertainment. Most STV operations book their own programs rather than work through a single supplier such as the HBO service.[35] A few offer a network pay service, as is. It is the ability to cater to the tastes of the local audience that distinguishes stand alone STV from most pay cable operators which rely on national services. This prompts a comparison of pay cable operations with network-affiliated television relying on central sources of programming, and STV stations with independent stations that create a more locally oriented mix of programming.

Some STV stations are attempting to sell their service to cable.

STV and the Media Environment

At present, STV makes one or two additional television stations available to several large metropolitan areas. For the most part, it was the only pay-TV-type service available in these cities when the broadcasts started. In a few of the places pay cable TV and STV co-exist, but in these cases there are many parts of the metropolitan STV coverage area where cable is not available. Under the old FCC rules, only a few cities were eligible for STV. These cities were the bigger television markets (or locations within those markets), where four conventional television stations are already available and where television stations have been assigned but not licensed. Even now that the FCC rules are changed, it is not likely that STV will be a programming option for smaller media environments because it would take between 350,000 and 1,000,000 households in a market to support STV.[36]

If the cost of the STV technology is reduced, as predicted, more communities could be served. The number of communities could be calculated easily by determining the new break-even point (in terms of households at the lower cost per household served) and then counting the number of media environments (communities) that have a sufficient number of households to achieve the new break-even point.

Most people in the cable television industry, and some in the STV business, believe that cable television can provide the same service and more, at less cost, once cable systems are constructed in the major cities. Nevertheless, the development of major urban cable systems will be slow enough for STV operators to make an adequate return on the investment. The industry speaks of a "window" for STV that extends into the middle to late 1980s.

If cable television makes STV-type programming available in the major cities in the next few years, the most beneficial effect of STV on media environments in the longer term will be on the population areas not dense enough to support cable. As noted earlier, full-power STV services in these areas are precluded by the high cost of conventional broadcasting. The FCC has eliminated the "complement of four" rule, as well as the rule requiring unscrambled broadcasting, making STV somewhat more practical in low density areas. Another apparent solution to this problem, presently proposed by the FCC, is to create the opportunity for low-power TV stations in all communities. These stations would be free to become STV services without any restrictions. The number of existing conventional stations in the area would have no bearing on the function of these low-power stations as subscription services. It is possible that networks of low-power STV stations could be interconnected by satellite, perhaps with a full-power STV station, to share the administrative and operating costs of programming a subscription service. (For more details on low-power TV, see that discussion later in this chapter.)

In the STV service market, DBS is a possible competitive supplier. DBS might provide more channels, but perhaps at a higher cost. (See further discussion under MDS.)

MULTIPOINT DISTRIBUTION SERVICE

Definition

Multipoint Distribution Service (MDS) is a common carrier closed-circuit microwave system transmitting a signal addressed to multiple, fixed, receiving points.[37] Frequencies have been allocated for two MDS channels in the 2150- to 2162-mHz portion of the spectrum. Channel 1 is 6 mHz, and the second channel, depending on the location, can be either 6 mHz (channel 2) or 4 mHz (channel 2a).[38] MDS stations are intended to provide one-way transmission (usually in an omnidirectional pattern) from a stationary transmitter to multiple receiving facilities located at fixed points designated by the subscriber.

Economic Future

The important cost variables in MDS are the downconverter package, antenna, transmitter, installation and maintenance, marketing, and transaction costs. The costs for the downconverter can range from under $50 to $350 or more. Special equipment features such as low noise capability, automatic fine tuning (prevents drifting), or filtering add to the cost. Antennas cost from about $20.[39] Households farther from the transmitter need larger, more costly antennas.

Generally, power for MDS stations is limited to 10 watts.[40] Under some circumstances a waiver can be obtained to transmit at 100 watts. This requires an additional amplifier to upgrade the service. A 10-watt transmitter costs about $17,000 whereas a 100-watt amplifier costs $13,550.[41] An FCC staff study noted that, if initial construction grants were issued permitting carriers to use a single piece of equipment for 100-watt transmitters, instead of the add-on amplifier, there would be a cost savings of several thousands of dollars while increasing the technical reliability of the equipment.[42] To this cost must be added the costs, varying considerably on conditions and the service, of transmitting antennas, towers, and monitoring, switching and originating equipment. The total would be $150,000 or less.

In the past, costs for MDS have declined fairly steadily. This trend is expected to continue into the future but with a slower rate of decline. There is competition in the equipment manufacturing industry; thus hardware options are available at competitive prices. The big breakthrough was the dramatic cost reduction in installation packages (receiving antenna/downcoverter). Since 1976 costs have declined from about $1,500 per installation to an average price range of under $100 to about $300. At this price, it has become possible to market to single-family dwellings.[43]

Subscription prices for pay television delivered via MDS average about $15.00 per month and range from $7.00 to $26.50 in different communities. Deposits of $10–100 are sometimes required. Consumer costs vary as a function of the type of dwelling (single-family or multiple units), quality of equipment, and service tiers or packages purchased.

Usually it is significantly less expensive to provide service to apartments and other multiple-unit dwellings with a single antenna and downconverter for the whole group of dwellings. Discounts are then available to these groups in subscription and installation fees.[44] MDS subscribers usually have the option of owning or renting home receiving equipment from the pay TV company.[45]

MDS as a common carrier receives statutory protection against unauthorized reception.[46] Security for MDS systems adds to the total cost. Typical methods of guarding against piracy are the use of scrambled signals, addressable downconverters, or cards with encoded chips. Presently most MDS signals are not scrambled, but as the equipment becomes more available to the general public, piracy is more likely, and MDS systems will have to begin encoding the signals and installing decoders.

MDS systems can operate in a smaller market than can STV. Under 10,000 subscribers may sustain MDS at a break-even rate or better. This relatively small number of subscribers makes MDS viable in a larger number of cities than STV, which typically requires a base of 35,000–40,000 subscribers for break-even costs.[47] However, cable is usually well-established in these smaller communities. Initial investments in the MDS service are recouped after two to four years.[48]

To start a profitable MDS pay TV business in the average market costs half a million dollars. To lease transmission time over MDS facilities costs much less per hour than the rates for comparable service over STV facilities.[49]

The MDS industry has no restrictions on cross-ownership or multiple ownership, duopoly, or any other restrictions normally associated with broadcasting because of its common carrier status. The main restriction applicable to MDS carriers relates to business partners who are customers. Limitations are placed on the amount of time that affiliated subscribers (business partners) can have for resale.[50] To be eligible for station authorization, the MDS applicant must indicate that no more than 50 percent of the services offered will be consumed by these affiliated subscribers.[51] Block-time sales are permitted to the extent that they are not anticompetitive.

There is no restriction on the number of MDS licenses which can be awarded to any individual or group. Thus, networks can be developed. MDS is often used to provide a service which softens a market for cable service.[52]

The MDS business is fairly active. Between 1971 and 1980, some 131 MDS stations were authorized by the FCC, with 86 MDS stations completely constructed and offering service and another 467 applications pending. The FCC is considering a possible expansion of the spectrum allocated to this service.[53]

Technology

An MDS system has a fixed station transmitting omnidirectionally to fixed receiving stations. The receiving stations use directive antennas to pick up the microwave transmissions. The line-of-sight transmissions are picked up by parabolic antennas. The signal is converted by a down-converter from the microwave frequency to a selected lower frequency, then passed through a decoder (in an addressable or scrambled system), conducted by coaxial cable to the TV receiver, and displayed on an unused channel on the TV set. Master antenna system wiring, used for many years in apartment buildings, can sometimes serve as the link to TV receivers.

The service area extends from 15 to 25 miles or more, depending on the terrain. The picture quality is similar to cable service. One or two TV channels can be offered depending on the economic and regulatory circumstances. In some cases, the service area can extend to 70 miles. The transmission range is a function of transmitting power, the character and size of the receiving antennas, line-of-sight orientation, and obstructions such as terrain shielding, foliage, or intervening buildings.[54] MDS service is quite reliable up to the 25 mile primary service area.

MDS hardware varies, but although the equipment performs differently, it can be interfaced.[55] In some markets, such as Baltimore and Cleveland, line-of-sight problems (terrain shielding) preclude successful single-family-dwelling marketing.[56]

Presently, MDS has been allocated the spectrum space of 2150-2162-mHz. This permits two possible channels of service for major metropolitan areas.[57] An *FCC Notice of Inquiry* (Docket No. 80-112) proposed consideration of a possible reallocation of spectrum in the 2500-2690-mHz band among the MDS, instructional television fixed service (ITFS), and operational fixed services (OFS) services. Thirty-one underutilized channels may be reallocated between the other two services which would afford ten more channels to MDS for a total of twelve in each location.

Programming

MDS can offer subscription television programming on a 24-hour basis. HBO or Showtime are the most common services. Local programming, children's programming, and business data services are also offered. In some cases, MDS can be offered as an interim service until cable is sufficiently developed in a given market to provide an alternative service.[58] MDS is also quite active in data markets. Thus, MDS stands to lose if AT&T enters data markets in competition. MDS could be used in the future for high definition simulcasts of broadcast stations.

MDS and the Media Environment

MDS, STV, cable, and perhaps DBS could compete for the same pay television market. MDS might have a slight price advantage over some of the competitors. In comparison with the three competitors, MDS requires far less capital investment and, therefore, may serve smaller numbers of people. However, multiple dwelling units of any size are usually located in urban settings where cable and STV are sure to be eventually. Under these competitive circumstances, particularly against cable with multiple channel offerings, MDS is likely to be an interim service or a supplementary business of apartment and motel owners who hold out against cable, although multiple channel MDS systems, if permitted, could keep MDS competitive.

The cable industry is now quite concerned with the growing competition from MDS, STV, and satellite master antenna television (SMATV) systems. SMATV is practical in apartment complexes with as few as 150 units. These systems may provide five or more pay and advertiser supported channels (e.g., HBO, ESPN, CNN, WTBS, and USA) for about $15 per individual subscriber or $10 per unit on a bulk rate (where the apartment management adds the service into the rent). AML microwave (see Chapter 2) may serve many apartment complexes with 50 to 100 channels in direct competition with cable. Two-way services may also be provided in this type of system by using a reverse microwave path.

SMATV operators envision multichannel systems using high powered, high frequency satellites with inexpensive antenna dishes and receivers. DBS systems, using the high powered, high frequency satellites, one meter dish antennas and simple decoders, could make multiple channels available to every household in the U.S. at a reasonable cost.

If MDS were increased to five or ten channels, and to this were added ten off-air channels, the resulting 15- to 20-channel system would be quite competitive with cable; particularly at the lower rates that would be permitted by the minimal capital costs of the wireless MDS.

Apartment complexes using SMATV or MDS may attempt to exclude cable from the buildings. The right of the cable franchisee to wire and solicit customers in apartments is now being fought in courts and state legislatures. Cable systems operating on private property, within apartment complexes, are called *private cable systems*. The industry association is the National Satellite Cable Association (333 N. Michigan Ave., Chicago, Illinois 60601).

STV stations have been quite successful in competing with cable. Many STV customers actually believe they have "cable." Others see cable and STV as essentially the same service in terms of the principal attraction, uncut, uninterrupted movies. If an STV station has locked up the rights to desirable sports franchises, cable may be less attractive.

The value of the multichannel capability of cable has been questioned. A study by Browne, Bortz and Coddington found that five channels of programming would satisfy the needs of most consumers.[59] If this proves true, SMATV, multiple channel MDS, and DBS could all compete effectively with cable. Incidentally, this would help legitimize the cable industry contention that cable is not a market monopoly and, therefore, should be deregulated. Under these competitive circumstances the argument for leased channels, rate regulation, etc. has less strength.

TELEVISION BROADCAST TRANSLATOR AND LOW-POWER STATIONS

Definitions

A television broadcast *translator station* is "a station in the broadcast service operated for the purpose of retransmitting the programs and signals of a television broadcast station, without significantly altering any characteristic of the original signal other than its frequency and amplitude, for the purpose of providing television reception to the general public."[60] A few translators are allowed limited origination of programming.

A *primary* television station provides programs and signals which are then retransmitted on a different TV channel by a translator station to extend a service area. Translator stations operate in both the UHF and VHF bands. These stations have been in existence for years, and there are thousands now serving rural areas at a distance from television markets.

Low-power television stations (LPTV) rely on virtually the same technology but are different in that they may originate programming or receive and retransmit satellite programs without any limitation. They may be commercial or noncommercial and may be STV stations.

Economic Future

According to Corporation for Public Broadcasting (CPB) estimates, 10-watt VHF station transmission equipment would cost about $13,000 and a satellite receive station about $25,000, all installed (without the cost of the tower). (CPB recommends piggybacking on another tower when possible.) CPB's estimate for the maximum power UHF transmission equipment (without tower) is about $76,000 along with the $25,000 satellite earth station.

These capital investments would suffice for LPTV stations providing a satellite-delivered network, for example, ESPN or CNN. It would cost a few thousand dollars more to automate the insertion of local commercials.

If the station were an LPTV-STV station, it would make another investment in decoders of about $150 per subscribing household (see discussion of STV). This would be the major capital expense. Total cost for transmitting equipment, site lease, and antenna is $100,000 to $150,000.[61]

If the LPTV station wished to originate programming, production equipment would be necessary. These costs are most variable, depending on the quality and extent of production contemplated. The CPB cost estimate for broadcast-quality color studio equipment is $190,500.[62]

Operating costs would be dependent on programming. Cost to the station of a pay television satellite network would be about $4.00 per subscriber; an advertiser-supported network, perhaps 10¢ per subscriber. Operating expenses for the transmitting equipment would be about $5,000 annually.[63] Lease of the tower space could also be a significant cost. Administration and marketing of a passive station not originating any programming could be as low as $50,000. Production costs would be entirely dependent on the scale and whether the production crew were full-time or contracted for on an ad hoc basis.

Evidence that LPTV has an economic future, at least on paper, may be found in the applications for thousands of stations already filed with the FCC from the Neighborhood TV Company, partly owned by a subsidiary of Sears, Roebuck, Turner Broadcasting stations, and many other organizations. The backlog caused the FCC to put a "freeze" on applications. It is also possible, however, that the applicants have no clear idea of the economic viability of LPTV but are, in a manner of speaking, hoarding licenses in case viable services develop.

A few LPTV licenses have been granted. One, an STV station in Bemidji, Minnesota, is now in operation. It will take some time for all of the remaining applications to be evaluated. The FCC has been instructed by Congress to give preference to minorities, women, labor unions, and community groups.

Technology

Translators and LPTV stations are reduced scale broadcast television systems, limited in power to fit into the present allocation scheme and table of assignments for higher-powered VHF and UHF broadcast stations. The quality of the equipment for low-power transmission and low cost production has improved over the years to permit origination. The reliability of the transmitting equipment has also improved minimizing the risk of interference. Since translators and LPTV stations are assigned frequencies already in use by VHF and UHF television broadcasters, interference must be minimized. It is possible for a low-power station to interfere with the operation of an adjacent or co-channel television station for many miles beyond its effective service area. It should be noted that translators and LPTV stations can interfere with cable system, too. If a cable systems picks up, over the air, a distant TV station and a translator is put in the community on the same or an adjacent channel, it can interfere with the cable system's reception of that channel.

The service area, and potential for interference, is limited by power, antenna height, the type of transmitter used, and the quality of the receiving antenna installed by users of the service. Limits on power—10 watts for VHF and 1,000 watts for UHF—are placed on LPTV transmitters. Coverage, however, is determined by effective radiated power which is multiplication of transmitter power (called *gain*) as a result of the transmitting antenna concentrating the signal. The coverage of VHF and UHF low-power stations at varying power and antenna heights is illustrated in Table 16-1, prepared by CPB.[64]

Table 16-1. Illustrative Low-Power Television Station Coverage

Transmitter Power Output (watts)	Transmitting Antenna Gain	Effective Radiated Power[1]	Transmitting Antenna Height[2] (feet)	Approx. Useful Coverage Distance[3] (miles)
VHF (channels 2–13)				
1	5	5	100	3.5
1	5	5	500	8.0
1	5	5	1,000	11.0
10	5	50	100	6.2
10	5	50	500	14.0
10	5	50	1,000	19.5
UHF (channels 14–83)				
10	10	100	100	2.9
10	10	100	500	6.5
10	10	100	1,000	9.0
100	15	1,500	100	6.5
100	15	1,500	500	12.5
100	15	1,500	1,000	18.0
1,000	15	15,000	100	10.0
1,000	15	15,000	500	21.0
1,000	15	15,000	1,000	26.5

[1]Technically, the loss in the cable between the transmitter and the transmitting antenna should be taken into account in calculating the effective radiated power (ERP). The reduction in ERP that would occur has been approximated by using a lower than normal antenna gain.

[2]The "height above average terrain" which will coincide with the height above ground level only for flat terrain. Variation in terrain will cause variation in coverage.

[3]Distance is to the "Grade B contour." At the extremes of this coverage distance, outside antennas will generally be necessary for adequate reception.

Source: "Low Power Television Guidebook," Corporation for Public Broadcasting, Washington, D.C., 1981.

The low-power station provides a *secondary* service on a frequency that is in use by a full-powered station. It must regulate its signal, if necessary, to protect the primary station. If interference cannot be prevented, the LPTV station must go off the air.

Low-power or translator stations may retransmit another station's signal, a television translator relay station, a television intercity relay station, a television studio-transmitter link (STL) station, CARS (cable antenna relay service), common carrier microwave station, or satellite service. It appears that most of the applicants for LPTV licenses have in mind a satellite interconnected network of many stations. LPTV used for STV will have the same security problems discussed in the STV section.

Programming

At this point it is not clear what type of programming will be most feasible for LPTV. Everything is possible. The cost of production for small potential audiences rules out much original programming in the small towns, although production may be practical in densely populated urban areas where a coverage radius of a few miles would encompass millions of people.

Presumably, in urban areas with many broadcast television stations in service and cable bringing in more programming, LPTV would be narrowcast to special interests. In small town and rural areas, LPTV could supplement meager broadcast television station availability with some of the more generally popular programming available now to cabled communities.

The company in which Sears, Roebuck has invested intends to be country and western television with country music, comedy, and rodeos. A number of proposed religious and minority-owned networks have also filed applications. Other networks would be movie services. Some would be superstations—extending the programming of a present full-service station to a network of LPTV stations.

The FCC has deliberately kept LPTV stations free to try any kind of programming. There are only a few restrictions. They must observe the Fairness Doctrine if they broadcast controversial material. They must comply with the reasonable access and equal time requirements of the Communications Act. The same laws that prohibit obscenities and lotteries apply to LPTV. The copyright laws also apply.

LPTV and the Media Environment

As translators have already done, LPTV stations can add programming options to small communities and rural areas underserved by television. The cost of stations designed to broadcast satellite services may be sufficiently low to cover these media-poor areas with one or more additional signals, providing the most popular programs, available on cable, to noncabled homes on a subscription basis.

In urban areas, LPTV may have difficulty in competition with conventional broadcast television, STV, and cable. But LPTV might find a niche that could be sustained by subscription, advertising, or a combination. Although the FCC created the new service with rural areas unserved or underserved by regular television and cable principally in mind, the high demand for new video services in urban areas suggests that they, too, are underserved.[65]

VIDEODISCS/CASSETTES

Definition

Videodiscs and videocassette machines come under the broad label of home video equipment: "electronic equipment that enables the consumer to record and/or play back sound and images on a standard TV set."[66] These machines provide a service which enables the home viewer to "play" programs on the television screen in the manner of records played on a phonograph.

The videocassette recorders (VCRs) and disc systems differ both in the nature of their software and in their technical capabilities. The videocassette machines can record from the television set as well as play back existing cassettes. The VCR software medium is magnetic cassette tape of varying widths. Because the disc system cannot record, it must be used exclusively to play prerecorded material. The discs are manufactured with a protective coating that makes them almost indestructible.

The videodisc unit cannot duplicate or edit, capacities available on the videocassette recorder. The disc systems can support excellent stereo sound (not available on some videocassette recorders), good frame indexing, and fast random access, which makes the system desirable for industrial and educational uses as well as home entertainment. The stereo capability makes the discs preferred to most VCRs for preprogrammed musical productions.

The cassette recorders can record directly from the television set, even while another program is being viewed, and can duplicate other tapes as well as edit existing program tapes. Although cassette tapes are reusable, they have a limited life, and the newer, narrower tapes can be twisted or mangled.[67]

Economic Future

Both video systems vary in cost depending on the design features desired. However, predictions are that the disc system will remain substantially cheaper than the recorder systems, even though some fairly inexpensive recorders, longitudinal video recorders (LVR), are expected to enter the market. The LVRs are no-frills machines that record for only two or three hours as compared with six hours or eight hours for the newest videocassette machines.[68] Current list prices for videocassette machines are at a low of about $500, with the average price close to $1,000.[69] Optional equipment includes editors to eliminate commercials when television programs are recorded (about $250)[70] and portable home-movie-type cameras, which start around $400 and can go well over $1,000. To use the recording capability, machines without built-in tuning/timing mechanisms require a tuner-timer, which costs about $400 to $500. Blank tapes are about $20 each.[71]

Videodisc machines cost from $500 to $750.[72] Because discs themselves are manufactured inexpensively, the main consumer costs for disc use will be the actual program costs, which are applicable to cassette recorder owners also. Estimates are that discs will range from $5 to $30 each and that prerecorded tape cassettes will vary from $40 to $100 and up. Part of the difference lies in the blank software itself—factory costs for discs are $1 to $2 compared with $5 to $8 for cassette tapes. Other variables which can affect the cost of preprogrammed tapes or discs are royalty fees for performers, union fees, length of the recording, and promotion and distribution costs.[73]

Most predictions are that costs will rise for both hardware and software. As the market for certain preprogrammed material increases, the economies of scale might prevent prices from rising at a constant rate. Minority and other special interest groups could produce their own tapes if they are located in a community large enough to support a studio on a full-time basis.

Analogies to the price leveling experienced in the calculator industry are not expected to hold for VCR and disc machine prices. Production costs have risen for VCR equipment, and both systems are comprised of mechanical parts which require hand work and frequent inspection. The various industry leaders are producing incompatible systems. Some economies from mass production will not be realized until parts are interchangeable.[74]

The industry is fragmented. At least two specific types of cassette recorders and two technologically different disc machines are being marketed. The manufacturers are those that have been in the electronic industry for some time, and the potential for new firms seem slight. Many of the VCR manufacturers are located outside the United States, and the incentives to cooperate and to standardize have little effect.

The U.S. Court of Appeals has held that both videocassette manufacturers and consumers can be held liable for copyright infringement in recording television programs for home use.[75] This would significantly reduce the value of the videocassette machines if the ruling could be enforced.

Technology

The videocassette recorders read a magnetic tape: "Information is converted to modulations in an electric current which aligns molecules of a magnetic coating bonded onto a strip of plastic tape."[76] The original recorders were quadraplex (four-head) units which were large and cumbersome and suitable for commercial use only. Helical scanning, developed in Japan, enabled the machines to move from four-head readers to one head and from 2-inch-wide tape to ¾- to ½-inch tape. The cassette was marketed in 1972 with Sony's U-Matic, a ¾-inch tape system wound in a cassette. Several years before the cassette was introduced, the leading electronics companies had been experimenting with small playback recorders, but Sony in 1975 produced the Betamax recorder and began the home video industry. The Betamax used ½-inch tape and two heads which were oriented separately.

Competing with Betamax is VHS (JVC's "video home system"), which, although using the same technical components, has a slower speed. This increases the length of time available for recording. Other systems are Magnavox's Video 2000, with a longer-running tape, and longitudinal video recorder, which has an audio-type stationary head and shorter recording time.[77]

Technological advances predicted include smaller units and longer tape capabilities. The potential exists for metal tape as used in high-fidelity audio, digital video recording, ¼-inch tape, and many optional pieces of equipment.[78] The 8 mm home movie camera may be replaced by a ¼-inch video recorder and camera built into one unit.

The videodisc machine scans and plays encoded material from a disc by laser beam, electronic stylus (capacitance), or mechanical contact. The laser method involves no physical contact with the disc and thus no scratching or wear in the grooves. Once encoded, the disc is protected in a plastic sleeve. The encoded signal is converted to electrical impulses which are then modulated to a VHF frequency tunable on a television set. Playing time depends among other things on the rate at which the disc spins. Currently discs spin as fast as 1,800 revolutions per minute in the laser scanning system. The disc machine is the size and shape of an audiodisc turntable. Discs are available in different sizes. A 12-inch disc can hold up to 60 minutes of programming on each side. Discs are mass produced by molding from metal dies which have been etched by a master disc. The frames are numbered and addressable. The discs have dual audio potential (e.g., stereo sound). In the electronic stylus system a sapphire stylus reads the embedded images. This system does not have frame reference ability.

Predictions of new capabilities for disc machines include automatic changers, smaller equipment with comparable capacity for playing time, and extras such as microprocessing equipment.[79]

Although the home video function seems simple, the machinery is complex and hard to service. Parts are not interchangeable. Television repair services are generally not skilled in the requisite technical abilities needed to diagnose problems and make repairs.[80]

The consumer must decide the principal use of his or her video equipment: program diversity or time shifting of scheduled programs. If an intended use is time shifting, the videocassette recorder is mandated. However, if prerecorded programming is desired, the lower-cost videodisc machines with their more permanent software is a good choice.

Programming

The range of potential programming is limitless, but at present the movie industry dominates the software market.[81] Approximately 475 movie titles were available on tape during the 16 months preceding March 1980. Predictions are that movies may eventually be released on tape or disc even before they are released to theaters. The pay movie satellite channels are also expected to use home video to expand their market.[82]

Television programs recorded off air are considered to be a supplement to their audience by the broadcasters, and these audiences are being counted by the audience measurement companies.[83] Thus, the broadcast copying should not be an issue raised by broadcasters themselves. However, the software companies will be dealing with a variety of groups which will demand part of the disc or tape revenues. The unions, the performers, and those who hold copyright to any original works recorded will have to be part of the negotiation.

Disc programming, because of the stereo capability, may evolve heavily into the musical performance market and also serve markets for educational and other information-based programming.

Pornographic movies have been a very popular product for the home video industry, but family oriented programs are now being purchased more frequently. Recorded programs are generally used for time delayed viewing rather than for library stocking, but some people are keeping children's programs, specials, and major movies.[84] The number of videotape clubs and rental centers is rising.

ABC's Home View Network intends to make a pay television service available to videocassette owners. The network would broadcast scrambled programs over the ABC owned and operated stations and other ABC affiliates during the hours of 2 a.m. and 6 a.m. (ET). Subscribers would pay an installation fee for the decoder and a monthly fee of about $20 for the service. This would permit them to record programs from the schedule, as desired, by presetting the machines.

Videocassettes/Discs and the Media Environment

The videocassette or videodisc machines have the potential to equalize television programming availability, except for current affairs programming, across media environments. Presumably, everything that is now available on television, over the air, and via cable or satellites (that is not dependent for its value on immediacy) could be available on cassettes or discs. Thus limited television environments could have almost everything that is available in the television rich environments, except the most perishable of the content.

The cost of the playback machines and the cost and availability of tapes will determine whether this technology can function in this way. It is possible that, at high production levels, playback machines would come down to the cost of a good color television set. This might be an acceptable expense to households severely limited in television service, but the cost of programming must also be considered. Under present prices, the cost of television by cassette, for even a few hours of television weekly, would be prohibitive for the average household. There is not much hope for a reduction of these costs except through library distribution or rental systems. Experience with these forms of distribution in films, records, and even books would indicate that only a small proportion of the population would make use of them. It is possible that cable, where available, would provide an inexpensive delivery service for software using addressable descramblers. Channels which are blank late at night could be used to fill individual subscribers' requests for programming.

Across all media environments, videocassettes or discs can provide television programming to those who can afford it. Through this technology, highly specialized interests may be served. When the purposes of video content are served best by several replays, or start, stop, and freeze-frame playback, the tape or disc machines are necessary. When rental libraries of such materials may be the most efficient distribution system, persons in urban areas may have an advantage, although any area could be served by mail.

The time-shifting function of videocassette recording and playback devices may have slightly different functions in the different media environments. In the multichannel television environments, recording for playback at a different time may be most useful for an occasional program of special interest that is not scheduled for replay. In the case of a small town or rural television environment of only one or two stations, video recording may be used to create a new television schedule which fills up the available hours for viewing with programs of maximum appeal from among the limited offerings.

HOME COMPUTERS

Definition

The computer is considered the ultimate home appliance. "A computer is an incredibly complex set of switching circuits that take electrical impulses from the touching of a typewriter-like keyboard and step-by-step change them into some other impulses, then turn them back into letters and numbers on a video screen or a typewriter."[85] The *home computer* or *personal computer,* is a *microprocessor*—a small computer on a miniature silicone chip. The two-way cable communication services described in this book require computers.

Cable overcomes one of the major limitations of microprocessors, the limited *memory,* by permitting interconnection with larger mainframe computers. Telephone lines may be used for this purpose, but the narrow bandwidths (lower capacity) make the telephone impractical for some home uses. The marriage of telecommunications with computers is sometimes called *telematics.*[86]

Economic Future

Home computers sell for as little as $400, but with *peripheral* devices or *add-ons* to make the system functional for general purposes, the system would total about $2,000 to $3,000. Add-ons may include additional memory, a disk drive to provide high data capacity, a modem (modulator-demodulator) for sending and receiving over phone or cable, and a printer for hard copies (as opposed to characters on a CRT—cathode ray tube—or television screen).

In addition to the hardware, home computer owners must purchase *software*—the programs that instruct the computer what to do. The programs cost between $20 to $70. A computer hobbyist may also program the computer following instructions provided or having taken a course through the computer store or elsewhere.

Technology

The home computer is a small keyboard associated with a CRT or television screen. The input-output device, usually an audio cassette playback-recorder may be an integral part of the machine, or attached. A complete system would include the add-ons already identified.

The computer has a *memory* which, measured in *K*s, represents the number of characters (*bytes*, groups of binary digits—to encode, letters, numbers, spaces, instruction). A K is 1,024 characters. The capacity of a home computer may go as high as 64K memory cells within the machine (65,536 characters), which is adequate for many purposes. Secondary memory storage for a home computer (discs and tapes external to the machine) may extend the memory. However, larger computer systems, which would be necessary for referencing or manipulating large data bases, may have many millions of memory cells.

Programming

One of the difficulties in launching the home computer as a household utility has been the lack of software. It may cost as much as $50,000 to create a particular program. This cost must be spread over a great many users. At first, some hardware manufacturers attempted to control software for their machines, but the demand for software was greater than they could supply. Now most manufacturers encourage third party software suppliers.

At this point, the market for home computers has been among hobbyists. Some manufacturers have determined that the hobbyist market has peaked, concentrating for the moment on small business users. But there remains faith that software eventually will be developed to make the home computer a household utility as necessary as the hand calculator.

Computer literacy and *user-friendly machines* are necessary to reach the market beyond hobbyists. Few people are adept at using computers, and some have a fear of the computer technology. Home computer hardware and software must be designed to be more compatible with inexperienced users. A major problem in accessing information data bases is the cumbersome menu selection process.

Some of the uses for personal computers include computation, family finance (budgeting, keeping books balanced), securities analysis, home medical records, income tax preparation, games, conversion from English to metric units, conversion of recipes from standard servings to a particular number desired, personal telephone directories and appointment calendars, instruction, home energy control, travel, restaurant and hotel reservations, real estate, and job searches and license applications.

Through telephone or cable lines the home computer can access data banks of infinite variety. Many such data bases are already available. They are discussed in the section on videotext in Chapter 9. Several experiments are being conducted to test the market for such information.

Personal Computers and the Media Environment

Great stores of information are available to the home computer owner through telecommunication linkages. The personal computer working with other computers and data bases will supplement printed reference resources with more up-to-date information. Cabletext, in cabled communities, makes some of these data retrieval services available without any need for a home computer.

For communities without extensive reference resources, the home computer makes these resources more accessible. For those communities where the resources are available, the computer makes them much more convenient.

CABLE AND THE MEDIA ENVIRONMENT

In the previous chapters of this book, we have discussed the economic future, technology, and programming of cable communication systems. For this section we therefore go directly to a discussion of cable's effect on the media environment.

Number of Channels

Rural areas. As revenues per subscriber increase, it becomes feasible to include more and more of the less dense population areas adjacent to already cabled communities. This line extension activity will probably increase after cable has saturated the most economically desirable areas.

Even so, there will be some low density areas that will be impractical for cable for many years. The existence of cable in most other areas of the country, with the broad array of new services now available, will heighten the dissatisfaction of rural inhabitants with their own level of television and radio service. Already, a number of steps have been taken or proposed by the FCC to improve service to rural areas (low-power television, translators, frequency sharing on clear-channel radio, reduction of radio bandwidth from 10 kHz to 9 kHz to accommodate more stations, VHF short-spaced drop-ins, and allowing telephone companies to provide cable service in low population density areas.) The availability, or potential availability, of cable to most of the rest of the nation has stimulated this activity on behalf of the rural resident.

Small towns. Cable systems serving these communities are the classic 5- and 12-channel systems. These will be rebuilt gradually to modern standards of 35-plus channels. Some of this reconstruction will be forced on cable companies at franchise renewal time by competitive bids or by franchise authorities aware of better service elsewhere. A great many of these older franchises will be up for renewal in the next few years. Cable may have an effect on small market radio. People in those markets generally have access to only a few radio formats, mainly middle-of-the-road music. Cable can supplement the local stations by bringing in distant, urban stations filling out a complete range of radio formats: agriculture and farm, black, classical, "beautiful" music, country and western, golden oldies, jazz, middle-of-the-road, all-news, progressive, religious, Spanish, talk, top-40.[87] With cable, it will be easier for people in radio-isolated areas to satisfy programming tastes, although the classic cable systems serving these areas have not yet developed the market. Local radio stations may suffer some attrition of audience. The best prediction, however, is that the cable FM subscriber will listen to two stations, one of which will always be a local station.

Medium markets. These cities presently have the richest television environment. Most have 35-channel cable systems. The few that remain 12-channel systems will be rebuilding to accommodate additional revenue-producing tiers of service.

Suburbs. These are the newest cable systems, with 35 to 54 channels. Many suburbs have now franchised cable systems or will soon. In the mid-1980s almost all suburbs should be constructed.

Large cities. Cable is now being franchised or constructed in the large cities. Franchises and proposals for franchises in these cities offer 40, 52, 54, 80, and more than 100 channels. The franchising process may be delayed by overextension on construction commitments, but before the close of the decade, all areas of the urban markets should be wired.

In the meantime other technologies may supply service to large unit apartment dwellers. In building complexes with as few as 150 units satellite master antenna television (SMATV) is practical. These systems can provide up to about six pay and advertiser-supported satellite channels. Once the cable system is franchised and built, the SMATV systems may be sold to the operator or attempt to continue in competition. AML microwave (see Chapter 2) may serve many apartment complexes in a city with 50 to 100 channels over a long term in competition with cable. Two-way services may also be provided in this type system by using a reverse microwave path.

Diversity

Cable television means additional television fare for all media environments except for the lowest density population areas. For the most part, it will be much more of the same—movies, sports, network and syndicated program series, religious, cultural, children's, and public affairs programming. The principal advantage is in the much greater choice of these programs at any given time in the program schedule.

By far the greatest impact will be on the smaller communities. These communities have the least to begin with and, with rebuilding, will be eventually brought to near parity with all other cabled communities of greater size. In the largest cities, much of what cable offers is already available over the air, "free" or by subscription.

Because cable has more to offer in the limited television environ-ments, more people subscribe. In the town with fewer than three tele-vision stations available, cable subscription may be almost 100 percent of television households; in the metropolitan areas with five or more television stations, the subscription rate may be as low as 40 percent. Therefore, a multichannel cable system in the small-town, limited tele-vision environment brings proportionally more people more television channels than cable brings to the metropolitan community where a large percentage of the population may opt not to take advantage of the service because of its lesser increment in value. Of course, program producers and suppliers, as well as cable companies, are devoted to finding and supplying services to make the demand greater. In the time it takes to build cable in most of the larger cities, it can be assumed that penetration will be at a higher level, but never as high as in the television environ-ments that are severely limited without cable.

Localized Service

Cable television can provide community programming and message services by the cable company channels and public, education, and gov-ernment access channels. These services are very likely to be more or less present in all cabled media environments depending on local ordi-nances and franchise agreements and the level of community interest. The following may be the general case under particular environments, ignoring many atypical circumstances arising for the reasons just men-tioned.

Rural, small towns. Cable television systems are not likely to have the resources to produce much programming on their own nor will they have made extensive commitments in franchising agreements. Bulletin board type text messages can be expected to serve all institutions in the community. Sponsorship of these messages, with a crawl at the bottom or top of the message, and other text and crude graphic advertising and availabilities in satellite networks can be expected to give small local advertisers their first chance at television.

It is possible that some educational and governmental uses might be made of cable channels. Schools in small towns are likely to be housed in only one or two buildings, so the need for interconnection is not great. This would also be true of governmental units. There would be some value in television for continuing education, special education, and com-munity relations programs. The cost of equipment to produce such pro-gramming is low. Regional networks may develop so that program production is practical.

Medium towns. A full range of local service can be expected in the medium markets. Text messages or full-scale video productions in black and white or color may be made available in response to pressures from the city. The cable company and many of the community institutions will have the resources for production. Local advertisers may be able to take advantage of the low rates and greater opportunity to target messages to particular geographic areas or special interest groups.

Suburbs. The suburbs will probably experience service similar to small towns or medium sized towns depending on population, although there is some reason to believe that suburbs may be more likely to have utility for, and actually demand more, localized service than have small- to medium sized towns. The suburbs are generally more demanding of the franchisee than were the small and medium towns which franchised cable systems a decade or more ago with much less knowledge of the potentials. Furthermore, suburbs have a special problem receiving local information since most are swallowed up in large metro areas, where media, except for weekly newspapers, must serve millions of consumers. Therefore, local television news programs, alphanumeric text, and full audiovideo should have the greatest utility in the suburbs. And the middle- to upper-income residents of most suburbs are the greatest users of all types of media information.

Large cities. Large cities should have the institutional and human resources to develop all the types of localized services under discussion here. The community may be divided into districts (hubs) to provide a specialized service to neighborhood (and sometimes ethnic) groups. Interconnection of schools, medical and mental health clinics, police precincts, fire stations, courts and other government agencies, and private and public social services may serve many practical purposes.

Uses of broadband communication systems which supplant certain kinds of transportation needs and reduce the glut and cost of public and private transportation systems may have the most significance in the urban environments.

Small, local advertisers in large cities are the most disadvantaged by the lack of opportunity to use television efficiently. Cable may begin to serve these businesses.

Data Communication by Cable

Cable television could enter the data communication market in competition with common carriers in the major cities. A high-capacity alternative to telephone is needed for the local loop in satellite data communication networks. It is anticipated that this will be a $5 billion per year business. But the cable industry is reluctant to make the $200,000 to $500,000 capital investment per city.[88] Cable does not yet provide complete geographic coverage of the United States. Cable systems are not now as reliable as the telephone network. Modems for use on cable are only now becoming available, and they lag behind telephone modems in sophistication. Security is also a problem since the cable system is a broadband party line; anyone can intercept the transactions. Cable companies do not serve the right parts of town. The downtown areas, where most users of data communication are located, are often ignored by cable companies. Cable, for low speed data, may actually be more expensive than telephone networks. Cable's advantage is in the area of high speed data. Very few users of high speed data exist outside of major metropolitan areas where cable is not yet well established. The cable industry is now preoccupied with developing the entertainment and advertising aspects of the business and is hesitant to enter into direct competition with AT&T. While the cable industry is frying other fish, alternate technologies may arise to fill this need; the most probable is *cellular radio*. Cellular radio is a system of low power radio transmitters covering limited areas so that the same frequencies can be assigned over and over again to cells of a few miles in width. Cells with duplicate frequencies are separated by cells with a different frequency.

Despite the promise of cellular radio, it is believed by some that the demand for data communication channels will be sufficiently great to use *both* radio and cable technologies.[89] The cable industry will probably be brought into the market by the primary services, namely, companies organizing the networks and marketing the data communication service.

Cabletext

To all the media environments, videotext adds a new service. Although consumer demand in this format is unknown, the demand for certain of the reference-type information services is well established, for example, reference library information (atlases, encyclopedias), market reports, sports scores and statistics, weather, road conditions, traffic advisories, schedules, and calendars. Some of these services are currently available through other media; videotext is simply an alternative delivery system which may have economic advantages. In some of these cases, television text may be more current; for example, a continuously updated commodities market report may be superior to the newspaper report of yesterday's closing prices.

Some form of videotext could be available in almost all media environments. Teletext is available to any environment within reach of a television station, over the air or via cable. Videotext is available to environments with television and telephone. Cabletext, of course, is accessible only in the cable environments. Thinly populated areas would be excluded from cabletext service for the foreseeable future. For any of the videotext technologies, smaller communities may have less potential to generate the revenues necessary to justify the capital costs in providing *localized* information. Even these communities will be able to receive national services.

If one assumes that production and/or distribution costs in newspapers, television, and radio are major factors in the failure of urban media to cover the smaller units within the metro area (e.g., small suburbs, neighborhoods), then videotext may be a solution. Residents of these smaller neighborhoods could request a videotext budget of news for their neighborhood. While this news may not now be gathered, it might be feasible to do so when the low cost means of production and distribution are available. Some difficulty might be encountered in cultivating a demand for the service since residents of urban neighborhoods, for the most part, are not accustomed to such localized information. Furthermore, these people are likely to be of lower than average income. Few people in the United States are now accustomed to paying much money, out of pocket, for news. The concept would perhaps be hardest to sell to people of modest incomes.

Videotext could also serve persons in media environments whose principal source of local news is a weekly newspaper. The staffs of these newspapers could prepare reports, as they gather news, that could be processed and transmitted through a videotext system. In this case, the structure for news gathering is already in place. Videotext could substantially improve the timeliness of the news.

In videotext service, as with many other of the new communication services made possible by emerging electronic technologies, cable television environments are most advantaged. Cabletext has the largest capacity and the best response time. For these reasons, cabletext may have the broadest application and be most practical, although development of the technology and the markets may be slow.

SOCIAL IMPACT

Beyond the effects of new communication technologies on the numbers of communication channels and the amount of entertainment in the media environment lies the larger question of social impact. We have suggested at the outset that these technologies are not likely to be revolutionary in their influence on the human experience. None of the "revolutionary" communication advances since the Guttenberg press has had the predicted impact. But each technological change (high-speed presses, telegraph, telephone, color printing, radio, television, etc.) has made differences in the way in which people interact with one another and their world environment. It is important to contemplate the differences that may result from the newest wave of technology in the continuing effort to understand our milieu and in the need to manipulate the communication tools toward our deliberate purposes instead of ourselves being manipulated, unaware.

Impact on Children

Children are perhaps most vulnerable to communication impact, because they are relatively unformed, but also because they are more accepting of new technologies. We know a little about how children react to some of the new technologies. We can, however, make some educated speculation about other effects based on a knowledge of what new programs and services will be available.

The especially heavy television viewing of cable households may be a result of the slightly larger size of the cable household as suggested in Chapter 13. The fact that cable subscribers have to be especially interested in television and its content to begin with must also contribute. And we can expect that the new television menu available to the cable subscriber encourages even more viewing. Presumably the children are participating in this viewing.

Most people believe that parents have some responsibility to teach children how to use television to maximize its benefits and minimize presumed negative effects of particular programs or too much viewing. Some also believe that the schools have a responsibility here. Fully developed, multiple-channel, two-way cable greatly complicates the task. There is much more to select from and much more to avoid. Assigning priorities to the available material is made more difficult by the lack in most cable systems, of adequate program guides and descriptions. Where the cable operator, aided by program suppliers, does provide a full program guide, the programs are "promoted" rather than described. Perhaps various types of guides, developed independently of the industry, will supply an alternate, perhaps more critical perspective, helping children and adults to make more rational choices.

Psychiatrists and psychologists have long recommended family viewing of television as a means of helping children to adjust to the world presented by television. The presence of adults makes some of television less fearful. Dramatic license (whether in portraying violence or sex and racial and occupational stereotypes) may be discounted by parental comments. All the content can be explained and discussed. One can speculate what cable television will do to family viewing. On separate sets some of the children may be viewing Nickelodeon, and an older group of children may watch "The Shining" on a pay channel. Their mother may be viewing a women's channel or a talk show, while the father is engrossed in ESPN (with switchovers to Escapade), and the grandparents at still another set watching programs designed for that age group. This is of course, an extreme, but cable television *fragments* audiences, even within a household. It could have a negative effect on family communication patterns and parenting.

Children will be exposed to more sex on television. Where parental discipline is used to prevent viewing of these programs, it is likely to break down occasionally with even more excitement over the special permission or clandestine viewing. Broadcast television, lest its programming seems bland by comparison, is likely to be forced into further liberalities in programming despite the efforts of the moral majority.

Little is known about the effects of mediated sexual intimacy on children. Exposure to such content no doubt predates formal methods of teaching children about sex. But fragmentary information from peers has probably always done so anyway. There is no question that one of the uses of sexually explicit media and pornography is to stimulate sexual arousal. It should certainly have this effect on postpubescent teens.

On cable there is wider availability of programming attractive to children in all day parts. In the broadcast television world, the child must accommodate, most of the time, to programming aimed primarily at adults. With their greater buying power, the adults are more valuable to advertisers. Cable provides programs produced for children throughout day and adds greatly to the number of choices of off-network, syndicated programming carried by the broadcast stations available on cable. Among these programs are heavy child favorites (e.g., "Happy Days"). Movies are also appealing to children. Some of the pay channels run a number of G movies that are essentially child fare.

Commercial broadcast television was never able to offer much *age-specific* programming to children, that is, programs designed for the developmental level of a specific age group, for example, 4- and 5-year-old preschoolers. The commercial programming had to seek a broader group to assure commercially meaningful numbers in the audience—2 through 11 or even 2 through 17. Cable networks and local origination can be addressed to much more narrow audiences, making the programming more appropriate to those groups, be they preschoolers or adolescent rock music lovers.

Two-way participatory television could be very good for kids, making better use of their energy than passive television. Children may take special delight in manipulating images, as in TV games, in testing themselves in quiz programs, in voting along with others, or in ordering their own specialized information through a cabletext service. Instructional programs such as "Sesame Street" may be more engrossing in the two-way mode, and the learning enhanced through reinforcement. On the other hand, children could become more prone to interact with television than with peers or adults, delaying some kinds of social learning.

Traditionalists may view the personal computer, linked to reference resources through phone or cable lines, as a crutch for children which may prevent their familiarity with conventional library research methods. Children may be less motivated to learn traditional methods in the knowledge that many of the resources are available at the home keyboard and screen. Nevertheless, the child must learn both the traditional and new methods to take advantage of the breadth of research resources available.

Children seem to thrive on an identification with school and community. To the extent that cable television can provide news coverage of schools and neighborhoods within metropolitan areas, urban children should have the advantage of smaller town children where the media cover events, sports, and people from their own environment.

General Impact

The emergence of cable and its general acceptance may be quite disturbing to some people. We know that some older people are resistant to cable and sometimes excessively negative, suggesting suspiciousness, a vague fear of the new medium, and a clear unwillingness to make the change. They will be somewhat alienated from others in the society who have adopted the new technology.

Learning to use cable to the fullest advantage may be more difficult for adults than for children. Adults are less comfortable with electronic gadgetry than are children of the present generation. Adults are somewhat set in their habits, having practiced them longer. They may experience some "future shock" in adapting.

Most of the 30 year old social concerns about television are magnified by the prospect of *more* television via cable. Despite interactive television, most viewing will be passive. Viewers may give up even more of their leisure time to the enticements of popular culture. On the other hand, more channel space, the opportunity for the expression of intensity of demand through subscription fees or pay-per-view options, and the wider field for talent development may raise the general level of television and make a place for the highest levels of entertainment and information for those who demand it. At this level of quality, it may be argued that television can be as intellectually engaging as any of the arts and, therefore, *not passive*.

In the worst of the 1984 scenarios, the home with interactive broadband communication capability is self-contained. Its members need not leave the premises for most activities. Artists have drawn shocking pictures of the human being evolving from such an environment—enlarged head, popping eyes, tiny body. At the other extreme, one might take another view of this development as essentially liberating. The household may be freed from some of the demeaning commutes to a distant workplace, some routine shopping trips, and noisy classrooms. Working couples might be together for more time. Time saved may be devoted to other endeavors that would more satisfactorily replace all the lost values, mainly social contact, in a more satisfactory way.

The certainty of more available and explicit sex via television, in the privacy of homes, vastly expands the audience base for such material. While it is possible that this programming might relax attitudes toward human sexual desire and help to take away some of the embarrassment and hesitation that impedes real love, it is not in prospect with the present level of such programming that caters mainly to male appetites and seems to degrade the female sex role. However, it can be expected that both the quality and quantity of adult sexually oriented material will improve as the market develops.

Television may come to serve a broader purpose with its variety of formats. It is probable that video programming will be used as "background" as well as "foreground" in audience attentiveness. In this regard television may take over some of the function of radio. Television has been used, at times, as a background to other activities, with only casual attention paid. Certain programs—"Today," "Good Morning America," "Tonight"—are designed with an otherwise occupied audience in mind. Cable adds significantly to the kind of programming that might be on for long periods of time while engaging the attention only occasionally— CNN, the video music channels, weather, adult entertainment, public access programming, minor sports, gavel-to-gavel coverage of meetings, second and third viewings of movies, and religious networks may all be examples. This is perhaps a valuable function of television.

The new technologies, computer and cable, along with the larger channel capacity and capability for narrowcasting vastly expand the information available to the home. The home can have the capacity of a public library, and more. Information and news can be very local, giving even urban residents the neighborhood news on demand or on a regular schedule. This could bring local government, institutions, and people closer together. A better identification with the immediate community may enhance community pride and reduce alienation.

While new technologies can localize information more practically than can the old, they may also divert attention from the local news. We reported earlier the tendency of local audiences to be seduced from their local outlets by slicker, more dramatic news from larger metropolitan areas. Attendance to news material, electronic or print, may be a ritual act built on an habituated appetite for political intrigue, crime, scandal, and human interest features, all of which repeat endlessly in the news. Time and place may not be very important.[90] The best play on these interests may capture the audience. Local programming may have the least of the resources, in terms of the actual events and in gathering and producing the news, to attract these interests. If diversion from local news to a more exciting and fulfilling compendium of news from a wider area takes place, some of the potential for a more informed, less alienated local citizen is lost.

Information may be tailored better to individual interests. Through cabletext or videotext, a unique budget of information may be ordered by each household. This may greatly improve the efficiency of information seeking. At the same time it reduces the opportunity for random exposure to information, as we now have in broadcast and print news, that may broaden viewer interests. It can be hoped that individuals will plan exposure to general information as well as to highly specific news to meet specialized interests.

Whatever the case, new access to communication channels of much greater content diversity permits a much more individualized exposure. The media user is no longer *forced* into the entertainment and information formulas that have been shaped by mass tastes, limited channels, and the commercial system. The size of the "mass" audience may be greatly reduced; the concept of "mass" media may be less meaningful.

With the diverse media opportunities and the resultant highly individualized media exposure, we lose the common media experience that was once dictated by the system and may have had significant values related to community and national unity. Despite diversity, there will always be media events that will draw community and nation together for both serious purposes and the less serious entertainment. We will still have the opportunity to develop national symbols and a common ground for communication—through crisis news, blockbuster movies that both theater and home audiences view, and popular entertainers capable of finding a common denominator.

The advantages of the new communication technologies will not be shared equally across all members of the society. Almost all the new services bear a consumer cost, much beyond the cost of advertiser-supported broadcasting and print media. The full range of services—for example, the top tier of cable, cabletext, or videotext and interactive games, depending on usage—could cost $50 and more monthly per household. Low income persons will be excluded from the full benefit, thus widening the information gap between low income and high income people. At the lowest cost level of cable services (basic), much of the news and information services will be provided, principally advertiser supported. Basic may even be free, or almost free. It is in the higher levels of entertainment and in interactive information retrieval where the poor are most clearly disadvantaged. It is possible that some sort of "information subsidy" may be provided by government if the balance shifts too far in the direction of the higher income households.

The new costs of media and communication services will result in a major income redistribution for everyone. In just a few years, communication costs will rise from an inconsequential to a significant proportion of the household budget. Income will not rise at the same rate to accommodate this rapid cost increase, thereby creating a need to shift income from another budget area, a sacrifice of some magnitude.

In the optimistic view, the new communication technologies project a net social gain—in quality of entertainment, in the cultural level, in convenience, in conservation of resources, in education, in knowledge of public affairs, and in freedom of choice. There are, however, economic and perhaps social costs that must be monitored to maintain that gain.

NOTES

[1]Much of the material in this section was developed under Grant No. DAR 7910614 from the National Science Foundation. The beginning of the Media Environment section is reproduced, with some editing, from an article in the *National Forum* with permission from the publisher: see Thomas F. Baldwin, John D. Abel, and Ewart Skinner, "New Communication Technologies and Mass Media Environment: A Question of Access," *National Forum,* Summer 1980, pp. 28–30.

[2]Thomas F. Baldwin and John D. Abel, project leaders, "Mass Media Environment Study," All-University Research Initiation Grant, Michigan State University, Department of Telecommunication, East Lansing, 1978–1979.

[3]B. H. Bagdikian, "The Best News Money Can Buy," *Human Behavior,* October 1978, pp. 62-66; F. Gutierrez and C. C. Wilson, "The Demographic Dilemma," *Columbia Journalism Review,* Vol. 17, Jan–Feb, 1979, pp. 53–55.

[4]William A. Lucas and Karen B. Possner, "Television News and Local Awareness: A Retrospective Look," Rand R-1858-MF, Rand Corporation, Santa Monica, California, October 1978. See also Chapters 6 and 13.

[5]Most of the material on new communication technologies was written in collaboration with Richard Ducey. A good single introductory source of information on the new technologies is "New Technologies Affecting Radio & Television Broadcasting," National Association of Broadcasters, 1771 N Street, N.W., Washington, D.C. 20036, November 1981.

[6]International Telecommunications Union, *Final Protocol: Space Telecommunication* (197), 23 N.S.T. 1573–1574, July 17, 1971.

[7]"Broadband Communication in Rural Areas—National Cost Estimate and Case Studies," Denver Research Institute, Colorado, 1973.

[8]"Looking Skyward," *Broadcasting,* December 24, 1981, p. 42.

[9]David M. Rice, "Direct Broadcast Satellites: Legal and Policy Options," Communication Media Law Center of New York Law School, prepared for the FCC Network Inquiry Staff, Washington, D.C., 1979.

[10]"COMSAT's Satellite-to-Home Subscription TV Proposal," *System Operating Series,* National Cable Television Association, Washington, D.C., March 1980, p. 5.

[11]"To DBS or Not to DBS," *Broadcasting,* April 14, 1980, pp. 122–126.

[12]John P. Taylor, "Direct-to-Home Satellite Broadcasting," *Television/Radio Age,* (reprint of several articles), New York, New York, 1980.

[13]*Report and Order in Docket No. 16495,* 22 FCC 2d 86 (1970); *Second Report and Order in Docket No. 16495,* 35 FCC 2d 844, 847–50 (1972).

[14]Rice, "Direct Broadcast Satellites," p. 27.

[15]"COMSAT's Satellite-to-Home Subscription TV Proposal," p. 5.

[16]Rice, "Direct Broadcast Satellites," p. 25.

[17]Ibid., pp. 57–58.

[18]Roberto Grandi and Giuseppe Richeri, "Western Europe: The Development of DBS Systems," *Journal of Communication,* Spring 1980, p. 171.

[19]47 C.F.R. 73.641 (a) and (b).

[20]"FCC Repeals Curbs on Pay TV Stations," *New York Times,* June 18, 1982, p. 33.

[21]Kristin Booth Glen, *Report on Subscription Television,* prepared for the Network Inquiry of the Federal Communications Commission, Washington, D.C., October 1979, p. 1.

[22]"STV: Scratching Out Its Place in the New Video Universe," *Broadcasting,* April 7, 1980, p. 46.

[23]"FCC Letting STV Out of the Closet," *Broadcasting,* October 1, 1979, p. 23.

[24]Glen, *Report on Subscription Television,* p. 46.

[25]"STV Release," *Cablevision,* June 28, 1982, p. 18.

[26]44 F.R. 60069.

[27]"STV: Scratching Out Its Place in the New Video Universe," *Broadcasting,* April 7, 1980, p. 58.

[28]Ibid.

[29]Ibid., p. 46.

[30]Glen, *Report on Subscription Television,* pp. 34–35.

[31]Ibid., p. 47.

[32]Ibid., p. 8.

[33]"FCC Letting STV Out of the Closet," *Broadcasting,* October 1, 1979, pp. 23–24.

[34]The case regarding pay cable was *Home Box Office* v. *FCC,* 567 F. 2d 9 (D.C. Cir., 1977), cert. denied 434 U.S. 829 (1977).

[35]Glen, *Report on Subscription Television,* p. 5.

[36]Using the range of break-even figures reported in the discussion on the economic future of STV and assuming a 10 percent penetration of households.

[37]Kristin Booth Glen, *Report on Multipoint Distribution Service,* prepared for the Network Inquiry of the FCC, Washington, D.C., November 1979, p. 1.

[38]47 C.F.R. 21.901.

[39]Glen, *Report on Multipoint Distribution Service,* p. 71.

[40]47 C.F.R. 21.904.

[41]Glen, *Report on Multipoint Distribution Service,* p. 64.

[42]Ibid., p. 65.

[43]Ibid., p. 70.

[44]Ibid., p. 80.

[45]47 C.F.R. 21.903 (b)(4).

[46]47 U.S.C.A. 605.

[47]Glen, *Report on Multipoint Distribution Service,* p. 104.

[48]Sam S. Street, "MDS and CATV: Competition, Partnership or Coexistence?", *TVC* May 1, 1979, p. 60.

[49]Glen, *Report on Multipoint Distribution Service,* p. 105.

[50]47 C.F.R. 21.903 (b)(2).

[51]47 C.F.R. 21.900.

[52]Glen, *Report on Multipoint Distribution Service,* p. 9.

[53]"FCC Wants to Give MDS More Spectrum," *Broadcasting,* March 24, 1980, p. 69.

[54]Glen, *Report on Multipoint Distribution Service,* p. 64.

[55]Ibid., p. 59.

[56]Ibid., pp. 59, 73.

[57]47 C.F.R. 21.901(c).

[58]Glen, *Report on Multipoint Distribution Service,* pp. 81, 102.

[59]"Microband MDS System Set to Compete with Cable,"*Multichannel News,* May 10, 1982, p. 29.

[60]47 C.F.R. 74.701(a).

[61]"FCC's Grass Roots Ploy Sprouts Confusion Over TV's Future," *Cablevision,* April 20, 1981, p. 65.

[62]"The Low-Power Television Guidebook," Corporation for Public Broadcasting, Washington, D.C., 1980.

[63]"Comments of the Association of Maximum Service Telecasters" in FCC Docket No. 78-253, January 10, 1979.

[64]"Low-Power Television Guidebook," Corporation for Public Broadcasting.

[65]"LPTV: Special Report," *Broadcasting,* February 23, 1981, p. 43.

[66]Sheila Mahony, Nick Demartino, and Robert Stengel, "The Home Video Market," in *Keeping Pace with the New Television: Public Television and Changing Technology* (New York: The Carnegie Corporation of New York, VNY Books International, 1980). This section was written with Janet Bridges.

[67]"Videocassettes and Videodiscs—Companions or Competitors?" *Videoplay,* June 1980, pp. 51–53; Mahony et al., p. 153.

[68]Donald E. Agostino, Rolland C. Johnson, and Herbert A. Terry, *Home Video: A Report on the Status, Projected Development and Consumer Use of Videocassette Recorders and Videodisc Players in the United States,* report prepared for the Federal Communication Commission Network Inquiry Special Staff, *Preliminary Report on Prospects for Additional Networks,* Washington, D.C., February 1980, pp. 13–17.

[69]Videocassettes and Videodiscs," p. 52, Agostino et al., *Home Video,* pp. 34–35; Glen Spain, "The Social Implications of Videocassette Technology," *Journal of Community Communications,* February 1980, p. 15; Dwight M. Cosner, "Coping with the Complexity of New Video Technologies: A Pilot Study of U.S. Videocassette Recorder Usage," *The Nielsen Newscast,* no. 1, 1980, p. 2.

[70]"Videoplaytest: 'The Editor,' " *Videoplay,* June 1980, pp. 60–61.

[71]Ibid., p. 31.

[72]Mahony et al., *Keeping Pace with the New Television,* p. 162; Agostino et al., *Home Video,* p. 24.

[73]Mahony et al., *Keeping Pace with the New Television,* pp. 160, 169.

[74]Agostino et al., *Home Video,* pp. 35–57.

[75]Universal City Studios, Inc. *v.* Sony Corp. of America, U.S. Court of Appeals, 9th Circuit, decided October 19, 1981, Nos. 79-3683, 79-3735, 79-3762, Vol. 50 Radio Regulations 2nd, p. 543.

[76]Agostino et al., *Home Video,* p. 6.

[77]Ibid., pp. 7–17.

[78]Ibid., pp. 18–19.

[79]Ibid., pp. 19–25.

[80]Ibid., p. 17.

[81]Ibid., pp. 50–51.

[82]Mahony et al., *Keeping Pace with the New Television,* pp. 167, 170–171.

[83]Cosner, "Coping with the Complexity of New Video Technologies," pp. 2–3.

[84]Agostino et al., *Home Video,* pp. 50–51, 62–63.

[85]Wayne Green, "Now You'll Really Be Able to Use a Home Computer," *Popular Mechanics,* November 1978, p. 107.

[86]Craig J. Calhoun, "The Microcomputer Revolution? Technical Possibilities and Social Choices," *Sociological Methods and Research,* May 1981, p. 415.

[87]Format categories listed in *Broadcasting Yearbook 1981,* Broadcasting Publications, Inc., Washington, D.C., pp. D-75 through D-95.

[88]Frank Drendel and Gary Wienberg, "New Entrants in Distribution and Information Systems: What Role for Cable?" NCTA Convention, Los Angeles, May 31, 1981.

[89]Ibid.

[90]This concept, called the "ludenic theory of newsreading," is developed in William Stephenson, *The Play Theory of Mass Communication* (Chicago: University of Chicago Press, 1967), pp. 147–159.

PART VI

APPENDICES

Appendix A

Sample
Local Origination Equipment
Franchise Proposal
Tucson, Arizona
Cox Cable

FORM K

Cox believes that this easily accessible communications center where citizens will meet to take free basic and advanced cable workshops, exchange ideas, use equipment, and access instant replay programming service means active participation in community programming.

Studio and Master Control

Quantity	Description
1	821 ISI Master Control Switcher
1	ISI Master Sync Distribution System
1	15 × 12 3M Routing Switcher
1	2525 Microtime Frame Synchronizer
2	2020 Microtime Time Base Correctors
1	HR-200 Hitachi 1″ Recorder/Editor with Slow Motion, TBC, and Console with Monitoring
1	HR-200 Hitachi 1″ Recorder/Editor with Console and Monitoring
1	EA-3X Cezar Editing Controller
6	VO-2860A Sony Recorder/Editors
3	RM-440 Sony Automatic Editing Controllers
1	Film Island with Ikegami ITC-230 Camera, 16mm Film Chain Projector, and 35mm Slide Projector
1	X-10 Teac ¼″ Reel-to-Reel Professional Recorder
1	Thomson-CSF Videfont 4, Two-Channel Character Generator
4	RTS Master 8-Channel Intercomm Stations; Includes 860 System Interconnect 3 TWI 224 to 2 to 4 Wire Interconnect 2 PS-50RM Power Supply 5 SPK-501 Rack Mount User Stations
9	S-4105-XD Single Muff Headsets
9	7-1435-XE Dual Split Headsets
1	PVM-5300 Sony Triple 5″ Trinitron Color Monitors
3	VM-12PRO Videotek 12″ Trinitron Monitor
5	PVM-8022MB Sony Dual 8″ Trinitron Color Rack Mount Monitors
1	Master Control Audio Monitoring System
3	528 Tektronix Waveform Monitors
3	1420 Tektronix Vectorscopes
3	VM-8PRD Videotek Dual 8″ Trinitron Color Monitors
3	WV-5203 Panasonic Triple 5″ Monochrome Monitors
3	VS-6A Dynair 6 Position Passive Routing Switchers
3	14M939R Setchell Carlson 14″ High Resolution (800 and Lines)
3	Studio 12 Videotek 12″ Trinitron Professional Monitors

Studio and Master Control (Continued)

Quantity	Description
9	FP-60 Hitachi Professional Studio Cameras with Fujinon 10:1 Zoom Lens and Soft Cables
9	FB-60 Hitachi Camera Control Units
9	P4 ITE Pedestals with H6 Hydro Heads
3	902 ISI Special Effects Switchers with Encoded Chroma Keyer and Downstream Key Edger
15	ECM-50 Sony Lavalier Microphones
6	Electrovoice Shotgun Microphones
3	SR-101 Shure Audio Boards
9	WV5203 Panasonic Triple 5″ Monochrome Monitors
6	PRO-12 Videotek 12″ Trinitron Color Monitors
1	Two-Camera Teleprompter System
3	Strand Century Studio Lighting Systems
1	Package Console and Wiring to Provide a Complete Working System-Installation Included

Total Cost $ 898,850

Instant Replay

Quantity	Description
1	HP 250
1	1 Metro-Data 180 Character Generator

Total Cost $ 50,000*

*All modulators, other character generators, and control devices are budgeted in MTC (master tape control) and hub equipment costs.

Master Tape Control

Quantity	Description
30	JVC-CP5500 ¾″ Direct Drive Players
1	ISI-30-50 AFV Routine Switcher with Intelligent Control for Computer Control
50	Black and White Panasonic WV-5203 Monochrome Monitors
10	Sony RM-820-T Color Monitors
1	Custom Audio Control Center with 50-Channel Capacity
1	Package Necessary Interior and Hardware to Facilitate Installations

Total Cost $ 255,200

Six Editing Rooms

Quantity	Description
1	½ BR-6400UJVC Edit/Recorder
1	½ BP-5300UJVC Edit/Recorder
1	Control Unit
1	RM-88 Control Unit
2	CR 8200 ¾" Edit Recorders
4	TM-41 AU Monitors with Audio, Miscellaneous Speakers, Connection Cables, etc.

Total Cost $ 108,000

Bilingual Dubbing and Titling Studio

Quantity	Description
1	Sony 2011 Player
2	12" Sony Monitors
1	Audio Console
1	¾" Tape Machine
2	Shure Microphones

Total Cost $ 6,000

Tucson Telecommunications Center Community Programming Van

Quantity	Description
3	KY2000 P.S. JVC Portable Color Camera and Extra
1	1 CR-4400 U JVC Portable ¾" Recorder with AC
3	H-9 ITE Fluid Heads
3	T-6 ITE Elevation Tripods
3	D-6 ITE Dollies
3	RH ITE Right-Hand Handles for H-9 Head
3	VF-2500 JVC 5" Viewfinders
3	RS-2000 JVC Studio Control Units
6	VC-5550 U JVC 65' Camera Cables
3	HZ C 30 U JVC Rear Lens Controls
	Monitor and terminal equipment includes
1	D3106 3M Character Generator with Audio Interface
1	902 ISI 10 Input Production Switcher
1	660-4 ISI 4 Input Chroma Keyer
1	558 ISI Sync Generator
4	521 ISI Pulse Delay Distribution Amplifiers
1	519 ISI Pulse Distribution Amplifier
2	513-6 ISI Video Distribution Amplifiers

Quantity	Description
2	525 ISI Sub-Carrier Distribution Amplifiers
2	501 ISI Rack Frames
2	505 ISI Power Supply
2	VM-12 PRO Videotek 12″ Trinitron Rack Mount Professional Color Monitor
1	PVM-410 Sony Quad. 4″ Monochrone Monitors
1	ISM 5 Videotek Waveform Monitor
1	1420 Tektronix Vectorscope
1	RF Videotek Rack Frame
1	982 ISI 10X1 AFV Switcher
1	M-B Cezur Matchbox for Rapid Camera Matching
	Audio and distribution equipment includes
1	GR-101 Shure Professional Audio Control Console
4	ECM 50 PS Sony's Professional Omni-Directional
3	SM-50 Shure Hand-Held Microphones
1	316 Shintron Audio Distribution Amplifier 1 Output 6 Output
1	982 ISI Routing Switcher
2	MS-105 McMartin Monitor Amplifiers
1	F-87 Fraizer Monitor Speaker
1	PLS-1 Video Aids Power Supply/Intercom Amp
3	PL-1 Individual Stations
3	TEA-52 Single Muff Headsets
	Videotape equipment includes
2	VO2860A Sony Videocassettes Rec/Play/Edit
1	RM-430 Sony Edit Controller
1	CVS-520 Time Base Corrector with 16-Line Window
	Lighting equipment includes
2	TL-92 Lowell Light Kits
1	5KW ONAN Generator (Installed)
	Modification and turnkey installation includes
1	Carpet installation, windows with curtains, door installation, step installation, one 13,000-BTU roof air conditioner, split electric service for equipment and air. All equipment racks and equipment wiring, roof rack and ladder, ¼″ aluminum diamond plate, all power distribution, all video interfacing, cabling of all interface panels, slant mount for video switcher, and audio console. All miscellaneous cables, connectors, and hardware.

Total cost $ 149,500

FM Stereo Studio

Quantity	Description
1	Stereo FM Cablecasting Studio
1	AC-8D-5B-8 Channel Dual Stereo Console
2	280B-24 Reel-to-Reel Stereo Quarter Track Recorder/Reproducers
4	CT 3547B Carts NAB Type A and B Recorder, Reproducer Stereo
4	E.S.F. Electronic
4	DMT-13 Digital Message Timers
4	Mx-1 Monomax Dual Matrix-Dematrix
1	800A Orban/Optiomod-FM-Audio Processor
1	OPT-13 Dolby Port Installed
2	1650 16″ Turntables
2	S-260 Tone Arms
2	Alpha II Pre Amps
2	F-3EE Cartridges
6	RE 20 Microphones
6	Goosenecks
1	On-Air Right
2	Double Pedestals
1	Center Audio Table
1	Double Rack

Total Cost $ 42,317

Portable Downlink

Quantity	Description
1	Microdyne 3.6-meter antenna with noise temp of 29° K and dual polarized prime focus feed system. Also includes Mount and Trailer LNA 100° K DC Power Supply RX Agile with Built-In Modulator

Total cost $ 11,350

Total Cost for Tucson Telecommunications Center Equipment

Studio and master control	$ 898,850
Instant replay	50,000
Billingual dubbing and titling studio	6,000
Master tape control	255,200
FM studio	42,317
Six editing stations	108,000

Total Cost for Tucson Telecommunications Center Equipment (Continued)

Community programming van	149,500
Portable downlink	11,350
Total	$1,521,217
Sales tax	60,848
Grand total	$1,582,065

a. Will this equipment also be available for access use:

(X) Yes   ( ) No

Appendix B

Sample
Public Access Channel Rules

UNITED CABLE TELEVISION OF MID-MICHIGAN
PUBLIC ACCESS CHANNEL RULES,
EAST LANSING

I. PREAMBLE

1.1 The purpose of these public access rules is to clearly define the rights and responsibilities of the United Cable Company and the applicant in the use of public access facilities provided by United Cable. The primary purpose of these facilities is to encourage East Lansing residents to take the opportunity provided by public access in the production of localized television programming.

II. APPLICATIONS

2.1 A user will be defined as any East Lansing resident applying for use of the public access production facilities.

2.2 Any individual or group may use the access channel according to these rules. Access to this channel will be first-come, first-served and nondiscriminatory.

2.3 If the applicant is under 18 years of age, he or she must have an adult co-sign the application form and agreement. The co-signer is then responsible, along with the applicant, for any financial responsibility connected with the use of the company's facilities other than normal wear and tear.

2.4 Any user charged with one period of studio use during one week shall not be prevented from assisting in other studio productions during the same week.

III. USER RESPONSIBILITY

3.1 The applicant assumes full responsibility for use of United Cable production facilities, other than normal wear and tear.

3.2 Under the terms of the Public Access Channels Usage Agreement, the public access producer assumes all liability for program content and agrees to indemnify United Cable and the City of East Lansing and its representatives for all liability or other injury due to program content.

3.3 Persons utilizing the Public Access production facilities will, at all times, be under the supervision and authority of United Cable Public Access Coordinators. All handling of the facilities or granting of authority to do so will be done by the Public Access Coordinator in charge at the time of the production. Users of the channel may not present any material designed to promote the sale of commercial products or services. This includes any advertising by, or on the behalf of, candidates for public office.

3.4 The applicant must be sure that, if the use of music and non-music copyrighted material is involved, the appropriate copyright clearances have been obtained. Before presenting a program, s/he must have signed the Public Access Channels Usage Agreement (Appendix A).

3.5 Regarding the use of studio facilities the following stipulations will be observed:

   a. Users are requested to arrive at least 15 minutes before their scheduled times of appearance.
   b. Users and other participants are asked to keep the control room clear of non-essential personnel during the production.
   c. Technical help and users shall not smoke, snack, or bring drinks into the control room.
   d. Users and other participants may not interfere with the production and/or studio usage time of another user.

3.6 United Cable reserves the right to temporarily refuse the use of the Access Channel and facilities to any person under the influence of alcohol, drugs or otherwise not under full control of his/her senses.

3.7 Any individual/program is responsible for canceling reserved studio/porta-pak time if that time will not be used. All public access users are also expected to be prompt for their reserved activities; a grace period of 15 minutes from the scheduled time will be allowed after which the studio/porta-pak time will be given to other users. Any individual/program that does not cancel scheduled time will be kept record of; after three such violations the program/individual will be put on a 60-day probation during which if another violation occurs a 30-day suspension from public access will be authorized.

3.8 Removal of United Cable videotapes off the premises is strictly prohibited (except with use of porta-paks in the field). If absolutely necessary to sign them out full cost of tape is required as a deposit.

IV. UNITED CABLE COMPANY RESPONSIBILITY

4.1 Basically, there are two ways to provide programming in order to utilize public access time. A program may be produced by using United Cable's portable facilities or studios or a prerecorded tape (or film) may be supplied to United Cable. In either case, the tape (or film) is then scheduled for showing on the designated public access channel as outlined in the "Public Access Schedule Procedure."

4.2 United Cable will provide a qualified person to offer technical and programming assistance to channel users in order to assure optimum technical quality.

4.3 Applications to use the public access channel for the showing of a prerecorded program is outlined in the section designated "Public Access Schedule Procedure." The company will not edit, or alter in any way, the content of public access material without permission of the user. The necessity of duplication or any other type of alteration will be discussed with the public access coordinator when application is made.

4.4 United Cable will keep for public inspection all applications for use of the public access channel and a complete record of the names and addresses of all persons or groups who request access time. The company will retain all records for a period of two years.

V. FACILITIES MADE AVAILABLE BY UNITED CABLE

5.1 All facilities will be offered on a first-come, first-served basis. Public access facilities are to be used only in the production of public access programming.

5.2 For remote productions, "Porta-Pak" type equipment and the necessary supplemental production gear will be supplied free of charge to any applicant qualifying under the terms of these public access rules on 24 hours' notice for a period not to exceed 24 hours. Facilities will also be made available for electronic editing of the taped footage produced with the Porta-Pak.

5.3 In cases where studio production facilities are required, application should be made at least one week in advance, for the convenience of the user. This time limitation may be excepted in cases of public interest.

5.4 United Cable's public access production studio may be reserved one week in advance, by applicants for one continuous 90-minute period of time on any given workday free of charge.

5.5 Each finished program produced/recorded using the public access facilities will be allowed one free dubbing (copying) per episode; afterward a charge of $10 per hour (one-hour minimum required) will be levied. The dubbing of an episode must be approved by the program producer and time scheduled through a public access coordinator.

VI. PUBLIC ACCESS SCHEDULE PROCEDURE

6.1 First, all users must sign the Public Access Channel Use Agreement, included as Appendix A of these rules. Producers of live public access programs must complete the Public Access Channel Use Agreement prior to commencement of cablecasting.

6.2 Access programming will normally be videotaped; except in order to achieve the timeliness of a program, United Cable may permit live presentations.

6.3 There are no theoretical limitations imposed on the running time of any Public Access program. There are, however, several practical and logistical factors which may dictate the limitations on program length. These limitations may include:

a. Public Access production facility availability
b. Channel time availability

6.4 United Cable will deviate from the established telecast schedule only upon its approval of written request, by a group or individual affected by the deviation. It is not the intent of the Company to herein inhibit or restrict the use of the Access Channel, but to insure in as fair a manner as possible, that all persons and groups wishing to use the Public Access facilities have an equal and fair opportunity to take advantage of communication potentials in Public Access. The utilization in a monopolistic manner by one or a few select groups or individuals is not deemed to be in the public interest. Channel use limitations will be applied only in cases where the public interest is not being maintained.

6.5 United Cable assumes responsibility for rescheduling programming which is delayed or interrupted for a duration of 10% of its total time, if such delays or interruptions are beyond control of the user.

VII. REGULATION OF OPERATION

7.1 United Cable reserves the right to waive any self-imposed regulation when such waiver is judged by the Company to be in the public interest.

7.2 Any violation of these rules may, at the Company's discretion, cause United Cable to withhold the use of its facilities from the violator.

7.3 All applicants for use of United Cable facilities should be aware that they may be held accountable for their actions by the same laws that govern any public activity.

7.4 Any violation of an access volunteer's right to use the facilities in accordance with these Public Access Rules will be reported to the East Lansing Cable Communications Commission for appropriate action.

VIII. MISCELLANEOUS

8.1 As experience shows a need, these rules shall be subject to periodic revision, upon approval of United Cable and the East Lansing Cable Communications Commission.

8.2 The company will have available information regarding services offered to public access users by the East Lansing Cable Communications Commission. This information will be prepared and supplied by the commission.

PUBLIC ACCESS CHANNEL
USE AGREEMENT

NAME: _____PHONE: _____

ADDRESS: _____

_____

PROGRAM TITLE: _____LENGTH: _____

CONTENT: _____

_____

REQUESTED DATE OF PLAYBACK:

DATE: _____TIME: _____DATE: _____TIME: _____

MAY WE SCHEDULE YOUR PROGRAM AT ADDITIONAL TIMES?

YES_____ NO_____

FORMAT

TAPE: ½"_____¾"_____Cassette_____BETAMAX_____

LIVE STUDIO_____OTHER_____

"Applicant" herewith applies to United Cable Company for use of the designated public access channel on the following terms and conditions:

1. No charge shall be made for the use of United Cable's public access channel.
2. Applicant will not cablecast a lottery or any advertisement of or information concerning a lottery.
3. Applicant agrees to make all appropriate arrangements with, and to obtain all clearances from, broadcast stations, networks, or sponsors, without limitation from the foregoing, any and all other persons (natural and otherwise) as may be necessary to transmit its program material over the company's cable television system.
4. In recognition of the fact that the company has no control over the content of the applicant's public access cablecast, applicant agrees to indemnify and hold the company harmless from any and all liability or other injury (including reasonable costs of the defending claims or litigations) arising from or in connection with claims for failure to comply with any applicable laws, rules, regulations, or other requirements of local, state, or federal authorities; for claims of libel, slander, invasion of privacy, or infringement of common law or statutory copyright; for unauthorized use of trademark, trade name, or service mark; for breach of contractual or other obligations owing to third parties by company; and for any other injury or damage in law or equity which claims result from the applicant's use of the United Cable designated public access channel.

5. Applicant recognizes that the Federal Communications Commission requires the company to maintain available for public inspection a record of all persons applying for use of designated public access channel and agrees that this application may be used for such record.
6. Applicant states that he or she has read the company's "Public Access Rules" governing use of cable public access channel and agrees to abide by the terms and conditions contained therein.

_____

Signature

_____

UNITED CABLE REPRESENTATIVE

_____

Date

Appendix C

FCC Community Channel Rules

76.205 ORIGINATION CABLECASTS BY CANDIDATES FOR PUBLIC OFFICE

(a) General requirements. If a cable television system operator shall permit any legally qualified candidate for public office to use the system's origination channel(s) and facilities therefore, the system operator shall afford equal opportunities to all other such candidates for that office: *provided, however,* that such cable television system operator shall have no power of censorship over the material cablecast by any such candidate, *and provided, further,* that an appearance by a legally qualified candidate on any

(1) bona fide newscast,
(2) bona fide interview,
(3) bona fide news documentary (if the appearance of the candidate is incidental to the presentation of the subject or subjects covered by the news documentary), or
(4) on-the-spot coverage of bona fide news events (including but not limited to political conventions and activities incidental thereto) shall not be deemed to be use of the facilities of the system within the meaning of this paragraph.

NOTE—The Fairness Doctrine is applicable to these exempt categories. See §76.209.

(b) Rates and practices. (1) The rates, if any, charged all such candidates for the same office shall be uniform, shall not be rebated by any means direct or indirect, and shall not exceed the charges made for comparable origination use of such facilities for other purposes.

(2) In making facilities available to candidates for public office, no cable television system operator shall make any discrimination between candidates in charges, practices, regulations, facilities, or services for or in connection with the service rendered or make or give any preference to any candidate for public office or subject any such candidate to any prejudice or disadvantage; nor shall any cable television system operator make any contract or other agreement which shall have the effect of permitting any legally qualified candidate for any public office to cablecast to the exclusion of other legally qualified candidates for the same public office.

(c) Records, inspections. Every cable television system operator shall keep and permit public inspection of a complete record of all requests, for origination cablecasting time made by or on behalf of candidates for public office, together with an appropriate notation showing the disposition made by the operator of such requests, the charges made, if any, and the length and time of cablecast, if the request is granted. Such records shall be retained for a period of two years.

(d) Time of request. A request for equal opportunities for use of the origination channel(s) must be submitted to the cable television system operator within one (1) week of the day on which the first prior use, giving rise to the right of equal opportunities, occurred, provided, however, that, where a person was not a candidate at the time of such first prior use, he shall submit his request within one (1) week of the first subsequent use after he has become a legally qualified candidate for the office in question.

(e) Burden of proof. A candidate requesting such equal opportunities of the cable television system operator, or complaining of noncompliance to the commission, shall have the burden of proving that he and his opponent are legally qualified candidates for the same public office.

76.209 FAIRNESS DOCTRINE: PERSONAL ATTACKS; POLITICAL EDITORIALS

(a) A cable television system operator engaging in origination cablecasting shall afford reasonable opportunity for the discussion of conflicting views on issues of public importance.

NOTE—See public notice, *Applicability of the Fairness Doctrine in the Handling of Controversial Issues of Public Importance,* 29 FR 10415.

(b) When, during such origination cablecasting, an attack is made upon the honesty, character, integrity, or like personal qualities of an identified person or group, the cable television system operator shall, within a reasonable time and in no event later than one (1) week after the attack, transmit to the person or group attacked (1) notification of the date, time, and identification of the cablecast; (2) a script or tape (or an accurate summary if a script or tape is not available) of the attack; and (3) an offer of a reasonable opportunity to respond over the system's facilities.

(c) The provisions of paragraph (b) of this section shall not be applicable (1) to attacks on foreign groups or foreign public figures; (2) to personal attacks which are made by legally qualified candidates, their authorized spokesmen, or those associated with them in the campaign, on other such candidates, their authorized spokesmen, or persons associated with the candidates in the campaign; and (3) to bona fide newscasts, bona fide news interviews, and on-the-spot coverage of a bona fide news event (including commentary or analysis contained in the foregoing programs, but the provisions of paragraph (b) of this section shall be applicable to editorials of the cable television system operator).

(d) Where a cable television system operator, in an editorial, (1) endorses or (2) opposes a legally qualified candidate or candidates, the system operator shall, within 24 hours of the editorial, transmit to respectively (i) the other qualified candidate or candidates for the same office, or (ii) the candidate opposed in the editorial, (1) notification of the date, time, and channel of the editorial; (2) a script or tape of the editorial; and (3) an offer of a reasonable opportunity for a candidate or spokesman of the candidate to respond over the system's facilities, *provided, however,* that where such editorials are cablecast within 72 hours prior to the day of the election, the system operator shall comply with the provisions of this paragraph sufficiently far in advance of the broadcast to enable the candidate or candidates to have a reasonable opportunity to prepare a response and to present it in a timely fashion.

76.213 LOTTERIES

(a) No cable television system operator, except as in paragraph (c), when engaged in origination cablecasting shall transmit or permit to be transmitted on the origination cablecasting channel or channels any advertisement of or information concerning any lottery, gift enterprise, or similar scheme, offering prizes dependent in whole or in part upon lot or chance, or any list of the prizes drawn or awarded by means of any such lottery, gift enterprise, or scheme, whether said list contains any part or all of such prizes.

(b) The determination whether a particular program comes within the provisions of paragraph (a) of this section depends on the facts of each case. However, the commission will in any event consider that a program comes within the provisions of paragraph (a) of this section if in connection with such program a prize consisting of money or thing of value is awarded to any person whose selection is dependent in whole or in part upon lot or chance, if as a condition of winning or competing for such prize, such winner or winners are required to furnish any money or thing of value or are required to have in their possession any product sold, manufactured, furnished, or distributed by a sponsor of a program cablecast on the system in question.

(c) The provisions of paragraphs (a) and (b) of this section shall not apply to advertisements or lists of prizes or information concerning a lottery conducted by a state acting under the authority of state law when such information is transmitted (1) by a cable system located in that state, (2) by a cable system located in an adjacent state which also conducts such a lottery, or (3) by a cable system located in another state which is integrated with a cable system described in (1) or (2) herein, if termination of the receipt of such transmission by the cable system in such other state would be technically infeasible.

(d) For the purposes of paragraph (c) "lottery" means the pooling of proceeds derived from the sale of tickets or chances and allotting those proceeds or parts thereof by chance to one or more chance takers or ticket purchasers. It does not include the placing or accepting of bets or wagers on sporting events or contests.

76.215 OBSCENITY

No cable television system operator when engaged in origination cablecasting shall transmit or permit to be transmitted on the origination cablecasting channel or channels material that is obscene or indecent.

76.221 SPONSORSHIP IDENTIFICATION, LIST RETENTION, RELATED REQUIREMENTS

(a) When a cable television system operator engaged in origination cablecasting presents any matter for which money, service, or other valuable consideration is either directly or indirectly paid or promised to, or charged or accepted by such operator, the operator, at the time of the cablecast, shall announce (1) that such matter is sponsored, paid for, or furnished, either in whole or in part, and (2) by whom or on whose behalf such consideration was supplied, provided, however, that "service or other valuable consideration" shall not include any service or property furnished either without or at a nominal charge for use on, or in connection with, a cablecast unless it is so furnished in consideration for an identification of any person, product, service, trademark, or brand name beyond an identification reasonably related to the use of such service or property on the cablecast.

For the purposes of this section, the term "sponsored" shall be deemed to have the same meaning as "paid for."

(b) Each cable television operator engaged in origination cablecasting shall exercise reasonable diligence to obtain from employees, and from other persons with whom the system operator deals directly in connection with any matter for cablecasting, information to enable such system operator to make the announcement required by this section.

(c) In the case of any political origination cablecast matter or any origination cablecast matter involving the discussion of public controversial issues for which any film, record, transcription, talent, script, or other material or service of any kind is furnished, either directly or indirectly, to a cable television system operator as an inducement for cablecasting such matter, an announcement shall be made both at the beginning and conclusion of such cablecast on which such material or service is used that such film, record, transcription, talent script, or other material or service has been furnished to such operator in connection with the transmission of such cablecast matter, provided, however, that in the case of any cablecast of 5 minutes' duration or less, only one such announcement need be made either at the beginning or conclusion of the cablecast.

(d) The announcement required by this section shall, in addition to stating the fact that the origination cablecasting matter was sponsored, paid for or furnished, fully and fairly disclose the true identity of the person or persons or corporation, committee, association or other unincorporated group, or other entity by whom or on whose behalf such payment is made or promised, or from whom or on whose behalf such services or other valuable consideration is received, or by whom the material or services referred to in paragraph (c) of this section are furnished. Where an agent or other person or entity contracts or otherwise makes arrangements with a cable television system operator on behalf of another, and such fact is known or by the exercise of reasonable diligence, as specified in paragraph (b) of this section, could be known to the system operator, the announcement shall disclose the identity of the person or persons or entity on whose behalf such agent is acting instead of the name of such agent. Where the origination cablecasting material is political matter or matter involving the discussion of a controversial issue of public importance and a corporation, committee, association or other unincorporated group, or other entity is paying for or furnishing the matter, the system operator shall, in addition to making the announcement required by this section, require that a list of the chief executive officers or members of the executive committee or of the board of directors of the corporation, committee, association or other unincorporated group, or other entity shall be made available for public inspection at the local office of the system. Such lists shall be kept and made available for a period of two years.

(e) In the case of origination cablecast matter advertising commercial products or services, an announcement stating the sponsor's corporate or trade name, or the name of the sponsor's product, when it is clear that the mention of the name of the product constitutes a sponsorship identification, shall be deemed sufficient for the purposes of this section and only one such announcement need be made at any time during the course of the cablecast.

(f) The announcement otherwise required by this section is waived with respect to the origination cablecast of "want ad" or classified advertisements sponsored by an individual. The waiver granted in this paragraph shall not extend to a classified advertisement or want ad sponsorship by any form of business enterprise, corporate or otherwise. Whenever sponsorship announcements are omitted pursuant to this paragraph, the cable television system operator shall observe the following conditions: (1) Maintain a list showing the name, address, and (where available) the telephone number of each advertiser (2) Make this list available to members of the public who have a legitimate interest in obtaining the information contained in the list.

(g) The announcements required by this section are waived with respect to feature motion picture film produced initially and primarily for theatre exhibition.

NOTE—The waiver heretofore granted by the commission in its Report and Order, adopted November 16, 1960 (FCC 60-1369, 40 FCC 95), continues to apply to programs filmed or recorded on or before June 20, 1963, when §73.654(e), the predecessor television rule, went into effect.

(h) Commission interpretations in connection with the provisions of the sponsorship identification rules for the broadcasting services are contained in the commission's Public Notice, entitled "Applicability of Sponsorship Identification Rules," dated May 6, 1963 (40 FCC 141), as modified by Public Notice, dated April 21, 1975 (FCC 75-418). Further interpretations are printed in full in various volumes of the Federal Communications Commission reports. The interpretations made for the broadcasting services are equally applicable to origination cablecasting.

Appendix D

Procedure for Assessment of Communication Needs

ASSESSMENT OF COMMUNICATION NEEDS:
MEETING WITH INFORMED CITIZENS

To determine communication needs initially, the advisory body may convene a meeting of representatives of various interests in the community to discuss local needs. One or two meetings with a variety of persons should provide an inventory of communication needs and also serve a community education function.

STEP 1. SELECTION OF PARTICIPANTS

Potential participants should be discussed and selected at an advisory body meeting. Agreement to participate should be secured from at least one community leader or informed citizen in all areas of interest in the community. As a checklist of such areas, the following categories might be helpful:

Economic (e.g., business, labor, agriculture)
Social services
Government
Education
Religion
Recreation
Health
Human relations (e.g., minority-majority relations)

The checklist will have to be adapted to the particular community and the range of interests in that community. Backup persons should be identified in case the originally selected persons are not available.

STEP 2. INVITATION OF PARTICIPANTS

The participants selected should be invited by phone, letter, or personal visit, at which time they should be informed of the responsibility of the advisory body to assess communication needs. They should be assured that they are not expected to be communication experts—that the greatest interest is in their knowledge of the needs and problems of the community and the various communication and public information techniques presently being used.

The invited participants should be made to feel that their participation is important and the results of the inquiry will be reflected in the cable franchise agreement.

STEP 3. MEETING

To be most productive, the meeting should be structured somewhat so that the participants know the interests of the advisory body and to ensure that all the potential uses of cable communication are covered.

Introduction

Begin by reminding people of the information supplied in the invitation to participate: (1) the advisory body responsibility to assess communication needs, (2) the importance to potential applicants of knowing the special communication needs of a community, and (3) the importance to the city government of knowing communication needs prior to evaluating franchise applications.

Background on Cable Communication

Many of the participants will need to know more about cable television. A few minutes should be spent reviewing how cable works and the kinds of services it can provide. (Literature provided by the MCCB might be helpful here.)

Present Communication Methods

The discussion should be opened by asking the participants about present communication methods and problems in the community. Specific types of communication should be suggested. For example,

Public relations and public information
Communication of ideas, plans, advice, news, etc. Seeking feedback or response.

Citizenship information: political office campaigns and platforms, public meetings, hearings, public safety information, speeches, committee, commission and board meetings, "know your government" programs, news conferences, patriotic and holiday events, etc.

Specialized news and announcements
Announcements, news, meetings, special events and other information intended for specialized groups such as trade or professional associations, employees, unions, school parents' associations, civic groups, service clubs, youth groups, church groups, etc.

Education

Job training, adult education, cultural enrichment, remedial programs, etc.

Data transfer

Moving information from one place to another within a community: business records, real property descriptions, court calendars, school schedules, inventories, medical records, etc.

Weather and disaster information

Tornado, flood, hail, and other storm warnings. Civil defense information.

Communication resources in the community

Audio and video equipment in private and public organizations (e.g., schools, government agencies, businesses, hospitals, libraries).

General Needs and Problems

Since it may not occur to all participants that specific problems may be addressed by certain communication techniques, the participants should be asked about the most important problems and needs in the community, not necessarily those related to communication. As these problems are expressed, in some cases it may become apparent that there are aspects of the problem that may be approached by communication. The group process of attempting to apply cable communication to these general problems may produce some creative ideas. And, at the same time, some thoughts that may later bear fruit will have been planted.

STEP 4. RECORDING AND SUMMATION

During the meeting, one of the advisory body members will have to take notes. At another meeting of the advisory body, an "initial statement of communication needs" should be prepared, with each need described in as much detail as the assessment meeting provided.

STEP 5. PUBLIC COMMENT

The "initial statement" should be read at a city council meeting and given to the local newspaper and other media. It should be available thereafter at city hall. The public should be invited to comment on the statement and make additions. After a suitable period has elapsed, if comments and additions have been received, the advisory body should include the "statement" on the agenda for a meeting. The "initial statement" should be revised accordingly and a final "statement of communication needs" agreed upon.

STEP 6. DISTRIBUTION

Each cable system making inquiry about the franchise should receive a copy of the "statement of communication needs." The final statement should also be available at city hall and given to the local newspaper and other local media.

Appendix E

National League of Cities
Code of Good Cable Television
Franchising Conduct

I. PURPOSE

Cities around the country are currently engaged in various phases of cable television franchising or renegotiation. The cable franchising process is a complex one, involving a broad range of technical, economic, and social issues. The decisions made by local officials will have a long-term effect on the types of cable services available to the people. While this code focuses on the franchising process, city officials must be aware throughout that process of the many ongoing issues of cable regulation, franchise administration and enforcement, and quality of services.

The bidders in the franchise process are typically well financed and exceedingly competitive. Extreme marketing pressure is sometimes exerted on city officials. Allegations of competitive abuse on the part of the cable industry and conflict of interest on the part of city officials and influential citizens have frequently arisen.

This National League of Cities' Code of Good Cable TV Franchise Conduct is intended to serve as a guide for cities in dealing with the cable industry during franchise negotiations. This code attempts to articulate basic principles and identify related options for cities. The code is a guideline and adherence to it is strictly voluntary on the part of cities.

II. THE ROLE OF CITIES IN CABLE TV FRANCHISING AND REGULATION

Cities have an important and proper role in cable television franchising and regulation. Several factors set the context of that role: cable operations have a quasi-monopoly status. The kinds of services delivered over cable systems are becoming increasingly desired by and essential to the public. Cable provides unique opportunities for locally originated and locally oriented programming and uses. Each of these factors makes it imperative that cities have and retain the ability to franchise and regulate local cable systems in order to assure that the public interest is protected and served. The federal level also has an appropriate role in establishing minimum technical standards. Among the powers that should reside with city government are

1. the power to franchise,
2. the power to regulate, including rate regulation of cable services, and
3. the power to assure local public, community, educational, municipal, and leased cable access and to promote local programming.

III. GUIDELINES FOR THE FRANCHISING PROCESS

A. The Franchising Process Should Be Open

The process should be planned so as to allow for and encourage participation by the public, community groups, and governmental agencies and institutions. The following are some (nonexclusive) procedures which have been used:

1. A prefranchising educational process aimed at both local officials and the public. The purpose of such a process is to inform relevant officials, community groups, and the citizens about the potentials of cable and about the franchising process itself.
2. Public hearings both at the outset, when the structure of the process is being planned, and after proposals have been received and are being evaluated.
3. Appointment of citizen task forces to assess community needs and evaluate the potential of cable for serving those needs, and to continue after the cable system is established to help mobilize community resources in meeting the identified local needs.
4. Appointment of an interagency task force to assess municipal government needs and evaluate the potential of cable for serving those needs and to continue after the cable system is established to help mobilize local governmental resources in meeting the identified local needs.
5. Appointment of a citizen advisory group and/or cable consultant to evaluate proposals and recommend an award.

B. The Franchising Process Should Be Structured, Should Provide Certainty for Parties, and Should Provide Full Information Needed by Applicants

The rules which will govern the process should be made clear at the outset, and all parties should be informed of them. A reasonable time frame for the process should be predetermined which lists the steps to be taken and projects their timing. The timing should be changed only if necessary and with adequate notice. The announced period between the issuance of the Request for Proposals (RFP) and the deadline for proposals should be especially firm. The RFP should include full information needed by potential applicants, including the criteria which will be used in evaluating proposals. Once the RFP is issued, changes in rules or requirements should be avoided if possible. If changes must be made, they should be formally adopted, made in writing, and publicized.

C. The Franchise Fee, if Any, Should Be Predetermined

It is reasonable for cities to collect a franchise fee from cable operators. These revenues may be needed to defray the costs of cable franchising, regulation, and monitoring and to support local cable programming. However, it is preferable to predetermine the size of the franchise fee, in terms of percentage of revenues, and to state the level of the fee in the RFP. In this way, the franchise fee does not become an item of competitive bidding. Thus, a potential appearance of inappropriate motivation on the part of the city is avoided, and greater attention can be paid to the substance of the proposals. Additionally, the RFP should state whether any prepayment of franchise fees will be required or accepted. The franchise agreement or ordinance should include provisions to take effect should federal regulations concerning franchise fees be changed. Any other applicable taxes or fees should be fully explained in the RFP.

D. Procedures and Formulas for Recovering the Costs of Franchising, if They Will Be Used, Should Be Predetermined and Uniformly Applied

It is typically the case that the city's franchising costs will be recovered from the applicants. Any nonrefundable application fee should be specified in the RFP. If additional costs not covered by the application fees are to be reimbursed by the company eventually awarded the franchise, this should also be specified and a reasonable upper limit set. The types of costs to be covered should be enumerated.

E. The Franchising Process Should Be Deliberate

Adequate time is needed for all interested parties to be heard and for city officials and staff to become familiar with the issues, economics and technology. Experience in various cities has suggested that a common time period is 9 to 12 months; however this can be expected to vary widely.

F. Elected Officials Should Be Involved in and Informed About Every Step Throughout the Process

The franchising process is likely to require significant staff work, and citizen advisory groups and independent cable consultants may be involved. However, the ultimate responsibility typically rests with the appropriate elected officials, so their continuing involvement is important.

G. Any Inquiries Made to Other Cities About Applicants' Performance Should Be Formal and Uniform

Inquiries to other cities about the level of performance of cable companies operating within their jurisdictions can provide important information on applicants. However, the inquiry procedure must be fair to all applicants. The inquiries should be formal, with the same questions asked in each case, and a reasonable sample of cities should be asked.

H. Any Inquiries Made to Other Cities About Consultants' Performance Should Be Formal and Uniform

In deciding whether to engage a professional cable consultant and in choosing a particular consultant, cities may wish to inquire about the performance of consultants in other jurisdictions. In order that effective information be gathered, and that the process be fair to potential consultants, this inquiry process should be formal, with the same questions asked in each case, and a reasonable sample of cities should be asked.

IV. OWNERSHIP ISSUES

A. If a City Decides to Require or Give Preference for Specified Ownership Interests Clear Guidelines Need to Be Established

In assuring that the franchisee will serve the public interest, cities may determine that certain types of ownership interest in the cable company are either necessary or preferred. A city may decide to own the cable system itself. If the city decides to grant a franchise, however, it may also decide that certain ownership interests are desired.

Ownership involvement on the part of local citizens in general, minorities and women, community groups, or public institutions are factors which have been required in RFPs or been given preferential weight in competitive evaluations. Some cities have concluded that such ownership involvement can be beneficial in encouraging the cable system to be more responsive to local needs. If such ownership preferences or criteria are adopted, the city should consider adopting safeguards regarding later sale of the cable system which might thwart the city intent. Some cities have barred ownership transfers for some specified number of years. Others require that city approval be obtained for significant transfer of ownership.

Allegations have arisen that, in some cases, showings of local ownership have not indicated functional involvement in the proposed cable operation. This allegation has arisen especially in cases where the ownership interest is given to local citizens or institutions free or for far less than actual value. A related issue is whether future cable subscribers should be required to pay, through increased subscription fees, for such equity "giveaways."

Among (nonexclusive) options for dealing with these local ownership issues are

1. make clear in the RFP any preferences which will be given for local ownership or for particular types of local ownership.
2. require full and timely disclosure of all parties with any ownership interest and the amount of investment made by each party and any other inducements or considerations given to any party.
3. state in the RFP that bona fide investment by local citizens or institutions is desired and therefore proposals containing any of the following elements would be looked on with disfavor
   a. if any investor's percentage of stock is greater than the percentage of dollars or services actually invested.
   b. if investors have received loans from the cable company with which to purchase stock.
   c. if the cable company guarantees investors little or no financial risk.
   d. if the interests of the local owners can be bought out readily or at a guaranteed price.
4. state in the RFP and provide in the franchise agreement that a portion of investment equal to the proportion of uncompensated transferred equity will be excluded from the investment base on which the rate of return is calculated for purposes of rate regulation. This approach reflects the apparent willingness of the cable firm to forego the profits on the portion of equity "given away."

B. Applicants Should Be Required to Disclose
   All Present and Former Corporate Parents,
   Owners, Partners, Affiliates, Subsidiaries,
   and Ownership Interests in Any Other Firms
   or Ventures

Such disclosure should be required of applicants, their principals and their immediate families.

C. Cross-Ownership of Local Communications
   Media Is an Appropriate Concern of
   Franchising Cities

In safeguarding the public interest, cities should consider whether granting a cable franchise to a particular applicant would result in an increased concentration of media ownership. Cable has become an important medium for the dissemination of inf rmation to the public. If one individual or firm controls multiple information sources in a locality, the public interest may be adversely served.

V. GUIDELINES FOR FINANCIAL DISCLOSURE REQUIREMENTS

Clearly, a franchising city must require sufficient information from applicants to be assured that adequate funds are available to build and operate the proposed system. In order that potential conflicts of interest can be discovered and competitive activities evaluated, applicants should be required to disclose certain other financial and expense information. Similarly, public officials, key staff, consultants, and members of official citizen advisory groups should disclose any potential conflicts. The particular approach to financial disclosure adopted by a city, of course, must be compatible with applicable state and federal law.

A. Applicants Should Be Required to Disclose
   All Transfers or Agreements for Transfers of
   Cash or Other Assets

Certain transfers of assets may be commendable while others may raise questions of conflict of interest or influence peddling. In any case, the city should require full and timely disclosure of all transfers or agreements for future transfers of stock or stock options, cash, property or other considerations or inducements on the part of applicants or affiliated persons or entities.

B. Applicants Should Be Required to Disclose All Expenses Made in Seeking the Franchise Award

Applicants should be required to provide periodically information on expenses incurred by the local company, its parent company, partner(s) or joint venturer(s) in seeking the award. The disclosure should include expenses for lobbying, public relations, marketing, advertising, research, salaries, legal fees, personal service agreements, contracted services, campaign contributions and donations or gifts to local individuals, groups or institutions.

C. City Officials, Key Staff, and Members of Official Citizen Advisory Groups Should Be Required to Disclose Any Potential Conflicts of Interest

Such disclosure by public officials is often already required by local laws and procedures. If it is not, or if key staff members are not covered, special requirements may be needed. Disclosure of any financial interests in applicant or affiliated firms and any potential conflict arising from professional or personal affiliations should be required. Any financial or other consideration given by applicants or affiliated parties should also be disclosed, including any trips taken at an applicant's expense, such as to tour operating cable facilities. During the franchising process and throughout the franchise term, campaign contributions made by franchise bidders, cable operators, or any affiliated parties should also be disclosed.

D. Any Consultants Used by the City in Relation to the Franchising Process or Ongoing Cable Administration or Regulation Should Be Required to Disclose any Potential Conflicts of Interest

Disclosure by consultants should include any corporate, financial, professional, or personal affiliation with any persons or firms holding any interest in cable companies or affiliated firms. Any financial, professional, or personal relationship with any local official or responsible staff should also be disclosed. Disclosure of all other governmental jurisdictions, firms, or other parties for whom the consultant has consulted or is currently consulting or has otherwise been engaged should be required. If the consultant has recommended franchise awards to one or more bidders in other jurisdictions, a complete listing of the firms previously recommended in each instance should also be required.

VI. GUIDELINES FOR LOBBYING RULES

A. Clear Rules Governing Lobbying Activities Should Be Established

The purpose of clear lobbying rules is both to protect the public interest and to make the franchising process fair to all bidders. On many questions arising during the franchising process, the best sources of information are the applicants. It is important that city officials and staff have access to that information. It is also important that all of the applicants have an equal opportunity to be heard. A number of approaches have been taken on the lobbying issue. Whatever specific approach is adopted, the rules must be made clear at the beginning of the process and must be uniformly applied. Among lobbying rules that have been adopted by cities are:

1. *Lobbyist registration.* Any person who is paid or otherwise compensated to make statements or otherwise influence action in favor of an applicant can be considered a lobbyist. Some cities require that all cable lobbyists register with the city and disclose any money spent in the course of contacts with city officials or personnel.
2. *Disclosure of all spokespersons.* Applicants may have a number of spokespersons who may not commonly be considered to be lobbyists. Some cities require a periodic listing of all persons who will be speaking on behalf of an applicant to avoid this definitional problem.
3. *Disclosure of contacts with elected officials or key staff.* Contact by applicants can be allowed, but disclosure of all such contacts required. Often, a transcript or summary of these discussions is required to be filed.
4. *Assuring fairness in industry contacts with elected officials.* Contacts with elected officials can be handled in a number of ways. Some cities have prohibited all contacts after some predetermined point in the franchising process when all parties have had a fair opportunity to be heard. Others have prohibited contact with individual council members, or have required that all contacts be made in public sessions only. Another approach has been to require that all contacts not made in a public session be in written form and included in the public record.
5. *Assuring fairness in contacts with city staff.* The same procedures which are adopted regarding contacts with elected officials can be made to

apply to staff as well. Some cities have required all applicant contacts to be made through a single designated staff member. Others have required applicants to submit information requests and then arranged to provide the same information to all applicants.

B. All Applicants Should Be Given a Fair Opportunity to Be Heard

Typically, a public hearing is held at some point after the proposals are received to allow applicants to present their proposals verbally. All applicants should be given an equal opportunity and time to make such presentations.

Index

DATE DUE